Media Violence and Children

Recent Titles in
Advances in Applied Developmental Psychology
Irving E. Sigel, Series Editor

Media Violence and Children

A COMPLETE GUIDE FOR PARENTS AND PROFESSIONALS

Edited by Douglas A. Gentile

Advances in Applied Developmental Psychology, Number 22
Irving E. Sigel, Series Editor

Westport, Connecticut
London

Library of Congress Cataloging-in-Publication Data

Media violence and children : a complete guide for parents and professionals / edited by
    Douglas A. Gentile
        p. cm. —(Advances in applied developmental psychology)
    Includes bibliographical references and index.
    ISBN 0–275–97956–3 (alk. paper)
        1. Children and violence. 2. Violence in mass media. I. Gentile, Douglas A., 1964–
II. Series.
HQ784.V55M43   2003
303.6—dc21   2003051067

British Library Cataloguing in Publication Data is available.

Library of Congress Catalog Card Number: 2003051067
ISBN: 978–0–313–36152–4 (pbk.)

First published in 2003

Praeger Publishers, 88 Post Road West, Westport, CT 06881
An imprint of Greenwood Publishing Group, Inc.
www.praeger.com

Printed in the United States of America

The paper used in this book complies with the
Permanent Paper Standard issued by the National
Information Standards Organization (Z39.48–1984).

P

In order to keep this title in print and available to the academic community, this edition
was produced using digital reprint technology in a relatively short print run. This would
not have been attainable using traditional methods. Although the cover has been changed
from its original appearance, the text remains the same and all materials and methods
used still conform to the highest book-making standards.

The truth knocks on the door and you say,
"Go away, I'm looking for the truth," and so it goes away. Puzzling.

Robert M. Pirsig, *Zen and the Art of Motorcycle Maintenance*

Contents

Introduction

A clear and consistent pattern of empirical results has emerged from over four decades of research on the effects of media violence. It is therefore surprising that many people still resist the idea that media violence has negative effects. A simple test will demonstrate that people are reluctant to accept this idea. Ask a large group of people, "How many of you think the media have a really large effect on people?" and most will raise their hands. Then ask, "How many of you think the media have a really large effect on *you*?" and many of the hands will go back down. This can also be replicated with parents, asking about media effects on "children" and "*your* children." Why does the public remain resistant to the idea that we or our children might be affected by the media in general, and by media violence in particular? Perhaps many don't think watching media violence can change attitudes. Or perhaps some recognize that media exposure does change attitudes about aggression, but don't think that those changes will be reflected in behavior.

In contrast, most people will readily admit that advertisements work (though perhaps not on them personally!), and we all know that the goal of an ad is to motivate us to change our behavior—to stop buying "brand X" and start buying "brand Y." Advertisements work through exactly this process of changing attitudes slowly over time; these altered attitudes are later reflected in product awareness, preferences, purchases, and brand loyalty. As demonstrated by the chapters in this book, this same process is one of the mechanisms by which media violence affects individuals.

Similarly, most people recognize that changes in information and attitudes about physical health can lead to altered behaviors. For example, we routinely hear stories in the news that broccoli reduces the risk of cancer, that calcium supplements increase bone mass, or that a low-fat diet is good for one's health. Many people immediately trust these stories, and change their behaviors as a result.

Two important points should be apparent after reading this book. First, the evidence for or against any of these types of health issues is often much more flimsy than the evidence regarding the effects of a steady diet of media violence. Second, often the size of the effect of diet on health issues (e.g., *how much* changing your diet really helps, or *how much* a calcium supplement actually reduces your risk of osteoporosis) is much smaller than the size of the effect of media violence (see chapter 11).

Youth violence is a complex phenomenon. Multiple factors influence aggression, and multiple perspectives inform the role that media violence plays in affecting aggression. This complexity means that research is particularly valuable. Research-based information can cut through all of the opinions and rhetoric surrounding this issue. While individuals may continue to ignore or disbelieve the accumulated evidence, many credible organizations have reviewed the research and are on record stating that media violence is one of the *causes* of aggression in society. A partial list of these organizations includes:

- The American Medical Association
- The American Academy of Pediatrics
- The American Psychological Association
- The National Institute of Mental Health
- The National Institutes of Health
- The American Academy of Child and Adolescent Psychiatry

Perhaps what needs to be recognized is that media violence *is* a health issue, just as diet is. As with changing diets, changing media habits is difficult. But with much of media violence, as with medicine, prevention is often the best cure.

It has often been suggested that children are more vulnerable to the effects of media violence because they cannot tell the difference between fantasy and reality. It is certainly a true research finding that children under eight generally do not have the same understanding of fantasy and reality that adults do. This matters a great deal when thinking about what types of issues might scare them more (see chapter 10). But many parents say, "It is a little violent, but we think he [the child] can differentiate between a game and real life" (Leland, 2000). The notion that the ability to distinguish between fantasy and reality inoculates a person from media effects is a false one. For example, adults all know that advertisements are "fake," but they still work. Similarly, knowing that a program or game is "only entertainment" does not ameliorate its effects. In fact, we often notice emotional and sometimes physical effects of watching violent entertainment—we get scared, we get excited, we laugh, we notice our palms sweating or hearts racing. Ironically, some of the effects of media violence may be so obvious that we fail to notice them.

This book is designed to provide a complete and up-to-date picture of the field of media violence research. The book has three goals. First, it is designed to be an interdisciplinary review of media violence research across a variety of media (e.g., TV, video games, music, etc.). It is intended to give the reader a sophisticated understanding of the complexity of these studies, applying advances in modern developmental theory to the vast body of knowledge that has been generated by psychologists, physicians, and communications scholars. Second, it is intended to be useful as a textbook for undergraduate and graduate students in a range of disciplines, including psychology, education, communication, journalism, medicine, public health, and other related fields. Third, it is intended to define the course of future research by describing what we know, what remains to be studied, and how we can utilize limited resources most effectively by drawing on the advances from several disciplines.

The success of any undertaking of this size requires the support of many people, only some of whom I have space to thank personally. I am grateful to each of the contributing authors for sharing their expertise and time in this venture. My longtime friend and colleague Irving Sigel provided the opportunity for this book to be written. David Walsh and the National Institute on Media and the Family provided the time and resources I needed. Many students have challenged my thinking, helping me to integrate many points of view. In particular, I wish to thank Jamie Ostrov, Elizabeth Jansen, Mari Cary, Ingrid Hoffman, Amelia Alexander, and Gina Lazar, all of whom gave a great deal of their time and consideration. I also must thank my family for their support, especially my wife, Tara van Brederode, and my father, J. Ronald Gentile. Finally, this book is dedicated to my daughter, Lauren, because trying to learn the truth so that we can do the right thing for our children is the most important job we can perform.

Douglas A. Gentile

CHAPTER 1

The Proliferation of Media Violence and Its Economic Underpinnings

Bruce D. Bartholow, Karen E. Dill,
Kathryn B. Anderson, and James J. Lindsay

Violence in entertainment is as old as civilization itself. The Romans delighted in watching Christians do battle with hungry lions. Dramatic theater—from the ancient Greeks to Shakespeare to Andrew Lloyd Webber—has always been thick with jealousy, retribution, and violence. However, it was not until the mass media explosion of the twentieth century that heavy doses of violence were made available to everyone, every day. Over the past 100 years, as media have become more available, they also have become more violent (e.g., Bushman & Anderson, 2001). This chapter reviews the amount of violence in the media, the impact of violent media, and the economic mechanisms that perpetuate media violence, focusing on media industry beliefs that violent program content attracts more viewers (and hence their dollars) than does nonviolent program content.

THE RISE OF MASS MEDIA CONSUMPTION

In the early part of the twentieth century, motion pictures and radio provided an interesting diversion for those who could afford them. However, relatively few people considered these commodities to be an essential part of their lives. With the introduction of television in the middle of the century, however, mass media availability (and consumer demand) began to skyrocket. Although America's entry into World War II delayed this boom by approximately a decade (television was first introduced in 1939), by 1955 two-thirds of all homes in the United States contained a television set. This figure increased to around 93 percent by the end of that decade, and today television is a part of the daily lives of virtually all Americans (Nielsen Media Research, 1998).

The rise in media availability of all kinds has gone hand in hand with a steep rise in media consumption among both children and adults, such that media consumption is now the great American pastime. The numbers are startling. The television is on for 7 hours and 40 minutes each day in the average American household (TV Turnoff Network, n.d.). Forty to 60 percent of Americans watch television during dinner, a time traditionally devoted to family interactions (Gentile & Walsh, 2002; Roberts, Foehr, Rideout, & Brodie, 1999), and 25 percent of people regularly fall asleep with the television on (TV Turnoff Network, n.d.). One recent study indicates that the average American child spends upward of 40 hours per week consuming some type of mass media, not including that related to school and homework (Roberts et al., 1999). Indeed, children spend more time watching television than doing any other waking activity, including time spent in school (TV Turnoff Network, n.d.; Walsh, 2001a). In contrast, the National Institute on Media and the Family reports that in an average week, kids spend one-half hour interacting directly with dad, two-and-one-half hours with mom, four hours on homework, and one-half hour reading (Walsh, 2001a).

During weekday evenings, the first hour of prime time television—the time when networks and their advertisers are targeting adults specifically—is seen by 33 percent of American children ages 2–11 (Hamilton, 1998). Consumption of television rises for all age groups on the weekend, but especially for children. One particularly telling statistic is that at 10:00 A.M. on any given Saturday, approximately 60 percent of all American children are watching television (Comstock & Scharrer, 1999). At the rate Americans watch television, a child who grows up and lives to be 75 will have spent 9 years of his life in front of the TV (Kubey & Csikszentmihalyi, 2002).

Since its inception, television has been the dominant form of media. However, it is no longer the near "single source" of entertainment and information that it once was (Groebel, 2001). More recently, other types of media, including computers and video games, have become commonplace. According to the U.S. Census Bureau, by the year 2000, 42 percent of American households contained at least one member who routinely used the Internet at home (Fox, 2002). Recent analyses indicate a trend among children and adolescents to spend more time with computers and less time with television. Youth also report preferring computers to more traditional media like television (Strasburger & Wilson, 2002).

In the past 10 years, the video game industry has boomed, as video games of all kinds have become extremely popular among young people. Annual video game industry sales consistently outpace sales of movie tickets (Elmer-Dewitt, 1993; Hettrick, 1995; Walsh, 2001b). Despite the recession, video game sales increased by 43 percent in 2001, skyrocketing to $9.4 billion in the United States alone (Markoff, 2002). Recent surveys of video game consumption are consistent with these enormous dollar figures, showing that upward of 90 percent of American children between the ages of 2 and 17 play video and computer games regularly and/or have video game systems in their homes (Funk, 1993; Walsh, 2001b). Older teens and college students also play a lot of video games. According to one report, approximately 15 percent of young men entering college play at least one hour of video games per day in an average week (Cooperative Institutional Research Program, 1999). This figure appears to have been steadily rising in recent years. Video game industry executive Doug Lowenstein attributes some of the growth of the industry to the fact that two generations of children have now grown up with video games and interactive technology (Markoff, 2002).

HOW MUCH VIOLENCE IS IN THE MEDIA?

The rise in media consumption has important implications for society. Cultural norms and values are reflected in (and some say determined by) the media. As such, increases in violence depicted in the media have raised concerns over the impact of this violence on society. Before discussing this issue in detail, it is important to first outline what constitutes media violence.

Defining Media Violence

The National Television Violence Study (NTVS) (1998)—a comprehensive examination of the content of American television programs—defines media violence as:

Any overt depiction of a credible threat of physical force or the actual use of such force intended to physically harm an animate being or group of beings. Violence also includes certain depictions of physically harmful consequences against an animate being or group that occurs as a result of unseen violent means. Thus there are three primary types of violent depictions: credible threats, behavioral acts, and harmful consequences. (p. 41)

Although some other definitions differ slightly (e.g., Center for Media and Public Affairs, 1999), most scholars generally agree with the definition provided in the NTVS. Jo Groebel, director general of the European Institute for the Media, concludes that, over a broad range of research methodologies (e.g., content analyses, behavioral research, cultural studies) and settings (e.g., North American, Western European, Asian, African), the terms "aggression" and "violence" in the media are defined generally as "behavior that leads to harm of another person" (2001).

Potter (1999) analyzed how theorists, content analysts, and the public define violence and aggression. Starting with a scholarly definition that focuses on causing harm to another, he notes that scientists disagree over specifics such as whether intent matters, whether both physical and verbal aggression should be included, and whether nonhuman targets and off-screen events should be included. Such differences may affect the outcomes of content analyses, and as such, reports can vary in their conclusions concerning the amount of violence on television and in other media. Potter also found what he called a "profound" difference between what the public considers violent and how scientists conceptualize violence. For example, the public does not consider cartoons to be violent, although scientists note that cartoons feature some of the highest rates of violence found in the media. The public becomes concerned when they are shocked or offended by what they see, and hence the graphicness of media violence is the most important factor for many. Critics, then, conclude that scientists use poor definitions of media violence; but Potter contends that the scientists' definitions are not poor, but reflect different concerns: The public is concerned with being shocked by what they watch, and scientists are concerned that the public will be harmed by what they watch, whether or not it is perceived as shocking.

Violence on Television

As television became more widely consumed over the past half-century, it also became increasingly violent, a fact that has raised concerns among many social policymakers. Over 30 years ago, consensus was already building as to the dangers of violence on American television, as indicated by the National Commission on the Causes and Prevention of Violence in 1969: "The preponderance of the available research evidence strongly suggests . . . that violence in television programs can and does have adverse effects upon audiences" (cited in Berkowitz, 1993, p. 199). Nevertheless, entertainment industry officials have been reluctant to embrace this conclusion. Still, following a 1972 report by the Surgeon General of the United States, which concluded, "there is a causative relationship between televised violence and subsequent antisocial behavior," some industry executives appeared convinced of the evidence and pledged to "manage program planning accordingly" (Communications Subcommittee, 1972). In a more recent policy statement, the National Cable Television Association (1993) condemned the "gratuitous use of violence depicted as an easy and convenient solution to human problems" and vowed to "strive to reduce the frequency of such exploitative uses of violence" (p. 1). The Network Television Association (1992) made similar promises.

What has been the outcome of this careful program planning? The answer, unfortunately, is that violent programming has steadily increased over the past 30 years. Research reports published in the early 1970s indicated that by age 14, the average child had witnessed more than 11,000 murders on television (Looney, 1971). This figure has dramatically increased, with more recent reports indicating that the average American child now witnesses more than

10,000 violent crimes (e.g., murder, rape, and assault) each year on television—about 200,000 total violent crimes by the time they are in their teens (Signorielli, Gerbner, & Morgan, 1995). Moreover, the authors of the NTVS (1998) reported that 61 percent of television programs contain violence. Other reports contend that the figure for prime time network programs—those that young people are most likely to watch—is more than 70 percent (Gerbner, Gross, Morgan, & Signorielli, 1994). Violent acts occur 5 times per hour in prime time programs and 20 times per hour in children's programs (Strasburger & Wilson, 2002). Fully two-thirds of children's programming contains violence, making these shows more violent than all other genres except feature films and drama series. All indications are that these figures will continue to climb.

The 1990s saw an increase in the number of popular children's programs with violent themes, and particularly those in which the "heroes" use violent means to solve problems or settle disputes (e.g., Power Rangers, Power Puff Girls). According to the NTVS (1998), at least 10 percent of the perpetrators of violence can be categorized as "heroes." Furthermore, the majority (68 percent) of children's programming with violent content was presented in a humorous context. Trotta (2001) explains that this combination of violence and humor plays a major role in desensitizing children to violence (an issue discussed in more detail later in this chapter). Signorielli, et al. (1995) also explain that media producers often mix violence and humor to increase the appeal of the violence to the audience (see also Jhally, 1994). This helps create the illusion that violence is fun and largely without negative consequences, thus encouraging violence in the viewer. Bushman and Huesmann (2001) agree that unpunished violence perpetrated by attractive heroes provides what they call the "best" prescription for encouraging imitation of violent scripts and adoption of proviolence beliefs and attitudes.

Table 1.1 contains percentages of the main types of violent content as a function of program genres and contextual variables identified by the NTVS (1998). Percentages are reported by program genre to illustrate how children's programs compare to other types of programs. As shown in Table 1.1, the percentage of children's programs containing excessive violence (nine or more violent interactions) exceeded that found in comedies, music videos, and reality programs. The majority of violent interactions (58 percent) in children's programs involved repeated attacks from the same perpetrator on the same target (e.g., repeated punching). Most violent children's programs show only short-term negative consequences for targets of violence (67 percent), only 6 percent show long-term negative consequences for targets, and 26 percent show no negative consequences at all. Use of the body as a weapon in violent interactions in children's programs (43 percent) is more frequent than in violent interactions in dramas (31 percent), movies (39 percent), and reality shows (25 percent), which are more likely to depict guns as weapons. These depictions have real consequences for aggression in society. Research on ob-

Table 1.1
Percentages of Violent Television Programs by Content and Program Genre

Type of Violent Content	All	Children's	Comedy	Drama	Movies	Music Videos	Reality
				Program Genre			
Excessive violence	32	31	5	40	59	3	17
Fantasy violence	45	87	14	11	19	12	0
Realistic violence	55	13	86	89	81	88	100
Punishment of "bad" perpetrators	55	59	47	66	56	27	45
Long-term negative consequences for targets	16	6	8	33	33	10	7
Short-term negative consequences for targets	55	67	44	49	49	41	47
No negative consequences for targets	29	26	48	18	17	49	45
Violence with blood and gore	14	1	1	21	24	9	16
Violence with humor	42	68	89	16	32	14	8
Use of guns in violent interactions	26	12	15	41	33	18	45
Use of body as a weapon	39	43	53	31	39	56	25
Repeated perpetrator-target violence	61	58	51	59	63	62	71
Overall proportion of programs with violent content	61	67	37	75	89	53	39

Note: Figures are taken from the National Television Violence Study (NTVS) (1998). Excessive violence was defined in the NTVS as nine or more acts of violence in a given program.

servational learning suggests that children who view aggressive behavior involving the body (e.g., biting and kicking) are likely to imitate the behavior (e.g., Bandura, 1973, 1983), which is likely to result in harm to child peers. Other research indicates that the repeated pairing in the media of guns with violence leads to the formation of permanent links in memory, such that the mere presence of a gun enhances the likelihood of aggressive responding (e.g., Anderson, Benjamin, & Bartholow, 1998; Bartholow, Anderson, Carnagey, & Benjamin, in press; Berkowitz & LePage, 1967).

In a recent report, the Parents Television Council (PTC) examined the content of television's traditional family hours of programming, defined as between 8 and 9 P.M. Monday through Saturday and 7 to 9 P.M. on Sunday (Parents Television Council, 1999). The study found that the major TV networks' family hour programming has grown increasingly more sexual, explicit, profane, and violent. The PTC study found that the percentage of violent programs broadcast per hour on the major networks (ABC, CBS, Fox, NBC, UPN, and WB) had nearly doubled since 1997, the last time the family hour content had been studied. In all, only 24 percent of family hour programs were deemed "family friendly," which was defined as "programs that promote responsible themes and traditional values" (Parents Television Council, 1999, "Overview and Background," p. 1). The authors cite the reason for this "coarsening" of the family hour as economic in nature: because advertisers want to market to a young adult audience, programmers have created content they think will attract that audience.

Violence in Other Forms of Media

More recently developed forms of entertainment media for young people can be even more graphic and violent than television programs. This is particularly true of video games. As mentioned previously, an overwhelming majority of children play video games daily or weekly. Perhaps the most alarming aspect of the popularity of these games is that a majority of the most popular ones are extremely violent in nature, involving brutal mass killings as a primary strategy for winning the games, and containing extremely gory graphics to depict it all (e.g., Anderson & Bushman, 2001; Bartholow & Anderson, 2002; Buchman & Funk, 1996; Dietz, 1998; Funk, Flores, Buchman, & Germann, 1999; Provenzo, 1991). This fact came to light very publicly in the 1993 U.S. Senate hearings hosted by Joseph Lieberman (D-Connecticut) examining whether violence in video games poses a public health risk. Although at that time only 10 percent of video games available for the home market were identified as violent in nature, the violent games—particularly *Mortal Kombat* and *Street Fighter II*—overwhelmingly dominated the market (Kent, 2001). One outcome from these hearings was the industrywide rating system for video games, which was intended to give parents the information necessary to determine which games were age-appropriate for their kids. Unfortunately, the rating system so far appears to have failed to protect most kids from exposure to violent games. Parents and the video game industry both hold some of the responsibility to protect children. In a recent survey of eighth and ninth graders, only 15 percent said their parents "always" or "often" check the ratings before allowing them to buy or rent video games (53 percent said "never"), and fewer than one in five parents (19 percent) have ever prevented purchase because of a game's rating (Gentile, Lynch, Linder, & Walsh, 2003; also see Gentile & Walsh, 2002). Even when parents do check the ratings, children may be exposed to inappropriate material because the ratings provided by the video game industry often do not match those provided by parents or their game-playing kids (Anderson & Bushman, 2001; Funk et al., 1999; Walsh & Gentile, 2001).

Another outcome of the Senate hearings of 1993 was the strong encouragement from both the Senate panel and several media experts who testified for industry officials to institute a voluntary, industrywide cap on the level of violence in their games. Just as television executives have done for over 30 years, video game industry heads have ignored this advice. A recent content analysis of top-selling video games for personal computers (PCs) found that 60 percent of the games contained a main theme of violence, with 17 percent of those depicting sexualized violence (Dill, Gentile, Richter, & Dill, 2001). Believing that realistic depictions of violence are theoretically more likely to incite violence in the player, Dill et al. (2001) rated the realism of game content, finding that two-thirds of the violent games portrayed realistic (defined as existing or able to exist in the real world) targets and that 92 percent portrayed realistic weapons. Dietz (1998) analyzed the content of top-selling console video games and found that 79 percent of the games included aggression and that 21 percent of the games depicted violence toward women.

Finally, there is some discrepancy in the literature as to the amount of violence contained in music videos. For example, some reports indicate that, overall, about 15 percent of the videos on popular cable music channels (e.g., MTV, VH-1, BET) contain violence (e.g., Durant et al., 1997; Smith & Boyson, 2002). On the other hand, findings from the NTVS (1998) indicated that 53 percent of music videos contained violent scenes (see Table 1.1) (also see Strasburger & Wilson, 2002). This apparent discrepancy could be a function of different methods of coding what is violent, as discussed previously. In addition, part of the discrepancy might reflect differences in the music genres examined. For example, whereas nearly a third of rap and heavy metal music videos contain violence, less than 10 percent of adult contemporary and rhythm and blues videos contain violence (Strasburger & Wilson, 2002).

WHY IS THERE SO MUCH VIOLENCE IN THE MEDIA?

> We live in a violent society. Art imitates the modes of life, not the other way around: It would be better . . . to clean up society than to clean up the reflection of that society.
> —Zev Braun, CBS television executive

> The television industry is merely holding a mirror to American society.
> —Howard Stringer, CBS television executive

Media executives publicly claim that the reason for violence in the media is that society is filled with violence, and that the media, in their products, have a responsibility to accurately depict society. Here, we offer what we believe to be the underlying reasons, based on economic realities of the media industry, for the unrealistic levels of violence depicted in television, movies, and video games.

Media Marketing: Economic Reasons for Violence in Media

If the average person were asked, "What is the purpose of the media?" chances are the response would be something like, "to inform and entertain the public." Indeed, broadcasting licenses are awarded (at essentially no cost) to television networks on the understanding that they broadcast in "the public interest, convenience, and necessity" (Hamilton, 1998, p. 33). From this perspective, it would appear that networks determine what to broadcast based on what the public appears to want. Beth Waxman Bressan, vice president and assistant to the president at CBS/Broadcast Group, expressed this sentiment when accounting for the presence of violence on television to a U.S. Senate panel: "TV looks like it does because we try to respond to the wants of viewers" (Violence bill debated in Washington, 1990, p. 78). However, the true purpose of television is not so much to inform and entertain as to provide an audience for product advertisements. Perhaps the most obvious clue to this fact is the daytime drama, or "soap opera." The first televised soap opera *(Search for Tomorrow)* aired on CBS in 1951, though the concept was actually borrowed from radio programs dating back many years. As implied by their name, soap operas were invented as a vehicle for marketing cleaning products, and they aired during the daytime hours when men were presumed to be at work, while most women—those presumed most likely to care about and buy cleaning products—stayed home. To this day, advertisements accompanying programs that air during the daytime hours are primarily for household products, and they are primarily aimed at women. Thus, from the start, media and marketing executives have been targeting specific audiences with the types of programs they are assumed to like in order to sell specific kinds of products.

It is an understatement to note that advertising is a huge business. Annually advertisers spend approximately $150 billion to sponsor TV and radio programs, in the hopes of making two to three times as much in return from media consumers who buy their products and services (Fox, 2002). From the 1970s to the 1990s, the daily number of ads targeted to the average American jumped from 560 to 3,000 (Fox, 2002). In that same time frame, the number of ads to which children were exposed increased from 20,000 per year (Adler et al., 1977) to more than 40,000 per year (Kunkel & Gantz, 1992; also see Strasburger, 2001). Children represent an especially captive audience for TV ads, because research shows that children (especially those younger than five years) do not discriminate between programs and advertisements (e.g., Levin, Petros, & Petrella, 1982; Ward, Reale, & Levinson, 1972). Even somewhat older children who can discriminate programs from ads at a perceptual level often do not recognize the persuasive intent of those ads (see Kunkel, 2001). Findings such as these prompted the Federal Communications Commission (FCC) in 1978 to attempt to ban all advertising aimed at children (Fox, 2002).

However, precisely the opposite has come to pass. For example, since its inception in 1989, Channel One—a television network ostensibly meant to inform children about current events—has been broadcast directly into American school classrooms. The main purpose of Channel One, as with all television, is selling. As the president of Channel One told an audience of youth marketers in 1994, "The biggest selling point to advertisers [is that] . . . we are forcing kids to watch two minutes of commercials. The advertiser gets a group of kids who cannot go to the bathroom, cannot change the station, who cannot listen to their mother yell in the background" (cited in Fox, 2002, p. 25). Hence, when viewing time at school and home is considered, the average child can virtually never escape television and the marketing machine that powers it.

In his book *Selling Out America's Children*, Walsh (1994) discusses how television programming and advertising, two key influences in American culture today, work together to shape our values. The job of media executives is to hold an audience in order to sell their advertisers' products. In order to hold their audience, they do what it takes to get the audience's attention. The most common attention-grabbing topics are sex, violence, and humor, and consequently these topics are commonly featured on television (Walsh, 1994, 2001a; see also Jhally, 1994). In the end, as a result of seeking the most profitable programs, media executives are creating programming that promotes violence, irresponsible sex, and materialism. In this respect, media executives are profiting from a product that is unhealthy for those who consume it, particularly children. Younger viewers are often sought after because their relative inexperience with ads and the fact that their product and brand-name preferences are less firmly entrenched make them potentially more easily influenced than older audiences.

Hamilton (1998) provides a detailed analysis of the use of violence on television as a marketing strategy to ensure a viewing audience. He explains, "the portrayal of violence is used as a competitive tool in both entertainment and news shows to attract particular viewing audiences" (p. 3), and that these audiences are chosen based on the kinds of products and services they are likely to purchase. This, then, determines what kinds of ads will be shown during particular time slots, and what prices will be charged by the networks for showing these ads. Demographic characteristics of those who appear to prefer violent programs are thus very important to television executives. There are some data to suggest that a large audience of young men and women—the demographic groups considered most attractive by advertisers—watches violent programs. Hamilton (1998) reports the results of a large survey in which adults in three age categories (18–34, 35–50, and 50 and over) were asked about their viewing habits. Results showed that 73 percent of men in the 18–34 group were heavy consumers of violent programming and that overall, men in this age category answered yes to an average of almost 5 out of 10 questions related to viewing violent shows. The next-highest violence-viewing group was women in the 18–34 age group, 60 percent of whom were considered heavy consumers of televised violence.

Why Violence Sells

Groebel (2001) cites many factors that explain why violence is an effective marketing tool. He explains that violent media are successful in part because violence attracts the attention of male adolescents, a highly sought-after demographic for marketers (Hamilton, 1998; Strasburger & Wilson, 2002). Violence is also easier to produce and has a more universal language than what he calls "complex, dialogue-based stories" (Groebel, 2001, p. 255). According to noted media expert George Gerbner, violence is a preferred commodity in a global media market because violent scenes essentially speak for themselves, needing very little in the way of verbal translation (e.g., Gerbner, 1994b, 1999; see also Jhally, 1994). On the other hand, even though humor is a very popular and proven way to gain attention in the media, what is funny is often culturally specific and can be difficult to translate.

Why Do We Watch? Psychological Mechanisms

> Perhaps the most ironic aspect of the struggle for survival is how easily organisms can be harmed by that which they desire. The trout is caught by the fisherman's lure, the mouse by cheese. . . . Realizing when a diversion has gotten out of control is one of the great challenges of life.
> —R. Kubey and M. Csikszentmihalyi

From our review above, it is safe to conclude that media consumption is the primary free-time activity of most Americans. The question is, why do we watch so much? Kubey and Csikszentmihalyi (2002) say that we are psychologically addicted to the electronic screen. They cite the example, familiar to many of us, of people trying to have a conversation in a room where a television is turned on. Periodically, during both interesting and uninteresting conversations, talking ceases and everyone turns to the television screen. As we will see, this is largely because media executives are experts at getting our attention.

Kubey and Csikszentmihalyi (2002) explain that TV repeatedly triggers our orienting response—the instinctive reaction to pay attention to any sudden or novel stimulus. This orienting response evolved in the species because it helps us identify potential threats and react to them. Producers of media use features such as edits, cuts, zooms, pans, and sudden noises to continually trigger our orienting response. In short, they exploit basic psychological and biological mechanisms to get and keep our attention. In ads, action sequences, and music videos, the orienting response is triggered at an average rate of once per second (Kubey & Csikszentmihalyi, 2002); essentially, this amounts to a continuous cueing of attention.

Similarly, the National Institute on Media and the Family (NIMF) describes what they call "jolts and tricks" (National Institute on Media and the Family, n.d.; Walsh, 2001a). Jolts are devices used by the media that are designed to engage our emotions. The most common emotional jolts are appeals to sex, violence, humor, and belonging needs. Tricks are technical features designed to grab our attention, including those triggering the orienting response. Common tricks used to grab our attention include special effects, edits, pacing, music, camera angles, graphics, color, volume, lighting, makeup, and animation (National Institute on Media and the Family, n.d.; Walsh, 2001a). It is not only the content of programs that attracts attention, but also the way in which that content is presented. Media producers know that when an audience's emotions are engaged, that audience is more vulnerable to suggestion (e.g., Cialdini, 2001). In this case, the suggestion takes the form of advertised products. In short, media producers believe that grabbing our attention eventually translates into grabbing our money.

So what might be wrong with allowing the media to grab our attention? After all, as Kubey and Csikszentmihalyi (2002) point out, sometimes television is enjoyable and can offer an outlet for fun and relaxation. When, then, does it become a problem? Kubey and Csikszentmihalyi report that 2 out of 5 adults and 7 out of 10 children say that they watch too much TV. Also, viewers often feel that they can't stop watching TV. Furthermore, while people report increased good moods after activities such as sports and hobbies, they report being in the same mood or in a worse mood after watching TV (Kubey & Csikszentmihalyi, 2002).

Studies show that prolonged viewing is less relaxing and satisfying than low or moderate viewing. However, this may not be apparent to the viewer because the relaxation response occurs soon after viewing begins, thus the viewer associates relaxation with watching television. Turning off the TV after a viewing session is associated with more stress and with dysphoric rumination. However, this is not because turning off the TV is stressful, but because the initial relaxation response has faded with prolonged exposure. Thus, people end up watching television for longer than they say they want to, under the incorrect assumption that more television will increase relaxation. Ironically, heavy TV viewers enjoy TV less than light TV viewers do (Kubey & Csikszentmihalyi, 2002).

Economic Costs of Violent Media

Although media executives publicly deny that market pressures drive the levels of violence in their programs, privately they often point out that such pressures impair their ability to reduce television violence (Hamilton, 1998). In a 1988 congressional debate on television violence, representative Dan Glickman observed, "An obstacle to voluntary reduction in violence by networks is that, in this intensely competitive business, it is commonly held that violence sells" (Congressional Record, 1988). Despite this prevailing industry ethos, recent data indicate that media executives may be hurting themselves, in addition to their viewing audiences, by broadcasting violence.

The argument that programs are violent in response to public demand appears to be unfounded. For example, Gerbner (1994a) notes, "the most highly rated programs are seldom violent" (cited in Hamilton, 1998, p. 32). Gerbner compared the average Nielsen ratings (the industry standard for determining viewership of particular programs and networks) and shares (i.e., proportion of the television market at any particular time) for 104 violent programs and 103 nonviolent programs aired between 1988 and 1993, and reported that the average rating for violent programs was 11.1, whereas the average rating for nonviolent programs was 13.8. Similarly, the average share for violent programs was 18.5 compared to 22.5 for nonviolent programs. Consistent with these findings, Hamilton (1998) reported that when theatrically produced movies are shown on television along with warnings about content (for violence, nudity, or language), "broadcasters run more network promotions and fewer general product ads, consistent with the theory that warnings cause advertiser pullouts that lower prices" (p. 165).

It is generally thought that advertisers pull product ads during programs with warning labels out of fear that consumers will be offended by the programs and potentially associate them with their products (Hamilton, 1998). However, recent findings suggest an even better reason for advertisers not to sponsor violent programs. In a series of three experiments, Bushman (1998) exposed participants to commercials embedded in either violent or nonviolent film clips, and later asked them to recall as many of the commercial messages as they could. Across experiments, participants who saw the violent film clips consistently showed poorer memory for commercials than those exposed to the nonviolent film clips. Moreover, Bushman reported that violent film clips made participants angry, and that level of anger served to impair memory (i.e., anger was a mediating variable). These findings were confirmed by those of a recent meta-analysis (Bushman & Phillips, 2001), showing that all types of TV viewers (children, adults, those who do and do not like to watch violent TV) are less likely to remember the content of advertisements during shows that contain violence. Other recent findings indicate that sexual content produces similar impairment of memory for ads (Bushman & Bonacci, 2002). The implication is that although violent (and sexually explicit) television shows may attract large audiences and exposure to the commercials, the viewers may not remember the content of the commercial messages, which ultimately will decrease the likelihood that investment in commercials will result in increased product sales.

In addition to potential revenue losses associated with decreased advertisement effectiveness, it can be argued that the constant broadcasting of violence in the media produces economic and other costs for society for which media corporations are not held responsible. Media corporations profit from sponsorship of their programs with little regard for how their products affect viewers. Hamilton (1998) has argued that this phenomenon—products or by-products resulting in costs to those who don't profit from the products—is not unlike the health and monetary costs incurred by the public through industrial pollution. Just as an industrial process can produce wastes that pollute the local air and groundwater (resulting in acute and chronic health problems to local inhabitants) while generating commercial products, so too do programs and other events portrayed by the media produce costs to individual viewers and society as a whole. Hamilton has labeled this phenomenon the *theory of negative externalities.*

According to Hamilton (1998), television and cable networks operate according to a relatively simple formula involving the number of viewers for a given program (within a given demographic), the number of competing networks offering a similar type of program, the amount that advertisers or cable subscribers are willing to pay for a program, and the costs involved in producing or acquiring a program. What these economic formulas miss are the costs borne by viewers. For one, television generally increases passivity among viewers, leading to less exercise, increased food intake (generally of high-calorie snack foods), and ultimately a less healthy populace. The link between television viewing, decreased physical activity, and obesity (particularly in children) is well documented (e.g., Andersen, Crespo, Bartlett, Cheskin, & Pratt, 1998; Crespo et al., 2001; Dennison, Erb, & Jenkins, 2002; Dietz & Gortmaker, 1985). Furthermore, a recent study showed that children who were randomly assigned to watch less television showed less weight gain over seven months than children whose television viewing was not altered (Robinson, 1999). Other costs associated with media violence, particularly those related to increased societal violence, have been reviewed elsewhere (e.g., Gentile & Anderson, chapter 7, this volume; Strasburger & Wilson, chapter 4, this volume). However, the tools that economists, accountants, and public health officials use to determine health risks associated with hazardous wastes (e.g., animal testing and lifetime excess cancer risk calculations) cannot be used by researchers to determine risks associated with violent television programs, video games, and music lyrics. Although many of the elements are present to estimate such risks, the fact that media violence may have substantial long-term effects brought about through repeated exposure to violent programs, and that such risks can only be estimated through correlational data, hinders researchers' ability to effectively estimate the degree to which a particular program is responsible for a person's actions.

Hamilton (1998) states that estimates by the Environmental Protection Agency regarding "lifetime excess cancer risk" due to a particular hazardous-waste site are fraught with controversy. Estimates of risks associated with a given television program, video game, or music lyric may be even more controversial due to sparse or nonexistent data on long-term effects of specific programs and consumers' general belief that they are immune to such effects (as discussed in the next section). Producers of violent media capitalize on this missing element in the research. We suspect that to the degree that the risks and costs associated with violent content of a television show, movie, video game, or song lyric remains uncertain, those in the media industry will continue to base their decisions concerning whether to broadcast violence on profits and direct costs without considering the costs to consumers or ultimate costs to society at large.

The Impact of Violence in the Media on Society

The ill effects of media violence on society are well documented (e.g., Anderson & Bushman, 2002; Gentile & Anderson, chapter 7, this volume; Strasburger & Wilson, chapter 4, this volume; see also Bushman & Anderson, 2001; Bushman & Huesmann, 2001; Smith & Donnerstein, 1998). On the basis of the accumulating evidence, six major professional organizations that focus on public health issues—the American Psychological Association, the American Academy of Pediatrics, the American Academy of Family Physicians, the American Psychiatric Association, the American Medical Association, and the American Academy of Child and Adolescent Psychiatry—recently signed a joint statement attesting to the dangers of media violence for children: "At this time, well over 1,000 studies . . . point overwhelmingly to a causal connection between media violence and aggressive behavior in some children (*Joint Statement*, 2000, p. 1).

The evidence (and endorsement of the evidence by experts in the field) apparently does not convince media executives, however. Just as tobacco company CEOs did for decades, media executives have consistently told the public that there is no proof that dangerous content of their products leads to any ill effects on society. For example, in a May 12, 2000, interview, Doug Lowenstein, president of the Digital Software Association, told CNN's *The World Today*, "There is absolutely no evidence, none, that playing a violent video game leads to aggressive behavior" (Time Warner, 2000). Similarly, Jack Valenti, president of the Motion Picture Association of America, has said, "If you cut the wires of all TV sets today, there would be no less violence on the streets in two years" (Moore, 1993, p. 3007). Apparently, media executives believe that although the advertisements that they sell to corporations have an influence over the behavior of viewers, the violent content of their programs has no such influence (see Berkowitz, 1993; Bushman & Anderson, 2001).

Media executives are not alone in their apparent belief that media violence is harmless. Many individuals in the lay public also seem largely unaware of the deleterious effects of consistent exposure to violence in the media. For example, in one recent poll conducted by *PC Data* magazine, respondents indicated that they believed video games do not cause aggression ("Poll says games are safe," 1999). Such beliefs likely are based on personal experience; that is, "I've been watching violent shows all my life, and I've never killed anyone." However, media violence effects are often more subtle than such statements would imply, sometimes leading indirectly to increased aggression, or to decreased helping and compassion, via psychological mechanisms or processes that can be slow to develop and difficult to recognize. For example, many scholars have hypothesized that, over time, repeated exposure to violence in the media can desensitize viewers to real-world violence (see Bushman & Anderson, 2001). That is, although viewing violence is thought to initially provoke fear, anxiety, disgust, or other negative affective states, repeated exposure to violence appears to reduce its psychological impact, such that violent images eventually do not elicit these negative responses (e.g., see Berkowitz, 1993; Griffiths & Shuckford, 1989; Rule & Ferguson, 1986).

The concept of desensitization has been applied to understanding a number of phenomena in the psychological literature. Perhaps the most well-known example is the use of systematic desensitization to treat patients in a phobia or anxiety clinic. Behavioral therapists have known for decades that systematic exposure to a threatening stimulus (e.g., a snake), coupled with relaxation and/ or enjoyment, is effective in reducing the fear and anxiety associated with that stimulus. According to Wolpe (1982), after repeated exposure to an anxiety-provoking stimulus under relaxing conditions, "the stimulus eventually loses its ability to evoke anxiety. Successively 'stronger' stimuli [can then be] introduced and similarly treated" (p. 133).

The long behavioral tradition of systematic desensitization suggests that repeated exposure to increasingly gory and realistic portrayals of violence in the mass media may desensitize people to violence in the real world. Research shows that media violence initially provokes fear, anxiety, and sleep disturbances (e.g., Cantor, 1998, 2001; Harrison & Cantor, 1999). However, violent media are typically consumed in conditions of relaxation and pleasure, and with no apparent adverse consequences for the individual. As such, repeated exposure may cause the initial adverse reactions to fade such that people become less responsive to real violence. A number of studies have found support for this basic premise, in that participants exposed to violent media (e.g., slasher films, televised police action, violent boxing matches) are less physiologically aroused by subsequent real-world violence than are participants initially exposed to nonviolent media (e.g., Carnagey, Bushman, & Anderson, 2003; Cline, Croft, & Courrier, 1973; Lazarus, Speisman, Mordkoff, & Davison, 1962; Linz, Donnerstein, & Adams, 1989; Thomas, 1982; Thomas, Horton, Lippincott, & Drabman, 1977). In addition, playing a violent video game causes a decreased likelihood of helping victims of violence (Carnagey et al., 2003), suggesting a negative behavioral consequence of media violence desensitization.

As noted previously, the public becomes concerned about the level of violence in the media only when they are shocked or offended by what they see. Over years of exposure to violent media, the process of desensitization changes what shocks or offends, and indeed changes people's very definitions of what is violent (see Bushman et al., 2002; Linz et al., 1989). This process leads to a kind of induced complacency, whereby violence may seem more commonplace and appropriate, aggressive thoughts and feelings may come to mind more easily, and aggressive responses (including verbal, gestural, and physical responses) in interpersonal situations may become more likely. It is therefore understandable why most people believe they are not harmed by media violence, despite scientific evidence to the contrary.

WHAT'S REALLY REAL?

Recently, there has been a growing interest in the media to depict "real life." "Reality" television, as it is called, has included such popular shows as the *Survivor* series. Nielsen recently reported *Survivor II* as the most popular program for children aged 2 to 11 in the 2000–2001 viewing season (Strasburger & Wilson, 2002). MTV broadcasts *Real World*, and even the Learning Channel promises "life unscripted."

Ironically, while audiences long for reality in their media, their own lives are becoming less real. Educator Roy F. Fox claims, "In today's culture, reality plays second fiddle to representations of reality" (Fox, 2002, p. 24). Fox explains:

The images, voices and sounds of electronic media overwhelm their real counterparts. While Huck [Finn] may have ruminated over his last conversations with Tom Sawyer, the minds of today's kids reverberate with messages, impressions and values from an infinite number of electronic sources, each one clamoring, in uniquely compelling ways, to be heard, to be believed, to be real. (pp. 23–24)

While the audience desires depictions of reality, what we see on television is often patently unreal. Bushman and Huesmann (2001) speak to the unreality in the world of media violence, noting that the frequency of aggressive crimes occurring in the real world is significantly lower than that depicted on television. For example, FBI statistics show that 0.2 percent of the crimes occurring in the real world are murders, whereas 50 percent of the crimes occurring on "reality-based" television are murders (Oliver, 1994). To put these figures into perspective, if the murder rate depicted on TV were applied to real life, the entire population of the United States would be wiped out in just 50 days (Medved, 1995).

With children spending the majority of their free time plugged into media, the unreal world becomes theirs. For example, Fox (2002) tells how children often "replay" commercials they've seen on television by acting them out, singing the slogans, or even including them in their art projects at school. Some kids, he relates, even dream about commercials, and one boy, when asked to do a self-portrait, created a replica of a character from a television commercial for potato chips (Fox, 2002). Rather than actively participating in life during their own free time through involvement in sports, art, and outdoor play, children in our culture watch other people do things, with the increasing hope that what they watch will be "real." Perhaps kids hope that someday others will watch them on television, thus completing the cycle. Advertisers are fully aware of this dynamic, as illustrated by commercials for Gatorade-brand sports drinks that appeared a few years ago, suggesting that kids all want to be "like Mike" (referring to basketball star Michael Jordan), and that drinking Gatorade would magically make this happen. Not only does this turn media representations of reality into kids' actual reality, it also fills their minds with a distorted view of the world they live in as a hyperviolent, hypersexual, hypermaterial place. In the end, this may become a self-fulfilling prophecy.

CONCLUSION

As media play more prominent roles in our lives over the coming decades, history shows that we can expect the violent content of media to increase as well. The most important challenges for parents in such an environment will revolve around how to model and enforce responsible media consumption, with special emphasis on helping children avoid unnecessary exposure to violent programs and games. Media professionals and policymakers also must begin to recognize the impact of increasingly violent content on the public (see also Bushman & Anderson, 2001), and take responsibility for limiting violence in programming. Ultimately, media choices boil down to economics. A media industry powered by profits will produce whatever it believes to be most profitable. As indicated by recent research, the apparent belief among media corporations that "violence sells" may be largely unfounded (e.g., Bushman, 1998; Bushman & Phillips, 2001; Gerbner, 1994a). Perhaps if more research were dedicated to illustrating the economic costs, as well as societal costs, of media violence, eventually media executives would take notice and begin to change programming accordingly. Media will always be aimed at turning children (as well as adults) into consumers above all else. We might hope, however, that in the process children are not also turned on to violence.

CHAPTER 2

Developmental Approaches to Understanding Media Effects on Individuals

Douglas A. Gentile and Arturo Sesma Jr.

A 12-year-old boy in Florida brutally kills a 6-year-old girl by imitating professional wrestling moves (*Stiff Sentence*, 2001). Two teenagers in Littleton, Colorado practice shooting everything in sight by repeatedly playing the violent video game *Doom* before they embark on a shooting spree that kills 13 adolescents and themselves at Columbine High School (Gibbs & Roche, 1999). A 17-year-old in Texas sets himself on fire while being videotaped in an attempt to duplicate a stunt called the "human barbecue" from the MTV show *Jackass* (Brachear, 2002). Four youths, aged 13 to 17, watch the violent film *Menace II Society* on videotape, then commit a carjacking and shoot two other youths in a manner that parallels the film very closely (Means Coleman, 2002). These and countless other tragedies are the types of incidents that often come to mind when one mentions the effects of media violence on people. While such stories suggest an immediate, direct effect of media on the perpetrators, these highly publicized "media effects" stories may actually demonstrate more about how *not* to think about media effects, because they oversimplify complex situations.

In order to more fully understand media effects on children, it is first necessary to dispel some myths regarding media influences. Thus, we address some common beliefs regarding media effects, and how these beliefs—though simple, persuasive, and sometimes partly true—may actually hamper a fuller comprehension of how various media influence youth. Following this discussion, we describe two general approaches to development—one based on normative developmental theory (the developmental tasks approach) and the other focused on individual differences among children (the risk and resilience approach). We will use these models as frameworks for understanding the intersection of media effects and development.

SEVEN MYTHS ABOUT MEDIA EFFECTS

Myth 1. Media effects are simple and direct.

Each of the examples above describes what appear to be simple and direct effects on children imitating what they have seen. Yet the effects of media are not simple; neither are they usually direct. Most media effects are cumulative and subtle, even when they are designed to influence behavior. This subtlety masks remarkable power and persuasiveness. For example, research on advertisements demonstrates that attitudes and purchase behavior can be altered by as few as two or three exposures to an advertisement (Woodward & Denton, 2000). Yet, as we watch or drive past advertisements we don't *feel* our opinions changing. The effects of media usually happen at a level of which we are not consciously aware.

Advertisements, for example, are designed to influence and are successful at influencing brand awareness, brand preferences, brand usage, and brand loyalty (e.g., Gentile, Walsh, Bloomgren, Atti, & Norman, 2001). We rarely notice that advertisements affect us (aside from the rare pizza commercial that immediately makes us crave pizza). This is because ads are generally presented as entertainment, so that viewers are less likely to notice any effect or to resist their messages. Research suggests that the more one participates in this charade, by claiming that advertisements don't affect one's self, the *more* likely one is to be affected (Greene, 1999).

Thus, to the extent that we expect media effects to be simple and direct, we are probably failing to notice the strongest and most powerful media influences.

Myth 2. The effects of media violence are severe.

Each of the events mentioned at the beginning of this chapter is extreme, and it is certainly true that most people who watch media violence never seriously injure other people or themselves. Since media violence does not make them commit the same kinds of violence, many people draw the inference that it has no effect on them or on most other people. Potter (1999) described this issue clearly, stating that, "People know that others are committing violent acts, but they also know that they personally have never committed any atrocities. The problem with this reasoning is that people equate [media] effects with atrocities" (p. 122). Watching violent media can have many effects, and we should not expect that exposure to media violence will cause people to begin killing each other. For every child who picks up a gun and shoots someone, thankfully there are millions who do not. But anecdotally, most seasoned educators will tell you that schoolchildren have become more disrespectful, more verbally aggressive, and more likely to push and shove each other over time. In fact, the largest effect of media violence is probably not illustrated by individual examples of violent behavior, but by the "culture of disrespect" it has fostered and nurtured (Walsh, 2001). Interpersonal violence is just the endpoint on a continuum of disrespectful behavior. As can be seen in Figure 2.1, for every single example of a school killing, there were over 7,000 serious injuries, 28,000 thefts, 44,000 physical fights, and 500,000 reports of bullying (W. Modzeleski, personal communication to the authors, January 9, 2003). Killing someone is just the most visible tip of the phenomenon—there is a great deal of aggressive behavior that is not so extreme.

While media effects on aggression are most likely to arouse concerns, violent media affect us much more broadly. Any time that you have laughed, felt excited, become scared, or otherwise aroused while watching a violent movie, *you have just been affected*. Positive and negative emotional and physiological reactions to violent media are media effects. Clearly, many people seek out this type of stimulation. After all, who wants to watch a "boring" movie? Violent media have many effects, including emotional, physiological, cognitive, attitudinal, and behavioral effects (see chapters 4 and 7 for more details). To the extent that we expect media effects to be exhibited through atrocities, we may be missing opportunities to see the more typical effects of media.

Figure 2.1
Incidents of Violent Behaviors in American Schools, 1998

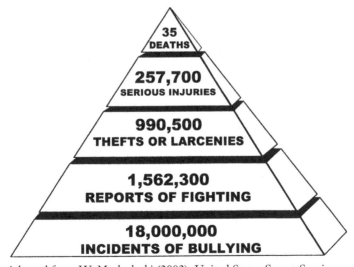

Source: Adapted from W. Modzeleski (2002), United States Secret Service.

Myth 3. Media effects are obvious.

In each of the examples at the beginning of this chapter it was obvious (usually from the perpetrator's own admission) what media product had influenced the subsequent behavior. This leads many to expect that such links should usually be obvious, and thus they take the absence of a direct and obvious link as evidence that no media effects should be implicated. Because the effects of violent media are usually indirect, subtle, and cumulative (and thus not obvious), many people then argue that researchers and policymakers are trying to find an easy scapegoat to explain violent behaviors. Indeed, even when the link is obvious, many people make this argument. The following anonymous quote was posted in response to the *Jackass* copycat burning: "TV shows are not responsible for copycat attempts of dangerous stunts they portray . . . Blaming TV shows for the actions of minors is just passing the buck" ("Texas talkback," n.d.).

Because the effects tend to be subtle and cumulative, even if people notice that someone is becoming more aggressive over time, they may not infer that the gradual change could be due partly to watching violent media. Nevertheless, cause-effect relationships need not be obvious to be significant. Most people accept that smoking causes lung cancer, even though the effect is subtle and cumulative (for a description of the many parallels between smoking and media violence, see Bushman & Anderson, 2001). One cigarette does not change a person's health in any particularly noticeable way, but years of smoking can have dire consequences (but, importantly, not for all people!). To the extent that we expect media effects to be exhibited in an obvious manner, we are missing opportunities to see other less obvious and perhaps more pervasive effects.

Myth 4. Violent media affect everyone in the same way.

Many people assume that, to be considered valid, media violence effects must be unidimensional—that is, that everyone must be affected by becoming more aggressive and violent. While that is one of the documented effects, it is not the only one. Meta-analyses (studies that analyze data presented across large numbers of studies) have shown that there are at least four main effects of watching a lot of violent media. These effects have been called the *aggressor effect*, the *victim effect*, the *bystander effect*, and the *appetite effect* (Donnerstein, Slaby, & Eron, 1994).

The *aggressor effect* describes how children and adults who watch a lot of violent entertainment tend to become meaner, more aggressive, and more violent.

The *victim effect* describes how children and adults who watch a lot of violent entertainment tend to see the world as a scarier place, become more scared, and initiate more self-protective behaviors (including going so far as to carry guns to school, which, ironically, *increases* one's odds of being shot).

The *bystander effect* describes how children and adults who watch a lot of violent entertainment tend to habituate to gradually increasing amounts of violence, thereby becoming desensitized, more callous, and less sympathetic to victims of violence (both in the media and in real life).

The *appetite effect* describes how children and adults who watch a lot of violent entertainment tend to want to see more violent entertainment. Simply put, the more one watches, the more one wants to watch.

These effects are well-documented in hundreds of studies. What is less well known is which people are more prone to which effects (although these effects are not mutually exclusive). In general, females tend to be more affected by the *victim effect*, whereas males tend to be more affected by the *aggressor, bystander,* and *appetite effects.* But it is still unclear how to predict exactly how any given individual will be affected by any given media violence presentation. However, the fact that we cannot yet make this prediction reliably should not be taken as evidence that there is no effect. Furthermore, that everyone is not affected in the same way does not mean that everyone is not affected.

To understand where children learn their attitudes, values, and patterns of behavior, we can consider the effects of various proximal and distal sources of influence (see Figure 2.2). The family is closest to children, and children clearly have their attitudes, values, and behavior patterns shaped and modified by their families. The behaviors defined as "normal" within each family affect

Figure 2.2
Multiple Spheres of Influence on Children

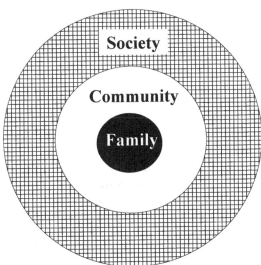

the behaviors of the individuals within that family. Beyond the level of the family, the norms of the community affect the norms of families and individuals within it. Beyond the level of the community, the norms of society affect the norms of communities, families, and individuals within it. The media operate at this societal level, and media effects can be seen at all levels. Thus, the media can affect us not only one-on-one, when we are watching TV, for example, but they also affect us by affecting the norms, expectations, and patterns of behavior of our families and communities. This is another aspect of the media's subtlety—they can affect us through multiple directions at once. Although this makes it likely that everyone will be affected by violent media in some way, it also makes it likely that the effects may not be identical for all people.

Myth 5. Causality means "necessary and sufficient."

Determining if and when something "causes" something else is a problem that has plagued philosophers and scientists for centuries. In the social sciences, it is a surprisingly complex problem to solve. For many people, however, it has become oversimplified—something is a cause if it can be shown to be necessary and/or sufficient as a precursor. This position has been used to argue against the effects of media violence. Ferguson (2002), in a response to Bushman and Anderson's (2001) meta-analyses of media violence and aggression, stated that: (a) because humans have always been violent, "violent media, then, are not a necessary precursor to violent behavior" (p. 446), and (b) because many people who are exposed to media violence never commit violent behavior, "violent media, then, are not sufficient to cause violent behavior" (p. 446).

This argument seems, on its surface, to be reasonable. Yet this argument actually betrays a grossly oversimplified idea of causation. Consider, for example, a rock on the side of a hill. Assume that you give the rock a push and it begins rolling down the hill. Did you cause the rock to roll down the hill? By the argument laid out above, you did not. Rocks have rolled down hills for centuries without someone coming along and pushing them. Therefore pushing it is not necessary. Furthermore, many rocks that are pushed do not roll down hills. Therefore, pushing it is not sufficient. Although pushing the rock was neither necessary nor sufficient to make it roll down the hill, that does not mean that it was not a cause of the rock's beginning to roll.

Most complex issues of interest (such as aggressive behavior) are multicausal. In the present example, many other issues interact to determine whether the push you gave to the rock caused it to roll down the hill: the force of gravity, the mass of the rock, the shape of the rock (round rocks require less of a push than square ones), the friction of the hill surface, the slope of the hill surface, the direction of the push, the force of the push, how deeply the rock is embedded into the ground, and so on—all interact to determine whether your push makes the rock begin to roll or not. Recognition that the issue is multicausal does *not* mean that your push is not one of the causes; in fact, it may have been a significant determiner or catalyst for the ultimate outcome, without which the other causes would not have been activated or sufficient. Aggressive behavior, too, is multicausal. Media violence is likely to be one of the pushes that interacts with other forces at work. In most situations, it is neither necessary nor sufficient. However, that does not mean that it is not a cause—it just means that it is *one* of the causes.

This conception of causality is similar to the idea of "proximate cause" in law, where the goal is to assign legal responsibility for an action. The proximate cause is the last action to set off a sequence of events that produces an injury. Yet, the goal of social science is not the same as that of law. Social science is concerned with all of the causes for some behavior, not only the necessary, sufficient, most recent, or largest causes. Because media violence has been shown to increase the likelihood of aggressive behavior, it can be a cause of aggressive behavior, even if it alone is not a necessary or sufficient cause.

Myth 6. Causality means immediacy.

Many people also expect that causality requires immediacy, as in a fall causing a broken bone. As noted in the smoking and cancer example, however, physical symptoms may become visible only after some threshold of disease process is attained, which may take a long time. With regard to media violence, many people assume that the effects must be seen in the short term in order to be caused by exposure. For example, Ferguson (2002, p. 447) states, "If media violence is a necessary and direct cause of violent behavior, a significant decline in violent crime should not be occurring unless violence in the media is also declining." We have already seen that media violence can be a cause without being a "necessary" cause. The issue of whether it is a "direct" cause seems to be the relationship between the amount of media violence and the incidence of violence in society. From the 1950s until about 1993, both the amount of media violence and the number of aggravated assaults rose in the United States (Grossman, 1996). In the latter half of the 1990s, the aggravated-assault rate fell somewhat while the amount of media violence stayed constant or increased (especially in video games—see chapters 4 and 7). This was taken by many to be "evidence" that media violence does not cause aggressive behavior.

Yet many causes have long-term effects. Consider smoking and lung cancer. Or consider water, salt, and your car. Over many years, cars that are repeatedly exposed to salt rust at a higher rate than those that are not exposed. But if you pour saltwater on your car, will you see it rust? No, it is a long-term effect. Some researchers have presented evidence that the effects of media violence may be long term. For example, Centerwall (1989) has documented

that the murder rate appears to double about 15 years after the initial introduction of television to communities or countries. It has been hypothesized
that about 15 years must elapse before the full effect is revealed, as that is the
time it takes for a generation to grow up with the violent media and to reach
a prime crime-committing age. If this hypothesis is correct, then we shouldn't
expect to see immediate effects. To the extent that we expect causation to
appear as immediate or short-term effects, we may miss a number of important long-term effects.

Myth 7. Effects must be "big" to be important.

Many people have agreed that the accumulated research shows that there
is a systematic effect of violent media on aggressive behavior, yet they also
insist that it is not a large enough effect to be important. These discussions
often include a statistical approach. For example, Ferguson (2002) notes that
the amount of variance in violent behavior explained by media violence in
meta-analyses is somewhere between 1 and 10 percent. This means that if we
drew a circle representing all the reasons why someone might act violently,
media violence would account for between 1 and 10 percent of the pie. (It
should be noted that some meta-analyses have reported larger numbers, and
that there are a number of methodological reasons why these numbers may
be underestimates; see Paik & Comstock, 1994, for a detailed explanation.)
Ferguson (2002, p. 447) states that these effect sizes are "small and lack practical significance." Ferguson is not alone in making this type of value judgment
(e.g., Freedman, 2002), but it is unclear on what basis it is made. In epidemiological terms, if only 1 percent of the people watching a violent TV show
become more aggressive, and one million people watch the program, then
10,000 people were made more aggressive. That does not seem to us to "lack
practical significance." Indeed, many (if not most) medical studies on the effects of drugs or diet are concerned with such small effects. Supplementing
one's diet with calcium can increase bone mass, but the effect is "only" about
one percent (Bushman & Anderson, 2001). Hormone replacement therapy in
women may increase the odds of breast cancer, but across the whole population, the effect is probably less than one percent. A daily aspirin may reduce
the risk of heart attacks, but again, the effect is less than one percent (Hemphill, 2003). The medical profession regards these small effects as clearly important and having a great deal of practical significance.

In fact, there are probably hundreds of reasons for any aggressive act (e.g.,
abuse, poverty, history, gang membership, drug use, etc.). If there are hundreds of reasons, then any single one of them should not account for much
variance. That media violence consistently appears to account for at least 1
to 10 percent of the effect is actually surprisingly large!

Summary

These persistent myths underscore the importance of thinking carefully about what the effects of media violence on individuals may be. We must understand that everyone may be affected, yet not in the same way. We must recognize that most children may be affected, although we may only notice the effects in extreme cases. Two developmental theoretical approaches show a great deal of promise for helping researchers to understand the effects of media violence on children: the developmental tasks approach, and the risk and resilience approach. Each will be described in turn, and their relevance to media effects will be discussed after each.

DEVELOPMENTAL TASKS APPROACH

Overview

Most children learn to talk. Most children become attached to a primary caregiver. Most children develop relationships with peers. Each of these capacities—language acquisition, development of attachment relationships, and the formation of peer relationships—is a *developmental task*—a capacity or skill that is important for concurrent and future adaptation (Sroufe, 1979). Masten and Braswell (1991, p. 13) define developmental tasks in the following manner:

In developmental psychopathology, adaptation is often defined in terms of developmental tasks. . . . The basic idea is that in order for a person to adapt, there are developmental challenges that must be met. Some arise through biological maturation, others are imposed by families and society, while others arise from the developing self.

Researchers have used this approach for at least two purposes. First, it provides a set of criteria by which to judge adaptation at any particular point in development. All children of a particular society are presumed to face these tasks at some point in development; thus, these tasks serve as a barometer from which to infer competence (Masten & Coatsworth, 1998). Second, the developmental task approach provides researchers and practitioners with a framework for understanding how development unfolds over childhood. For example, those interested in understanding the etiology of depression can use such a framework to inform how development went awry (Cicchetti & Toth, 1998).

A number of principles are specific to a developmental task approach. First, there is a hierarchy to these tasks (Sroufe, 1979; Sroufe, 1995). Different issues rise in importance depending on the developmental level of the child. Thus, for infants, the most important task that must be negotiated is developing a trusting relationship with a primary caregiver. As can be seen in Table 2.1, this task recedes in importance as other tasks arise.

This does not mean, however, that early tasks are irrelevant at later stages; to the contrary, later tasks are *contingent* on the success with which earlier tasks were negotiated. That is, any measure of competence is implicitly measuring the totality of adaptation that occurred prior to that measurement. This idea—that development is cumulative and builds on prior adaptation—can also be seen in Table 2.1. Here, the degree to which a child is able to form a trusting relationship with a primary caregiver has direct implications for how she negotiates the next tasks, such as active exploration of her environment. If a child has established a healthy sense of trust and this helped her to actively explore her environment, then the child is in a good position to deal with issues of self-regulation, which are typically encountered in the preschool period. Development proceeds in this way, building on past resolutions and negotiations.

Although current adaptation is predicated on prior adaptation, change is still possible; future developmental progress is not determined or fixed as a result of how earlier developmental tasks are organized (Sroufe, 1997). Rather, the successful negotiation of earlier tasks sets the child on probabilistic pathways for future competence, and these can change depending on the severity of contemporaneous circumstances (e.g., parental death; Cicchetti & Toth, 1998). The implication of this is that it is erroneous to think of adaptation (or maladaptation) as something a child "has." Instead, adaptation is a dynamic process, predicated both on past history and current context.

Finally, while change is possible, it is constrained by prior adaptation (Erikson, 1963; Sroufe, 1997). The longer a child is on an adaptive pathway (i.e., successful negotiation of prior developmental issues), the less likely it is that dire, current circumstances can bump the child onto a maladaptive pathway. This line of reasoning informs current efforts at early prevention projects (Zigler & Styfco, 2001).

Summary of Major Developmental Tasks

The effects that violent (or other) media may have on children and youth may be very different depending on the age of the child in question. As children face different developmental tasks, media are likely to have a greater or lesser effect depending on the specific issues the children are facing at that time. A brief summary of the key developmental tasks at each of five ages is presented below. Because of space limitations, we are unable to describe each task in detail, but have made an effort to include most of the major tasks at each age in a number of categories. The developmental tasks have been adapted from Masten and Braswell (1991), Sroufe, Cooper, and DeHart (1996), Sroufe, Egeland, and Carlson (1999), and Aber and Jones (1997).

Table 2.1
Examples of Developmental Tasks

Key Developmental Tasks of Infancy (0–12 Months)
- Attachment to caregiver(s)
- Regularity of patterns
- Transition from reflex to voluntary behavior

Key Developmental Tasks of Toddlerhood (1–2½ Years)
- Curiosity, exploration, and mastery
- Differentiation of self from world
- Independence of actions, such as self-care and feeding
- Learning of language

Key Developmental Tasks of Early Childhood (2½–5 Years)
- Learning behavioral self-control and compliance with external rules
- Learning emotional self-control
- Learning gender roles and stereotypes

Key Developmental Tasks of Middle Childhood (6–12 Years)
- Learning how to build loyal friendships and to be accepted by peers
- Learning social rules and norms
- Adjusting to school
- Learning the importance of academic achievement and real-world competence
- Moral development
- Consolidating self-concept (in terms of the peer group)

Key Developmental Tasks of Adolescence (13–18 Years)
- Learning to build intimate and committed friendships/relationships
- Adjustment to pubertal changes
- Transition to secondary schooling
- Developing strong and coherent personal identity

Source: Adapted from Aber & Jones (1997); Masten & Braswell (1991); Sroufe, Cooper, & DeHart (1996); Sroufe, Egeland, & Carlson (1999).

Infancy (approximately 0–12 months)

During infancy, developing a trusting relationship with a caregiver is the key developmental task for healthy development. This is not to belittle other important developmental functions at this age. In physical development, the brain is undergoing a tremendous amount of neural network development. In cognitive development, infants exhibit learning by classical conditioning, operant conditioning, and imitative learning. In emotional development, the expression of emotions begins to develop, and we see the beginnings of emotional regulation.

Toddlerhood (approximately 1–2½ years)

During toddlerhood, children develop a number of capacities that could be affected by media. In cognitive development, children at this age develop the capacity for symbolic representation, including language. Children also grow in their ability to use language in a competent communicative manner to conduct conversations in a socially appropriate and culturally specific manner. Social gestures begin to emerge, including conventional social gestures and symbolic gestures. Children also begin to understand themselves as distinct from others. However, children's cognition is still constrained by limited memory abilities, a lack of logic, and a difficulty distinguishing what is real and what is fantasy.

In social development, children's independence of action and feelings of competence are particularly important during toddlerhood. This is also the period when children begin to be expected to learn to regulate and control their behaviors and expressions of emotions. Toddlers begin to acquire the rules, norms, and values of society through socialization processes. Children begin to look to others for cues about how to act in new or ambiguous situations, and begin to internalize the rules and values.

In emotional development, the so-called self-conscious emotions such as shame, guilt, and pride emerge. Early attachment relations and the further development of those attachment relations continue to be important.

Early childhood (approximately 2½–5 years)

In cognitive development, children at this age begin to learn to classify things by shared characteristics, such as color, size, and shape (classification). They also begin to be able to organize things along a particular dimension, such as size or height (seriation). Learning to deploy attention with intention begins at this age, although "the tasks of selecting information to attend to, staying focused on it, and ignoring irrelevant stimuli all pose challenges to preschoolers" (Sroufe et al., 1996, p. 348). Children at this age continue to have difficulty solving appearance-reality problems, and reality is usually defined by the surface appearances of things. In addition, children at this age tend to only be able to focus on one piece of information at a time.

In social development, children of this age begin to develop what has been called a theory of mind. The idea is that preschoolers begin to understand that some things happen that cannot be directly observed, such as the idea that other people can make errors. However, preschoolers continue to have difficulty differentiating their own point of view from that of others.

Children at this age begin to learn "scripts" for types of behaviors, such as what happens in restaurants or what happens to get ready for bed. Similarly, preschoolers also begin acquiring a gender-role concept and to conform to sex-typed behavior. Related to this, preschoolers begin to explore adult roles in their play, including identifying with adults and mimicking adult attitudes and behaviors.

However, probably the most important developmental task for early childhood is learning self-control and self-regulation, including reflecting on one's actions, delaying gratification, tolerating frustration, and adjusting or inhibiting one's behaviors to suit particular situational demands. These actions are part of the preschooler's growing social competence, where children begin to be able to coordinate and sustain interactions with individuals and groups of peers.

In emotional development, preschoolers begin to regulate their own emotions, including learning to be aware of the standards for behavior and using those standards to guide their words and actions. This internalization of standards is a critical part of learning to be able to feel genuine guilt or pride. True empathy and aggression begin at this age, by which we mean actions that have no other purpose than to commiserate with another person or to cause the other person harm or distress.

In moral development, children enter Kohlberg's stage 1 of preconventional moral reasoning, in which "good" behavior is based on a desire to avoid punishments from external authorities (e.g., Sroufe et al., 1996).

Middle childhood (approximately 6–12 years)

In cognitive development, children at this age begin to understand the distinction between appearance and reality and to look at more than one aspect of things at the same time. They also gain a sense of industry, which Sroufe et al. (1996) define as a basic belief in one's competence, coupled with a tendency to initiate activities, seek out learning experiences, and work hard to accomplish goals. Ideally these actions would lead to a sense of personal effectiveness.

In social development, learning how to form friendships is probably the main developmental task of middle childhood. This includes learning how to be part of a peer group, and how to learn and adhere to the group norms. These foster the development of the self-concept, in which one's sense of self is defined in part by the context of the peer group to which one belongs.

These peer relations are also important for moral development, in that the peer groups help to impart cultural norms and values. They also provide opportunities for children to see other points of view and to grow in understanding emotion and having empathy for others. Children continue to develop through Kohlberg's preconventional moral reasoning (stage 2, in which actions are motivated by desires for rewards more than desires to avoid punishment) and begin conventional moral reasoning (stage 3, in which the child's goal is to act in ways others will approve of and to avoid disapproval). Although the peer group is important as part of the engine of moral development, it is important to remember that peer groups exist within cultures and usually reflect those cultures. In fact, Sroufe et al. (1996, p. 472) have stated clearly that "the particular moral principles that children adopt are largely a product of their culture."

Adolescence (approximately 13–18 years)

In cognitive development, adolescents gain the ability to think about abstract concepts and relationships among abstract concepts. Attention skills also make major gains during adolescence.

In social development, the main developmental task is probably learning how to achieve deep levels of trust and closeness with both same-sex and opposite-sex peers. At home, adolescents gain more autonomy and responsibility for homework, finances, jobs, and choices affecting their futures. Personal identity makes additional gains during adolescence, in which adolescents begin to find a fit for themselves within the larger social context as well as defining themselves as unique and independent of their peer groups. Body image also begins to become important as children adjust to pubertal changes.

In moral development, adolescents continue through Kohlberg's conventional moral reasoning (stage 4, in which actions are defined as good to the extent that they perform one's duties as prescribed by the laws of society), and may begin to develop into Kohlberg's postconventional moral reasoning stages.

Media Violence and Developmental Tasks Example

Using a developmental tasks approach can help guide research and theories about media effects in a number of ways. When asking the question, "how will this show/game/movie affect children?" it becomes clear that the answer is unlikely to be unidimensional. The effects are likely to differ greatly depending on the age of the child. Consider the following example taken from a nationally broadcast episode of professional wrestling (*WWF Smackdown*, October 7, 1999). Wrestling was selected as an example of media violence here because it is highly watched by children (it has historically been the highest-rated show on cable; Keller, 2002).

A male wrestler, Jeff Jarrett, is angry at his wrestler girlfriend, Miss Kitty, because she lost a wrestling match the previous week. In order to "get back on [his] good side," he requires Miss Kitty to participate in a mud-wrestling match. He asks the reigning ladies' champion, Ivory, to stand near the ring to watch. He then announces that the goal of the match is to remove the opponent's shirt and bra in order to win. Jarrett then throws Ivory into the mud, to her apparent surprise. Miss Kitty immediately attacks Ivory, removing Ivory's dress. Meanwhile, Jarrett makes comments about women being the lowest form of life and the announcers make lascivious comments about the women's bodies. Ivory eventually removes Miss Kitty's bikini top, "winning" the match. Incensed older-women wrestlers arrive to confront Jarrett, who promptly throws them into the mud, while making comments about them being fat old sows. Ultimately, another lady wrestler, Chyna, sneaks up behind Jarrett, and pushes him into the mud. How would children who repeatedly watch shows like this be affected? The developmental tasks approach provides a framework to understand how children may be affected at different ages.

For infants, it is unlikely to have much effect, unless the parents watch programs like this so much that it interferes with their ability to care for the infant or disrupts the infant's ability to set regular patterns. For toddlers, who are beginning to use language, there were a number of derogatory terms used that children might learn. However, children at this age are just beginning to acquire the standards and values of society through the socialization process. This type of program shows violence as the solution to interpersonal conflict, as well as the "normality" of verbal and physical abuse toward women (especially scantily clad or nude women). Habituation and desensitization processes have begun.

In early childhood, where the main developmental tasks are about behavioral self-control, emotional self-control, and gender roles, this type of program may have a number of negative effects. Very little self-control is displayed. Words are not used to resolve problems, but only to enhance problems. In this specific example, the male was the one with all the power—he set the rules for the engagement, and even though Ivory was "tricked" into the ring, there was no reason she needed to comply with Jarrett's rules—yet she did. The entire episode was derogatory toward women, and even though some might say that the women won in the end, they did it on his terms, not theirs. Children at this age may begin to see women as needing to do whatever men say they should to gain the approval of men and that such behaviors are normal or natural.

In middle childhood, social rules and norms take on increased importance, and they are likely to learn lessons about the importance of physical domination and humiliation of others as an acceptable method of conflict resolution; that is, if they have not already habituated to this level of physical and verbal abuse and therefore do not see it at all. Furthermore, in this example, competence was defined only in terms of ability to fight (although there is also a subtext of sexuality as competence).

In adolescence, the major developmental task is learning how to have intimate and committed relationships. This type of show portrays the relationships between men and women very stereotypically, where the male has the power and the females are submissive. Furthermore, it portrays physical aggression between the sexes as acceptable (and sexual). By this developmental stage, physical and verbal violence in the media will likely appear unremarkable—a natural part of our culture and only a mirror of our society.

We do not mean to suggest that watching one episode of any program is likely to have a large, immediate effect. But any immediate effects as well as long-term effects are likely to be different based on the age of the child, and the developmental tasks approach provides a framework for designing and testing hypotheses about the types of effects we might expect at different ages.

A RISK AND RESILIENCE APPROACH TO DEVELOPMENT

Another approach to viewing development is via a risk and resilience perspective (see reviews by Glantz & Johnson, 1999; Masten & Coatsworth, 1998). As opposed to the normative approach of the developmental tasks framework—every child is presumed to go through these phases, each with varying degrees of ease—a risk and resilience approach focuses on differential life experiences among children that may put them at risk for future maladaptation (risk factors), and those factors that serve to "protect" children from this risk exposure (protective factors). This approach is likely to be useful to help explain why we may see greater effects of media violence on some children than on others. Exposure to media violence is likely to be a "risk factor" for all children. However, some children may have additional risk factors that enhance the effects of media violence exposure, whereas other children may have protective factors that attenuate the effects of exposure to media violence.

One of the strongest and most robust findings in the risk and resilience field is that of the risk gradient, also called a cumulative risk model (Masten, 2001). The premise behind a cumulative risk model is simple: the more risks encountered by a child, the greater the likelihood of problematic functioning (Masten & Wright, 1998; Rutter, 2000; Sameroff & Fiese, 2000). Though simple in premise, the strength in such an approach lies in its acknowledgment that a true challenge to the developmental system comes from the interaction of multiple risk factors, and that this cumulative risk process is greater than any one single-risk factor in derailing development (Belsky & Fearon, 2002). Typical risk factors studied include marital discord, low socioeconomic status (SES), maternal psychological distress, single parent status/divorce, low maternal education, and exposure to violence (Masten, 2001; Masten, Miliotis, Graham-Bermann, Ramirez, & Neemann, 1993; Rutter, 2000), as well as genetic risk factors for psychopathology or aggression (Rutter et al., 1997). Seldom do these risk factors occur in isolation; children experiencing one risk factor are likely also to experience a variety of other risk factors (Masten, 2001).

These studies have also found that there are individuals who aren't as vulnerable to risk factors as other individuals. This phenomenon, termed resilience, refers to the observation that despite experiencing severe adversity, some children display normal or above normal levels of competence across an array of domains (Masten et al., 1999). Early perspectives on resilience erroneously labeled such children as stress-resistant or invulnerable; such labels incorrectly implied that there was something special about these children, such as hardy constitutions that rendered the children impervious to stress and adversity (e.g., Anthony, 1974). Current thinking regarding resilience assumes that successful outcomes despite stress exposure arise out of dynamic interactions between the child and the environment (Masten, 2001). That is, resilience occurs as a result of multiple protective factors—genetic, interpersonal, contextual, and societal—that impinge on the child as well as interact with the child to counteract the negative effects of stress (Sameroff, Seifer, & Bartko, 1997).

One of the interesting findings to come out of studies of resilience is that there are no extraordinary children or circumstances that account for successful development in the context of adversity; rather, factors such as good self-regulation, close relationships with caregivers and other adults, and effective schools are all implicated as characteristics contributing to resilience processes (Masten & Coatsworth, 1998; Masten & Reed, 2002). In fact, Masten has called this whole process "ordinary magic" (Masten, 2001) due to the normal adaptive processes needed to overcome risk.

With regard to media violence, our view is that exposure to entertainment media violence is a risk factor for aggressive behavior and other negative outcomes. The presence of this single risk factor is not sufficient to cause children to pick up guns and begin shooting. However, with each additional risk factor children have for aggressive behavior (e.g., gang membership, drug use, poverty, history of being abused, access to guns, etc.), the risk of that child acting violently compounds. In contrast, with each additional protective factor children have (e.g., stable family environment, good school performance, open communication with parents, etc.), the risk of violent behavior decreases.

This approach may serve to answer the comment most people make about media violence: "I watched a lot of media violence as a kid, and I never shot anyone." We need to remember that "shooting someone" is a highly extreme behavior. Most people will never engage in such an extreme behavior, and exposure to media violence is not such a powerful effect as to be able to make such extreme changes in people. One possible metaphor for this process is to consider the thermometer shown in Figure 2.3.[1] At the lowest end, a child's behavior is routinely respectful and polite. At the highest end, a child engages in the ultimate disrespectful behavior of shooting someone. It is likely that regular exposure to media violence might be able to shift someone about three spots on the thermometer. It certainly isn't a strong enough effect to shift

Figure 2.3
Metaphorical Aggressive Behavior Thermometer

Shooting or stabbing someone

Hitting with intent to injure

Occasional threats of violence

Pushing and shoving

Occasional violent thoughts/fantasies

Verbally aggressive behavior

Occasional aggressive thoughts/fantasies

Occasional rude behavior

Routinely respectful and polite behavior

someone from routinely respectful behavior to shooting someone, but it might change someone to begin showing rude and verbally aggressive behavior. If, however, an individual starts out with other risk factors for violent behavior, and is already at the verbally aggressive spot on the thermometer, regular exposure to media violence may just add enough additional risk to get him to start pushing and shoving others around. The child may also have additional protective factors, which help to keep the level lower.

We have described a number of commonly held beliefs about media effects, and how those beliefs can hamper the ability to accurately predict and interpret the effects of violent media portrayals on children. These myths include the beliefs that media effects must be simple, direct, obvious, severe, and affect everyone the same way. They also include errors in the idea of what a "cause" must be, or how large an effect must be to be important. While the research is clear that media violence can have a negative impact on children, it has been less clear why some children may show a larger effect than others, or why some children may be affected in different ways. The persistence of the myths has made it difficult to understand why we should not expect children to be affected identically. To begin to come to a deeper understanding of the effects of media violence on children, we have provided a brief discussion of two developmental frameworks that can help us to understand how the processes of media effects and development interact. The developmental tasks approach helps to describe why children at different developmental stages would be expected to be affected differently. The risk and resilience approach helps to describe why children at any given age could be affected the same way, but that one child would show the effects behaviorally and another might not. These two developmental approaches have great promise for the field of media effects research, as they help us to understand why children may be affected differently by exposure to media violence, and also why even though most children will not become seriously violent from exposure to media violence, they may nonetheless be affected in an important and negative manner.

NOTE

1. This metaphor is used in the understanding that it is imperfect. For example, this thermometer describes a hierarchy most typical of male aggression, whereas females are more likely to engage in relational aggression rather than physical aggression (e.g., Crick, 1995; Crick & Dodge, 1996). It is intended solely to help describe how different risk factors can increase the likelihood of more severe aggressive behaviors, and how protective factors can decrease the likelihood of aggressive behaviors.

CHAPTER 3

Media Effects on Societies and Communities

Tannis M. MacBeth

When considering possible media effects, most people think of effects on individuals. That has been the focus of most research and is the domain of the preceding chapter. It is possible, however, that media can also have an impact at a broader level, on a society and its communities. In keeping with the model presented in Figure 2.2 of the previous chapter (Gentile & Sesma, chapter 2, this volume), there are multiple spheres of influence surrounding individuals, including family, community, and societal levels. This chapter addresses media effects on the societal and community levels. Such effects may not be simply an additive effect across individuals; the whole may be greater than the sum of the parts. The research examples and issues raised in this chapter focus primarily on media violence and children, in keeping with the emphasis of this book. For theoretical and methodological reasons, however, it can be instructive to consider positive or prosocial effects when thinking about the potentially negative impact of various media. As well, research on media violence and children may benefit, methodologically or otherwise, from consideration of other possible negative media effects (e.g., body image and eating disorders). Some examples of positive and other negative media effects occurring at a more macroscopic level in various cultures therefore have been included.

NEGATIVE AND POSITIVE EFFECTS: THEORY

One of the reasons for discussing positive media effects when asking about negative ones, such as the impact of media violence on attitudes, fear, and behavior, is theoretical. For example, on the positive side, watching educational television programs, such as *Sesame Street*, in the preschool years provides a positive advantage for children upon entering school, and this benefit continues for years. This has been found in longitudinal research in which the same children were studied on several occasions, more recently in the United States (Anderson, Huston, Smith, Linebarger, & Wright, 2001) as well as earlier in Sweden (Jönsson, 1986; Rosengren & Windahl, 1989). On the negative side, researchers in both countries found that watching a lot of entertainment programming in the preschool years had the opposite effect. In other words, depending upon the type of programming children watched in the preschool years, the relationship between their TV viewing and subsequent school achievement could be described as an upward or downward spiral (MacBeth, 1996a), or, to use Rosengren and Windahl's phrase, a series of positive or vicious circles. Theoretically, it is likely that some of the processes through which media content has an intended positive impact are the same processes through which other media content has a negative impact on some people, whether this is an intended or unintended effect on the part of the producers of that content. This, to my mind, was one of the brilliant aspects of the *Report from the [U.S.] Surgeon General's Scientific Advisory Committee on Television and Social Behavior* (National Institutes of Mental Health [NIMH], 1972). Prior to the publication of that five-volume report, representatives of the television industry had strongly argued their case for "no effects"; they said that television is a mirror of society, but not an agent for change. They discounted the evidence that filmed violence can have an impact on children's aggressive behavior through vicarious reinforcement and imitative learning (e.g., Bandura, Ross, & Ross, 1963). Then, in research commissioned for the Surgeon General's report, Stein and Friedrich (1972) demonstrated evidence of prosocial learning from television in the preschool years, consistent with social learning theory (Bandura, 1977, 1994). It became much more difficult for the industry to argue that there are no negative effects, in the face of positive effects theorized to occur through similar learning processes.

NEGATIVE AND POSITIVE EFFECTS: METHODOLOGICAL DIFFICULTIES

In addition to theory, there is another reason to consider positive effects when asking about negative ones. In my opinion, it usually will be more difficult to obtain research evidence of negative than of positive effects, for two reasons.

First, antisocial behaviors such as aggression are disapproved; families, schools, religious institutions, and the society's legal systems work hard to socialize children to inhibit aggressive impulses. It is against the law not only to aggress physically but also to threaten to do so. It's also true, of course, that children receive many mixed messages; for example, they are told both "don't hit" and "stick up for yourself"; they may see sports such as boxing in which the goal is to render your opponent unconscious; and some have observed violent models in their homes. Nevertheless, for researchers to be able to demonstrate a link between media violence and aggressive or other negative behaviors, the effect must be strong enough to overcome the person's inhibitions against those behaviors. Note that these inhibitions vary among groups (e.g., Buddhists who try to "do no harm" versus criminal organizations) as well as among individuals. It is likely that media violence leads to aggressive behavior more often, and sooner, for those with the fewest inhibitions against behaving aggressively, whether that is expressed verbally, physically, and/or psychologically. The impact on others may occur later, for example, through retaliation, as a result of interaction with individuals whose inhibitory threshold for aggression is lower. In other words, there may be ripple effects that go far beyond an individual viewer. Exposure to media violence may influence the attitudes and/or behavior of a particular person, who then interacts with one or more others, who change in response to those attitudes/behaviors. The others may thus be affected by the media violence, even though they themselves weren't exposed to it.

With regard to aggression, a ripple effect may have occurred in the town my colleagues and I called Notel and studied in 1973 and 1975, just before and two years after it first received television reception (MacBeth, 1996a, 1996b, 2001; Williams, 1986).[1] Most nonisolated communities in Canada had obtained television reception by the late 1950s or early 1960s, but this particular town did not get TV reception until November 1973. We took advantage of this unusual opportunity to conduct before-and-after research. If we had only studied Notel, however, we would not have been able to rule out the possibility that any changes we observed were really due to some other co-occurring change in Canadian society, rather than television. So we extended this natural experiment to include Unitel, a town of similar size an hour's drive away, which had had one TV channel for about seven years, and Multitel, a town closer to the border with the United States, which had had four channels for about 15 years. We found that many changes occurred in Notel but not in Unitel or Multitel over the two-year period of our research. These changes included increases in verbal and physical aggression on the school playground and are described in more detail later in this chapter.

A similar process in which those least inhibited about a negative behavior may acquire it first through TV portrayals, and others may acquire it later in part through interaction, may have occurred in the natural experiment regarding disordered eating studied by Becker and her colleagues in Fiji (Becker, Burwell, Herzog, Hamburg, & Gilman, 2002; Bosch, 2000) (also described later in this chapter). Note, however, that in neither the Notel/Unitel/Multitel study nor in the Fiji natural experiment is it possible to discern from the data whether this hypothesized two-step ripple pattern of effects occurred. Unfortunately, it also is difficult to imagine how researchers could in future research disentangle the processes.

A second reason that makes it difficult to study and demonstrate the effects of media violence is that, ethically, researchers cannot expose children or even adults to media content as violent as is routinely available through videos and films. For example, Bushman (1995) conducted three laboratory experiments with university students. He found that: (1) individuals who scored higher on trait aggression were more attracted to media violence than were those lower in trait aggression; (2) media violence elicited aggressive emotion/affect, and to a greater extent for those high than those low in trait aggression; and (3) aggressive behavior was greatest for those who saw the violent film, were high in trait aggression, and had higher habitual exposure to TV violence. He pointed out that the magnitude of these effects is very impressive, given that the violent videotape (an excerpt from *Karate Kid III*) did not contain graphic violence (no blood, none of the characters killed or seriously injured) and was rated PG-13. In addition to the ethical issues involved in using extreme violence in research, he noted the methodological problem that it is difficult to find nonviolent movies that are similar in arousal value to graphically violent ones.

Finally, it is important to realize that whether our focus is on a positive effect, such as literacy (discussed toward the end of this chapter), or a negative effect, such as aggression (its main focus), even if only a small percentage of viewers is affected directly, the impact on communities may be substantial from an epidemiological point of view. For example, if only one percent of those who see an advertisement change their buying habits, that may be very profitable for the company. If aggression increases for only one percent of those who watch a violent TV program, and there were one million viewers, then 10,000 people would act more aggressively, with substantial impact on their victims, as well as through any subsequent ripple effects.

GENERAL METHODOLOGICAL ISSUES FOR MEDIA RESEARCH ON COMMUNITIES

New Media Technology

Both historically and recently, when researchers have studied media effects at the community or societal level, the impetus has been the advent of new media technology or even a new medium. Before discussing examples of such research I want to raise some general methodological issues that apply to many if not all such studies.

Penetration of the technology

Occasionally, when a new technology becomes available, it does so universally, that is, to all households in the community. This is most likely to occur if that particular community lags behind others in getting access to the new technology, as was the case for Notel in the natural experiment we studied (MacBeth, 1996b, 2001; Williams, 1986). We did not have the usual problem that penetration covaries with other important variables, especially socioeconomic status (SES), because Notel obtained television reception so late that the residents knew what TV was, had watched it elsewhere, and almost all had television sets in their homes awaiting the arrival of a signal, via a new transmitter. Usually, however, it takes some time for any new technology to reach full or almost complete penetration, and the problem for researchers is that the process is not random. New technologies are acquired first by better-educated, more affluent families, that is, those of higher SES. It is crucial, therefore, when evaluating research evidence, to consider this issue. For example, I recently read a newspaper article stating that a poll had revealed that most Canadian parents monitor their children's computer and Internet use. But parents can only do so if they have the technology, and many don't. So it's not true that most Canadian parents monitor their children's use, though it may be true that most who have the technology say that they do so. If monitoring children's behavior varies with SES, then SES will be important to consider when evaluating the results of research on technologies new to any community.

Effects envisioned and studied

Unfortunately, a problem for all of us, as researchers or concerned individuals, is that the development of new technologies is always far ahead of our awareness of the consequences of its use, whether they are positive or negative (MacBeth, 1996b). For example, when television was new, people were much more concerned about its impact on eyesight than on aggression. As a consequence, the results of the classic natural experiments studied then in the United Kingdom (Himmelweit, Oppenheim, & Vince, 1958) and in the United States and Canada (Schramm, Lyle, & Parker, 1961) tell us disappointingly little about the topic of this book, media violence and children.

These days, we find ourselves frustrated and angry about the impact of computer viruses and worms on our lives, in terms of both time and money, at both the individual and corporate level. This problem has arisen, in large part, because e-mail and Internet technology was developed in a university setting where the primary concerns were freedom of speech, universal access, and exchange of ideas, rather than privacy and security. Those who developed the technology did not envision the current large number of ill-intentioned users.

Even when regulatory bodies such as the Federal Communications Commission (FCC) in the United States and the Canadian Radio-Television and Telecommunications Commission (CRTC) are willing in principle to regulate new technologies, they may be unable to do so. For example, the CRTC did restrict the use in Canada of automated telephone-dialing devices because of a court ruling concerning invasion of privacy. But when faced with the Internet, the CRTC said that although it was well within their mandate to regulate it, they concluded that it is impossible to do so.

In some cases, regulatory bodies in two otherwise fairly similar cultures have taken different decisions about new technologies, creating an ideal opportunity to study the resulting natural experiment. For example, Tim Collins's invention of V-chip technology at Simon Fraser University has made it possible to block television programs that have been encoded on certain dimensions. Currently, these are: V-violence; FV-fantasy violence (science-fiction, cartoon, etc.); D-dialogue (sexual innuendo); S-sexual behavior (depicted); and L-offensive language (swear words, racist epithets, etc.). The V-chip was not, however, implemented in the same way across North America. In the United States, all television sets with screens larger than 13 inches sold after 1999 must carry the V-chip. In Canada, the CRTC said that this step would unfairly advantage those of higher SES, who would more likely be able to buy a new TV set. Instead, since most Canadians subscribe to a cable system, the CRTC requires the cable companies to make the V-chip technology available to all subscribers. One might hypothesize that the different implementation of the V-chip in two similar countries might result in different effects. It will be interesting to see whether the greater availability of this technology in Canada will change the content or the effects of the content to a greater extent than in the United States.

Distinguishing Media from Real-Life Effects

Whether talking about the effects of new or older technologies, it will be difficult to isolate media effects if the messages are similar to, albeit perhaps narrower or more extreme than, messages from real life. In part this is because of the gradual, cumulative nature of the effects of media with similar content. Greenberg (1988) described this as a *drip, drip, drip* process. He contrasted this more typical usual effect with the occasional, strong *drench* effect of an unusually powerful portrayal (e.g., the serial *Roots*). A more recent, vivid example would be the televised images of the airplanes hitting the World Trade Center towers in New York on September 11, 2001.

One way to isolate media from other effects is to find communities where most people have little or no knowledge from their own life experience about certain topics, making it more likely that their knowledge of those topics has been influenced by media. An interesting study of this sort was conducted by Tate and Trach (1980). It was based on the premise that relatively few Canadians have personal experience with court and other criminal legal procedures. At that time, there were no television programs depicting Canadian procedures, some of which differ from those common in the United States. Tate and Trach found that Canadians who were regular viewers of U.S. TV programs involving lawyers as characters were more likely to respond to questions about legal procedures with an answer that would be correct for the United States but not for Canada.

In a different domain, but based on the same principle, Armstrong, Neuendorf, and Brentar (1992) found that different types of media content were related differently to white university students' beliefs about the SES of African Americans. Greater exposure to entertainment content was associated with beliefs that they enjoy a relatively higher position with regard to average income, social class, and educational achievement, whereas greater exposure to TV news was associated with perceptions that, relative to whites, they are worse off in SES. These media effects were stronger for respondents who had little or no opportunity for direct interracial contact.

DOMAINS OF MEDIA EFFECTS ON COMMUNITIES

Cultural Identity

In some countries/cultures, residents have access to a lot of foreign media, which sometimes raises concern about cultural identity. For example, most Canadians receive U.S. as well as Canadian television channels, and more of the former than the latter. Winter (Winter & Goldman, 1995) conducted research in Windsor, the Canadian city across the river from Detroit, with university students and a stratified sample of community residents. He found that U.S. politicians were more often correctly identified than Canadian ones, and this was also true for national TV news figures. More Canadian residents (57 percent) could name the first U.S. president, George Washington, than could name the first Canadian prime minister, Sir John A. MacDonald (38 percent). Whereas most said that Canadians should preserve their culture (88 percent) and that broadcasting should contribute to Canadian culture (85 percent), 56 percent couldn't name their favorite Canadian TV program or didn't have one, and 82 percent couldn't name the last Canadian film they'd seen. This is perhaps not surprising, as 97 percent of the films shown in Canadian movie theaters are foreign, most are from the United States, and the United States controls film distribution in Canada.

An example of an opportunity "to assess the long-run effects of introducing television on a whole society" (Katz, Haas, & Gurevitch, 1997, p. 45), occurred in Israel, where television was established in 1968 by the Israel Broadcasting Authority (IBA), as one channel, operated during daytime hours by the Educational Broadcasting Service of the Ministry of Education. Subscription cable TV was introduced in the early 1990s, along with a second channel in 1993. It is similar to ITV channels 3 and 4 in the United Kingdom, financed by advertising but overseen by a public board.

Katz et al. (1997) compared the findings of two surveys of Jewish Israelis, the first conducted in 1970, and the second in 1990, that is, before the introduction of the additional channels. As I mentioned earlier in this chapter, causal inferences may be made, in natural or other quasi-experiments, but only when all possible threats to internal validity, that is, other possible explanatory variables, can be ruled out. Katz et al. noted that, over the 20-year period of this study in Israel, there were many such variables: two wars; a doubling of the population; the mean level of education increased by three years; political shifts; greater cultural pluralism; an additional hour of daily leisure; a second day off from work (Friday); and a rise in the standard of living.

Katz et al. (1997) concluded that over the first 20 years of television exposure, Jewish Israelis and their culture had changed in the following ways. Values had changed, slowly, in an individualistic direction—in the direction of concern with self at the expense of concern with collectivity (the communal good), and in the direction of pleasure at the expense of civic obligation. But rather than attributing this to the impact of foreign TV, which did not arrive until after their 1990 data collection, they argued that this process probably was *slowed* by television, given the emphasis on promoting collectivism by the IBA. Katz et al. expect that the new multichannel television, with its emphasis on choice and consumerism, will support the trend toward individualism. Over the 20 years of their study, more than a third of leisure time in Israel was spent watching TV, which subsumed some functions of other media.

Mean World Syndrome

Gerbner and his colleagues (Gerbner, Gross, Morgan, & Signorielli, 1994) contend that both in the United States and around the world, television is a source of the most broadly shared images and messages in history, and the common symbolic environment into which children are born. Through its content, much of which is about power relationships, including those involving violence, it *cultivates* certain expectations and beliefs about the world. They call one set of such beliefs the *mean world syndrome*, that is, believing that the world is a dangerous place. They have demonstrated this in part by showing that in the United States heavy exposure to television cultivates exaggerated perceptions of the number of people there involved in violence in any given week, as well as other inaccurate beliefs about crime and law enforcement. Given the much lower rates of violent crime in Canada (even relative to the population), and given that most Canadians watch a lot of U.S. television, it seems reasonable to hypothesize that this exposure would result in an even greater overestimation by Canadians of the number of people in Canada involved in violence. To the extent that this affects their behavior, it is likely to affect their culture and communities. For example, if overestimation of the probability of encountering violence contributes to a decision to stay at home rather than to go out for the evening, there will be fewer people on the streets, which in turn may make the community seem less vibrant and going out less attractive—another version of a ripple effect. In this case, Canadians watch U.S. programs on Canadian and U.S. channels they receive through their Canadian cable company. But in many other countries, television programs have been imported from the United States or other Western countries (e.g., in Fiji, from the United States, United Kingdom, and Australia; Becker et al., 2002; Bosch, 2000). Gerbner argues that violent TV is more likely to be exported/imported because it "travels well" and is easier to understand across cultural boundaries than are humor and other culturally linked characterizations.

Natural Experiments: Aggression and Conceptions of Criminal Behavior

As I mentioned earlier, I was fortunate to hear in July 1973 of an unusual research opportunity. The *U.S. Surgeon General's Report on Television and Social Behavior* had just been published (NIMH, 1972), and its authors lamented the lack of opportunity to study a before-and-after natural experiment. They believed that since penetration of the medium was so complete in North America, this was no longer possible. Soon afterward, I heard about a community in British Columbia that did not yet have television reception. "Notel" was located in a valley, so the repeating transmitter that was supposed to provide (English) CBC, the national public channel, failed to do so. A new transmitter was going to be installed that November. My colleagues and I jumped at this opportunity to study the impact of the arrival of TV in Notel. As in any quasi-experiment, however, we would not have been able to rule out the possibility that other variables co-occurring with the arrival of television (e.g., general or local historical events), that is, third variables or *threats to internal validity*, accounted for any changes observed in Notel (MacBeth, 1996a, 1998, 2001; Williams, 1986). So in addition to studying Notel just before and two years after the arrival of TV, we studied two control or comparison towns at both times. Unitel, an hour's drive from Notel, had had one channel, CBC (English) for about seven years, and Multitel, located closer to the border with the United States, had had (English) CBC and the three private U.S. networks, ABC, CBS, and NBC, for about 15 years. *Statistics Canada* data indicated that the three towns were similar in size, demographic variables such as SES, cultural backgrounds of the residents, and types of industry in the area. Each town, with about 700 residents in the town, served a population about four times as large through its schools, stores, and services. We studied the impact of television on both children and adults in a variety of domains, including creativity, acquisition of reading skills, participation in community activities, attitudes about gender roles, and aggression (Joy, Kimball, & Zabrack, 1986).

We studied aggression by observing children's natural play behavior on the school playgrounds. Both before (Phase 1) and two years after (Phase 2) the arrival of TV in Notel, we observed the physical and verbal aggressive behavior of girls and boys in the early elementary grades in all three towns. Each child (120 in total for the two phases) was observed on several occasions over two weeks, for a total of 21 one-minute intervals. We also obtained ratings on these children from their teachers and peers on a variety of positive and negative behaviors, and found that those whom we observed to be more physically and verbally aggressive were rated so, lending ecological and construct validity to our observations. Following the introduction of TV to Notel, both verbal and physical aggression on the school playground increased substantially for both girls and boys and for those who were initially low as well as those initially high in aggression relative to their classmates. Similar increases did not occur in Unitel and Multitel, although amount of television viewing by children in those towns in Phase 1 did add significantly to prediction of aggressive behavior in Phase 2, over and above the child's level of aggression two years earlier. Taken together, these findings indicate that television affected children's aggressive behaviors on these school playgrounds. Moreover, this was not, as is sometimes argued, limited only to children already high in trait aggression.

What were the processes through which aggression increased following the arrival of TV in Notel? We cannot be sure, as we did not observe them, but we think that the change for the entire community in exposure to aggression may have reduced the effectiveness of the social controls previously established. It is likely, as I mentioned earlier, that the children with the fewest inhibitions against aggression were initially affected, and that the others were influenced in part through exposure to aggression on TV and in part through interaction with their peers, in a ripple effect.

In an Australian natural experiment, 8- to 12-year-olds were interviewed about their conceptions of crime (Murray, 1998; Murray & Kippax, 1977, 1978). The design of this study was similar to ours; three towns were studied before and two years after one of them obtained television reception. The researchers called them a no-TV town, a low-TV town (two years experience with one channel of public television), and a high-TV town (five years experience with both public and commercial television). Two years after the no-TV town had become a new-TV town, and the others had had four and seven years experience with TV, respectively, children were interviewed about crime. Their responses to questions about the similarity of various crimes indicated that those in the new- and low-TV towns had a two-dimensional conceptualization of crime: its degree of seriousness, and whether its focus was on property or persons. Children in the high-TV town, the only ones with exposure to the more violent commercial channel, produced a more differentiated three-dimensional conceptualization. The first two dimensions were similar to those for children in the other towns, but the "seriousness" and "property versus person" dimensions were overlaid by a third dimension, "drunkenness, spying, and shoplifting," which seemed to be a mélange of the real and television worlds. The researchers concluded that the high-TV-town children had a much more complex conception of crime than did their peers in the low- and new-TV towns.

Copycat Crimes

Media events are sometimes imitated by those who have read or heard about or seen them, in such a way that there is good reason to believe that the media portrayals/descriptions played a role in the imitation. The phrases *copycat crimes* and *bizarre replications* refer to such reenactments, which have taken many forms. Sometimes these reenactments are rare, and only one or a few are documented. For example, in a made-for-TV movie, *The Burning Bed*, a woman whose husband had beaten, assaulted, and terrorized her for years set fire to him and his bed. After watching the movie, a man who had been similarly violent toward his wife set fire to her, and she died. He told the police that he was afraid that she would have done that to him. This was the only replication publicized, to my knowledge. In other cases, however, depictions in the media have been followed by a series of similar events in a variety of communities and countries. I will mention a few here as examples of copycat crimes in which media may have had an impact at the societal level, rather than just upon individuals.

Suicides and homicides

Phillips (e.g., 1985), a sociologist, has used the paradigm he calls *found experiments* to study the impact of mass media stories on fatal antisocial behavior, which he divides into three categories: (1) self-directed violence (suicide), (2) other-directed violence (homicide), and (3) a combination of self-directed and other-directed violence (murder-suicide).

In a lengthy series of studies, Phillips (1985) obtained evidence (e.g., from the U.S. National Center for Health Statistics) regarding the incidence of suicide, homicide, and apparently purposeful car and plane accidents following publicized stories in newspapers and on television about suicide, murder-suicide, and championship heavyweight prizefights. With regard to suicides, motor-vehicle fatalities, and private plane crashes, he found statistically significant evidence (a) of increases following publicized suicide stories; (b) that the greater the publicity in the United States, the greater the increase; and (c) that the greatest increases occurred in the geographic areas where the suicide was most heavily publicized.

Murder and murder-suicides by parents

Over the last two years or so, North American media have publicized a number of homicides in which a parent has killed his or her children, and/or the other parent, and sometimes him/herself as well, in both the United States and Canada. It is difficult to know to what extent the publicity given to such killings has contributed to this recent spate.

Anthrax

Beginning in the fall of 2001, following the attacks on September 11 in the United States, there was considerable publicity about both the general possibility of biological weapons being used there and specific incidents in which anthrax was distributed in the mail system and caused illness and, in some cases, death. Some of the anthrax incidents may have been copycat crimes. There also, however, were many more incidents in which harmless powders were distributed by mail following media stories about the serious anthrax events and threats. Reports in newspapers, and on radio, television, and the Internet, indicated that a great many people were afraid to open their mail. This seems to be a clear example of the impact of media on communities, beyond the individual level.

School shootings

Beginning in about 1975 there has been a lengthy series of school shootings in North America in which one or more youths have gone to a school and shot and injured or killed students and/or teachers. In some cases they have also killed their parent(s) and/or themselves. Almost all of the aggressors have been male. Most of the widely publicized attacks have occurred in the United States, but a similar crime was enacted April 26, 2002, in Germany. One of the Canadian shootings occurred in Taber, Alberta, a small Canadian town, in May 1999. I received a phone call within a couple of hours from CBC television, asking whether they could interview me about my thoughts on this event. The reporter who called me began by saying, "We have stopped publicizing suicides and are very concerned about the role of the media. What should we do?"

The role of media in copycat crimes of violence occurs at two levels. The first is the initial portrayal, that is, the choice by the film/television producer or newspaper/magazine editor to portray the violence, whether in the context of fiction or nonfiction. If any copycat crimes occur following that initial portrayal, the media then have the responsibility of deciding whether to publicize the replications. With regard to the series of school shootings in North America, Grossman (1998), a former U.S. Army officer expert on the psychology of killing, who lived in one of the communities (Jonesboro, Arkansas), wrote:

In the days after the [March 24, 1998] Jonesboro shootings, I was interviewed for Canadian national TV, the BBC,[2] and many U.S. and international radio stations and newspapers. But the U.S. television networks simply would not touch this aspect of the story [the media's responsibility for copycat crimes]. Never, in my experience as a historian and a psychologist, have I seen any institution in America so clearly responsible for so many deaths, and so clearly abusing their publicly licensed authority and power to cover up their guilt. Time after time, idealistic young network producers contacted me, fascinated by the irony that an expert in the field of violence and aggression was living right here in Jonesboro and was at the school almost from the beginning. But unlike the stories in all the other media, these network items always died a sudden, silent death when the powers-that-be said, Yeah, we need this story like we need a hole in the head.

Para-Social Murder

Media provide the illusion to their users of knowing and interacting with the characters depicted, whether they are real or fictional. Horton and Wohl (1956) described these as *para-social interactions*, and said they are especially important for the "socially isolated, the socially inept, the aged and invalid, the timid and rejected" (p. 223). Meyrowitz (1985) found this para-social framework helpful in explaining why it is that when a *media friend* dies, millions of people experience a great sense of loss. In most cases the death is from an accident (e.g., Princess Diana) or health-related causes (e.g., Elvis). But the "para-social relationship has also led to a new form of murder and a new type of murder motive," the *para-social murder* (Meyrowitz, 1985, p. 121). John Lennon's murderer was a complete stranger who had never met Lennon physically, but for Mark David Chapman there was a powerful para-social tie between them. Meyrowitz notes that a similarly bizarre relationship existed for John Hinckley, who attempted to murder the U.S. President Ronald Reagan, to cement his perceived "personal" relationship with actress Jodie Foster.

Eating Disorders

A medical anthropologist has been studying eating habits in Fiji for about 12 years (Becker et al., 2002; Bosch, 2000). Traditionally, Fijians have preferred robust body shapes for both women and men, reflecting the importance in their culture of generous feeding and voracious eating. Television came to Fiji in 1995, in the form of one channel that primarily broadcasts programs from the United States, Australia, and the United Kingdom. In their prospective, multiwave, cross-sectional study, Becker and her colleagues assessed two different sets of school girls in Nadroga aged 15 to 19 years, the first 64 in 1995 within a few weeks of the arrival of TV, and the other 65 in 1998. There was an increase in the proportion who reported ever having vomited to control weight (0 to 11.3 percent), and in those who scored high on a test of risk for disordered eating (13 percent to 29 percent). In 1998, those who lived in a house with a television set were three times more likely to show symptoms of eating disorders, though they were not more overweight. Three years after the arrival of TV in Nadroga, 69 percent of the young women said that they had dieted to lose weight at some time, and 74 percent reported feeling "too big or fat" on occasion. They also said in interviews that they were interested in weight loss as a means of modeling themselves after the dramatic-fiction television characters whom they admired.[3] The authors said that the impact of television seems to have been especially strong, given the longstanding cultural traditions that previously had seemed to protect the Fijian population against dieting, purging, and body dissatisfaction.

Media Imperialism

One of the ways in which mass media from foreign cultures may affect other cultures is to encourage unfavorable lifestyle comparisons, promoting emigration to wealthier areas, depriving poorer areas of needed expertise and labor (Katz & Wedell, 1977). Snyder, Roser, and Chaffee (1991) challenged this assumption of simple, direct, powerful effects of foreign media, arguing that social change in developing countries involves a more complex interplay between mass media and interpersonal communication. They also noted that much foreign news is negative, making it unlikely to create a desire to emigrate to a country with such crime and disaster. They conducted their study in Belize in 1982, a year after U.S. television had arrived,[4] before there was any Belize-produced TV. Prior to the arrival of U.S. TV, some Spanish-language TV from other countries was available near Belize's borders. Snyder et al. (1991) assessed 11- to 19-year-olds' desires to emigrate to the United States. Almost all listened to local radio (98 percent) and read local newspapers (96 percent), but their entertainment media were foreign dominated. U.S. programs were predominant among their favorite TV shows, and more than half had attended a movie in the past week (36 percent made in the U.S., 16 percent in Hong Kong, 3 percent in Latin America). The most popular music was American-style soul and disco (60 percent cited it as favorite), with Caribbean music being about as popular (14 percent) as other U.S. genres (rock, 13 percent; Western, 10 percent). When asked if they would like to move to another country, 47 percent said no; 45 percent said they'd like to live in the United States; and 9 percent mentioned other countries. The most important predictor of a desire to move was interpersonal contact with people in the United States. Viewing entertainment television also positively predicted wanting to emigrate, whereas reading news magazines was a negative predictor. The highest probability of wanting to emigrate (81 percent) occurred for those having many interpersonal sources in the United States, watching U.S.-dominant entertainment television, and reading U.S. newspapers. These results indicate that in the case of Belize and the United States, interpersonal contacts are much more strongly associated with emigration than is mass media exposure, although after being available for a year, U.S. entertainment TV also did contribute to young people's interest in moving there.

Entertainment-Education Soap Operas

So far in this chapter, most though not all of the examples of research on various media effects on communities have been examples of unintended negative effects on antisocial attitudes and/or behavior. But there also have been some very interesting and impressive large-scale studies of intended positive effects on prosocial behavior. Miguel Sabido (1981) developed his methodology for combining entertainment with education in soap operas when he was a vice-president at Televisa, Mexico's privately owned commercial television network, in the 1970s. Sabido's entertainment-education methodology has also been used in India (Brown & Cody, 1991; Singhal & Rogers, 1988) and, more recently, has been transferred to Kenya, Tanzania, Malawi, Brazil, Jamaica, Indonesia, Nigeria, China, Turkey, Egypt, and the Philippines. Many of these programs focus on family planning. The Mexican and Indian projects are described below. More detailed information about the methodology and the projects in all of the countries above mentioned is provided by Nariman (1993).

Mexico

In Mexico, Televisa broadcast six series of prosocial programs called *tele-novelas* (TV soap operas) from 1975 to 1981 to promote adult literacy, family planning, and gender equality. These prodevelopment soap operas used Sabido's entertainment-education strategy to induce cognitive and behavioral changes in viewers (Ryerson, 1994).

Of the six Televisa entertainment-education soap operas, two focused on adult literacy, and one each focused on family planning, responsible parenthood, adolescent sexual education, and women's equality. Nariman (1993) has described their development and effectiveness in detail. The results include research evidence of: (1) a 63 percent increase in new students enrolled in adult literacy programs during the year that *Ven Comingo* (*Come with Me*) was on air (compared with an increase of only 7 percent in the preceding year and 2 percent in the subsequent year); (2) 2,500 new volunteers as aides in family planning clinics; (3) an increase of 23 percent in condom purchases (by comparison with 7 percent in the preceding year); and (4) a continued decline in the birth rate. Many viewers also spontaneously said that the entertainment-education soap operas were better than others because of their educational content. It is noteworthy, as well, that rather than being a budget drain, as are educational and social government-sponsored resources, entertainment-education soap operas generate income from advertising and foreign sales.

India

Based on the Mexican experience, the soap opera *Hum Log* (*We People*) was created in India and broadcast twice a week over 17 months in 1984–1985 on Doordashan, the private Indian television network. It became the most popular program in the history of Indian television (Mitra, 1986). An average episode was watched by 50 million people. It was sponsored by Food Specialties Ltd., a Swiss subsidiary of Nestlé, who used it to introduce *Maggi*

2 minute Noodles to India. Its financial success led to the commercialization of television in India and the proliferation of other privately sponsored dramatic serials. *Hum Log* resulted from "a marriage between Indian television and Bombay's film industry" (Brown & Cody, 1991, p. 118).

The goal of *Hum Log* was to improve the status of women in India, with episodes which confronted the problem of women's abuse (e.g., 1,319 recorded bride-burning fatalities in 1986); promoted women's employment outside the home; encouraged women to make decisions for themselves and their families; criticized the dowry system; and promoted women's freedom of choice and equality.

Unfortunately, research evidence of the effectiveness of *Hum Log* is weaker than that for the Mexican series. For example, Indian television viewers were not consciously aware of the beliefs about women that the program was trying to promote, or, if they were, they focused more on other themes. And, whereas in Mexico viewers preferred the characters who promoted positive as opposed to negative sides of prosocial behavior, that was not the case in India. The mother in the *Hum Log* family, Bhagwanti, "represented the stereotypical, self-effacing, self-neglecting Indian wife/mother who was a negative role model for female equality" (Brown & Cody, 1991, p. 118). In contrast, Badki, the eldest daughter, was a nontraditional, independent, hard-working woman and represented the positive role model. But Brown & Cody found that 18 percent of their survey respondents identified Bhagwanti as the positive role model to emulate, and 80 percent of those who did so were women. Only 11 percent of the respondents chose Badki, and 5 percent chose Chutki (a career-minded young woman). Brown and Cody surmised that this was because both of the younger women occasionally suffered negative consequences when attempting to promote women's status. Many female viewers apparently took away the message that it is better to be self-sacrificing like Bhagwanti so as to avoid the occasional troubles brought on by nontraditional roles. Brown and Cody noted that their findings are reminiscent of the evidence that the Archie Bunker character in *All in the Family* did not necessarily have the effect Norman Lear had intended. Bigots identified positively with him and his discriminating views, whereas liberals saw him as Lear had hoped, that is, as sexist and racist (Vidmar & Rokeach, 1974).

CONCLUSION

The main goal of this chapter has been to raise awareness that, in addition to the impact media violence may have on individuals exposed to it, media may also affect people indirectly, as a result of the broader impact on communities and cultures. It is my hope that the methodological issues and research examples discussed in this chapter provoke thought, discussion, and further research, with an eye toward maximizing positive media effects and minimizing negative effects on attitudes and behaviors.

NOTES

1. This study is described in greater detail later in the chapter in the section on natural experiments.

2. The national public broadcasting system in the United Kingdom, the British Broadcasting Corporation.

3. As I cautioned earlier in the chapter, full penetration of new technologies is not immediate and varies with SES. In Western culture, eating disorders are more prevalent among higher than lower SES groups, and higher SES characters or role models (in terms of careers, clothing, etc.) are more prevalent on television.

4. An entrepreneur in Belize City bought a used satellite dish antenna, put it in his backyard, and retransmitted the signal to subscribers, bringing Chicago television to the country.

CHAPTER 4

Television Violence

Victor C. Strasburger and Barbara J. Wilson

The debate about media violence has been raging for nearly 50 years. In 1954, Senator Estes Kefauver, then Chairman of the Senate Subcommittee on Juvenile Delinquency, held hearings on whether television violence was contributing to real-life violence in the United States. When questioned, network executives claimed that the available research was not conclusive (Liebert & Sprafkin, 1988). A half-century later, hundreds of research studies and several government reports provide conclusive evidence that media violence *can* have harmful effects on viewers (e.g., Bushman & Anderson, 2001; Federal Trade Commission, 2000; Pearl, Bouthilet, & Lazar, 1982; Strasburger & Wilson, 2002). Yet some industry representatives continue to argue that television violence is harmless entertainment (see Figure 4.1). How much is actually known about the impact of media violence on children and adolescents, what sorts of studies have been done, and how convincing are the data? Are the media part of the problem of violence in society? Or, as some TV executives suggest, does television merely reflect the violence that is occurring in society?

VIOLENCE IN AMERICAN SOCIETY

In the debate over television violence and its impact, observers cannot even agree on the answer to this simple question: Is American society becoming more or less violent? For example, the rate of juvenile crime among 12- to 17-year-olds decreased in 1997 to 31 serious crimes per 1,000, the lowest rate since 1986 (Forum on Child and Family Statistics, 1999). At the same time, this lower crime rate still translates into more than 700,000 violent crimes committed by teenagers in 1997 (Forum on Child and Family Statistics, 1999).

Figure 4.1

Among 15- to 24-year-olds, homicide remains the second leading cause of death (National Center for Injury Prevention and Control, 2000), and the United States ranks first among all industrialized nations in youth homicides (Snyder & Sickmund, 1999). The outbreak of school shootings in the last few years only serves to reinforce many people's notion that there is a "culture of violence" afoot in the United States (Ginsburg, 2001).

Although the nature of recent trends in violence may be debatable, what is clear is that violent crime has increased dramatically since the advent of television 50 years ago. From 1960 through 1991, the U.S. population increased by 40 percent, but the violent crime rate increased by 500 percent (Grossman & DeGaetano, 1999). Moreover, homicide rates may not be the best indicator of whether violence is increasing. For one thing, murder is the least frequently committed crime. For another, people are now able to survive being shot because of extraordinary advances in medical care (Grossman & DeGaetano, 1999). Some experts contend that levels of *aggravated assault* provide a far more appropriate index of how violent society has become (Grossman & DeGaetano, 1999), and these levels have risen dramatically during the past 50 years (see Figure 4.2).

Figure 4.2
Rates of Aggravated Assault, Imprisonment, and Murder

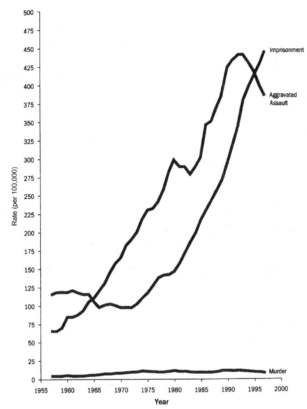

Source: Grossman & DeGaetano (1999).

In some provocative research, Centerwall (1992) has argued that historical changes in violent crime can be tied to television violence. In a 1992 study, he examined white homicide rates in South Africa, Canada, and the United States and found that in the latter two countries, 10 to 15 years elapsed between the introduction of television and a subsequent doubling of the homicide rate—exactly what one would expect if TV violence primarily affects young children (see Figure 4.3). As Centerwall predicted, urban homicide rates rose before rural rates (television was first introduced into urban areas), rates rose first among affluent whites (minorities could not afford early TV sets), and rates increased earlier in those geographical areas where TV was first introduced. South Africa was used as a "control" nation because it closely resembles Western countries, yet it did not have any television until 1973. Predictably, homicide rates in South Africa have now begun to climb as well (Strasburger, 1995). Based on his statistical analyses, Centerwall (1992) asserts

Figure 4.3
The Impact of TV on Homicide Rates

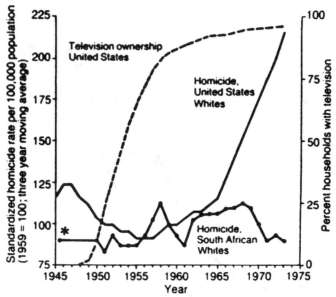

Source: B. S. Centerwall (1992). Television and violence: The scale of the problem and where to go from here. *Journal of the American Medical Association*, 267, 22–25. Copyright © 1992, American Medical Association.

that long-term exposure to TV violence is a causal factor in approximately half of all homicides in the United States and that 10,000 homicides could be prevented annually if television were less violent. These are intriguing arguments based on data that go well beyond typical correlational analyses. Still, the findings do not meet stringent cause-and-effect criteria and thus are open to alternative explanations.

HOW VIOLENT IS AMERICAN TV?

American television is arguably one of the most violent media landscapes in the world. Early estimates indicated that the average American child or teenager viewed 1,000 murders, rapes, and aggravated assaults per year on television alone (Rothenberg, 1975). A more recent review by the American Psychological Association puts this figure at 10,000 per year—or approximately 200,000 by the time a child graduates from high school (Huston et al., 1992).

In the earliest efforts to quantify violence on television, Gerbner and his colleagues analyzed a week of programming each year from 1967 until the

late 1980s (e.g., Gerbner, Gross, Morgan, & Signorielli, 1980). The researchers found a great deal of consistency over time, with 70 percent of prime time
programs and 90 percent of children's programming containing some violence. Rates as high as 20 violent incidents per hour in children's programming
and 5 violent incidents per hour in prime time programming were found (see
Figure 4.4).

More recently, researchers at four universities collaborated on the National
Television Violence Study (NTVS), which represents the most comprehensive
content analysis ever attempted of American television. From 1994 to 1997,
over 2,500 hours of content were assessed each year across 23 different channels, including the broadcast networks, independent broadcast, public broadcasting, basic cable, and premium cable (Smith et al., 1998; Wilson et al.,
1997, 1998). Over the three years of the study, a steady 61 percent of programs
contained some violence. However, the prevalence of violence varied considerably by channel type. More than 80 percent of programs featured on premium cable contained violence, whereas fewer than 20 percent of programs
on public broadcasting did (see Figure 4.5).

Figure 4.4
**Violence on Television Based on Annual Content Analyses by George
Gerbner and Colleagues**

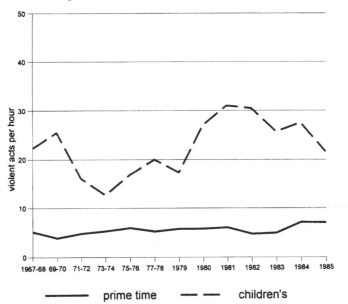

Source: Original data from N. Signorielli and M. Morgan, *Cultivation analysis: New
directions in media effects research* (Sage, 1990). Adapted by V. C. Strasburger and B. J.
Wilson, *Children, adolescents, and the media* (Sage, 2002). Reprinted by permission of
Sage Publications, Inc.

Figure 4.5
National Television Violence Study

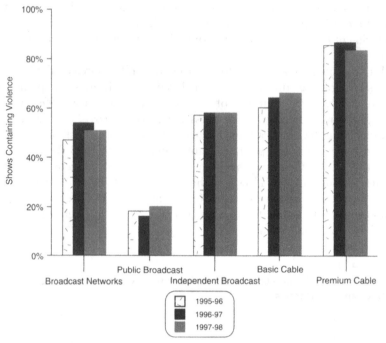

Source: Original data from S. L. Smith et al., Violence in television programming overall: University of California, Santa Barbara study. In *National television violence study: Vol. 3* (Sage, 1998). Adapted by V. C. Strasburger and B. J. Wilson, *Children, adolescents, and the media* (Sage, 2002). Reprinted by permission of Sage Publications, Inc.

The researchers also examined *how* violence is portrayed on television. As it turns out, in trying to understand the potential harm a portrayal might pose for viewers, contextual features such as whether a perpetrator is attractive and whether the violence is punished are more important than the sheer amount of aggression (see Wilson et al., 1997). Several conclusions were drawn from the three-year content analysis:

- *Violence on television is frequently glamorized.* Nearly 40 percent of the violent incidents were perpetrated by "good" characters who could potentially serve as role models for young viewers. In addition, a full 71 percent of violent scenes contained no remorse, criticism, or penalty for violence at the time that it occurred.

- *Violence on television is frequently sanitized.* Nearly one-half of the violent incidents failed to show physical harm or pain to the victim. And less than 20 percent of the violent programs portrayed any long-term negative consequences of violence to the victim or the victim's family.

- *Violence on television is often trivialized.* More than half of the violent incidents featured physical aggression that would be fatal if it were to occur in real life. Yet 40 percent of the violent scenes included some form of humor.
- *Very few programs emphasize an antiviolence theme.* Across the three years of the study, less than 5 percent of violent programs featured an antiviolence message. In other words, almost all TV violence is shown for entertainment rather than for educational or prosocial purposes.

Two genres of programming bear special mention because they are so popular among youth. First, shows targeted specifically to children under the age of 13, most of which are animated cartoons, contain a great deal of violence. Nearly 70 percent of children's shows contain some violence, whereas 57 percent of nonchildren's shows do (Wilson et al., 2002). Furthermore, a typical hour of children's programming contains 14 different violent incidents, compared with 6 per hour in all other programming. The context of violence is also different in children's programs. For example, children's shows are even less likely than other types of shows to depict the serious consequences of violence. Children's programs are also more likely to portray violence as humorous.

Second, music videos are quite popular with preadolescent and adolescent viewers. Overall, only 15 percent of all music videos on BET, MTV, and VH-1 contain violence (Smith & Boyson, 2002). However, that figure jumps to nearly 30 percent when looking just at rap or at heavy metal videos in particular (see Figure 4.6).

THE IMPACT OF TV VIOLENCE ON VIEWER AGGRESSION

No single factor propels a child or a teenager to act aggressively. Instead, the causes of such antisocial behavior are complex and multifaceted. Hormonal and neurological disorders, impulsivity, and even child temperament have been identified as risk factors (Raine, 1997; Shaw & Winslow, 1997), as have environmental forces such as poverty, drug use, and lack of parental affection (Archer, 1994; Guerra, Huesmann, Tolan, Van Acker, & Eron, 1995). But because the expression of aggression is a *learned* behavior (Eron, 1997), the media too have been identified as a risk factor.

Several methodologies have been used to study the effects of TV violence on aggression. Experiments are controlled studies in which people are randomly assigned to receive a treatment (e.g., watch something violent on television) or to serve in a control group, and afterward their responses are measured. Experiments can be conducted in a laboratory or in a more naturalistic setting in the field. Because all other variables are held constant and only the treatment is manipulated, experiments are the best method for establishing cause-and-effect relationships. However, experiments can be criti-

Figure 4.6
Music Video Violence, National Television Violence Study

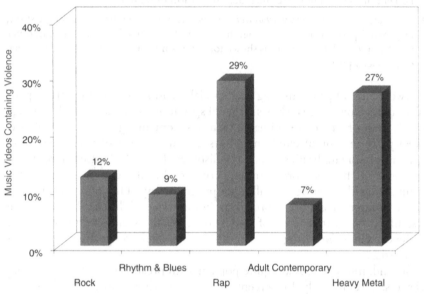

Source: Original data from S. L. Smith and A. R. Boyson (2002), Violence in music videos: Examining the prevalence and context of physical aggression, *Journal of Communication, 52* (1). Adapted by V. C. Strasburger and B. J. Wilson, *Children, adolescents, and the media* (Sage, 2002). Reprinted by permission of Sage Publications, Inc.

cized for being artificial and for focusing on short-term effects only. Correlational studies typically involve large-scale surveys that ask people about their media habits and about their aggressive behavior. The samples are commonly more representative than those used in experiments, and the results reflect more natural, ongoing behaviors in the real world. Yet it is difficult to ascertain causality when variables are simply correlated or shown to relate to one another at a single point in time: Do media habits influence aggression, or do aggressive people seek out violent media? To address this issue, longitudinal studies follow the same sample of individuals over time. This approach allows for the testing of long-term effects and for ascertaining whether early media habits predict subsequent behavior or vice versa.

Given that each method has particular strengths but also certain limitations, no single approach can definitely address the problem. However, by aggregating research across the different methods, we can draw certain conclusions about the impact of media violence (Bushman & Huesmann, 2001). Using each of the methods as a framework, we provide an overview of the evidence below.

Experimental Studies

Some of the earliest research on television violence was conducted in the 1960s by Albert Bandura and his colleagues. In a series of classic experiments (Bandura, Ross, & Ross, 1961, 1963a, 1963b), Bandura observed the behavior of nursery-school children in a playroom that was filled with toys, among them a Bobo doll (a punching bag with a sand-filled base and a red nose that squeaked). The purpose of the experiments was to investigate the circumstances under which children would learn and imitate new aggressive behaviors. To test imitation, children typically watched the following filmed sequence on a TV set before being allowed to play:

The film began with a scene in which [an adult male] model walked up to an adult-size Bobo doll and ordered him to clear the way. After glaring for a moment at the noncompliant antagonist the model exhibited four novel aggressive responses, each accompanied by a distinctive verbalization. First, the model laid the Bobo doll on its side, sat on it, and punched it in the nose while remarking, "Pow, right in the nose, boom, boom." The model then raised the doll and pummeled it on the head with a mallet. Each response was accompanied by the verbalization, "Sockeroo . . . stay down." Following the mallet aggression, the model kicked the doll about the room, and these responses were interspersed with the comment, "Fly away." Finally, the model threw rubber balls at the Bobo doll, each strike punctuated with "Bang." This sequence of physically and verbally aggressive behavior was repeated twice. (Bandura, 1965, pp. 590–591)

Bandura and his colleagues varied the endings to this film across different experiments. In one study (Bandura, 1965), for example, children were randomly assigned to one of three conditions: (a) a model-rewarded condition, in which the model was called a "champion" and was treated with a soft drink and an assortment of candies, (b) a model-punished condition in which the model was severely scolded and called a "bully," or (c) a neutral condition in which the model received no rewards or punishments for his behavior. Afterward, each child was escorted to the playroom, which contained the plastic Bobo doll, along with three balls, a mallet, a dollhouse, and assorted other toys. The results revealed that children in the model-rewarded and neutral groups displayed significantly more imitative aggression than did children in the model-punished group. The fact that the no-consequences condition resulted in just as much aggression as the model-rewarded condition suggests that so long as no punishments occur, children are likely to imitate a model's behavior.

Other research by Bandura et al. (1963a) found that children could learn new aggressive behaviors as easily from a cartoonlike figure as from a human adult, a result that clearly implicates animated TV shows as an unhealthy reservoir of violence. Although Bandura's experiments have been criticized as artificial because children were merely hitting an inflated punching bag, other laboratory research has shown that young children will aggress against a human being dressed as a clown just as readily as they will against a Bobo doll (Hanratty, O'Neal, & Sulzer, 1972). Furthermore, field experiments that have been conducted in more naturalistic settings indicate that aggression can be targeted to peers as well. In one study, preschoolers who watched ordinary, violent TV programs during breaks at school displayed more aggressiveness on the playground than did children who viewed nonviolent programs over the same 11-day period (Steuer, Applefield, & Smith, 1971). More recently, elementary-school children exposed to a single episode of *The Mighty Morphin' Power Rangers* displayed more verbal and physical aggression in the classroom than did children in a no-exposure control group (Boyatzis, Matillo, & Nesbitt, 1995). In fact, the treatment group committed seven times the number of aggressive acts, including hitting, kicking, shoving, and insulting fellow students, than did the control group.

In summary, a large number of well-controlled experiments, dating back to the 1960s, demonstrates that television violence can *cause* short-term aggressive behavior in some children. In addition, by carefully manipulating the program content in some of these studies, researchers have found that certain types of portrayals are more likely to encourage the learning of aggression than others (for review, see Wilson et al., 1997, 2002). In other words, not all television violence is alike in the risk that it poses to viewers. Table 4.1 summarizes some of the contextual features of violence that encourage the learning of aggression in viewers as well as features that can actually discourage such learning.

A Unique Quasi Experiment

In 1986, an unusual study was conducted in Canada to assess the effect that the introduction of television would have on a particular community (Williams, 1986; see MacBeth, chapter 3, this volume, for a more detailed review). Children in a Canadian town that had no television (labeled "Notel") were compared with children in two nearby communities that had only one station ("Unitel") or multiple channels ("Multitel"). The three communities were similar in size and socioeconomic characteristics; the major difference was the presence and amount of television available. However, the study is called a "quasi experiment" rather than a true experiment because children were not actually randomly assigned to the different communities at the outset, which is the only way to ensure truly equal groups.

Data were collected on children in all three communities prior to 1974, when television was first introduced in Notel, and then in a two-year follow-up. In each town, children received scores for aggression based on observations of their play behavior, teacher ratings, and peer ratings. The researchers found that Notel children showed significant increases in physical and verbal aggression after the introduction of television (see Figure 4.7), whereas children in the other two communities showed no significant change in aggression during this same time period (Joy, Kimball, & Zabrack, 1986).

Table 4.1
Risky Versus Educational Depictions of Violence in the Media

Media themes that *encourage* the learning of aggression
  "Good guys" or superheroes as perpetrators
  Violence that is celebrated or rewarded
  Violence that goes unpunished
  Violence that is portrayed as defensible
  Violence that results in no serious harm to the victim
  Violence that is made to look funny
Media themes that *discourage* the learning of aggression
  Evil or bad characters as perpetrators
  Violence that is criticized or penalized
  Violence that is portrayed as unfair or morally unjust
  Violence that causes obvious injury and pain to the victim
  Violence that results in anguish and suffering for the victim's loved ones

Source: Strasburger and Wilson (2002).

Correlational Studies

In the 1970s, many researchers studied large populations of children and teens to determine whether heavy viewers of TV violence were more likely to show aggressive behavior. Such studies were partially a response to criticisms that laboratory experiments were too artificial, used "play" measures of aggression, actually condoned aggression by having adult experimenters encourage violent viewing, and only measured short-term effects (Freedman, 1984, 1986). One critic of the research put it more graphically: "Viewing in the laboratory setting is involuntary, public, choiceless, intense, uncomfortable, and single-minded. . . . Laboratory research has taken the viewing experience and turned it inside out so that the viewer is no longer in charge" (Fowles, 1999, p. 27).

Nevertheless, the correlational studies support many of the same patterns that have been documented in laboratory experiments. Some of the major early studies include the following:

- *A survey of 2,300 junior and senior high school students in Maryland* (McIntyre & Teevan, 1972). Each student was asked to list four favorite TV programs, which were then analyzed for violent content. Self-reports of aggressive behavior, ranging from fights at school to serious encounters with the law, were obtained. The study found that aggression scores were positively associated with the degree of violent content in favorite programming.

- *A national sample of 1,500 19-year-old males* (Robinson & Bachman, 1972). Those who expressed a preference for violent programming were significantly more aggressive in their self-reported behavior.

Figure 4.7
Mean Levels of Physical and Verbal Aggression before (Time 1) and after (Time 2) the Introduction of Television in the Notel Community in Canada

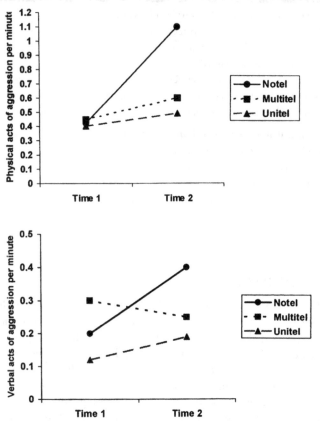

Source: Adapted from Joy et al. (1986).

- *A study of 850 fourth through sixth graders in Michigan* (Dominick & Greenberg, 1972). The researchers found that the greater the exposure to TV violence, the more the children perceived violence as an effective solution to conflict and a viable option for themselves. The findings held up for both boys and girls.

- *A combined Maryland/Wisconsin study of more than 600 adolescents* (McLeod, Atkin, & Chaffee, 1972). The adolescents were asked how often they viewed 65 prime-time programs, which had been rated for violent content by independent coders. The teens also were asked how often they had engaged in various forms of aggressive behavior as well as how they would likely respond to a series of hypothetical situations. A modest positive correlation was found between violent TV viewing and overall aggressive behavior, even when variables such as IQ, academic performance, and socioeconomic status were statistically controlled.

- *A large-scale study of more than 1,500 English 12- to 17-year-old males* (Belson, 1978). Originally commissioned by the CBS television network, this project involved a representative sample of adolescent males and employed meticulous measures of TV exposure and aggressive behavior. Exposure to TV violence was positively associated with less serious forms of aggression, but the relationship to more serious forms of aggression (antisocial and criminal acts) was even stronger. Males who viewed large amounts of violent TV content committed a far greater number of seriously harmful antisocial and criminal acts than did matched peers who were light viewers.

The samples in most of these correlational studies are impressively large and the measures of aggression are presumably more realistic than those collected in lab studies. However, correlational research suffers from the so-called chicken-and-egg dilemma: do aggressive children choose to watch more TV violence, or does TV violence cause aggressive behavior? To help untangle the direction of causality, longitudinal studies are useful because they assess the same sample of children or teens over time.

Longitudinal Studies

Some of the most powerful evidence that television has an impact on young people's behavior comes from longitudinal studies. Several major studies have been conducted by different groups of investigators on different samples of children and teens, and most of them point to a strong connection between early exposure to TV violence and subsequent aggressive behavior.

In one of the earliest studies, Huesmann and his colleagues followed a cohort of children over a 22-year period (Huesmann & Eron, 1986; Huesmann, Lagerspetz, & Eron, 1984; Lefkowitz, Eron, Walder, & Huesmann, 1972). The original study began in 1963, with a sample of 875 third graders (age 8) in upstate New York. The researchers were initially interested in the impact of different parenting styles on children's aggressive behavior. As a means for disguising their purposes, the researchers included what they thought were some "innocent" questions about media use in their interviews of parents. But when the data were examined 11 years later, the researchers realized that TV viewing habits seemed to have played a substantial role in the development of aggression. In other words, the findings showed that exposure to TV violence during early childhood was predictive of higher levels of aggressive behavior at age 19 (see Figure 4.8). By contrast, the reverse was not true: being more aggressive at age 8 did *not* predict greater consumption of violent programming at age 19. Consequently, the notion that more aggressive children tend to view more violence on TV was not substantiated. Interestingly, the TV-aggression link held only for boys, not for girls. This may be due to the types of aggression shown on TV and the types measured (physical aggression rather than other forms of aggression). However, the TV-aggression link persisted even when IQ, socioeconomic status, and overall exposure to TV were statistically controlled.

Ten years later, this same cohort was again studied, only this time the data revealed a link between exposure to TV violence at age 8 and self-reported aggression at age 30 among males (Huesmann, 1986; Huesmann & Miller, 1994). In some of the most provocative data reported, childhood TV habits also predicted criminal arrests for violent behavior at age 30 (see Figure 4.9). Based on these longitudinal patterns, Huesmann (1986) argued that "aggressive habits seem to be learned early in life, and once established, are resistant to change and predictive of serious adult antisocial behavior. If a child's observation of media violence promotes the learning of aggressive habits, it can have harmful lifelong consequences" (p. 129).

In a separate cross-cultural study, Huesmann and Eron (1986) followed more than 1,000 children in the United States, Australia, Finland, Israel, the Netherlands, and Poland over a 3-year time period. For every country except Australia, early viewing of TV violence was significantly associated with higher levels of subsequent aggressive behavior, even after controlling for a child's initial level of aggressiveness. This widespread pattern was found despite the fact that crime rates and TV programming differed substantially among the different nations. Furthermore, the pattern was found just as often for girls as for boys in three of the countries, including the United States. Thus, Huesmann's earlier findings that seemed to pinpoint only boys now could be extended to girls as well. Contradicting the earlier 22-year longitudinal study, there was some evidence in this cross-cultural study that early aggression did predict subsequently higher levels of violent viewing. In fact, Huesmann now argues that the relationship between TV violence and aggression is probably reciprocal: Early viewing of violence stimulates aggression, and behaving aggressively then leads to a heightened interest in violent TV content (Huesmann, Lagerspetz, & Eron, 1984).

Figure 4.8
Does Watching Violence on TV at Age 8 Affect Behavior at Age 19?

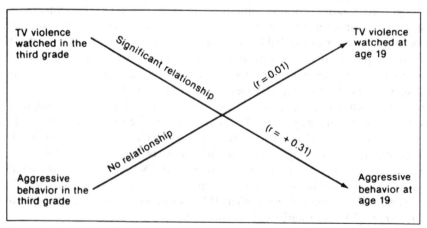

Figure 4.9
Does Preference for Violent TV at Age 8 Correlate with Criminal Activity at Age 30?

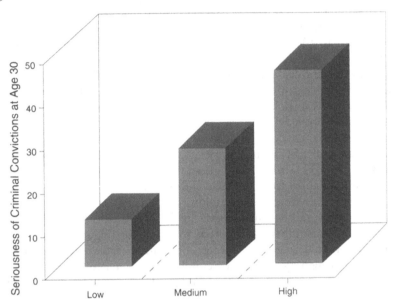

Preference for Violent TV at Age 8

Source: Adapted from Huesmann (1986).

Other longitudinal studies have not been nearly as ambitious but have found similar results. In 1981, Singer and Singer (1981) studied 141 children from nearly 50 different New Haven, Connecticut kindergartens over a one-year period. The researchers found a significant relationship between children's viewing of TV violence (as recorded in daily diaries by parents) and their aggressive behavior, observed in free play at school. The relationship held for both sexes and was strongest in those viewing the most violence on TV. In a subsequent five-year study, Singer, Singer, and Rapaczynski (1984) tracked 63 boys and girls from age 4 to age 9. Again, the researchers found that those who watched the most violent programming as preschoolers displayed the most aggression at age 9, even when controlling for initial levels of childhood aggression.

Only a controversial study sponsored by the NBC television network seems to stand out against this trend (Milavsky, Kessler, Stipp, & Rubens, 1982). The research was conducted over a three-year period and involved a large sample: 2,400 elementary-school children and 800 teenage males from Minneapolis, Minnesota and Fort Worth, Texas, respectively. Self-reports of exposure to TV and to violent programming were collected at several points in time, as were self-reports and peer ratings of aggression. Positive correlations between TV violence and aggression were observed at each single point in time. But when the researchers applied a variety of statistical controls, they concluded that the over-time relationships were generally weak or inconsistent. However, other researchers have reexamined the NBC data and reached the opposite conclusion—that the findings in fact support the link between early exposure to TV violence and subsequent aggressive behavior (Comstock & Strasburger, 1990; Kenny, 1984).

The most recent evidence that early viewing can predict later aggression comes from a 17-year study by Johnson and his colleagues (Johnson, Cohen, Smailes, Kasen, & Brook, 2002). The researchers tracked a random sample of 707 children from two counties in the state of New York. The children were between the ages of 1 and 10 at the outset of the study. They were assessed repeatedly, beginning in 1975, with family interviews, personality profiles, individual interviews, and questionnaires. In addition, adult criminal records were obtained from the state and the FBI in 2000. Results revealed that the amount of time spent watching TV during early adolescence was associated with a subsequent increase in the likelihood of committing aggressive acts against others, particularly for males (see Figure 4.10). This relationship persisted even when other important variables were controlled, such as previous aggressive behavior, childhood neglect, family income, neighborhood violence, parental education, and psychiatric disorders. Notably, the study assessed total TV-viewing time rather than viewing of *violent* content, but the results are still quite impressive, especially given that it is the first longitudinal study to link adolescent TV habits to adult aggression (Anderson & Bushman, 2002).

Meta-Analyses

A meta-analysis is a quantitative review of the research on a given topic, in which the results from a number of separate studies are summarized (see chapter 11 of this volume). Using meta-analytic statistical techniques, a researcher can combine individual studies to yield a picture of the overall pattern across different investigations (O'Keefe, 2002). Meta-analyses result in numerical estimates of the size of an effect across all the studies taken together.

A number of meta-analyses have been conducted on the literature pertaining to the impact of media violence on aggression. All of them have found support for the hypothesis that exposure to TV violence increases the likelihood of subsequent aggressive or antisocial behavior. The earliest meta-analysis looked at 67 studies, involving a total of about 300,000 subjects altogether (Andison, 1977). Cumulatively, the results revealed a weak positive relationship between exposure to TV violence and subsequent aggression.

Nearly 10 years later, Hearold (1986) examined 230 studies, of which some looked at the impact of TV on prosocial behavior and others examined the impact on antisocial behavior. Isolating just those involving antisocial behavior, Hearold found an average effect size (analogous to a correlation coeffi-

Figure 4.10
Most Recent Longitudinal Study

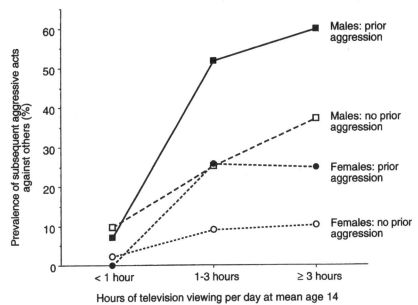

Hours of television viewing per day at mean age 14

Source: Johnson, Cohen, Smailes, Kasen, & Brook (2002). Copyright © 2002 American Association for the Advancement of Science.

cient) of 0.30 (see Figure 4.11). According to scientific convention, an effect size of 0.10 is considered to be small, 0.30 is medium, and 0.50 is large, although an effect size of 0.30 is large when considered empirically (Hemphill, 2003). In an update several years later, Paik and Comstock (1994) examined 217 studies and found an almost identical effect size of 0.31.

Two smaller meta-analyses focused only on a subset of the published studies on the impact of TV violence. Wood, Wong, and Chachere (1991) looked at those experiments in which children's aggressive behavior was actually observed in social interactions with peers after exposure to TV violence. The researchers' goal was to isolate causal studies that employed the most realistic measures of aggression. Once again, across 23 such experiments, there was a significant effect of media violence on aggression. Hogben (1998) examined only those studies that measured naturalistic viewing of TV violence, eliminating any investigation in which viewing was controlled or manipulated. Even with this limited group of studies, he too found a significant relationship between viewing of TV violence and aggressive behavior. However, the effect size was smaller than that observed when all types of studies were considered (Hearold, 1986; Paik & Comstock, 1994).

The most recent large-scale meta-analysis by Bushman and Anderson (2001) examined 212 studies of the effects of media violence, looking for

Figure 4.11
A Meta-Analysis of 230 Separate Studies to Examine the Effect Size of Television's Influence on Aggressive Behavior at Different Ages

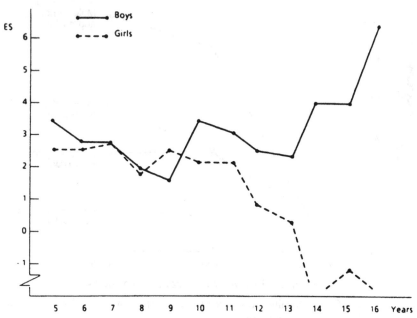

Note: In childhood, males and females appear to be equally at risk, whereas adolescent males are more susceptible than females.
Source: Hearold, S. (1986). Antisocial treatments and physical aggression by age and sex. In G. Comstock, *Public Communication and Behavior: Vol. 1. Academic Press.* Elsevier Science (USA).

patterns over time. The researchers found that since 1975 the size of the effect between media violence and aggressive behavior has steadily increased. There are at least three possible explanations for this trend: people may be spending more time with the media and consequently with violent portrayals; the sheer amount of violence in entertainment programming may be increasing; and/ or the entertainment industry may be changing the way in which violence is portrayed by making it more graphic or realistic, hence heightening the potential for harmful effects on viewers (Bushman & Anderson, 2001).

In general, all six of the meta-analyses reported here have documented a positive and significant relationship between media violence and aggression. The size of the effect has varied, although two studies agree that it is roughly around 0.30. Another way to interpret this statistic is that roughly 10 percent of the variance (0.3^2) in aggressive or antisocial behavior can be attributed to exposure to TV violence. In other words, in the midst of all the complex and multiple causes of violence, television is responsible for roughly 10 percent of the aggression observed in a typical sample of individuals. And conceivably this figure represents an underestimate for several reasons (Comstock & Strasburger, 1993). First, the unreliability of measurement reduces the degree of association that can be determined. In media research, the measures of behavior and of exposure are far from perfect. Second, there are virtually no control subjects available with truly low or zero exposure to TV. Even low-exposure groups have a substantial amount of viewing and knowledge about TV violence, thus narrowing the range of associations possible. Nevertheless, even a 10 percent effect can be significant when considering large populations of children or adolescent viewers.

As it turns out, the link between media violence and aggressive or antisocial behavior is actually stronger than many commonly accepted cause-and-effect associations, such as the relationship between calcium intake and bone mass, or between condom use and decreased risk of contracting HIV (Bushman & Huesmann, 2001). And the effect is only slightly smaller than that between smoking and lung cancer, which is nearly 0.40 (see Figure 4.12). Just as not everyone who smokes will develop lung cancer, not everyone who views violence on TV will become violent. But the risk is there and it appears to be quite significant.

Cumulation of Evidence

Collectively, then, there is a great deal of evidence linking media violence to aggression. Experimental studies have established a cause-and-effect relationship in short-term situations, surveys have documented this pattern in large samples of youth, longitudinal studies show that early exposure is predictive of increases in aggression over time, and meta-analyses of all this research show a consistent link between exposure to media violence and aggressive behavior. To be sure, no media researcher today would claim that watching a single violent film or television show directly and immediately *causes* a person to commit aggressive behaviors. Instead, repeated and cumulative exposure to media violence is seen as a risk factor that contributes to the development of aggression over time. A number of governmental and professional organizations, including the National Institutes of Mental Health (Pearl et al., 1982), the U.S. Surgeon General (Elliott, Hatot, Sirovatka, & Potter, 2001), the American Psychological Association (1993), the American Academy of Pediatrics (2001), and the American Medical Association (1996), have reviewed the evidence and drawn similar conclusions.

WHY DOES TV VIOLENCE ENCOURAGE AGGRESSION?

There are now several well-supported theories that help explain how media violence can contribute to aggression. Observational or social learning theory is perhaps the oldest and most popular theoretical explanation. According to

Figure 4.12
How Strong Is the Link between Media Violence and Real-Life Aggression?

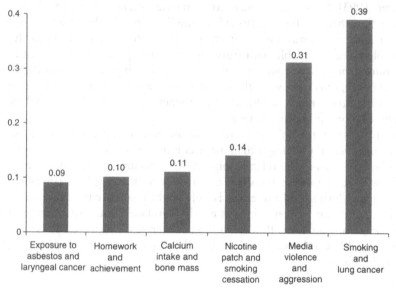

Source: Bushman & Anderson (2001).

Bandura (1977), children learn new behaviors by direct experience or by observing and imitating others in their social environment. The rewards or punishments that role models experience are crucial in determining whether certain behaviors will be imitated. As discussed above, children are more likely to imitate a behavior that is rewarded or that goes unpunished (Bandura, 1965). Even Hollywood seems to accept this theory. As one well-known producer once stated:

I'd be lying if I said that people don't imitate what they see on the screen. I would be a moron to say they don't, because look how dress styles change. We have people who want to look like Julia Roberts and Michelle Pfeiffer and Madonna. Of course we imitate. It would be impossible for me to think they would imitate our dress, our music, our look, but not imitate any of our violence or our other actions. (cited in Auletta, 1993, p. 45)

In recent years, Bandura (1986) has revised his theory to include cognitive processing variables in observational learning. Now called social cognitive theory, Bandura acknowledges that differences in a child's attention to and retention of a model's behavior can help explain imitational responses. This larger framework also allows the theory to extend beyond behavioral outcomes, and to include the learning of aggressive attitudes and normative beliefs from observing a model (Bushman & Huesmann, 2001).

As an extension of social learning, Huesmann (1986, 1988) has proposed a theory involving cognitive scripting. Cognitive scripts are mental routines that are stored in memory and are used to guide behavior (Abelson, 1976). According to Huesmann (1998), violent television programs provide young people with scripts that encourage the use of aggression. Once learned, these scripts can be retrieved from memory at any time, depending on the similarity between the real situation at hand and the fictional event, as well as the circumstances surrounding when the script was first encoded (Huesmann, 1998). When an aggressive script is retrieved, it can be reinforced and broadened to a new set of circumstances (Geen, 1994). In this way, repeated exposure to media violence can encourage a child to develop a set of stable cognitive scripts that emphasize aggression as a typical response to social situations.

Two other theories focus more on how the media might prompt or trigger already learned aggressive behaviors. Zillmann's (1991) excitation transfer theory maintains that media violence can have an impact simply because it is arousing in nature. According to the theory, exposure to TV violence can generate excitement that, because it dissipates slowly, can transfer to other emotional experiences. If a person is already feeling angry or hostile, a stimulating violent TV show can increase the intensity of those feelings and thereby increase the potential for aggressive responding (Zillmann & Johnson, 1973). Because of its arousal properties, Zillmann (1971) has found that even erotic media content can increase aggressive responses in angry or frustrated individuals.

Berkowitz (1984) has proposed a cognitive cueing or priming theory to account for the short-term instigational effects of media violence (also known as cognitive-neoassociation theory). According to Berkowitz, a violent television program can activate or "prime" aggressive thoughts in a viewer. Several conditions can encourage these aggressive thoughts to be turned into aggressive action, including intense feelings of negative affect or anger (Berkowitz, 1990), justification for aggressive behavior (Jo & Berkowitz, 1994), and cues in the environment that relate to the program just viewed (Jo & Berkowitz, 1994). In one of the first tests of this theory, Berkowitz and Rawlings (1963) conducted a classic experiment using *Champion*, a boxing film starring Kirk Douglas. One group of college males viewed a scene in which Kirk Douglas is brutally beaten; another group viewed a nonviolent track meet. An experimental assistant—named either "Bob" or "Kirk" Anderson— angered some of the subjects beforehand. The researchers accurately predicted that aggression (as measured by willingness to give electric shocks to the assistant) would be triggered when the subjects were angered, when they saw a violent movie that primed aggressive thoughts, and when there was a "cue" in the environment (i.e., name of the target) that resembled the movie. Dozens of similar experiments have been conducted since, with similar results (Comstock & Strasburger, 1990).

Together these four theories can account for most of the processes by which media violence might contribute to aggression. Social learning theory focuses on how particular television programs can teach novel aggressive behaviors to a child, whereas script theory helps explain how cumulative exposure can foster the development of aggressive habits and routines during childhood. In contrast, excitation transfer and cognitive priming are applicable to those situations in which media violence seems to trigger immediate violent responses, particularly among those who are predisposed to act aggressively as well as those who already have a repertoire of aggressive behaviors at their disposal. Recently, Anderson and Bushman (2002) have developed the general aggression model (GAM), which attempts to integrate these smaller theories into one unifying framework. GAM focuses on both individual and situational factors that can influence aggression; it acknowledges that cognitions, emotions, and arousal interact in ways that produce aggression, and it accounts for the initial development as well as the persistence of aggressive behavior (see chapter 5 of this volume).

THE MYTH OF CATHARSIS

In his *Poetics*, Aristotle suggested that theatergoers could be purged vicariously of their feelings of grief, fear, or pity. The idea that aggression can be "purged" through exposure to fantasy violence is derived from psychoanalytic theories of various "energies" coursing through the body like ancient "humors," just waiting to be drained. Obviously, this is an idea that has been quite popular in the Hollywood community (Plagens, Miller, Foote, & Yoffe, 1991).

A few early studies seemed to support the notion of catharsis (Feshbach, 1955, 1961). In one experiment (Feshbach, 1961), college students were insulted and then viewed either a violent film or a neutral film. Those who saw the violent film responded with *fewer* aggressive words on a subsequent word-association test than did those who saw the neutral film. In another study, Feshbach and Singer (1971) found that boys living in institutionalized settings who watched a steady diet of violent TV shows for six weeks were less aggressive than were those who watched nonviolent programs during the same time period. However, this field study has been critiqued extensively for methodological problems (see Liebert & Sprafkin, 1988). Furthermore, the scientific evidence reviewed above overwhelmingly shows that media violence has quite the opposite effect than that which is predicted by catharsis. In other words, in over 40 years of research *there has been no substantiation of the catharsis theory.*

MEDIA VIOLENCE AND FEAR OF VICTIMIZATION

By far, most of the research to date has concentrated on the impact of media violence on aggression. However, in recent years increasing attention has been paid to two other types of effects that can occur as a result of watching violent programs and movies: fear and desensitization (Potter, 1999; Smith & Donnerstein, 1998; Wilson et al., 1997).

Experiencing short-term fright reactions to the media is a common occurrence and often is a consequence of viewing material that is violent. According to a recent study, more than 90 percent of college students could vividly remember a film or TV program that caused them intense fear when they were young (Harrison & Cantor, 1999). Chapter 10 by Cantor provides an overview of short-term and even long-term fright reactions to the media, particularly those experienced by children. Such fear, which is intensely emotional and often physiological, can be contrasted with another type of fear that is more cognitive and even attitudinal in nature—fear of victimization (Potter, 1999).

Gerbner and his colleagues have coined the term "mean world syndrome" to explain how heavy viewers of TV develop a greater sense of mistrust and apprehension about the real world (Gerbner et al., 1994). According to their theory, television "cultivates" a view of social reality in viewers. Studies of children as well as adults support this idea; heavy viewers of television routinely perceive the world as a more violent place and give higher estimates of their own risk of being a victim of violence than do light viewers (see Signorielli & Morgan, 1990). Though most of the evidence to support cultivation theory is correlational in nature, there are a few experiments demonstrating that repeated exposure to television violence can elevate fear and anxiety about real-world violence (Bryant, Carveth, & Brown, 1981; Ogles & Hoffner, 1987). And there is even longitudinal research showing that early exposure to adult-oriented violent TV programs is positively correlated with children's beliefs that the world is a fearful and dangerous place (Singer, Singer, & Rapaczynski, 1984).

Cultivation theory has been critiqued on both methodological and conceptual grounds (Hawkins & Pingree, 1981; Hughes, 1980; Potter, 1993), and in 1980 the theory was refined so as to acknowledge that the cultivation relationship might vary across different subgroups of individuals (Gerbner, Gross, Morgan, & Signorielli, 1980). More recently, researchers have been testing cognitive processing models to help explain the cultivation effect (Mares, 1996; Shrum, 2001). In spite of these rigorous challenges to the theory, the data have been remarkably consistent over time (Potter, 1999). Indeed, a meta-analysis of over 20 years of cultivation research found a small but consistent relationship between exposure to television and perceptions of violence in the real world (Morgan & Shanahan, 1996). As Shrum (2001) recently stated, "The notion that the viewing of television program content is related to people's perceptions of reality is virtually undisputed in the social sciences" (p. 94).

MEDIA VIOLENCE AND DESENSITIZATION

Desensitization refers to the idea that repeated exposure to a certain stimulus can lead to reduced emotional and physiological responsiveness to it. In clinical settings, desensitization techniques are used to treat people's phobias.

If desensitization to media violence exists, it could explain the public's apparent callousness toward this issue and its acceptance of even more violence in television programming and movies (Comstock & Strasburger, 1993). In their book *High Tech, High Touch: Technology and Our Search for Meaning*, three critics of modern culture write (Naisbitt, Naisbitt, & Philips, 1999):

> In a culture of electronic violence, images that once caused us to empathize with the pain and trauma of another human being excite a momentary adrenaline rush. To be numb to another's pain—to be acculturated to violence—is arguably one of the worst consequences our technological advances have wrought. That indifference transfers from the screen, TV, film, Internet, and electronic games to our everyday lives through seemingly innocuous consumer technologies. (pp. 90–91)

Do studies support the notion of desensitization? The answer is an unqualified yes. Research shows quite clearly that physiological arousal becomes lessened with continued exposure to media violence (Cline, Croft, & Courrier, 1973). Subjects' heart rates and skin conductance decrease over time during prolonged exposure to violence, even within a single program (Lazarus & Alfert, 1964). In one study, both children and adults showed less physiological arousal during a scene of real-life violence after viewing a violent drama on TV (Thomas, Horton, Lippincott, & Drabman, 1977).

A far greater concern, of course, is whether this physiological numbing translates into a callousness or indifference to violence (see Figure 4.13). Numerous experiments suggest that it can. In one early study, children who had been exposed to a violent television show were less ready to intervene when a pair of preschoolers broke into a fight than were children who had seen a nonviolent TV program (Thomas & Drabman, 1975). In fact, many of the children in the violent viewing group never left the room to go get help even though they had been instructed to do so. Other studies also have documented a callousness to real-world aggression in children after exposing them to fictional portrayals of violence (Drabman & Thomas, 1974; Molitor & Hirsch, 1994).

Perhaps not surprisingly, adults show the same effect. Several experiments have shown that exposing college students to a series of slasher films makes them less sympathetic toward an alleged rape victim and more inclined to hold her responsible for her own rape (Donnerstein & Smith, 2001; Linz, Donnerstein, & Penrod, 1984).

Clearly, desensitization is not only a real and verifiable process, it also has important implications for society. Have levels of media violence increased because the American population has become desensitized? Have Americans become less empathic with victims of violence? Are Americans less willing to come to the aid of a victim now than they were 50 years ago? Could desensitization explain some of the recent schoolyard shootings (Strasburger & Grossman, 2001)? Could it also explain why certain elements in society are willing to consider inflicting the death penalty on mentally ill perpetrators or

Figure 4.13
Desensitization

Source: By permission of Mike Luckovich and Creators Syndicate, Inc.

imprisoning 12-year-old juvenile offenders for life? These are all debatable issues that underscore the importance of continuing to examine desensitization as a harmful outcome of repeated exposure to media violence.

One interesting question remains: is desensitization a transitory or a permanent byproduct of media violence? Can people become *re*sensitized to real-world violence? In a 1995 experiment, male college students were exposed to three slasher films during a six-day period (Mullin & Linz, 1995). In a supposedly unrelated experiment, they were then asked three, five, or seven days later to watch a documentary about domestic abuse. Results revealed that those who had seen the slasher films only three days earlier were less sympathetic to domestic violence victims and rated their injuries as less severe than did a control group (see Figure 4.14). However, those who had viewed the slasher films five and seven days earlier showed levels of sympathy that had "rebounded" to the baseline level of the control group. In other words, desensitization seemed to diminish after a three-day period. Of course, the notion of *re*sensitization requires that a person no longer be exposed to violent media during the "recovery" period, something that is virtually impossible these days if any media are consumed.

One important element of desensitization is that it appears to be a relatively automatic (and autonomic) process. Therefore, people are not aware that they have become desensitized—although they may be perfectly willing to accept that others have been. This tendency is called the "third person effect," a well-documented phenomenon whereby people assume that others are influenced more by the media than they themselves are (Perloff, 2002). The challenge, then, is to discover ways in which viewers can be made aware of the potential for desensitization to occur, especially among those who consume a great deal of media violence.

CAN TELEVISION VIOLENCE BE PROSOCIAL?

One common technique in many violent programs, especially those targeted at children, is to include a prosocial message or lesson at the end of the plot. Superhero shows such as the *Power Rangers, Wild Force,* and *Batman: The Animated Series* employ this strategy in nearly every episode. It is tempting to assume that such devices might encourage children to behave in prosocial

Figure 4.14
Resensitization

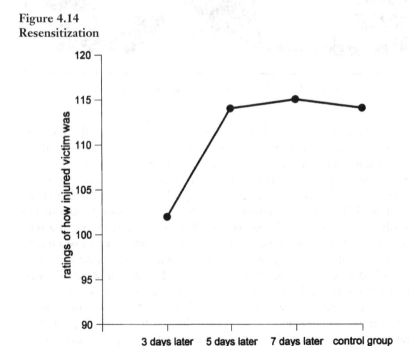

Source: Original data from C. R. Mullin and D. Linz (1995), Desensitization and resensitization to violence against women, *Journal of Personality & Social Psychology, 69,* 449–459. Adapted by V. C. Strasburger and B. J. Wilson, *Children, adolescents, and the media* (Sage, 2002). Reprinted by permission of Sage Publications, Inc.

ways, as is true of many nonviolent programs on television (Mares & Woodard, 2001). However, research cautions against this assumption. In one study, 68 children between the ages of 4 and 10 were exposed to an episode of *Power Rangers* and interviewed about it afterward (McKenna & Ossoff, 1998). When asked about the most important thing they remembered from the show, younger children referred mostly to the fighting sequences in the show. Only the 8- to 10-year-olds referred to the moral theme of the episode—that it is more important to work than to play. When asked directly what the main theme or message of the episode was, once again strong age differences emerged. The oldest children were significantly more likely to recognize the theme than were those under age eight.

Though younger children may misunderstand these messages, even more troubling is the potential impact of "prosocial" violence on viewer aggression. In two experiments, Liss and her colleagues (1983) exposed kindergarten, second grade, and fourth grade children to different versions of a cartoon: (a) a purely prosocial one with no violence in it, (b) a prosocial one with violence in it, and (c) a purely violent one with no prosocial theme in it. After viewing television, children had an opportunity to "help" or "hurt" a peer in a game situation. The researchers found that, regardless of age, children had more difficulty comprehending the prosocial message when it was couched in violence than when it was seen with no violence. Consistent with the confusing nature of such messages, the youngest children were more likely to engage in aggression than prosocial helping behavior after viewing the prosocial-violent cartoon. In other words, the superhero's violent behavior was more salient than his prosocial words were. In fact, the prosocial-violent cartoon produced more imitative aggression among kindergartners than did the purely violent cartoon.

These findings suggest that one of the most potent ways to teach aggression to young viewers is to couch the behavior in a moralistic context. Indeed, violence that is depicted as being justified is one of the most strongly reinforcing elements in whether it will be learned or imitated (Berkowitz & Rawlings, 1963). According to Comstock (1991), key factors that determine how violence will be interpreted by viewers include *efficacy*, or whether violence results in the achievement of desired goals, and *normativeness*, or whether the violence is portrayed as socially acceptable. Both of these factors are highlighted in most action-adventure programs that feature superheroes.

Is it possible then for violent programming ever to have a positive impact on children and adolescents? One unique study suggests that under certain circumstances, it is possible. In June 1998, Court TV funded a study to assess this issue (Wilson et. al., 1999). More than 500 teenagers from three different California middle schools were randomly assigned to receive or not receive the "Choices and Consequences" curriculum in school (see www.courttv.com/choices). The three-week curriculum involved viewing videotaped court cases about real teens who have engaged in risky behavior that resulted in someone dying. For example, in one case a group of teens pushed a young boy off of a railroad trestle and he drowned. Each week, the students watched portions of the trial, discussed the cases, engaged in role-playing, and completed homework based on the cases. Compared with the control group, the teens involved in the curriculum showed significantly reduced verbal aggression and physical aggression. They also had increased empathy. In other words, exposure to programming that emphasizes the lifelong negative consequences of antisocial behavior can have prosocial effects on teens.

Twenty years ago, Huesmann, Eron, Klein, Brice, and Fischer (1983) demonstrated that a slightly different curriculum could work with even younger age groups. In the study, second and fourth graders wrote essays about the unrealistic nature of violent programming as well as the impact of TV violence on young viewers. They were then videotaped reading their essays. Compared with a control group, these children displayed more negative attitudes about TV violence and decreased their aggressive behavior up to four months after the intervention.

Thus, violent programming can be used in structured situations to teach children about the dangers associated with it and with antisocial behavior more generally. And research suggests that even parents can employ critical viewing strategies that will decrease the impact of media violence on their children (Nathanson, 1999). Yet some programs may teach these lessons without the need for adult intervention. Hollywood pundits would point to such movies as *Boyz 'N the Hood*, *Schindler's List*, and *Unforgiven* as being powerfully antiviolent. Although there are no formal studies of the impact of any of these films, all are examples of the fact that sometimes violence needs to be portrayed in order to convey an antiviolence message. Clearly, the *context* of how violence is portrayed is crucial in determining its impact.

CONCLUSIONS

During the 1990s, the United States was shocked by an apparent epidemic of schoolyard shootings, ranging from Jonesboro, Arkansas to Springfield, Oregon to Littleton, Colorado. In January, 2001, a 13-year-old boy was found guilty of murdering a 6-year-old girl. He said that he was imitating wrestling moves he had seen on *WWF Smackdown* by Dwayne "The Rock" Johnson. The boy weighed 180 pounds, the girl 48 pounds (Clary, 2001). American society seems to be asking the same question in 2003 as Senator Kefauver asked in 1954: does media violence cause real-life violence?

As we have seen, the scientific literature is large, robust, and consistent in supporting the idea that media violence can contribute to the development of aggressive attitudes and behaviors in childhood and even adulthood. Effect sizes range from small to medium in size, depending on the types of studies involved (see Figure 4.15) (Anderson & Bushman, 2002; Comstock & Strasburger, 1993). Certainly, other factors are at work too, including poverty,

Figure 4.15
Effect Size According to Type of Study

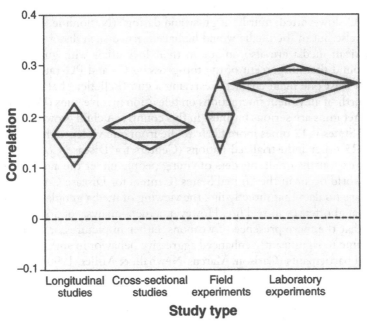

Source: Anderson & Bushman (2002). Copyright © 2002 American Association for the Advancement of Science.

racism, drugs, and unique personality factors. Witnessing violence is important as well (Buka, Stichick, Birdthistle, & Earls, 2001). In one study of 175 9- to 12-year-olds who visited a large urban pediatric primary care clinic, 97 percent reportedly had been exposed to real-life violence (Puigguan, Stein, Silver, & Benenson, 2000). In fact, 31 percent had witnessed someone being shot, stabbed, or killed. Obviously, the media also provide abundant opportunities to witness violence, and these portrayals can have an impact as well. A recent study found that demographic variables, parental monitoring, television viewing habits, and exposure to real-life violence explained nearly half of 2,245 children's self-reported violent behaviors (Singer et al., 1999). Media violence and real-life violence are intricately connected, along with many other factors.

A *New York Times* study of the 102 teen and adult rampage killers from 1949 to 2000 found that only 13 percent had an interest in violent media (Fessenden, 2000). However, this statistic may be misleading. The findings were based on self-reports of media use, and because of the third person effect, teenagers are likely to deny that they themselves are ever influenced by the media. Yet after his arrest, 16-year-old Luke Woodham of Pearl, Mississippi, (who killed three and wounded seven classmates) was quoted as saying, "I am not insane. I am angry. I killed because people like me are mistreated every day. I did this to show society: push us and we will push back. Murder is not weak and slow-witted; murder is gutsy and daring" (Nationline, 1997, p. 3A). Where else but in the media would he have learned such distorted notions?

American media are also unique in their love affair with guns. A recent study found that 40 percent of the top-grossing G- and PG-rated films featured at least one main character carrying a gun (Pelletier et al., 1999). And one-fourth of all violent interactions on television involve guns (Wilson et al., 1998). Yet guns are serious business in this country. A child growing up in the United States is 12 times more likely to die from gun violence than a child in any of 25 other industrialized nations (Centers for Disease Control, 1997). And three-fourths of all murders of young people under the age of 14 years in the world occur in the United States (Centers for Disease Control, 1997). There are no data that directly link the viewing of media gunplay with actual gun-related offenses in real life. However, a meta-analysis of 56 experiments found that the mere presence of weapons, either in pictures or in the actual environment, significantly enhanced aggressive behavior in angered and non-angered participants (Carlson, Marcus-Newhall, & Miller, 1990).

Obviously, not all children will develop aggressive habits even after watching extensive amounts of television violence. But other outcomes such as fear of victimization and desensitization are well documented in the literature and may actually occur more often and among greater numbers of viewers. Donnerstein and his colleagues (1994) offer one way to appreciate how widespread the impact of media violence can be across different types of individuals. After reviewing the scientific literature, they identified the following effects:

- *an aggressor effect* of increased meanness, aggression, and even violence toward others;
- *a victim effect* of increased fearfulness, mistrust, or "mean world syndrome," and self-protective behavior;
- *a bystander effect* of increased desensitization, callousness, and behavioral apathy toward other victims of violence; and
- *an appetite effect* of increased self-initiated behavior to further expose oneself to violent material. (p. 240)

To return to the beginning of this chapter, Senator Kefauver's question from nearly 50 years ago seems somewhat narrow today. Yes, there is a relationship between media violence and real-life aggression. But the relationship is certainly complex and probably reciprocal. The more critical questions for researchers, parents, and public policymakers in the twenty-first century are these: What types of violent portrayals pose the greatest risk of viewers learning aggression, becoming frightened, or experiencing desensitization? What types of individuals are most at risk for these effects? What can we do to ameliorate such harmful outcomes?

CHAPTER 5

Theory in the Study of Media Violence: The General Aggression Model

Nicholas L. Carnagey and Craig A. Anderson

A large portion of this book reviews empirical research on the effects of media violence. Researchers have used many tools in this effort to understand the media violence phenomenon. Creative lab designs and advancement of technology have allowed laboratory researchers to manipulate exposure to media violence and view the short-term results of brief exposure. Cross-sectional and longitudinal studies have allowed the research world to document the "real life" consequences of repeated exposure to large amounts of filmed violence. Although these empirical research tools have resulted in great advances in understanding by media violence researchers, it is important to remember that the theories guiding and being revised by such research are as important to the scientific enterprise as the data they generate.

Theory is typically defined as an organized set of hypotheses that allow a scientist to understand, explain, and predict a wide variety of phenomena (Shaw & Costanzo, 1982). Theory serves the scientist in a number of ways. First, theory organizes a researcher's thoughts, hypotheses, and existing knowledge. Such organization has many benefits, such as making the researcher more efficient in developing a strategic plan of analysis.

Not only does a good theory help organize concepts, but it also indirectly organizes researchers and their products. Think of knowledge as a tower of building blocks, with each block constituting a small piece of empirical knowledge. The more blocks there are, the more is known about a subject. Without theory to guide them, researchers are forced to individually build their own knowledge about a subject, starting from the ground up. However, with one theory guiding several researchers, they are empowered to build on each other's blocks, with theory establishing the foundation and basic structure for scientific advancement. With scientists able to add blocks to one single tower and indirectly work as a team, the amount of knowledge grows at a greater rate and with greater efficiency than if the scientists were working at individual levels.

In every field of science, including psychology, the purpose of research is to gain an understanding of a particular phenomenon, with the end result being the ability to predict future outcomes involving the phenomenon and to influence those outcomes, depending on how much control exists over particular variables (Shaw & Costanzo, 1982). Theory is useful in this respect because it attaches meaning to the data collected, enabling researchers to look beyond the numbers and understand the phenomenon at a deeper level. This understanding and advancement of knowledge make both prediction and control more accurate and useful.

As Kurt Lewin noted over 50 years ago, "There is nothing so practical as a good theory" (Lewin, 1951, p. 169). Of course, although a "good" theory is eminently practical, a "bad" theory can lead to major mistakes, ranging from poor individual decisions to public policy blunders that affect large populations (e.g., Anderson & Arnoult, 1985; Anderson & Sechler, 1986; Gilovich, 1991; Janis & Mann, 1977). This chapter is not the place for detailed discussion of good theory-building practices, but a key element of a good theory is its ability to account for (and then predict) empirical data obtained from rigorous scientific research.

The purpose of this chapter is to examine past and current theories in the aggression domain. Particular attention will be paid to the theories that have been used to explain media violence effects, identifying both their strengths and their weaknesses. Finally, the General Aggression Model will be introduced as a comprehensive theory that employs central elements from several of the earlier aggression theories. The chapter concludes with a brief section on applying current theory to public policy discussions.

EARLY AGGRESSION THEORIES

Human aggression was a much-discussed topic throughout the twentieth century, in part because of the two world wars. Several broad theories of aggression emerged in the early part of the century, and persisted (especially in the popular mind) despite a lack of scientific support for and considerable scientific evidence against their applicability to human aggression.

Instinct Theories

In his early writings, Freud (e.g., 1909) proposed that all human behavior stems from the life-giving or self-preservation instinct, called eros. "Libido" was defined as the energy of this life-giving instinct. Freud initially did not posit the presence of an independent instinct to explain the darker side of human nature. He wrote: "I cannot bring myself to assume the existence of a special aggressive instinct alongside the familiar instincts of self-preservation and of sex, on an equal footing with them" (Freud, 1909, p. 140). World War I, however, changed his views. By 1920, Freud had proposed the existence of a truly independent death or self-destruction instinct (the "death wish"), called thanatos. Freud viewed aggression as the redirection or displacement of the self-destructive death instinct away from the individual toward others. In a similar vein, Nobel prizewinner Konrad Lorenz (1966) suggested that animals (including people) possess an aggressive or fighting instinct. His evidence came primarily from observation of animal behavior and from evolutionary arguments.

Although the catharsis idea can be traced to the early Greeks, the modern notion comes from both Freud and Lorenz, particularly their hydraulic metaphors for the necessity of releasing aggressive energy by aggressing against others. Indeed, the catharsis notion is the only part of these broad models that is relevant to the modern issue of media violence. The main catharsis ideas are that: (a) instinctive self-destructive (Freud) or aggressive (Lorenz) energy is continually added to a closed emotional or energy system; (b) observing, enacting, or releasing aggressive behavior or aggressive emotions against others releases some of this energy, thereby reducing pressure on the system; and that (c) without such releases, the pressure will build until the system explodes, either in self-destructive behavior (e.g., suicide) or extreme violence against others (e.g., homicide, war). There is no scientific evidence of an instinctual death wish or aggressive energy, of a closed (hydraulic) emotional or motivational pressure system, or of behavioral catharsis (see Bushman, 2002; Geen & Quanty, 1977). Indeed, one major problem with Freud's and Lorenz's catharsis theory is that its basic tenets are largely empirically untestable, due to the inability to measure or detect variables such as thanatos or aggressive energy. Furthermore, the most important testable aspect of catharsis theory, the idea that observing or enacting aggressive behavior will reduce later aggression, has been repeatedly disconfirmed (Bushman, 2002; Geen & Quanty, 1977). Nonetheless, this idea persists and has been perhaps one of the most damaging "bad" theoretical ideas in all of psychology. It is still invoked by the purveyors of violent entertainment media to children, and is frequently cited by parents, school officials, and public policymakers as justification for exposing youth to violent media, promoting violent sports, and downplaying the significance of aggressive playground behavior (i.e., bullying).

Frustration

A much more empirically testable approach emerged in the form of the frustration-aggression hypothesis (Dollard, Doob, Miller, Mowrer, & Sears, 1939): (a) "the occurrence of aggressive behavior always presupposes the existence of frustration" (p. 1), and (b) "the existence of frustration always leads to some form of aggression" (p. 1). Miller (1941) revised the second statement to "Frustration produces instigations to a number of different types of response, one of which is an instigation to some form of aggression" (p. 338). The scientific framing of this theory enabled better empirical testing and subsequent revision than the instinct theories of Freud and Lorenz. It has also fared considerably better over time (Berkowitz, 1989). For instance, Dill and Anderson (1995) demonstrated that even a fully justified frustration can produce an increase in aggressive behavior, as predicted by Berkowitz's reformulated frustration-aggression model (1989). Despite its importance to the understanding of human aggression in general, the frustration-aggression model has little relevance to media violence effects, other than the methodological implication that media violence experiments need to account for potential frustration-inducing properties of their violent and nonviolent stimuli.

Learning

The extensive literature on learning essentially began in 1898 with E. L. Thorndike's *Animal Intelligence* and continues in various forms to the present day. Here, we confine ourselves to a discussion of the learning theories that emerged from Thorndike's time through B. F. Skinner's. At the risk of oversimplifying, two types of learning were seen as the building blocks of all animal behavior, including human aggression. These two types are respondent (or classical) conditioning and operant (or instrumental) conditioning. (See Hilgard & Bower, 1975, for an excellent overview of this work.) Classical conditioning consists of pairing an unconditioned stimulus with a conditioned stimulus until the unconditioned response (which is automatically elicited by the unconditioned stimulus) is elicited by the conditioned stimulus. Operant conditioning is stimulating (or inhibiting) a behavior based on the reward or punishment received after the behavior. The contributions made by these early theories to the understanding of human behavior are both impressive and important, but they fall far short of constituting comprehensive explanations of human aggression or other forms of human behavior. The most obvious problem is that they do not adequately account for the huge effects that the development of language has on human behavior. Despite this obvious limitation of traditional learning theories, they do contribute to our understanding of the processes underlying some media violence effects.

RECENT THEORETICAL DEVELOPMENTS

In the following sections, each of the modern theories that have been utilized to explain the effects of media violence will be discussed. It is important to note that none of these theories have been developed to specifically examine media violence effects; however, each has contributed to our understanding on the effects of watching simulated violence in television, movies, and video games.

Social Learning Theory and Social Cognitive Theory

Social learning and social cognitive theories (e.g., Bandura, 1973, 1983; Mischel 1973; Mischel & Shoda, 1995) contend that children learn behavioral responses by observing others or through direct experience. Furthermore, these approaches emphasize how a person "construes" events is also learned and is crucial in determining how that person responds to those events. Children witness social interactions from numerous sources: parents, peers on the playground, older siblings, and fictional characters on television and in movies. Along with these behaviors, children also witness the repercussions of these behaviors. Children are more likely to imitate a witnessed behavior if they also witness a reward for the action, and they are less likely to imitate a witnessed behavior if they witness the action being punished (e.g., Bandura, 1965; Bandura, Ross, & Ross, 1963). Over time children learn how to perceive and construe events in their social environment and start to assemble a detailed set of rules of behavior. These rules of behavior are then reinforced or inhibited based on the results they encounter in their own social interactions.

The primary strength of both social learning theory and social cognitive theory is that they can account for the acquisition of novel or unusual aggressive behaviors even in the absence of immediate rewards. For example, seeing someone else rewarded or punished is sufficient to "learn" the likely consequences of a particular behavior (even if the portrayed consequences are inaccurate, as is frequently the case with media violence). Another strength is that the theory provides an excellent set of constructs to understand thoughtful behavioral choices. In this sense, it works especially well for instrumental types of aggression (usually defined as thoughtful, planned, or goal-oriented aggression).

Cognitive-Neoassociation Theory

Berkowitz (1989, 1993) proposed that a variety of aversive events (i.e., frustrations, provocations, loud noises, uncomfortable temperatures, unpleasant odors) could lead to negative affect, and subsequently to aggression. Negative affect becomes linked (through learning and conditioning during other life experiences) to a variety of thoughts, memories, expressive motor reactions, and physiological responses. When negative affect becomes linked to these other responses, it automatically activates them when negative affect is present. These responses give rise to two immediate and simultaneous tendencies, fight or flight. The fight associations give rise to rudimentary feelings of anger, whereas the flight associations give rise to rudimentary feelings of fear. If the fight tendency is the stronger of the two, the individual will most likely aggress. If the flight tendency is stronger, aggression will be inhibited.

Cognitive-neoassociation theory contends that cues present during the initial aversive events become linked with the thoughts, memories, and motor reactions through processes like classical conditioning. If these cues are present later in different situations, they may trigger those same thoughts and emotions present during the initial aversive event. For example, Geen and Berkowitz (1966; also Berkowitz & Geen, 1967) showed that the effect of watching a boxing match on subsequent aggression in a different context was larger when the aggression target in that later context had the same name as the losing boxer. In other words, the boxer's name served as an aggression cue in the later context.

In addition, cognitive-neoassociation theory takes into account higher-order cognitive processes, such as appraisal and attribution processes. If motivation is present, people may use these higher-order cognitive processes to further analyze their situations. For example, they might think about how they feel, make causal attributions for those feelings, and consider the consequences of acting on their feelings. This more deliberate thought produces more clearly differentiated feelings of anger, fear, or both. It can also suppress or enhance the action tendencies associated with these feelings.

Script Theory

Borrowing from the cognitive and artificial intelligence literature (e.g., Schank & Abelson, 1977), Huesmann (1986, 1998) proposed that people's behavior is guided by the acquisition, internalization, and application of scripts. Scripts are sets of particularly well rehearsed, highly associated concepts, often involving causal linkages, goals, and action plans (Abelson, 1981; Anderson, Benjamin, & Bartholow, 1998; Schank & Abelson, 1977). Scripts define situations and guide behavior in the following way: the person first selects a script that most closely resembles the current situation and then assumes a role in the script. Once a script has been learned, it may be retrieved at a later time as a guide for perception, interpretation, and behavior.

One factor involved in the retrieval and implementation of a script is the similarity of the current situation to the situation in which encoding originally occurred. As a child develops, he or she may observe cases in which violence has been used as means of resolving interpersonal conflicts. If the child is then presented with his or her own conflicts, an aggressive script may be selected as a guide of an appropriate behavioral response. Retrieval of a particular script depends on the similarity between the cues encoded in the original script and the cues present in the current situation.

Script theory also utilizes some ideas from established cognitive-associative models that describe memory as a network consisting of nodes and links (Anderson et al., 1998; Berkowitz, 1993; Collins & Loftus, 1975). In these network models, it is assumed that each concept in memory has an activation threshold. A concept can receive activation energy from the various sources to which it is linked. When the total activation exceeds the threshold, the concept is activated and used. Concepts with similar meanings (e.g., hurt and harm), and those that frequently are activated simultaneously (e.g., shoot and gun), develop strong associations. When a concept is activated, its activation energy spreads to related concepts, as a function of how strongly they are associated. When items are so strongly linked that they form a script, they may be thought of as a unitary concept in semantic memory as well. Semantic memory is defined as "general knowledge of facts and concepts that is not linked to any particular time and place" (Schacter, 2000, p. 170). A frequently rehearsed script gains accessibility strength in two ways: increasing the number of paths by which it can be activated and increasing the strength of the links themselves. Thus, a child who has witnessed several thousand TV instances of using a gun to settle a dispute is likely to have a very accessible conflict–gun–resolve conflict script, one that has generalized across many situations. In other words, the script becomes chronically accessible.

Research has confirmed several aspects of script theory. Of course, the early social learning theory studies of learning aggressive behavior from observation of violent television and movie clips can readily be reinterpreted in script theory terms (e.g., Huesmann & Miller, 1994). Individual differences can also be interpreted as scriptlike phenomena. For example, one study (Dill, Anderson, Anderson, & Deuser, 1997) found that aggressive individuals were more likely to complete ambiguous story stems with aggressive content than nonaggressive individuals. Similarly, Bushman and Anderson (2002) found that playing a violent video game increases the amount of aggressive content in this same story-completion task. Completing a story stem is essentially a script-completion task, and violent media are essentially violent scripts.

Excitation Transfer Theory

Excitation transfer theory (Zillmann, 1983) rests on the fact that physiological arousal dissipates slowly. If two arousing events are separated by a short period of time, some of the arousal caused by the first event may transfer to the second event and add to the arousal caused by the second event. When this occurs, arousal from the first event may be misattributed to the second event. If the second event is related to anger, then the additional arousal should make the person even angrier. The notion of excitation transfer also suggests that anger may be extended over long periods of time, if the person has attributed their heightened arousal to anger. Thus, even after the arousal has dissipated the observer may remain ready to aggress for as long as the self-generated label of anger persists. The relevance to understanding media violence effects derives from the fact that violent entertainment media are generally arousing. Zillmann's work goes further, however, in predicting that nonviolent media may also increase aggression via excitation transfer principles if they increase arousal. Studies have confirmed this prediction (Bryant & Zillmann, 1979; Zillmann, 1971). For example, Zillmann (1971) found that arousal from viewing an erotic film can increase provoked aggression.

Cultivation Theory

All of the modern theories discussed so far have been theories of general behavior that have been applied to media violence. Cultivation theory is somewhat different because it has been more specifically developed to examine effects of exposure to media violence. A central assumption of cultivation theory is that the number of different messages produced by the media is a fairly small, consistent set. For example, prime time dramas display over ten times as much crime as actually occurs in the real world (Gerbner, Gross, Morgan, & Signorielli, 1982). Police officers, lawyers, and judges are over-represented as occupations on television while engineers or scientists are rarely shown (Gerbner et al., 1982).

When these messages are presented consistently over long periods of time, viewers can come to believe the messages they see in the media reflect the real world. Research has shown that exposure to heavy amounts of television can lead people to overestimate amounts of crime and victimization and conclude the world is a violent place (e.g., Bryant, Carveth, & Brown, 1981; Gerbner, Gross, Jackson-Beeck, Jeffries-Fox, & Signorielli, 1978).

These distortions of reality can have a variety of effects on the viewer. Potentially, overestimations of the amount of violence in the real world could lead to feelings of fear, anxiety, and suspicion. Combined with inaccurate estimations of violence in society, these feelings of fear and anxiety can have numerous effects on an individual's other beliefs and behaviors. It is reasonable to speculate that people who are overestimating the amount of crime in the world are more likely behave in a more defensive manner, such as purchasing extra locks or firearms for protection, restricting travel to certain areas they believe are high crime areas, or being more suspicious of strangers. Gerbner, Gross, Morgan, and Signorielli (1980) surveyed television viewers in suburban neighborhoods concerning their media usage and perceptions of danger in their neighborhood. Results showed that among both low and high-income groups, people who consistently view larger amounts of television consider their own neighborhoods to be more dangerous than people who view smaller amounts of media. Another study by Gerbner and his associates has shown that heavy television viewers have stronger beliefs than light viewers that more money needs to be spent on fighting crime (Gerbner et al., 1982).

Desensitization Theory

Techniques of systematic desensitization have been used in the treatment of anxiety disorders for decades. Wolpe (1958) describes systematic desensitization in two parts: first, relaxing the patient through both physiological and emotional relaxing procedures, and then introducing a weak anxiety-producing stimulus. After several series of exposures, the stimulus loses its anxiety-invoking abilities. After desensitization of the initial stimulus has occurred, relatively stronger anxiety-producing stimuli are introduced and also treated through the same manner (Wolpe, 1958). There have been refinements and variations in therapeutic techniques. For example, Bandura has emphasized the utility of modeling and guided participation techniques (e.g., Bandura, 1971, 1973). These techniques have been proven to be effective in reducing (and in many cases eliminating) avoidance behavior of individuals with phobic fears of snakes, spiders, dogs, and flying, among others. Without doubt, these techniques are extremely effective.

Similar desensitization processes appear operative in the media violence context. In this context, desensitization is defined as the process of becoming less physiologically and emotionally aroused to media violence due to extended exposure (Anderson & Huesmann, in press). This phenomenon has been demonstrated by measuring both the decrease in physiological responsiveness to violence (Carnagey, Bushman, & Anderson, under review; Cline, Croft, & Courrier, 1973; Lazarus, Speisman, Mordkoff, & Davison, 1962; Linz, Donnerstein, & Penrod, 1988; Thomas, 1982; Thomas, Horton, Lippincott, & Drabman, 1977) and emotional responsiveness (Smith & Donnerstein, 1998). Although a reduction in anxiety is a positive outcome in many contexts, such as when a fear of spiders is so extreme as to prevent an individual from taking walks or going on picnics, the reduction that occurs in the media violence context is viewed with concern for at least two reasons. First, in choosing among various behavioral alternatives in a conflict situation, anxiety associated with violent alternatives usually serves to inhibit such behaviors. Therefore, a reduction in that anxiety may well increase aggressive behavior (e.g., Anderson & Huesmann, in press). Second, such reductions in anxiety reactions to violence create an emotional blunting that may lead to an underestimation of the seriousness of observed violence, and may therefore reduce the likelihood of coming to the aid of a victim of violence (e.g., Bushman et al., under review). Other research has shown that after viewing several sexually violent movies, participants rated the last movies in the set as less violent (e.g., Cline et al., 1973; Linz et al., 1988) and showed less sympathy for and attributed more responsibility to a rape victim compared to those who viewed nonviolent movies (Dexter, Penrod, Linz, & Saunders, 1997; Linz et al., 1988).

THE GENERAL AGGRESSION MODEL: AN INTEGRATION

All of the recent theories discussed in the previous section have made important contributions. For example, one strength of social learning theory is that it can account for the acquisition of novel or unusual aggressive behaviors even in the absence of immediate reward. However, each theory focuses on a relatively narrow aspect of aggression. For example, Berkowitz's (e.g., 1993) cognitive-neoassociation theory does an excellent job of integrating much of the large body of affective-aggression literature, but has somewhat less to say about instrumental aggression. What is needed is a theory that incorporates the strengths of the theories discussed earlier, thereby accounting for a broader range of aggression. Such a theory must also avoid the pitfalls of the early, broad aggression "theories," which were largely not subject to empirical testing.

A theory developed in recent years, the General Aggression Model (GAM) (see Anderson & Bushman, 2002; Anderson & Huesmann, in press), is an integration that combines key ideas from earlier models: social learning theory and related social-cognitive theory concepts (e.g., Bandura, 1971, 1973; Bandura, Ross, & Ross, 1961, 1963; Mischel 1973; Mischel & Shoda, 1995); Berkowitz's Cognitive-Neoassociationist Model (1984, 1990, 1993); Dodge's social information-processing model (e.g., Crick & Dodge, 1994; Dodge & Crick, 1990); Geen's affective aggression model (1990); Huesmann's script theory (Huesmann, 1986); and Zillmann's excitation transfer model (1983). GAM describes a cyclical pattern of interaction between the person and the environment. Three main points compose the cycle: *input variables* of person and situation, *present internal state* of the individual, and *outcomes* resulting from various appraisal and decision processes.

Input Variables

GAM suggests that a person's behavior is based on two main kinds of input variables: the person and the situation (see Figure 5.1). The person variables are composed of all the things a person has with them when they enter a particular situation, including traits, current states, beliefs, attitudes, values, sex, scripts, and aggressive personality. The situation variables are simply composed of the environment surrounding the individual, including factors in the environment that could affect the person's actions, like aggressive cues, provocation, pain, rewards, and frustration.

Routes

Input variables, sometimes interactively, affect an individual's appraisal of a situation and ultimately affect the behavior performed in response to that appraisal, primarily by influencing the present internal state of the individual. According to GAM, there are three main routes of impact in which present internal states may be altered: cognition, affect, and arousal.

Figure 5.1
The General Aggression Model: Episodic Processes

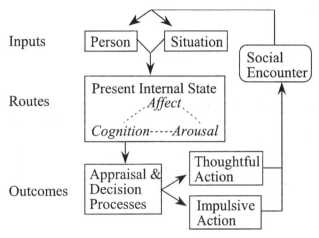

Cognition

Input variables can influence internal states by making aggressive constructs more readily accessible in memory. Constructs can be either temporarily or chronically accessible (e.g., Bargh, Lombardi, & Higgins, 1988; Sedikides & Skowronski, 1990). As a construct is repeatedly accessed, its activation threshold decreases. This means that the construct requires less energy necessary for activation, making it chronically accessible. A situational input (e.g., a violent film) results in a temporary lowered threshold of activation, making the construct accessible for a short time. This temporary increase in the accessibility of a construct is often called "associative priming."

As script theory has contended, situational variables may also activate aggressive scripts (Huesmann, 1986). As noted earlier, activating aggressive scripts can bias the interpretation of a situation and the possible responses to that situation. Similar to aggressive constructs, repeated access of aggressive scripts makes them more readily accessible and more likely to be activated in future situations.

Affect

Input variables can also influence affect, which in turn can have an impact on later behavior. For example, pain increases state hostility (anger) (K. Anderson, Anderson, Dill, & Deuser, 1998). Uncomfortable temperatures produce a small increase in general negative affect and a larger increase in the more specific affect of state hostility (C. Anderson, Anderson, & Deuser, 1996). Exposure to violent movie clips also increases state hostility (Anderson, 1997; Bushman, 1995; Bushman & Geen, 1990; Hansen & Hansen, 1990).

Many personality variables are also related to hostility-related affect. For example, trait hostility as measured by self-report scales is positively related to state hostility (Anderson, 1997; K. Anderson et al., 1998).

Arousal

There are three main ways in which increases in arousal can affect aggressive behavior. First, an increase in arousal can strengthen the already present action tendency, which could be an aggressive tendency. If the person has been provoked or otherwise instigated to aggress at the time this increased activation occurs, aggression will be a likely outcome. Geen and O'Neal (1969) provided an early example of this phenomenon by showing that loud noise increased arousal and aggression. A second possibility was already mentioned when discussing excitation transfer theory. Arousal elicited by other sources (e.g., exercise) may be mislabeled as anger in situations involving provocation, thus producing anger-motivated aggressive behavior. A third, and as yet untested, possibility is that unusually high and low levels of arousal may be aversive and may therefore stimulate aggression in the same way as other aversive or painful stimuli.

Interaction between routes

As mentioned earlier, input variables can influence cognition, affect, and arousal, but these three routes may also influence one another. The idea that cognition and arousal influence affect dates back all the way to William James (1890) and was first popularized among social psychologists by Schachter & Singer (1962). Affect also influences cognition and arousal (Bower, 1981). Research has shown that people often use their affective state to guide inference and judgment processes (Forgas, 1992; Schwarz & Clore, 1996). At a theoretical level, one can view affect as a part of semantic memory that can be primed via spreading activation processes. Thus, hostile cognitions might make hostile feelings more accessible, and vice versa.

Outcomes

Figure 5.2 presents a more detailed look at the appraisal aspects of GAM. Typically, before a behavior is emitted the individual will appraise the current situation and then select a behavior appropriate for the situation. Depending on the situational variables present, appraisals may be made hastily and automatically, without much (or any) thought or awareness, resulting in an impulsive behavior. However, frequently the individual will have the time and resources to reappraise the situation and perform a more thoughtful action. Of course, impulsive behavior may be aggressive or nonaggressive, just as thoughtful action may be either aggressive or nonaggressive.

Immediate appraisals are automatic, which means they are spontaneous, relatively effortless, and occur without awareness of the underlying process.

Figure 5.2
The General Aggression Model: Expanded Appraisal and Decision Processes

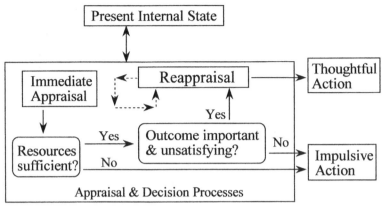

As Krull and colleagues have demonstrated, the spontaneous inference process is a flexible one; its outcomes depend largely on the perceptual set of the perceiver (Krull, 1993; Krull & Dill, 1996). Under some circumstances a behavior of another person is likely to be identified and attributed to that person simultaneously (e.g., Uleman, 1987). For example, if the target person has been thinking aggressive thoughts and is bumped by another person (actor), the target is likely to perceive the "bump" as an aggressive act by the actor. If the target person has been thinking about how crowded a room is, the same bump is likely to be perceived as an accidental consequence of the crowded situation.

However, what occurs after immediate appraisal depends on the resources available to the individual. If the person has sufficient time and cognitive capacity, and if the immediate appraisal outcome is both important and unsatisfying, then the person will engage a more effortful set of reappraisals. If resources are insufficient, or if the outcome of immediate appraisal is unimportant or satisfying, then action will be dictated by the immediate appraisal and the knowledge structure accessed in that appraisal.

Reappraisal consists of searching for additional information in order to view the situation differently. Reappraisal can include a search for relevant information about the cause of the behavior, a search for relevant memories, and a search for features of the present situation. The outcome of reappraisal determines, in part, affective, cognitive, motivational, and behavioral responses. The reappraisal process itself may go through a number of cycles as alternatives are considered and discarded, as long as resources are sufficient and the outcome of each cycle is both important and unsatisfying. At some point, of course, the recycling process ceases, and a thoughtful course of action occurs (including the possibility of "not reacting" to the provocation).

Regardless of immediate appraisal or reappraisal, a decision about the situation will be made and a behavior will soon follow. This action will then be followed by a reaction from the environment, which is typically other people's response to the action. This social encounter will alter the input variables, depending on the environment's response. This encounter could then modify the situation variables, the person variables, or both, resulting in a reinforcement or inhibition of similar behavior in the future (Anderson & Bushman, 2002).

Short-term vs. Long-term Effects

Even though GAM has a central focus on the episode, GAM is not restricted to short-term effects. The cyclical process of GAM lends itself to addressing long-term effects of exposure to media violence. With repeated exposure to certain stimuli (e.g., media violence), particular knowledge structures (e.g., aggressive scripts) become more readily accessible. Figure 5.3 dis-

Figure 5.3
The General Aggression Model: Personality Processes

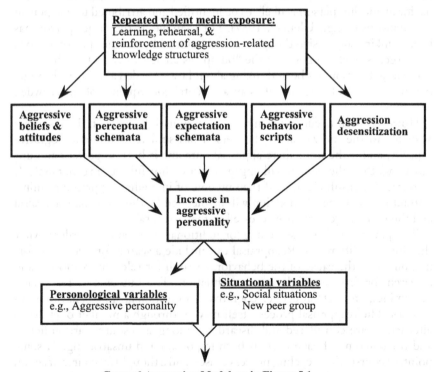

General Aggression Model, as in Figure 5.1

plays this process and several common types of long-term changes that may occur. Over time, the individual will employ these knowledge structures and possibly receive environmental reinforcement for their usage; these knowledge structures will then become strengthened and more likely to be used in later situations. Research supports this notion by demonstrating that repeatedly exposing children to media violence produces aggressive adults (Huesmann & Miller, 1994). Such long-term effects result from the development, automatization, and reinforcement of aggression-related knowledge structures. In essence, the creation and automatization of these aggression-related knowledge structures and the desensitization effects change the individual's personality. Long-term consumers of violent media, for example, can become more aggressive in outlook, perceptual biases, attitudes, beliefs, and behavior than they were before the repeated exposure, or would have become without such exposure.

Applying GAM to Media Violence

This model can be used to interpret the effects of virtually anything the person comes into contact with in his or her environment, including exposure to violent media. Theoretically, violent media can affect all three components of internal state. By itself, the relatively small research literature on violent video games has shown that playing them can temporarily increase aggressive thoughts, affect, and arousal (Anderson & Bushman, 2001). For example, Anderson & Dill (2000) showed that playing a violent video game increased the speed with which the person could read aggression-related words (aggressive thoughts). Similarly, Kirsh (1998) and Bushman & Anderson (2002) found that playing a violent video game subsequently increased hostile interpretations of ambiguous social events (aggressive schemata). And as noted earlier, exposure to violent media can reduce arousal to subsequent depictions of violence. Playing a violent video game can also influence the person's internal state through the affective route by increasing feelings of anger, and through the arousal route by increasing heart rate (Anderson & Bushman, 2001).

In sum, GAM accounts for the wide variety of effects seen in the media violence literature, including both short- and long-term effects on aggressive thoughts, feelings, and behaviors; on anxiety desensitization and subsequent declines in prosocial behavior; and on changes in the social environment that occur as the developing child becomes more habitually aggressive. There are two other media violence domains that have not been specifically discussed in past presentations of GAM—the effects of media violence on fear, and broader societal issues concerning the role of violent media in modern society. The former can easily fit into GAM, as will be seen in the next section. The latter falls outside the intended domain of GAM, and will be discussed in a later section.

Fear

Exposure to media violence can initially cause sleep disturbances, anxiety, and fear (e.g., Cantor, 1998, 2001; Harrison & Cantor, 1999; Owens et al., 1999; Singer, Slovak, Frierson, & York, 1998). Cantor (1994) has identified several moderating factors (see also Cantor, chapter 10, this volume). First, violent media are more likely to evoke fear in viewers if the stimuli are similar to real-life fears. For example, live-action sequences of violence are more likely to produce fear in viewers than animated cartoon violence (Gunter & Furnham, 1984; Osborn & Endsley, 1971; Surbeck, 1975). Second, motivation for viewing potentially frightening scenes of violence also affects whether the stimuli will evoke fear. People who seek out frightening material may voluntarily reduce their own cognitive defenses to enable themselves to be frightened. Those who try to avoid scary scenes may try to discount them when confronted with scenes of violence. A third set of factors that can contribute to fear while viewing media violence is other characteristics connected to the presentation, such as stressful music and sound effects (Cantor, 1994). Whereas all of these factors may contribute to an individual being frightened by viewing particular scenes of violence, the most recognized factor is developmental maturity.

As children mature, their fears develop as well, changing from fears of the dark and intangible monsters, to fears of personal injury, to fears of global and political issues (see Cantor, Wilson, & Hoffner, 1986). Based on her research, Cantor has developed some broad generalizations concerning developmental maturity and viewing fear-evoking violence (Cantor, 1994). First, Cantor contends that as a child matures, the importance of perceptible characteristics of media violence decreases. This means that younger children are more likely to become frightened of stimuli that look scary, but could be harmless, whereas older children base their fears on more conceptual information (Cantor & Sparks, 1984; Sparks & Cantor, 1986). As children mature, they develop the ability to distinguish fantasy from reality. Due to this development, children are also likely to develop more realistic fears (e.g., war, kidnappings) as fantasy fears (e.g., monsters under the bed) depicted in the media diminish (Cantor & Sparks, 1984; Cantor & Wilson, 1984; Sparks & Cantor, 1986). Third, as children mature they become more frightened of abstract concepts portrayed in media, such as nuclear attack and its consequences (Cantor, Wilson, & Hoffner, 1986).

All of these fear effects fit neatly into the early stages of GAM. For instance, some of the diminution of fantasy fears likely arises from standard desensitization effects. More broadly, as children develop, the knowledge structures they use to perceive and understand media violence also change and develop in predictable ways.

BROADER ISSUES

There is a host of media violence issues that fall outside of the domain of the General Aggression Model. One set of these issues is nicely described by

Potter's Lineation Theory (1999). Another set more directly involves public policy issues.

Lineation Theory

Lineation theory (Potter, 1999) examines five major facets of the media violence situation: content of media, media industry practices, psychological processing of media violence messages, factors influencing media violence effects, and the effects of viewing media violence. The General Aggression Model fully addresses the psychological processes underlying media violence effects raised by Potter (1999), and other behavioral science research has examined the content of the U.S. media landscape (e.g., Wilson et al., 1997, 1998). However, behavioral sciences have not thoroughly addressed the practices of the media industry. These issues, however, are important ones that should be addressed.

It is not clear to us how one should go about an empirical examination of how the media industry decides to include violence in its movies, television programs, and video games. Such an effort falls well outside our range of expertise. However, Potter's book provides some interesting ideas on this topic, and a recent book by James Steyer (2002) gives an insider's view of the processes, a quite disturbing view indeed. Interested readers should certainly examine these works carefully.

Although empirical examination of the media industry from a behavioral science perspective may not be possible, information from behavioral science may be one way in which social scientists can influence the industries. For example, Bushman and colleagues (Bushman & Bonacci, 2002; Bushman & Phillips, 2001) have found that violent and sexual content in television shows reduces the viewer's recall of advertisements in that show.

Public Health and Public Policy

Scientifically derived findings concerning media violence are relevant to public health issues, and therefore are relevant to public policy. Media violence researchers find themselves drawn into these debates despite a reluctance to participate in them. Such researchers sometimes must defend themselves from well-financed attacks by individuals and groups who have no training or real expertise in conducting media violence research, but have considerable funding and expertise in influencing public opinion and public policy. Perhaps even more damaging are those behavioral scientists who have made careers out of attacking media violence research despite having never conducted a major original empirical study of media violence effects. Their scholarly credentials (albeit in other domains) make them particularly attractive partners to the media industries who produce and profit from violent media, and they are frequently supported by those industries.

Despite the unpleasantness often associated with such nonscientific encounters, we believe that it is important for legitimate researchers to remain involved. After all, what is the point of doing good research if it is going to be either misrepresented to the general public or totally ignored by public policymakers? This section outlines some of the issues, one of which concerns the role of theory in such debates.

What is the proper role for media violence researchers in such public policy debates? We don't pretend to have an answer for all such researchers. However, we believe that in our role as scientists, it is important to provide an accurate and unbiased assessment of the scientific state of knowledge to any group that requests it, whether it is the local PTA, a state psychological association, child advocacy groups, the U.S. Senate, or even the Entertainment Software Association (though they haven't asked us yet). We also believe that most behavioral scientists (including ourselves) are not very good at this, largely because we often fail to hear the question that is being asked. Here are several things we have learned in such encounters.

First, many participants in public debates about media violence fail to make the crucial distinction between psychological science versus relevant personal values. The result, all too often, is a concerted effort by the media violence industry and their supporters to denigrate the scientific enterprise as well as the scientists involved. Similarly, child advocacy groups occasionally claim that the scientific research itself directly supports certain public policy actions. In fact, such public policy issues revolve around a host of factors, only one of which is the media violence research literature. Media violence researchers should be willing to share their special expertise concerning the scientific issues. However, media violence researchers do not have special expertise concerning legal issues or concerning a host of personal values that are also relevant to making an informed (and personal) decision about appropriate public policy. Reasonable people may well have different personal values relevant to a given issue, and so may come to very different conclusions concerning public policy even if they agree on the scientific conclusions. For example, two people can agree that repeated exposure of children to violent media leads to a significant increase in their propensity to aggress as adults, while simultaneously disagreeing about whether the government should impose restrictions on the kinds of video games youngsters can purchase or rent without parental consent. One person may value children's rights to choose so highly that they are willing to accept higher societal violence rates in order to let children choose. Another may decide that children need protection in this domain, and may be willing to reduce children's right to choose (and thereby increase parents' rights to control access to their children) in order to have a less violent society. Our role as behavioral scientists is to answer the question concerning what the research tells us about violent media effects, but we cannot tell others how highly they should value children's rights versus parents' rights or societal violence rates. For this reason, we try very hard to not make public statements about what politicians or other public policymakers ought to do, and instead confine our contributions to the scientific ones in our areas of expertise.

Second, the role of theory in such public policy debates is often misrepresented or underutilized. Sometimes this happens for fairly obvious motivational reasons, such as when the 40-plus years of research on TV and movie violence is categorically dismissed by the video game industry as irrelevant. Good psychological theory about how exposure to media violence influences aggression makes that larger and more developed research literature very relevant. After all, the practicality of a good theory derives from the fact that good decisions in the design of interventions, treatments, or programs—their success in achieving desired results—depends on well-integrated theories whose basic principles generalize.

Third, the entertainment media industries are using essentially the same tactics that the tobacco industry used for many years. One major tactic is to separate each type of video game study from the rest, and then attack each type individually. So laboratory experiments are "bad" because no one is actually killed in such studies; cross-sectional studies are "bad" because they are merely correlational; and longitudinal studies of violent video games don't yet exist. Similarly, studies with college students are "irrelevant" because they are legally adults and we're really only concerned about kids; studies with children are "irrelevant" because the industry already provides age ratings of video games. This divide-and-conquer strategy is very effective in misleading an audience about the true overall state of scientific knowledge. What researchers must do, in our view, is not allow such tactics to divert us (or our audiences) from the scientific strategy of looking at the totality of the empirical evidence and the strength (or weakness) of the theory guiding the integration of that evidence.

Good theory generalizes, and therefore cannot be ignored. GAM provides one integrative framework for understanding the empirical research on media violence, and for guiding future research and development of intervention strategies. As other chapters in this volume demonstrate, the totality of research and theory on media violence effects is extensive, coherent, and amazingly consistent when one takes the broad view. The public needs to understand this so that the public policy debate can move to legitimate discussions of which public policy options (if any) are appropriate.

CHAPTER 6

The Case against the Case against Media Violence

L. Rowell Huesmann and Laramie D. Taylor

Even before the introduction of television into everyday life over 50 years ago, the question of whether exposure to violence in the media made the viewer more violent was being debated. But it was the introduction of television into the average American home in the early 1950s that really stimulated an explosion of scientific research on the topic. In this chapter we are not going to review that large body of research in detail; other chapters in this volume do that and show that the accumulated research indicts media violence as a cause of viewers' aggressive behavior. Rather, in this chapter we are going to deal with the writings of those who argue that media violence has no effect on aggression. Specifically, we will (1) summarize some of the most common flaws in their arguments and criticisms, (2) respond in detail to the criticisms of several of the most vociferous "naysayers," and (3) try to explain the psychology of why these naysayers find it so difficult to accept conclusions regarding media violence that are supported by large amounts of evidence while they find it easy to accept conclusions about other threats to public health supported by less compelling evidence. However, to accomplish these goals we need to begin by briefly summarizing what the empirical evidence shows, how the integration of different methodologies leads to a particularly strong indictment of media violence, and what psychological processes explain the effects of media violence on aggression. Let us start with an explication of the psychological processes through which exposure to media violence has an effect on viewers' violent and aggressive behavior. Understanding these processes is the key to understanding what the body of empirical data really shows.

PROCESSES ACCOUNTING FOR EFFECTS OF MEDIA VIOLENCE

To begin with one must realize that different processes explain *short-term effects* and *long-term effects*. Short-term effects are due to (1) priming processes, (2) excitation processes, and (3) the immediate imitation of specific behaviors (Bushman & Huesmann, 2000; Huesmann, 1988, 1998).

Briefly, priming is the process through which spreading activation in the brain's neural network from the locus representing an external observed stimulus excites another brain node representing aggressive cognitions or behaviors (Berkowitz, 1993). These excited nodes then are more likely to influence behavior. The external stimulus can be inherently aggressive, for example, the sight of a gun (Berkowitz & LePage, 1967), or something neutral like a radio that has simply been nearby when a violent act was observed (Josephson, 1987). A provocation that follows a *priming* stimulus is more likely to stimulate aggression as a result of the priming. While this effect is short-lived, the primed script, schema, or belief may have been acquired long ago and may have been acquired in a completely different context.

To the extent that observed violence (real world or media) arouses the observer, aggressive behavior may also become more likely in the short run for two other possible reasons—excitation transfer (Zillmann, 1979, 1983a, 1983b) and general arousal (Berkowitz, 1993; Geen & O'Neal, 1969). First, a subsequent provocation may be perceived as more severe than it is because the emotional response stimulated by the observed violence is misattributed as being due to the provocation (Zillmann, 1979, 1983a). Such excitation transfer could account for a more intense aggressive response in the short run. Alternatively, the increased general arousal stimulated by the observed violence may simply reach such a peak that the ability of inhibiting mechanisms such as normative beliefs to restrain aggression is reduced (Berkowitz, 1993).

The third short-term process, imitation of specific aggressive behaviors, can be viewed as a special case of the more general long-term process of observational learning (Bandura, 1986; Huesmann, 1998). In recent years the evidence has accumulated that human and primate young have an innate tendency to imitate whomever they observe (Butterworth, 1999; Meltzoff & Moore, 2000; Rizzolati, Fadiga, Gallese, & Fogassi, 1996; Wyrwicka, 1996). These theories propose that very young children are likely to imitate almost any specific behaviors they see. Observation of specific aggressive behaviors around them increases the likelihood of children behaving exactly that way (Bandura, 1977; Bandura, Ross, & Ross, 1963). Granted, not all aggression is learned; in children two to four years old, proactive-instrumental behaviors that might be called aggressive (e.g., pushing another child without any provocation to get a desired object) appear spontaneously (Tremblay, 2000), as may hostile temper-tantrums. However, the observation of specific aggressive behaviors at that age leads to the acquisition of more coordinated aggressive scripts for social problem-solving and counteracts environmental forces aimed at conditioning the child out of aggression. As the child grows older, the social scripts acquired though observation of family, peers, community, and mass media become more complex, abstracted, and automatic in their invocation (Huesmann, 1988, 1998). Additionally, children's social-cognitive schema about the world around them begin to be elaborated. In particular, extensive observation of violence around them biases children's world schemas toward attributing hostility to others' actions (Dodge, 1985; Gerbner, Gross, Morgan, & Signorielli, 1994). Such attributions in turn increase the likelihood of children behaving aggressively (Dodge, 1980; Dodge, Pettit, Bates, & Valente, 1995). As children mature further, normative beliefs about what social behaviors are appropriate become crystallized, and begin to act as filters to limit inappropriate social behaviors (Huesmann & Guerra, 1997). Children's own behaviors influence the normative beliefs that develop, but so do the children's observations of the behaviors of those around them including those observed in the mass media (Guerra, Huesmann, Tolan, Van Acker, & Eron, 1995; Huesmann, Guerra, Zelli, & Miller, 1992; Huesmann, 2003). In summary, social-cognitive observational-learning theory postulates long-term effects of exposure to violence through the influence of exposure on the development of aggressive problem-solving scripts, hostile attributional biases, and normative beliefs approving of aggression.

Long-term effects are due to (1) observational learning of social scripts for behavior, of schemas about the world (e.g., is it hostile or benign), and of normative beliefs about the appropriateness of aggressive behavior; (2) emotional desensitization to violence; and (3) justification processes based on social comparisons (Bushman & Huesmann, 2000; Huesmann, 1988, 1998). There is some overlap with short-term effects; long-term effects are also quite likely increased by the habituation process called "desensitization." Most humans seem to have an innate negative emotional response to observing blood, gore, and violence. Increased heart rates, perspiration, and self-reports of discomfort often accompany such exposure (Cline, Croft, & Courrier, 1973; Moise-Titus, 1999). However, with repeated exposure to violence, this negative emotional response habituates, and the observer becomes "desensitized." One can then think about and plan proactive aggressive acts without experiencing negative affect. Consequently, proactive aggression becomes more likely.

One other long-term process is probably important. Social comparison theory suggests that humans evaluate themselves by comparing themselves to others. The aggressive child is generally (with some exceptions) not accepted because others do not like to be around aggressive peers (Anderson & Huesmann, in press). Huesmann (1988, 1995, 1998) has suggested that, to counter this threat to self-worth, aggressive children seek out aggressive media. Observing others behaving aggressively makes the aggressive children feel happier and more justified. Viewing media violence makes them feel happier because it convinces them that they are not alone in being aggressive. Of course, the ultimate consequence of such a turn, toward more exposure to violent media, is more observational learning of aggressive scripts, schemas, and beliefs, and more desensitization to violence.

INTEGRATION OF EMPIRICAL RESEARCH RELATING MEDIA VIOLENCE TO AGGRESSION

Once these processes are understood, the wealth of empirical evidence implicating exposure to media violence as a cause of aggressive behavior does not seem so surprising. However, to understand how compelling the evidence really is, one needs to integrate the evidence from all the different empirical approaches that have been employed.

The methodologies used in studying the relation between media violence and aggression fall into three major classes: (1) experiments in which the researcher manipulates exposure to media violence, (2) correlational studies, or one-shot observational studies in which exposure to violence and concurrent aggressive behavior are measured with surveys or observations, and (3) longitudinal observational studies in which exposure and behavior are measured on the same sample repeatedly over long periods of time. It is critical to integrate the findings of all three bodies of research in reaching any conclusion.

Generally, experiments have demonstrated consistently that exposing children to violent behavior on film and TV increases the likelihood that they will behave aggressively immediately afterward (see reviews by Bushman & Huesmann, 2000; Geen and Thomas, 1986; Paik & Comstock, 1994; Strasburger & Wilson, chapter 4, this volume). The typical paradigm is that randomly selected children who are shown either a violent or nonviolent short film are then observed as they play with each other or with objects. The consistent finding is that children who see the violent film behave more aggressively immediately afterward. They behave more aggressively toward persons (Bjorkqvist, 1985; Josephson, 1987) and toward inanimate objects (Bandura, 1977). The effects occur for all children—from preschool to adolescence, for boys and girls, for black and white, and for normally aggressive or normally nonaggressive. The average size of the immediate effect produced is about equivalent to a 0.4 correlation (Paik & Comstock, 1994). In these well-controlled laboratory studies there can be no doubt that it is the children's observation of the violence that is *causing* the changes in behavior. As described above, the psychological mechanisms operating are priming, excitation transfer, and simple imitation.

The question then becomes whether these causal effects observed in the laboratory generalize to the real world. Do they have real significance in the world? Do they extend over time? Does real media violence cause real aggression in the real world, not just in the short run but in the long run as well?

Empirical correlational studies of children and youth behaving and watching media in their natural environments have demonstrated that the answer to both of these questions is "yes." The great majority of competently done one-shot survey studies have shown that children who watch more media violence day in and day out behave more aggressively day in and day out (Paik & Comstock, 1994). The correlations obtained usually are between 0.15 and 0.30. Such correlations are not large by the standards of variance explained, but they are moderate by the standards of children's personality measurement, and they can have real social significance (Comstock & Scharrer, chapter 11, this volume; Rosenthal, 1986). In fact, as Rosenthal (1986) has pointed out, a correlation of 0.3 with aggression translates into a change in the odds of aggression from 50/50 to 65/35—not a trivial change when one is dealing with life-threatening behavior. Moreover, the relation is highly replicable even across researchers who disagree about the reasons (e.g., Huesmann, Lagerspetz, & Eron, 1984; Milavsky, Kessler, Stipp, & Rubens, 1982) and across countries (Huesmann & Eron, 1986).

Complementing these one-time survey studies are the longitudinal real-world studies that have shown correlations over time from childhood viewing of media violence to later adult aggressive behavior (Eron, Huesmann, Lefkowitz, & Walder, 1972; Milavsky, Kessler, Stipp, & Rubens, 1982; Huesmann, Moise, Podolski, & Eron, 2003; for reviews see Huesmann & Miller, 1994; Huesmann, Moise, & Podolski, 1997). Analysis of longitudinal data has also shown that early habitual exposure to media violence predicts increased aggressiveness beyond what would be predicted from early aggressiveness.

In conjunction with the theories described above, the results from these three kinds of research—experiments showing unambiguous causation, one-shot surveys showing real aggression correlates with concurrent habitual exposure to violent media, and longitudinal studies showing that childhood exposure predicts increased adult aggression independent of childhood aggression—should lead objective scientists to conclude that exposure to media violence increases a child's risk for behaving aggressively in both the short run and long run. So why is there still a body of public intellectuals who refuse to accept this conclusion?

THE PSYCHOLOGY OF DENIAL

To begin with, one must note that there is a clear consensus of opinion among scholars who actually do research on the topic that exposure to media violence causes aggression. Most major health professional groups have issued statements citing exposure to media violence as one cause of youth violence. Two Surgeon Generals of the United States (in 1972 and 2001) have warned the public that media violence is a risk factor for aggression. For example, in March 1972, then Surgeon General Jesse Steinfeld told Congress, it is clear to me that the causal relationship between [exposure to] televised violence and antisocial behavior is sufficient to warrant appropriate and immediate remedial action. . . . *there comes a time when the data are sufficient to justify action. That time has come.* (Steinfeld, 1972)

Surveys have consistently shown that over 80 percent of those doing research on the topic have concluded from the evidence that media violence is causing aggression (Murray, 1984).

So who are the vocal minority denying that there can be any effects? The best-known social scientists who deny there are any effects (e.g., Cumberbatch, Fowles, Freedman, Jenks) generally have never done any empirical research on the topic. However, they are glib and compelling writers, and their opinions cannot simply be dismissed. Furthermore, there is a large body of other intellectuals who deny that there are any effects. They range from the president of the Motion Pictures Producers Association (Jack Valenti) to the president of the Entertainment Software Association (Doug Lowenstein); from movie directors (e.g., Rob Reiner) to comic book producers (e.g., Gerard Jones); from science writers (e.g., Richard Rhodes) to booksellers (e.g., Chris Finan, president, American Booksellers Foundation).

Later in the paper we will deal with the individual criticisms of the most visible critics, but we first want to offer a psychological perspective on why well-intentioned, generally intelligent, and well-informed people can hold and promote attitudes on this topic that are so discrepant from what the majority of scientists, health care providers, and parents believe. We see three explanations for the discrepancy which are all grounded in psychological theory: (1) the need for cognitive consistency, (2) reactance against control, and (3) susceptibility to the "third person effect" of human behavior. However, all of these psychological processes depend on two underlying facts—one grounded in economics and one grounded in political principle, American history, and constitutional law. The economic fact is that violence in entertainment attracts audiences and makes large amounts of money for its purveyors (see Hamilton, 1998). The political principle is the sacredness of free expression in American society and law.

We propose that individuals involved in the production or marketing of violence will find it difficult to believe that viewing violence could be damaging to audiences because that belief would be cognitively inconsistent with their behaviors. Cognitive consistency is a remarkably powerful force that affects behaviors and beliefs (Abelson et al., 1968); so it would not be surprising that the behaviors shaped by subtle economic forces would shape beliefs. Only if the economic forces are blatant, or other beliefs relieve the inconsistency, can effects be admitted. For example, the director Oliver Stone says that "of course his [violent] movies [e.g., *Natural Born Killers*] are dangerous." His movies are intended to affect people, and that is one of the costs of free expression (BBC Panorama, 1997). Similarly, the cognitive consistency process can lead to a denial of effects for those who believe strongly in free expression in the mass media. Many individuals with strong liberal beliefs about free expression in the mass media also have strong beliefs about society having a duty to protect children. If they accepted the fact that media violence harms children, they might have to rethink their beliefs about balancing freedom of expression and consider protecting children. It is easier for them to avoid this cognitive dissonance by denying that media violence has effects than it would be for them to resolve the dissonance. Furthermore, if the purveyors of violence accepted that violence has serious effects on children, they would have to categorize themselves with other purveyors of products that threaten health, for example, tobacco, which would produce even more dissonance.

The second psychological process we see as relevant applies only to the producers of violent media. Most humans at a young age develop an aversion to being controlled and respond to such attempts with reactance, or attempts to regain or increase their own control (Brehm & Brehm, 1981). We suggest that artists, writers, and producers are particularly susceptible to displaying such reactance when attempts are made to control their creative products, in which their egos are heavily involved. Artists often view as threats of control statements that their programs or films harm viewers. Suppose a researcher tells an artist that a program of theirs, which is a financial and critical success, is bad because it stimulates violence in the children watching it. The artist, rightly or wrongly, consciously or unconsciously, may interpret this statement as a threat of control. Therefore, a plausible response of the artist according to reactance theory would be to attack the researcher's thesis that the program has bad effects on the viewer.

The third psychological process we offer is intended more to explain a frequent opinion one hears from violence viewers who believe viewing violence cannot be bad. The opinion is that "media violence may affect some 'susceptible' people, but it will not affect 'me' or 'my children' because we are impervious to such influences." It is common in opinion surveys to find people reporting that a media message or personal communication might affect some people, but not the respondent. This phenomenon has been labeled the "third person effect" (Davison, 1983). Of course, as the research reported elsewhere shows, media violence can affect any child. The third person effect may be related to reactance theory. If viewers admit that they are being influenced by messages in the media, then they would have to admit they are being controlled to some extent by the media. Reactance would demand some action then. But if one denies that one is being controlled by the media, one does not need to act according to reactance theory.

We offer these three psychological processes only as suggestions that may help explain how many informed and intelligent people can read the reports of the studies done and still sincerely deny that media violence has serious effects on viewers. We certainly cannot offer any empirical evidence that these processes do operate among the noted critics. However, they are well-established psychological processes that are likely to operate among any of us. Of course, there are other plausible contributors to the dissents of specific critics. Some critics have invested a great deal in denying effects for a long time and have been paid by the violence purveyors to write dissenting books (e.g., Freedman). Obviously, it would be difficult for them to change. Others have alternative theories of violence that they are invested in and see media violence as a competitor (e.g., Rhodes). Probably, it is a combination of multiple processes that leads to the most vociferous dissents, which are obviously sincerely held.

Four Common Flaws in Critiques of Media Violence Research

Let us now turn to a discussion of a few of the most frequently repeated errors of reasoning that have been made by critics who challenge the conclusion that exposing children to media violence puts them more at risk to behave aggressively in the short run and in the long run.

1. *Assuming that the question is whether TV violence is the "only" cause of aggression, and arguing that TV violence can't matter because people who see the same TV shows differ in aggressiveness.* For example, critics say that "Detroit, Michigan and Windsor, Ontario see essentially the same TV shows. But the murder rate is much higher in Detroit. Consequently TV violence cannot be increasing serious aggression." This argument has been repeated over many years by intelligent people ranging from social scientists criticizing the research to politicians to network vice-presidents. Of course, this argument would only make sense if *nothing except TV violence* influenced murder—not guns, not poverty, not social support, not peer attitudes, not child rearing, not biological predispositions. The murder rate in Detroit has been higher for a lot of these reasons. It's puzzling how anyone could seriously offer this as an argument that TV violence has no effect. No reputable researcher of media violence has ever suggested that media violence is the only cause or even the most important cause of aggression. Serious aggressive behavior only occurs when there is a convergence of multiple predisposing and precipitating factors (Huesmann, 1998).

2. *Ignoring laboratory experiments.* It has been common among the naysayers (e.g., Freedman, 1984) to ignore completely the well-done laboratory experiments that have shown that exposure to violence stimulates aggressive behavior in the short run. Ignoring any of the different types of research (e.g., experiments, cross-sectional surveys, longitudinal studies) on media violence would be risky, but ignoring laboratory experiments is particularly inappropriate because it is the kind of study that most clearly tests causation. One typical rationale for ignoring laboratory experiments is the supposed artificiality of the aggression measures used in the laboratory, such as giving shocks

to another person. The critics most often mention only the measures with the least face validity and never offer any empirical evidence that the lab measures are not valid indices of real-world aggression. The truth is that there is substantial empirical evidence that the measures of aggression used in laboratory studies are quite valid indices of how aggressively the person would behave outside the laboratory (Anderson & Bushman, 1997; Berkowitz & Donnerstein, 1982).

The other common complaint used against experiments without any justification offered is that "laboratory work suffers from strong experimenter demands" that bias the results in the direction of showing effects of media violence (Freedman, 1984). In fact, this criticism runs counter to the empirical evidence that suggests that participants in aggression experiments are likely to inhibit aggressive impulses because they fear being negatively evaluated by the experimenter (Turner & Simons, 1974). Finally, excluding laboratory experiments in favor of focusing only on field research reflects critics' misplaced confidence in such studies. While field studies may often (but not always—see Berkowitz & Donnerstein, 1982) have greater external validity, it is much harder to confirm the internal validity of the conclusions of field studies. And causation can never be tested as conclusively with field research as with a well-controlled laboratory experiment. The critics who ignore experiments conveniently overlook this fact.

3. *Selective reporting of negative results and changing criteria for accepting results.* Another common flaw in the critics' analyses of the research is their tendency to change the criteria for reporting a study or evaluating it depending on how the results came out. One study with positive results is discounted because of supposed demand characteristics on participants to behave aggressively, while a study with negative results is praised despite the fact that there were clear demands placed on the participants not to aggress. Another study with positive results is discounted because the stimulus films may have differed in attractiveness to the viewers, while a similar study with negative results is praised even though differential attractiveness of the films could have accounted for the negative effects. While meta-analyses that systematically combine all studies on a topic uniformly show positive and significant effect sizes for media violence on aggression (see Comstock & Scharrer, chapter 11, this volume), the reviews of the naysayers often convey the impression that most studies do not have positive effects simply because, for one flimsy reason or another, they exclude many studies with positive results and include every study with no results.

4. *Analyzing studies in a theoretical vacuum.* Perhaps the most egregious common error made by the naysayers is to evaluate the research on media violence as if it is completely disconnected from our existing knowledge about learning, social cognition, and aggression. We have outlined earlier in this chapter the established theory that explains how media violence influences aggression. The psychological processes that account for the effect were not invented to

account for the effect; they had been established independently. Given what we know about priming of social cognitions (Bargh, 1982), it would be incredibly surprising if media violence did not prime aggressive cognitions. Given what we know about arousal processes and excitation transfer (Zillmann, 1983a, 1983b), it would be startling if media violence did not produce such effects. Given what we know about the innate propensity of primates to imitate (Meltzoff & Moore, 1977, 2000) and the developmental course of observational learning in the real world (Bandura, 1977, 1986), it would be a shock if children did not acquire social scripts, world schemas, and normative beliefs from the mass media. Given the research on how hostile attributional bias (Dodge, 1980, 1985) and normative beliefs promoting aggression (Huesmann & Guerra, 1997) influence children's behavior, it would be surprising if such cognitions acquired from the mass media did not influence the children's behavior. And finally, given the established continuity of aggression from childhood to adulthood (Huesmann et al., 1984), it would be very surprising if the effects of media violence on children were not detectable when they were adults years later. Yet, the naysayers seem totally unaware of such psychological facts.

Given this background and overview of the most common errors in the critics' reasoning, let us now turn to a discussion of the specific views of several of the most prominent critics who challenge the conclusion that exposure to media violence increases the aggressive tendencies of the viewer.

The Freedman Chronicles

Over the past 20 years no critic has played a more prominent role in denying that media violence has any effect on behavior than psychologist Jonathan Freedman at the University of Toronto. Since 1984 (Freedman, 1984), he has written and published numerous articles disputing the fact that media violence has any significant effect on aggression and has culminated that work with a recent book (Freedman, 2002). Like most critics, he has never done any empirical research on the effects of media violence, and his critiques contain numerous examples of the four general flaws of thinking that we described above. Additionally, Freedman's objectivity, at least in his recent summative book, must be questioned as he was paid to write the book by the Motion Picture Association of America. Freedman accuses some of the scholars who have done empirical research on media violence of "basing their whole careers on showing that television violence is harmful" and therefore of being biased. In fact, a large amount of the important empirical work on media violence and aggression has been done by psychologists whose careers were devoted to *understanding social behavior or aggressive behavior* and who branched out to study media violence (e.g., Anderson, Bandura, Berkowitz, Bushman, Eron, Geen, Huesmann, Huston, Lagerspetz, Malamuth, and Parke, to name a few). Freedman, on the other hand, has based an entire 20-year career on trying to show that media violence has no effect on aggression. Nevertheless, Freedman deserves some additional response because he is a social scientist and has attracted considerable attention. Because previous responses to his critiques (Huesmann, Eron, Berkowitz, & Chaffee, 1992; Huesmann & Moise, 1996) have focused on his early essays, we focus on his recent book here (2002).

The book is engagingly written, accessible to a nonscholarly audience, and presents glib arguments for not believing that media violence affects aggression based on some truths, many selective distortions and exaggerations, and a few outright untruths or misunderstandings. As always, Freedman points out some real flaws in research on the topic. Freedman also avoids some of the errors of his earlier reviews—he does now devote attention to laboratory experiments, for example. However, as before, his approach to the issue is a-theoretical, and he employs selective reporting and shifting criteria for evaluation of studies. Because he is an engaging and talented writer, probably sincere in his beliefs that there are no effects, and probably unaware of how selective his reporting is, he builds a bond with the reader. This allows him to shift from the third person to the first person and engage in "conversations" with the reader. When faced with a result inconsistent with his thesis that he cannot explain away, he relies on this bond to allow him to simply say things like, "It is a complicated study with very complicated results. I am confident that, overall, these results do not show that exposure to media violence increases aggression" (p. 29). Or in response to a published assertion he does not like, he may simply exclaim: "This is incredible," or "Scandalous," or "It is junk science." These are just some of the phrases Freedman uses to convey his feelings. His feelings are clear, but the justification for them is not made clear. What is worse, while he carefully qualifies every statement he makes concerning any kind of positive effect that might possibly be found between media violence viewing and aggression, he forgets about qualifying negative statements; as a result, he has a number of clearly false statements. To offer a few of his statements that are patently false unless qualified: "Virtually, no research shows that media violence desensitizes people to violence." "There is virtually no research on changes in attitudes due to viewing violence." "A majority of studies show no ill effects." "None of these reviews looked at hundreds of studies." (Paik and Comstock [1994] looked at 217, to give one counterexample.)

While his style contributes significantly to the dismissive message about media violence that he conveys, it is the more substantive review techniques he employs that really distort the truth. To begin with, Freedman completely dismisses meta-analysis as a viable review technique; for some time meta-analysis has been the accepted scientific mechanism for combining the results of many social science studies on a particular topic (see Comstock & Scharrer, chapter 11, this volume). In fact, in the early 1990s Paik and Comstock published an outstanding meta-analysis on this topic covering research through 1990. Essentially, Freedman ignores this analysis with the comment that "they do not provide any details for how they classified results; so it is not possible to comment" (p. 31). This statement in itself implies a lack of understanding of the nature of meta-analysis. In meta-analyses quantitative effect sizes are combined according to mathematical principles, and the outcome does not depend on an individual classifying any particular study as supportive or not supportive. The aggregate effect size speaks for itself. Freedman's rationale for dismissing existing meta-analyses are not only weak, but also self-serving, as Paik and Comstock's conclusions are quite at odds with Freedman's thesis. For example, Paik and Comstock report an overall effect size (as a correlation) of 0.37 for experiments and 0.19 for surveys (see Comstock & Scharrer, chapter 11, this volume, for details and an explanation of how to interpret how large these effect sizes are). Furthermore, while dismissing this fine meta-analysis of 217 studies without comment, Freedman spends some pages taking apart a less sophisticated meta-analysis of 23 studies by criticizing the author's conclusions about each study on the basis of nothing but his word that he agrees or disagrees. By dismissing meta-analyses and refusing to do one himself, Freedman greatly diminishes the value of his review. However, he could still have had an impact if he had presented consistent scholarly arguments in analyzing each study independently, but he did not.

Freedman's approach to analyzing a study is to mix together some quite appropriate methodological issues of concern with other unique value judgments of his own into a glib mix that might fool the lay reader but will not carry much weight with the informed reader. It is not that he is misleading the reader. He is quite straightforward. But the assertions he makes without supporting facts just do not hold up. Also, despite his statement that he attempted to overcome his own biases and review studies fairly, his biases remain readily apparent. He shifts his criteria for criticism depending on whether the study shows positive or negative effects. He emphasizes minor methodological errors and statistical errors in studies finding a positive effect but minimizes them in studies showing no effect. We can't go through every study he reviews, but let's consider two.

In his discussion of a study by Leyens, Camino, Parke, and Berkowitz (1975), Freedman dismisses the positive results, which fit perfectly with what theory would have predicted, by saying that "there are a number of serious problems . . . that make its result almost impossible to interpret" (p. 101). In this study Leyens reported that boys who watched a week of violent films in their cottages were observed behaving more physically aggressively afterward compared both to their behavior during a previous week and to boys who saw nonviolent films. What are the serious problems, according to Freedman? First, Freedman says, "it was a mistake" that the observers were instructed to code observed behaviors (hitting, etc.) without reference to what they imagined might be the intent of the act (p. 101). Freedman does not mention that this is the typical instruction used everywhere for behavior observations to reduce observer bias. No—instead he says that it is wrong because the boys may be hitting each other without real intent to hurt the other person, and that should not count as aggression. But, of course, no one knows the boys' intentions except the boys, and, regardless of intent, if boys hit each other more after watching the films, one has demonstrated exactly the effect that observational learning theory predicts. Second, Freedman says that "the boys were more aroused by the violent movies than by the non-violent" (p. 102). This seems reasonable, though the authors collected data showing that this is not true (Leyens, Camino, Parke, & Berkowitz, 1975). If it is true, it simply suggests that the effect may be partially due to "excitation transfer" rather than observational learning. That is still an important result. Freedman would not see it as such, however, because he has taken a completely a-theoretical approach to the topic. He does not seem to realize that many researchers arguing publicly for concern about media violence believe that "excitation transfer" is an important component to the short-term effects of violence. Finally, Freedman says simply: "The statistical tests . . . are all inappropriate" (p. 101). Why? The children in each condition were divided between two cottages and cottages were the units assigned to condition. The analysis should have treated the subjects as nested within cottages but did not. Indeed this is a statistical error, but how serious? The key interaction is statistically significant at the 0.001 level in this study. It seems likely that, given that level of significance, the results would have held with the correct analysis. However, the point about all these criticisms is that Freedman ignores or minimizes similar flaws in a study when it suits his purpose.

As our second example, consider the Feshbach and Singer study (1971) that Freedman calls a landmark study and "the best field experiment on the issue" (p. 89). In this study boys in residential institutions were again randomly assigned to watch violent or nonviolent films. However, this time it was the boys who were assigned instead of the cottages. Freedman does not bother to discuss the serious potential methodological problems that such a within "home" design produces in terms of dependencies of each child's behaviors on what his peers are watching. Freedman does not discuss here the dependencies that this introduces in any statistical analysis of social behavior such as aggression. Freedman does recognize one major flaw in this study—that many boys were forbidden to watch the popular violent programs that other peers nearby were watching and such boys became angry. Thus, to most observers it is not surprising that this study showed more aggression among the boys who watched the nonviolent films. However, Freedman still sees this study as strong evidence of no effect for media violence. When in subsequent years even the senior author of this study has changed his interpretation of the results, one does not find Freedman's conclusion credible though, again, to a nonexpert the arguments may seem compelling.

The third major problem that reduces the scholarly value of the book is that it is just about completely a-theoretical. Freedman neither attends much to the psychological theory that has been advanced to explain why observation of violence engenders aggressive behavior nor does he attempt to place the research in any theoretical framework. As we outlined at the start of this essay, a substantial body of psychological theory has developed that explains social behavior in terms of priming effects, arousal effects, observational learning, and conditioning and that attends to the acquisition of such cognitive structures as hostile biases, mean world beliefs, and normative beliefs. Freedman ignores this theory. Of course, if he did not ignore it, he would need to explain certain contradictions. For example, how could he reconcile his conclusion of no effects of media violence on behavior with the accepted psychological laws that all primates have an innate tendency to imitate from a very early age? Does Freedman reject observational learning entirely? Or is his argument that children learn from observing those in the real world but not from observing those in the mass media? If so, why? Does it have to do with perceived realism? And how could one reconcile a finding of no effects on attitudes and beliefs with the theory of persuasive communication on which everything from commercials to public service announcements is based?

Freedman's overall approach in this book is to a great extent anecdotal. In other words, he attempts to prove assertions with a series of carefully chosen examples. The examples may be select studies; the examples may be select issues about studies; the examples may be select statements of others. He may indeed have read most of the studies on this topic that have been published in the English language, but he presents them with different emphases and different attention to detail, all designed to advance his thesis. This allows him to selectively attend to evidence that supports his view and ignore equally compelling evidence that does not. For example, in the introduction he presents three examples of youths' violent acts in which laymen jumped to the conclusion that the youth must be imitating a media presentation—for example, an English toddler killed by older boys shortly after a similar act was portrayed on TV; a boy who killed his sister with a fire shortly after a program about boys setting fires; and the martial arts fighting that seems to follow viewing *Power Rangers* on TV. Freedman is, of course, completely correct that such examples are terrible evidence to use in science. Yet, he uses the first two himself to argue against any media effect by showing that the perpetrators could not have seen the supposedly imitated show. Of course, few reputable scientists would have argued otherwise. On the other hand, he completely ignores the case of *Power Rangers* after just mentioning it, implying that any conclusion about it must also be false. If he had gone further, he would have had a much tougher time dismissing the proposition that *Power Rangers* indeed does increase aggressiveness (Boyatzis, Matillo, & Nesbitt, 1995).

Freedman once again offers the fallacious argument that if media violence is having an effect, all communities with TVs in all countries should be showing similar violence rates. When writing about the fact that crime increased in the United States at about the same time as the first generation of "TV-children" were reaching young adulthood, Freedman says, "Television was also introduced to France, Germany, Italy, and Japan at around the same time as it came to the United States and Canada. . . . If television violence were causing the increase [in crime], surely it should have had the same effect elsewhere" (p. 7). There is no discussion here of how much violence children are being exposed to on the different television systems; there is no discussion of cultural differences in the other causes of aggression that we know must converge for aggression to become manifest; there is no discussion of cultural and social moderating factors for the effect. There is a listing of other social factors that Freedman asserts increase crime (without any critical discussion of the evidence), for example, the divorce rate doubling and the gap between rich and poor growing. He simply concludes, "These important social changes are certainly some of the causes of the increase in crime; television ownership may be irrelevant (p. 7)." Of course, this statement is almost certainly true, particularly with the word "may" in the sentence. What the statement illustrates is the different criteria that Freedman uses for evaluating media violence and for evaluating other possible causes of aggressive behavior.

What comes across clearly in all this is Freeman's anger. Now there is nothing wrong with an author being angry. Great essays and great exposés have often been motivated by anger. However, it is hard to understand the cause of his anger. While Freedman denigrates a lot of research and vociferously denies that media violence can be causing aggression, he does accept some of the most important empirical findings in the area and reaches some conclusions that are not very different from what the majority of researchers (whom he so harshly criticizes) have been saying. On page 46 he says, "the results of this review of the survey research seem to indicate . . . that exposure to or preference for media violence IS related to aggressiveness. The correlation is small, probably between .10 and .20. . . . It might conceivably be as large as .3." Now admittedly he uses many more qualifiers in his statements than most others, but this is exactly in the range concluded by others whom he criticizes, including Paik and Comstock (1994) as mentioned above. Similarly, in his discussion of the Leyens study, he says, "in general those shown the aggressive films became more aggressive immediately after the films were shown" (p. 100). And later on page 101, he says, "it is possible that the somewhat greater scores for aggression in the violent film group occurred because the boys were acting out what they had just seen in the movie." If he stepped back a little and looked at what he wrote, he perhaps would see that this is exactly what scholars and researchers in the area have been saying is happening.

In summary, we find, first, that buried in the negative rhetoric of Freedman's book is a grudging acceptance of some of the most important fundamental empirical facts about media violence viewing and aggression—that they are correlated and that exposure to media violence causes increases in aggressive behavior, at least in the short run. Second, we find that, while his writing is glib and compelling, the facts that back up his negative conclusions are lacking. He displays three of the general flaws of analysis we described earlier—lack of attention to psychological theory, selective presentation of results with shifting criteria for evaluation, and making implicit assumptions that scientists arguing for an effect believe that media violence is the only cause of aggression. At the same time he never tries to make the case that exposing children to media violence is beneficial.

Unfortunately, other critics of media violence research findings take a more radical position, arguing that media violence is not only harmless but also beneficial. Two such critics who have received attention recently are communications professor Jib Fowles and comic book producer and workshop organizer Gerard Jones.

JIB FOWLES AND *THE CASE FOR TELEVISION VIOLENCE*

Fowles's (1999) dismissal of the body of scientific research that supports a causal relationship between viewing media violence and real-world aggression rests on three premises. First, Fowles echoes Freedman's arguments about the quality and validity of such research. In fact, in the preface to his book Fowles justifies its writing by the recent emergence of "capable overviews of the empirical literature on television violence" that have "called the whole enterprise into question" (p. ix), a clear reference to Freedman's work. Having already addressed Freedman's arguments at some length, however, we will move on to Fowles's other, more unique arguments.

In addition to various methodological flaws, Fowles sees television violence research as flawed due to its political, public nature. After documenting rises and falls in public attention to media violence questions, he claims that television violence is a "whipping boy." Class, race, gender, ideology, and age conflicts, Fowles claims, are subverted and expressed as attacks on media violence. While Fowles never fully explains why this invalidates media violence research, the implication is that the findings of such research are a foregone conclusion due to political forces that motivate it.

In making this claim, Fowles makes a basic assumption, specifically that discourse about effects of televised violence determine scholarly attention to such effects as well as the conclusions that such attention will lead to. While public outcry may indeed spark academic interest in a topic, this assumption, in this case, seems to be fundamentally wrong. In an analysis that compared news reports about the effects of media violence on aggression to the cumulative findings of scientific studies of the same phenomenon, Bushman and Anderson (2001) found that while such effects have received progressively less news attention and have been described as less serious in that attention, research has continued to identify those effects. Scientific research on aggression effects of violent television has continued to provide consistent evidence of those effects in spite of declining support from the news media.

The balance of Fowles's attack on the conclusions of television violence research consists of a recitation of evidence, primarily historical and anthropological, that violence and violent entertainment did not begin with television. Fowles points out that interpersonal violence and warfare have been common among people belonging to what he refers to as primitive hunter-gatherer cultures such as the Bushmen of the Kalahari, American Plains Indians, Aborigines of Australia, and Inuit Eskimos. Violence, according to Fowles, is the natural state of human existence. Fowles also reminds us that cultures throughout history have had public displays of state-controlled violence, including the human sacrifices of the Aztecs and Incas, the gladiatorial games of ancient Rome, and the violent sporting contests that arose in nineteenth-century Europe and North America, and he presents media violence as their modern equivalent. This history of violence, both the spontaneous and personal and the staged and public, demonstrates a human violent streak that precedes the existence of television violence. People of all ages have needed an outlet for their violent impulses, and these needs are met quite nicely by violent television.

Fowles is making the first common error of the critics as we enumerated them above. He neglects to mention that *no* researcher studying the effects of violent television content pretends that television is the original, only, or even most important cause of human violence. In fact, most researchers emphasize the point that there are multiple causes for aggressive behavior, including biological predispositions (Gentile & Sesma, chapter 2, this volume; Huesmann, 1998; Huesmann & Miller, 1994; Huesmann, Moise, & Podolski, 1997; Paik & Comstock, 1994; Strasburger & Wilson, chapter 4, this volume). However, the existence of such factors certainly does not preclude the existence of environmental influences, including television content, on behavior.

Less tenable even than Fowles's criticism of the evidence demonstrating that television violence leads to an increase in aggression is the theory he proposes in its place. Fowles claims that television violence serves a prosocial function by providing an outlet for natural, inevitable violent impulses. Basically, according to Fowles, people who watch television violence do so because they need to. In support of this argument, he appeals to two different theoretical and empirical threads of research, each of which will be discussed here.

First, Fowles turns to the mood management literature developed by Dolf Zillmann and his colleagues. Mood management research has, among other things, documented that some people in some situations select media content that will help them return to a more comfortable or desirable mood state; in one study, for example, subjects who were made to feel bored subsequently selected mostly exciting programming (Zillmann, 1988). Under mood management theory, if one is uncomfortably aroused—whether stressed, angry, or frustrated—one should select calming media fare. If one is bored or lethargic, one should choose more exciting content, possibly that which contains violence. Doing so would increase generalized arousal.

Unfortunately for Fowles's argument for a fundamental need to view violence, however, mood management theory does not argue that viewing violence is good or even functional for everyone; in fact, any content that is arousing or exciting is sufficient to increase arousal, and violent content is unnecessary. Further, counter to Fowles's argument that viewing violence is largely an emotional release, the assumptions underlying mood management theory indicate that viewing violence may lead to increased aggression through a process of observational learning. One of the fundamental tenets of mood management, according to Zillmann (1988), is that it is based on learning, on a nonconscious level, the impact of various types of media content on one's own mood. In other words, after watching a variety of types of television content in a variety of mood states, the viewer learns that certain content makes her or him feel a certain way; thereafter, when she or he desires that feeling, she or he will seek out that type of content. Individuals who learn that violent content arouses them can be expected, when underaroused, to create violence themselves to reach a more desirable level of arousal.

More importantly, Fowles's explanation of violent television's place in mood management is flawed, as he believes that viewing the same violent content can lead to either increased or decreased levels of arousal depending largely on the immediate needs of the viewer. Apparently, one gets whatever one needs from violent television content.

Surprisingly, Fowles not only does not recognize these holes in his theorizing, he also does not seem to recognize the obvious contradiction between one view that media violence reduces aggression by arousing people, and another view advocating that watching violent television provides a catharsis effect, whereby the aggressive or stressed viewer is calmed. To support this catharsis hypothesis, he first cites research in which stressed men and aggressive teens were shown to select more violent television content than their less stressed or aggressive peers. To take this as evidence for a catharsis effect, of course, is not justified, since there is no indication that these stressed and angry folk were any less stressed or angry after viewing violence than they were before; it only demonstrates that stressed people are watching more violence. Claiming a causal relationship here seems unwarranted by Fowles's own standards for evaluating research, for, as he reminds us, "The great vexation about correlations is that they cannot in and of themselves specify causes" (p. 22).

A more important response to Fowles's claims for a catharsis effect, however, can be found in the aggregate body of scientific research into the phenomenon. Overall, research indicates that rehearsing or acting out aggression leads to an increase, rather than a decrease, in aggression. This is true when such rehearsal consists of watching violence (Doob & Wood, 1972) and when it is more actively carried out through physical behavior such as punching a punching bag (Bushman, 2002). The research demonstrating the antithesis of a catharsis effect is also amply documented elsewhere (e.g., Strasburger & Wilson, chapter 4, this volume). Catharsis simply doesn't occur.

GERARD JONES AND KILLING MONSTERS: WHY CHILDREN NEED FANTASY, SUPERHEROES, AND MAKE-BELIEVE VIOLENCE

The absence of scientific support for a catharsis effect of media and fantasy violence, however, doesn't stop Gerard Jones from dedicating a book to its celebration (2002). Jones argues that children need violent media content in order to facilitate emotional and psychological self-regulation. He writes that children use whatever media content is appropriate to provide for whatever emotional or psychological needs they are experiencing at the moment—specifically, he claims that when children feel a need for nurturance, they may watch *Mister Rogers* or *Teletubbies*; if they need to feel strong and empowered, they will choose *Power Rangers* or *Pokémon* instead. Watching these shows and then emulating them in play, according to Jones, meets the child's needs.

In order to argue for this positive function of media violence, Jones first addresses—and dismisses—the scientific research on the effects of media violence. Like Fowles, Jones's first move is to echo and cite Freedman's arguments about the validity of laboratory experiments and survey research designs. Jones's next tactic is to quote a number of individuals he holds up as experts, each of which is made to seem to claim that media content does not make children violent. However, upon more careful consideration, these experts' statements do not contradict the conclusions of most media violence researchers. For instance, Stuart Fischoff is quoted as saying that "there is not a single research study which is even remotely predictive of [events like] the Columbine massacre" (p. 28). Jones interprets this to mean that there is no support for claims that media violence influences real violence, an interpretation that stretches far, far beyond the scope of Dr. Fischoff's words, which refer, not to all aggression, but to a horrific incidence of mass murder and suicide. Other psychiatrists are quoted as cautiously suggesting that for some violent or aggressive children, violent media may be seen as a tool for coping. None offers any evidence for this, at least none that Jones cites. Almost none of the supposed experts cited have ever done empirical research on media violence.

The third point in Jones's attack on media violence research strikes at the base of all social scientific research. Jones asserts that each individual child and each individual act of media use is unique, and that generalizations about them are inappropriate. As Jones puts it, "people rarely obey generalizations" (p. 8). Obviously, at one level of meaning for "generalization," this statement is true. But that is not the meaning of "generalization" that most scientists accept. For example, exactly the same argument could be offered about the generalization that smoking causes lung cancer. Without entering into a protracted discussion of the nature of truth and the social world, we can respond to Jones's criticism with a simple question: If generalizations about children's viewing patterns are inappropriate, why has Jones written a book in support of the generalization that media violence is good for children? Should we trust generalizations based on Jones's careful, one-sided collection of anecdotes or those based on hundreds of studies involving thousands of individuals according to the best practices of social science (Paik & Comstock, 1994)?

The sample that Jones draws on to support his thesis is a carefully selected one. For the most part, Jones recounts anecdotes about the children he has known best—himself as a child and his own son, as well as a few of his son's friends. He also spends a great deal of time recounting anecdotes shared with him by other parents in which they express relief after relenting to their children's demands for access to violent media and toys. Typical of these is the tale told by Emily's mother; Emily obsessed about guns for years, but her mother refused to buy her a toy gun or allow her to play with one. Finally, when Mom gave in and bought Emily a toy gun, Emily became much more well adjusted, much less gun-obsessed, and everything was wonderful. Similar stories are related by adults who reflect on how violent media content helped them to become healthy, functioning adults. Finally, the effects of continued restriction are presented when Jones describes the case of Kip Kinkel, the Oregon teenager who murdered his father before opening fire in a school cafeteria. Though Kip expressed an avid interest in guns from a very early age, his parents strictly forbade him from using violent toys or media until he was a teenager, when his father relented and bought him a real gun. If only his parents hadn't forbidden him access to violent television programming and toy guns, Jones muses, things would have been different; Kip clearly needed violent television.

Two flaws with this type of support are readily apparent. First, of course, is that since these anecdotes were selected for the sole purpose of supporting Jones's argument, they are biased and nonrepresentative at best. The second, possibly more damning flaw deals with the conclusions themselves, and is raised by Jones himself when he reminds us, in his discussion of research that demonstrates that media violence *does* cause aggression, that "a correlation is not a cause" (p. 30). Emily's change in mood, if it happened, may have been caused by any of a number of factors other than the opportunity to play with a toy gun. A likely alternative explanation is that when her mother relented to her demands, it marked an end to a long-standing conflict that had been a source of tension in the mother-daughter relationship. Rather than being swayed to do violence by a childhood deprivation of violent media content and toys, perhaps Kinkel was moved to violence by the implicit approval of violence his parents demonstrated as they bought him real guns. As for adults who remember violent media content as an important part of their maturation process, how can they be sure that other elements of that media content, divorced from its violent elements, would not have been as effective?

Fortunately, we have ways of addressing questions like these. Through carefully designed laboratory research experiments, we can isolate individual elements of media content and measure its effects. Through carefully conducted survey studies, informed by developmental theory, we can identify patterns of relationships between specific considerations such as viewing violent television and mood in nonlaboratory settings. By adding parametric statistical techniques, we can even parse out the influence of other contributing factors. Finally, using longitudinal designs, we can see the effects of these factors across the life span. Of course, as is documented elsewhere in this book, such research has already been done, and when viewed collectively, it paints a picture far different than that presented by Jones's anecdote-based conclusions.

Not only is the supportive evidence Jones calls on suspect, but his overall model is flawed. First, it assumes that children are perfectly rational, active viewers of television content. Unable to conceive of an alternative, Jones, in reference to violent media content, raises the question, "If it's harmful, why do children love it so much?" (p. 144); the implication being that if it were harmful, it would be shunned. This is ridiculous; there is no shortage whatsoever of dangerous and harmful things that are dearly loved—junk food, tobacco, illicit drugs, and high-speed driving to name a few. One may as well ask, "If smoking is so harmful, why do people love it so much?" The answer is simple; the pleasure they derive from the immediate experience outweighs considerations of possible harm for the user. Does this make smoking safe or beneficial? Of course not.

The idea that children or even adults only watch television that is good for them is also contradicted by empirical evidence, which finds that viewing specific kinds of television content can lead to depression (Schweitzer, Zillmann, Weaver, & Luttrell, 1992), fear (Valkenburg, Cantor, & Peeters, 2000), and diminished sexual satisfaction (Baran, 1976), none of which seem to be particularly good outcomes.

Empirical evidence also belies the fundamental need for violent television content which Jones claims all children experience. Cantor and Nathanson (1997) report on a study in which parents were interviewed to reveal whether they restricted their children's television viewing, and whether violent shows in particular were forbidden. These parents were also asked to rate how interested their children were in various types of violent television fare. If Jones is correct and children have a fundamental need for violent television, then those children who are denied such content should be more interested in viewing it. In fact, parental restrictions on viewing violent programming did not predict interest in any kind of violent programming.

Finally, of course, we must recognize that the assumption underlying Jones's argument for violent television, specifically that play aggression is cathartic, is basically flawed. Physically acting out aggression on a neutral target simply does not decrease subsequent aggression (Bushman, 2002). This is true even for individuals who have been told (and believed) that aggressive action is effective at reducing stress and anger (Bushman, Baumeister, & Stack, 1999).

HOWITT AND CUMBERBATCH AND THE ENGLISH DISMISSAL OF EFFECTS RESEARCH

Another criticism of the conclusion that media aggression produces real-world aggression comes from England and is typified by the work of Dennis Howitt and Guy Cumberbatch (Howitt & Cumberbatch, 1975). Their analysis of research on the effects of violent media long ago led them to the conclusion that such effects, when observed, are probably spurious, and almost certainly irrelevant. To support this view, they rely on criticisms of specific studies as lacking in validity, apparent inconsistencies between the findings of various studies, and a criticism of the various mechanisms by which media effects have been proposed to operate.

These specific criticisms, however, are driven by an almost ideological belief that media do not have effects. Cumberbatch, writing in 1989 (Cumberbatch, 1989), asserts that since "evidence for direct influence is generally weak" and that such evidence, when found, consists of "trivial results" which are "controversial," "mass communication research has shifted from a search for effects to an attempt to understand how 'active viewing' operates" (p. 1). In short, according to Cumberbatch, media content has no effect whatsoever; this applies not only to violence, but also to sex roles, sexism, racism and racial stereotyping, ageism, sexuality, alcohol use, and prosocial behaviors and attitudes (Cumberbatch, 1989).

Howitt and Cumberbatch's emphasis on an active audience features several key components. First, according to Howitt and Cumberbatch, it means that media content is almost universally unproblematic. Cumberbatch (1989) argues that its nature as a market product assures that television content provides a reflection of audience values, beliefs, and concerns. It can't change attitudes or behavior because it is consistent with them already. The fact that people watch violent television content is held up as proof that audiences find it compatible with their beliefs and value systems (Howitt & Cumberbatch, 1975). The fact that most people report in surveys and polls that they find television excessively violent is dismissed as a social desirability effect (Howitt & Cumberbatch, 1975). An alternative explanation for this pair of findings (that people report that television is too violent yet watch it anyway), on the other hand, is that people aren't nearly as active in their television viewing as Howitt and Cumberbatch assume.

Regardless of content, however, the active television viewer will not be moved to violence by her or his viewing, according to Howitt and Cumberbatch (1975), in part because "we are taught that aggression . . . is wrong," and this teaching makes us "feel anxious at the prospect of acting aggressively"

(p. 35). What the authors fail to include in this equation is that much of aggressive content on television does not teach that aggression is wrong. The question, then, becomes a simple one: can aggression be learned from the media?

In order to answer, Howitt and Cumberbatch limit their attention to a single, simplistic model of learning and another, equally simple model of attitude change. First, they hold up Bandura's early Bobo doll experiments, in which learning was conceived as direct imitation of specific acts, as examples of research on learning aggression. Howitt and Cumberbatch (1975) argue that due to the artificiality of the setting in which they occurred, the results are not generalizable to real children really watching television. Fortunately, scores of subsequent laboratory studies have used more realistic paradigms and shown the same effects (e.g., Bjorkqvist, 1985; Paik & Comstock, 1994). Second, they argue that for attitude change to result from viewing television, the attitude-relevant information must be deliberately attended to, and the attitude change would be specifically and narrowly limited to the content—they argue that images of spousal abuse could only have an impact on attitudes toward spousal abuse, and only if the viewer focuses and reflects on those images. Given that most significant findings don't fit these requirements, Howitt and Cumberbatch (1975) conclude there is no mechanism by which violence can be learned from television.

More recent theoretical developments, supported by and consistent with research findings, show such a conclusion to be untenable. Attitude change through "peripheral processing" is now accepted as a major mechanism for media influence (Petty & Cacioppo, 1986). In Bandura's (1994) more recent articulations of his theory, for example, he asserts that the social learning process can extend beyond mere imitation of specific behaviors to the creation of guidelines for the generation of future, innovative behaviors. Huesmann's (1998) model of social information processing provides for the learning or acquisition of scripts which are selectively applied across a variety of situations. The general aggression model articulated by Carnagey and Anderson (chapter 5, this volume) includes many sites where aggression might be learned, including normative beliefs and attitudes about aggression, perceptual schemata, expectation schemata, and behavior scripts. Clearly, learning from television can extend beyond direct imitation and narrow, highly specific attitude changes. Images of spousal abuse on television may be incorporated into a script for interpersonal conflict or one for interactions between men and women generally. They might lead to an expectation of compliance as a response to aggression. The images are certainly not limited in their effect to direct imitation or changing an attitude about spousal abuse specifically.

Finally, the notions that all media use is active and purposeful and that content that is not actively attended to cannot have an influence on viewers are simply unfounded. If children, for example, were already perfectly active television viewers, why would parental coviewing increase learning from educational television (Buerkel-Rothfuss & Buerkel, 2001)? Why would critical discussions with parents about television reduce the value-shifting effects of highly sexual television (Bryant & Rockwell, 1994)? Chaiken's (1980) heuristic-systematic processing model provides for effects even when audiences are unmotivated or unable to "actively" process information.

Ultimately, then, Howitt and Cumberbatch base their dismissal of a media violence effect on critiques and misinterpretations of old outmoded theories, an unjustified contempt for and myopic reading of research findings, and a dogged commitment to the unsupported, largely ideological belief in perfectly active audiences. Like their peers Freedman, Fowles, and Jones, they make their argument seem to hold water only through careful inattention and misrepresentation.

SUMMARY

If one does not want to believe a truth about human behavior, one can always focus on exceptions. There are flaws in some of the research on media violence, and some people do overstate the results. No single study is ever perfect, particularly in the social sciences. Some writers, including some of those we address in this chapter, have made a reputation for themselves by burying the body of studies indicting media violence under a pile of supposed flaws, and a myth has arisen that research on media violence does not present a compelling case that media violence stimulates aggression. We have tried to show in this chapter why that myth should remain a myth. We have tried to describe the psychology of the nonbelievers as far as we can understand it, and have tried to respond to their specific criticisms. Media violence is a contributor to aggressive behavior in the short run and, for children, at least, to aggressive behavior in the long run and even into adulthood. It is not the only factor accounting for individual differences in aggressiveness, nor even the most important factor. But as the mix of laboratory experiments, field experiments, cross-sectional survey studies, longitudinal survey studies, and meta-analyses show, it is a significant factor.

CHAPTER 7

Violent Video Games: The Newest Media Violence Hazard

Douglas A. Gentile and Craig A. Anderson

In 1972, a new form of entertainment became commercially available with the release of the video game *Pong*. In *Pong*, two players tried to "hit" an electronic "ball" back and forth. From these humble beginnings, a revolution in the entertainment industry was born. Interactive game revenues are now significantly greater than the domestic film industry ("Industrial Strengths," 2000). Worldwide video games sales are now at $20 billion annually (Cohen, 2000). The PlayStation video game console, which began as a side project at Sony, now represents $6 billion of the company's $20 billion in annual sales (Cohen, 2000). It is reasonable to question whether video games may have similar effects to the effects of other entertainment media. In this chapter the term video game will be used to describe games played on video game consoles (e.g., PlayStation), on computers, or on hand-held video game devices (e.g., GameBoy).

TIME SPENT WITH VIDEO GAMES

Video games have become one of the dominant entertainment media for children in a very short time. In the mid-1980s, children averaged about four hours a week playing video games, including time spent playing at home and in arcades (Harris & Williams, 1985). By the early 1990s, home video game use had increased and arcade play had decreased. The average amount was still fairly low, averaging about two hours of home play per week for girls, and about four hours of home play per week for boys (Funk, 1993). By the mid 1990s, home use had increased for fourth grade girls to 4.5 hours per week, and to 7.1 hours per week for fourth grade boys (Buchman & Funk,

1996). In recent national surveys of parents, school-age children (boys and girls combined) devote an average of about seven hours per week playing video games (Gentile & Walsh, 2002; Woodard & Gridina, 2000). In a recent survey of over 600 eighth and ninth grade students, children averaged 9 hours per week of video game play overall, with boys averaging 13 hours per week and girls averaging 5 hours per week (Gentile, Lynch, Linder, & Walsh, in press). Thus, while sex-correlated differences in the amount of time committed to playing video games continue to exist, the rising tide has floated all boats.

Even very young children are playing video games. Gentile & Walsh (2002) found that children aged two to seven play an average of 43 minutes per day (by parent report), and Woodard and Gridina (2000) found that even pre-schoolers aged two to five average 28 minutes of video game play per day. Although few studies have documented how the amount of time devoted to playing video games changes with development, some studies have suggested that video game play may peak in early school-age children. Buchman & Funk (1996) found the amount of time was highest for fourth grade children and decreased steadily through eighth grade. Others have suggested that play is highest between ages 9 and 12, decreases between ages 12 and 14, and increases again between ages 15 and 18 (Keller, 1992). Surprisingly, the amount of time children devote to television has remained remarkably stable even as the amount of time devoted to video and computer games has increased.

Although the research evidence is still limited, amount of video game play has been linked with a number of risk factors for maladaptive development, including smoking (Kasper, Welsh, & Chambliss, 1999), obesity (Berkey et al., 2000; Subrahmanyam, Kraut, Greenfield, & Gross, 2000), and poorer academic performance (e.g., Anderson & Dill, 2000; Creasey & Myers, 1986; Harris & Williams, 1985; Lieberman, Chaffee, & Roberts, 1988; Gentile et al., in press; Roberts, Foehr, Rideout, & Brodie, 1999; Van Schie & Wiegman, 1997; Walsh, 2000). These results parallel those showing that greater use of television is correlated with poorer grades in school (e.g., Huston et al., 1992; Roberts, Foehr, Rideout, & Brodie, 1999; Williams, Haertel, Haertel, & Walberg, 1982).

In one study of eighth and ninth grade students (Gentile et al., in press), lower grades were associated both with more years of video game play and more hours played each week (by self-report). Path analyses showed a significant effect of amount of video game play on school performance, but no specific effect of violent game content on school performance. However, violent content showed an independent significant effect on aggressive behavior. This analysis lends support for considering amount of game play and content of game play as two independent potential risk factors for children.

Preferences for Violent Video Games

Although video games are designed to be entertaining, challenging, and sometimes educational, most include violent content. Recent content analyses of video games show that as many as 89 percent of games contain some violent content (Children Now, 2001), and that about half of the games include violent content toward other game characters that would result in serious injuries or death (Children Now, 2001; Dietz, 1998; Dill, Gentile, Richter, & Dill, 2001).

Many children prefer to play violent games. Of course, what constitutes a "violent" game varies depending upon who is classifying them. The video game industry and its ratings board (Entertainment Software Rating Board) claim to see much less violence in their games than do parents (Walsh & Gentile, 2001) and other researchers (Thompson & Haninger, 2001). Even within the research community there is some inconsistency in definition of what constitutes a violent video game. Generally, however, researchers consider as "violent" those games in which the player can harm other characters in the game. In many popular video games, harming other characters is the main activity. It is these games, in which killing occurs at a high rate, that are of most concern to media violence researchers, child advocacy groups, and parents. (See Appendix A for recent recommendations regarding features of violent video games.) In studies of fourth through eighth grade children, more than half of the children state preferences for games in which the main action is predominantly human violence or fantasy violence (Buchman & Funk, 1996; Funk, 1993). In surveys of children and their parents, about two-thirds of children named violent games as their favorites. Only about one-third of parents were able to correctly name their child's favorite game, and in 70 percent of the incorrect matches, children described their favorite game as violent (Funk, Hagan, & Schimming, 1999). A preference for violent games has been linked with hostile attribution biases, increased arguments with teachers, lower self-perceptions of behavioral conduct, and increased physical fights (Bushman & Anderson, 2002; Funk, Buchman, & Germann, 2000; Lynch, Gentile, Olson, & van Brederode, 2001).

POTENTIAL FOR EFFECTS OF PLAYING VIOLENT VIDEO GAMES

There have been over 280 independent tests involving over 51,000 participants of the effects of violent media on aggression (Anderson & Bushman, 2002b). The vast majority of these studies have focused on television and movies. Meta-analyses (studies that measure the effects across many studies) have shown four main effects of watching a lot of violent entertainment. These effects have been called the *aggressor effect*, the *victim effect*, the *bystander effect*, and the *appetite effect* (Donnerstein, Slaby, & Eron, 1994). To summarize each:

The *aggressor effect* states that people (both children and adults) exposed to a lot of violent entertainment tend to become meaner, more aggressive, and more violent.

The *victim effect* states that people (both children and adults) exposed to a lot of violent entertainment tend to see the world as a scarier place, become more scared, and initiate more self-protective behaviors (such as carrying guns to school, which, ironically, *increases* one's odds of getting shot).

The *bystander effect* states that people (both children and adults) exposed to a lot of violent entertainment tend to become more desensitized to violence (both in the media and in real life), more callous, and less sympathetic to victims of violence.

The *appetite effect* states that people (both children and adults) exposed to a lot of violent entertainment tend to get an increased appetite for seeing more violent entertainment. Simply put, the more one watches, the more one wants to watch.

The scientific debate over *whether* media violence has an effect is basically over, and should have been over by 1975 (Bushman & Anderson, 2001). The four effects described above have been demonstrated repeatedly (see Strasburger & Wilson, this volume). Heavy diets of violent television and movies clearly have a detrimental effect on children. Given the increasing amount of time children play video games and the preferences many children have for playing violent video games, researchers have begun to study whether violent video games have similar effects.

WHY VIOLENT VIDEO GAMES MAY HAVE LESS EFFECT THAN VIOLENT TV

Some have suggested that the effects of playing violent video games may be weaker than the effects of viewing violent television. Three arguments have been postulated. First, the graphic quality of video games is much poorer and less realistic than on television (e.g., Silvern & Williamson, 1987). Research on violent television has shown that children are more likely to be affected and more likely to imitate aggressive acts if the violence is depicted more realistically (Potter, 1999). To the extent that video game graphics are of poor quality or are cartoonish, we might expect them to have less impact on children's aggression. Second, some of the "violent" actions in video games are abstract and are therefore not easily imitated. For example, games that include shooting at space ships (e.g., *Galaxian*, *Space Invaders*) or shooting at incoming missiles to protect your cities (e.g., *Missile Command*) model behaviors that are difficult to imitate in everyday life. Third, many games involve violence against creatures that are not human (e.g., space aliens, robots, etc.) or are unrealistic humanoids (e.g., zombies).

However, even though some research suggests that realism can increase the negative effects of media violence, the research literature on this issue is not very strong. In fact, many TV and movie violence studies have shown that cartoonish, unrealistic characters can increase children's and adults' aggression (e.g., Kotler & Calvert, chapter 9, this volume). And, as will be seen shortly, although these three arguments are reasonable, they have become less relevant as video games have become more graphically realistic and involve more imitatable forms of violence directed against realistic human characters.

WHY VIOLENT VIDEO GAMES MAY HAVE A GREATER EFFECT THAN VIOLENT TV

The public health community has concluded from the preponderance of evidence that violent television leads to "increases in aggressive attitudes, values, and behavior, particularly in children" (AAP, APA, AACAP, & AMA, 2000). Although the research on violent video games is still growing, there are at least six reasons why we should expect violent video games to have an even greater impact than violent television (Anderson & Dill, 2000; Gentile & Walsh, 2002). These reasons are based on what we already know from the television and educational literatures.

1. *Identification with an aggressor increases imitation of the aggressor.* It is known from research on violent television that children will imitate aggressive actions more readily if they identify with an aggressive character in some way. On television, it is hard to predict with which characters, if any, a person will identify. One might identify most closely with the victim, in which case the viewer would be less likely to be aggressive after watching. In many violent video games, however, one is required to take the point of view of one particular character. This is most noticeable in "first-person shooter" games, in which the players "see" what their character would see as if they were inside the video game. Thus, the player is forced to identify with a violent character. In fact, in many games, players have a choice of characters to play and can upload photographs of their faces onto their character. This identification with the aggressive character is likely to increase the likelihood of imitating the aggressive acts.

2. *Active participation increases learning.* Research on learning shows that when one becomes actively involved in something, one learns much more than if one only watches it. This is one reason computer technology in the classroom has been considered to be educationally beneficial. Educational video games are theorized to be effective partly because they require active participation. With regard to violent entertainment, viewers of violent content on television are passive observers of the aggressive acts. In contrast, violent video games by their very nature require active participation in the violent acts.

3. *Practicing an entire behavioral sequence is more effective than practicing only a part.* If one wanted to learn how to kill someone, one would quickly realize that there are many steps involved. At a minimum, one needs to decide whom to kill, get a weapon, get ammunition, load the weapon, stalk the victim, aim the weapon, and pull the trigger. It is rare for television shows or movies to display all of these steps. Yet, violent video games regularly require players to practice each of these steps repeatedly. This helps teach the necessary steps to commit a successful act of aggression. In fact, some video games are so successful at training whole sequences of aggressive behaviors that the U.S. Army has licensed them to train their forces.

For example, the popular violent video game series *Rainbow Six* is so good at teaching all of the steps necessary to plan and conduct a successful special operations mission that the U.S. Army has licensed the game engine to train their special operations soldiers (Ubi Soft, 2001). Furthermore, the U.S. Army has created their own violent video game as a recruitment tool (Associated Press, 2002).

4. *Violence is continuous.* Research with violent television and movies has shown that the effects on viewers are greater if the violence is unrelieved and uninterrupted (Paik & Comstock, 1994; Donnerstein, Slaby, & Eron, 1994). However, in both television programs and movies, violent content is rarely sustained for more than a few minutes before changing pace, changing scenes, or going to commercials. In contrast, the violence in violent video games is often continuous. Players must constantly be alert for hostile enemies, and must constantly choose and enact aggressive behaviors. These behaviors expose players to a continual stream of violent (and often gory) scenes accompanied by screams of pain and suffering in a context that is incompatible with feelings of empathy or guilt.

5. *Repetition increases learning.* If one wishes to learn a new phone number by memory, one often will repeat it over and over to aid memory. This simple mnemonic device has been shown to be an effective learning technique. With few exceptions (e.g., *Blue's Clues*), children rarely see the same television shows over and over. In a violent video game, however, players often spend a great deal of time doing the same aggressive actions (e.g., shooting things) over and over. Furthermore, the games are usually played repeatedly, thus giving a great deal of practice repeating the violent game actions. This increases the odds that not only will children learn from them, but they will make these actions habitual to the point of automaticity.

6. *Rewards increase imitation.* There are at least three different processes involved. First, rewarding aggressive behavior in a video game (e.g., winning extra points and lives) increases the frequency of behaving aggressively in that game (see number 5, above). Second, rewarding aggressive behavior in a video game teaches more positive attitudes toward the use of force as a means of solving conflicts. Television programs rarely provide a reward structure for the viewer, and it would be rarer still to have those rewards dependent on violent acts. In contrast, video games often reward players for participating. Third, the reward patterns involved in video games increase the player's motivation to persist at the game. Interestingly, all three of these processes help educational games be more effective. The last process can make the games somewhat addictive.

THE EFFECTS OF VIOLENT VIDEO GAMES

Over the past 20 years, a number of scholars have expressed concern over the potential negative impact of exposing youth to violent video games (e.g., Dominick, 1984; Kestenbaum & Weinstein, 1985). The first comprehensive narrative review (Dill & Dill, 1998) found evidence that such concern was warranted, but also noted that there were a number of weaknesses and gaps in the extant research. One problem in summarizing the results of existing video game studies is that they are sometimes hard to interpret in an environment that is continually evolving in terms of violent content. In order to compare the violence in video games from different studies, it is useful to understand how violence in video games has changed with time.

A BRIEF HISTORY OF VIOLENT VIDEO GAMES

The very first "violent" video game, *Death Race*, was released in 1976 by Exidy Games. It was a free-standing, driving simulator arcade game. In it, one attempted to drive a "car" over little stick figures that ran around. When hit by the car, the stick figures would turn into tiny gravestones with crosses.

Every time you made a hit, a little cross would appear on the monitor, signifying a grave. Nice game. Fun. Bottom line, the game really took off when TV stations started to get some complaints from irate parents that this was a terrible example to set for children. The industry got a lot of coast-to-coast coverage during news programs. The end result was that Exidy sales doubled or quadrupled. (Eddie Adlum, publisher of *RePlay Magazine*, cited in Kent, 2001, p. 91)

In order to compare the violence in video games from different studies, it is useful to partition the console gaming history into three distinct eras.[1] We focus on console systems because of their dominance of the video game industry and widespread use by children. The first era (1977–1985) was dominated by Atari, the second (1985–1995) was dominated by Nintendo, and the third (1995–present) has been dominated by Sony (although at the time of this writing it may be changing). Throughout the Atari era, the graphic capability of games was very simplistic, to the point that video game violence was largely abstract (Dill & Dill, 1998). "The protagonist in many video games is a computer-generated blip on the screen under the control of the player" (Cooper & Mackie, 1986). In 1984, Dominick commented, "video game violence is abstract and generally consists of blasting spaceships of stylized aliens into smithereens. Rarely does it involve one human being doing violence to another" (p. 138).

According to Nolan Bushnell, founder of Atari, this was no accident. "We [Atari] had an internal rule that we wouldn't allow violence against people. You could blow up a tank or you could blow up a flying saucer, but you couldn't blow up people. We felt that was not good form, and we adhered to that all during my tenure" (Kent, 2001, p. 92).

The Nintendo era (1985–1995) began with the release of the Nintendo Entertainment System (NES) in America. Nintendo publicly listed insufficiencies of older game systems such as Atari, including limited graphics, few colors, and poor audio qualities. Nintendo improved the graphic and audio capabilities of home console systems. This era was one of experimentation with what the public wanted and would accept in video games. Although Nintendo targeted younger children as their core audience, violent taboos were tested one by one. Gradually it became clear that games sold better if they contained more violence. One-on-one fighting games such as *Double Dragon* and *Mortal Kombat* became all-time bestsellers while pushing the boundaries of violence. During this era, Nintendo sold over one billion video games, and by 1995 Nintendo had placed an NES in over 40 percent of American homes ("Nintendo sells one billionth video game," 1995). The violence in the games was still fairly stylized, although it began to become more realistic. In 1992, *Wolfenstein 3D*, the first "first-person shooter" game, was released. In a first-person shooter, one "sees" the action as if one was holding the gun, rather than seeing it as if looking on from afar (as in almost all of the previous fighting games). One could move around exploring a three-dimensional environment and shooting at various game characters. The effect is to make the game player feel as if he is in the game—that he is the one fighting. This additional realism was followed by other realistic touches. Video game historian Steven Kent noted that "part of *Wolfenstein*'s popularity sprang from its shock value. In previous games, when players shot enemies, the injured targets fell and disappeared. In *Wolfenstein 3D*, enemies fell and bled on the floor" (Kent, 2001, p. 458). This caused a revolution in the way violent games were designed. By 1993, the next major first-person shooter, *Doom*, included more blood and gore, and also allowed players to hunt and kill each other rather than attacking monsters and demons.

The Sony era (1995–present) began with the release of the Sony Play-Station. The PlayStation revolutionized the gaming industry by increasing the graphic capability of games, switching from a cartridge-based system to a CD-based system. With CD technology, PlayStation games were able to deliver fast video game action as well as motion-picture-quality prerendered screens. Sony targeted adults as their main audience, in a move that caused the children who grew up during the Nintendo era to switch to PlayStation as adults.

The advances in technology over the past few years have been remarkable. Electronic game images are composed of polygons, making polygons/second a good measure of graphic quality. The original Sony PlayStation processed 350,000 polygons per second (pg/s). Sega's Dreamcast, released in 1999, boosted that to over 3 million, and PlayStation 2 rocketed to 66 million pg/s. Microsoft's Xbox, released in 2001, increased graphic capability to 125 million pg/s. The stated goal for PlayStation 3 is 1 billion pg/s. The dramatic increase in speed and graphic capability has allowed for more realistic violence than ever before possible. For example, in 2000, the game *Soldier of Fortune* was released for personal computers, marking an all-time high in video game violence realism. This first-person shooter game was designed in collaboration with an ex–army colonel, and features 26 different "killing zones" in the body. The characters in the game respond realistically to different shots depending on where in the body they are shot, with what weapons, and from what distance. For example, shooting a character in the arm at close range with a shotgun rips the arm from the socket leaving exposed bone and sinew while blood rushes from the wound.

These changes in technology likely produced changes in the nature of empirical studies of violent video game effects across time. Consider the first experimental studies, in which participants played either a randomly assigned violent or nonviolent video game and then engaged in some task that allowed a measure of aggression to be obtained. The difference between the treatment condition (violent game) and the control condition (nonviolent game) was likely to be relatively small in early studies, mainly because the early violent video games were not very violent. Now consider correlational studies, in which video game habits and aggressive behavior habits of participants are simultaneously measured and compared. In early studies of this type, participants who preferred violent video games and those who preferred to play nonviolent games likely had fairly similar video game experiences because there weren't any extremely violent games available. Thus, in both types of studies, early studies probably had pretty small differences in the independent variable of interest (i.e., amount of exposure to video game violence) and therefore might have discovered fairly weak effects. In a later section, we present two somewhat different ways of addressing this potential problem in the analysis of what the video game research literature shows. First, we take a look at the most comprehensive meta-analytic summary of video game research.

META-ANALYTIC SUMMARY OF VIOLENT VIDEO GAME EFFECTS

Narrative reviews of a research literature, such as that by Dill and Dill (1998), are very useful ways of examining prior studies. Typically, the researchers try to find an organizing scheme that makes sense of the varied results that typically occur in any research domain. However, as useful as such reviews of the literature are, meta-analyses (studies of studies) are a much more powerful technique to find the common effects of violent video games across multiple studies (see chapter 11). Specifically, a meta-analysis uses statistical techniques to combine the results of various studies of the same basic hypothesis, and provides an objective answer to the questions of whether or not the key independent variable has a reliable effect on the key dependent variable, and if so, what the magnitude of that effect is. Only recently have there been enough studies on violent video games to make meta-analysis a useful technique. In 2001, the first comprehensive meta-analysis of the effects of violent video games was conducted (Anderson & Bushman, 2001). A more recent update to that meta-analysis produced the same basic findings (Anderson, 2003a). A consistent pattern of the effects of playing violent games was documented in five areas.

1. *Playing violent video games increases physiological arousal.* Studies measuring the effects of playing violent video games tend to show larger increases in heart rate and systolic and diastolic blood pressure compared to playing non-violent video games (e.g., Gwinup, Haw, & Elias, 1983; Murphy, Alpert, & Walker, 1992; Segal & Dietz, 1991). The average effect size across studies between violent game play and physiological arousal was 0.22[2] (Anderson & Bushman, 2001). For example, Ballard and West (1996) showed that a violent game (*Mortal Kombat* with the blood "turned on") resulted in higher systolic blood pressure responses than either a nonviolent game or a less graphically violent game (*Mortal Kombat* with the blood "turned off").

Other physiological reactions have also been found. Adult males' brains have been shown to release dopamine in response to playing a violent video game (Koepp et al., 1998). In addition, Lynch (1994, 1999) has found that the physiological effects of playing violent video games may be even greater for children who already show more aggressive tendencies. Adolescents who scored in the top quintile for trait hostility, measured by the Cook and Medley (1954) scale, showed greater increases in heart rate, blood pressure, and epinephrine and testosterone levels in the blood. There were also trends for increased levels of norepinephrine and cortisol in the blood for the higher hostile children. This interaction with trait hostility is important, because it suggests that the harmful effects of playing violent games may be even greater for children who are already at higher risk for aggressive behavior.

2. *Playing violent video games increases aggressive cognitions.* Studies measuring cognitive responses to playing violent video games have shown that aggressive thoughts are increased compared to playing nonviolent video games (e.g., Anderson & Dill, 2000; Calvert & Tan, 1994; Graybill, Kirsch, & Esselman, 1985; Kirsh, 1998; Lynch et al., 2001). The average effect size across studies between violent game play and aggressive cognitions was 0.27 (Anderson & Bushman, 2001). These effects have been found in children and adults, in males and females, and in experimental and nonexperimental studies.

Aggressive cognitions have been measured in several ways. For example, Anderson and Dill (2000) found that playing a violent game primed aggressive thoughts, as measured by the relative speed with which players could read aggression-related words. Calvert and Tan (1994) asked adults about their thoughts after they had played a violent virtual reality game, and found that they had more aggressive thoughts than control subjects.

Studies of children's social information processing have shown that playing violent games increases children's hostile attribution biases. Kirsh (1998), in an experimental study, had third and fourth grade children play either a violent video game or a nonviolent video game. Children were then presented with stories in which a same-sex peer caused a negative event to occur, but where the peer's intent was ambiguous. Children who had played a violent video game gave responses attributing greater aggressive intent to the peer (i.e., they had higher attribution biases) than children who played the nonviolent game, and they also were more likely to suggest retaliation. In a correlational study, young adolescents who exposed themselves to more violent games also had higher hostile attribution biases (Lynch et al., 2001). Hostile attribution bias is important because children who have this social problem-solving deficit are also more likely to act aggressively, and are likely to be socially maladjusted (Crick & Dodge, 1994). Along these same lines, Bushman and Anderson (2002) showed that young adults who had just played a violent video game generated more aggressive endings to story stems than those who had played nonviolent video games.

3. *Playing violent video games increases aggressive emotions.* Studies measuring emotional responses to playing violent video games have shown that aggressive emotions are increased compared to playing nonviolent video games. The average effect size across studies between violent game play and aggressive emotions was 0.18 (Anderson & Bushman, 2001). These effects have been found in children and adults, in males and females, and in experimental and nonexperimental studies. In one study, adults' state hostility and anxiety levels were increased after playing a violent game compared to controls (Anderson & Ford, 1986). In a study of third through fifth grade children, playing a violent game increased frustration levels more than playing a nonviolent game (Funk et al., 1999).

4. *Playing violent video games increases aggressive behaviors.* Studies measuring aggressive behaviors after playing violent video games have shown that aggressive behaviors are increased compared to playing nonviolent video games (e.g., Anderson & Dill, 2000; Cooper & Mackie, 1986; Irwin & Gross, 1995; Lynch et al., 2001; Schutte, Malouff, Post-Gorden, & Rodasta, 1988; Silvern & Williamson, 1987). The average effect size across studies between violent game play and aggressive behaviors was 0.19 (Anderson & Bushman, 2001). These effects have been found in children and adults, in males and females, and in experimental and nonexperimental studies.

In studies of children aged four through seven, violent game play has increased both aggressive play with objects and aggressive behaviors toward peers (e.g., Schutte et al., 1988; Silvern & Williamson, 1987). Studies with elementary school-age children have found similar effects. For example, in a study of second grade boys, those who played a violent video game were more likely than those who played a nonviolent game to be both verbally and physically aggressive toward peers in a free-play setting and a frustrating task setting (Irwin & Gross, 1995). Neither arousal nor impulsivity moderated the effects.

In a correlational study, young adolescents who played more violent video games reported getting into arguments with teachers more frequently and were also more likely to become involved in physical fights (Gentile et al., in press). Exposure to violent video games was a significant predictor of physical fights, even when subject sex, hostility, and weekly amount of video game play were statistically controlled.

5. *Playing violent video games decreases prosocial behaviors.* Studies measuring responses to playing violent video games have shown that prosocial behaviors are decreased compared to playing nonviolent video games (e.g., Ballard & Lineberger, 1999; Chambers & Ascione, 1987; Silvern & Williamson, 1987; Wiegman & Van Schie, 1998). The average effect size across studies between violent game play and prosocial behaviors was − 0.16 (Anderson & Bushman, 2001). These effects have been found in both experimental and nonexperimental studies. In one study of 278 seventh and eighth graders, children who named violent games as their favorite games to play were rated by their peers as exhibiting fewer prosocial behaviors and more aggressive behaviors in the classroom (Wiegman & Van Schie, 1998).

CHANGES ACROSS TIME

As previously mentioned, early studies of violent video games probably tended to compare mildly violent games to nonviolent ones, resulting in relatively small effects, whereas later studies may yield somewhat larger effects because "violent" games have gotten much more violent. Anderson and Bushman (2001) did not find a significant time trend in their meta-analysis, but the small number of studies may well have hindered finding statistical significance. In this section we examine this question in two different exploratory approaches, one for experimental studies and one for correlational ones.

Experimental studies. The real question of interest is whether studies using video game stimuli that differ greatly in violent content tend to yield larger effect sizes than those using stimuli that don't differ much in violent content. For experimental studies, in which we know what game was used in each condition, the best way to address this question is to create a rating scale to assess the amount of violence in treatment (violent) and control (nonviolent) games. Then, for each study, one can assess the magnitude of the violent content difference between the violent and nonviolent conditions. Across experimental studies, we can then see if there is a correlation between the violent content difference and the size of the violent versus nonviolent condition effect on aggressive behavior. Figure 7.1 displays the results of such an analysis (Anderson, 2002). It reveals that, indeed, studies that have a more powerful manipulation of violent content tend to produce bigger effects on aggressive behavior.

Correlational studies. One cannot do such a direct analysis of the violent content differences between violent and nonviolent video games played by participants in correlational studies, simply because such studies typically do not identify (or report) what games each participant most frequently plays. However, we know that video games have become much more violent over time, so one way to address this question for correlational studies is to see whether the effect sizes tend to be larger in the later studies. Figure 7.2 presents the results of such an analysis. As can be seen, there is a positive correlation between year and magnitude of effect size. Of course, there may well

Figure 7.1
Relation between the Violent Content Difference of Violent and Nonviolent Video Game Conditions and Effect on Aggressive Behavior: Experimental Studies

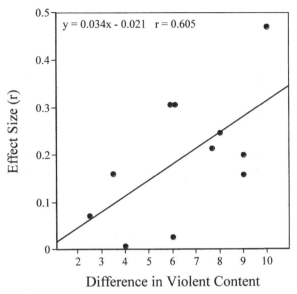

$y = 0.034x - 0.021$ $r = 0.605$

Source: Anderson (2002).

be other factors at work in this correlation, so one should regard this finding as somewhat tentative.

MODERATORS OF VIDEO GAME EFFECTS

The evidence reveals that violent video games can have negative consequences. The research literature is presently too small to allow sensitive tests of potential moderator effects (moderator variables can enhance or diminish other effects). Such effects, essentially interactions between exposure to video game violence and moderating variables (e.g., sex, age), require very large samples for adequate tests, and this research literature is simply too small. In fact, Anderson and Bushman (2001) reported finding no statistically significant evidence of sex or age moderator effects. Nonetheless, there are theoretical and empirical reasons to expect some groups to be somewhat more susceptible to violent video game effects than others, though there is no valid reason to expect any particular group to be totally immune.

Funk and her colleagues (Funk, 2001, 2003; Funk & Buchman, 1996; Funk, Buchman, & Germann, 2000) have described how many of the effects of video game play could be enhanced by other risk factors. These include player sex, age, status as bullies or victims of bullies, children with poor social problem-

Figure 7.2
Relation between Year of Study and Size of Effect of Video Game-Playing Habits on Aggressive Behavior: Correlational Studies

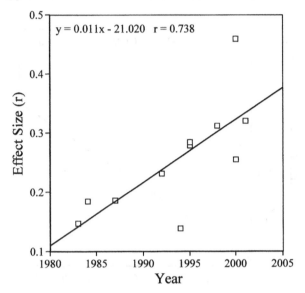

solving skills, and children with poor emotion regulation abilities. To this list we would add children who are generally more hostile in personality, who have a history of aggressive behavior, or whose parents do not monitor or limit their video game play. These risk factors will be described briefly below.

Although there is insufficient research to make strong claims about certain groups being more vulnerable to violent video game effects, there are a few individual studies that provide such evidence. For instance, a number of studies have shown that hostility may moderate the effects of playing violent video games. Lynch (1994, 1999) has shown that the physiological effects of playing violent video games are greater for children who are initially more hostile. Anderson and Dill (2000) found that the relationship between violent video game play and delinquent behaviors was greater for characteristically hostile individuals.

Longitudinal studies have repeatedly demonstrated that the best predictor of future aggressive or violent behavior is past history of aggression and violence (Anderson & Huesmann, in press; Surgeon General, 2001). There is evidence from the TV and movie violence literature that habitually aggressive youths are more susceptible to media violence effects than habitually non-aggressive youths (Bushman & Huesmann, 2000). There is also some evidence that repeated exposure to violent video games has a bigger negative impact on aggressive youth than on nonaggressive youth (Anderson & Dill, 2000).

Parental monitoring and limiting of children's media use has been shown to be an important moderating factor with other media such as television. Limits on the amount of time, coviewing, and mediation (discussion) of television messages have been shown to have beneficial effects (e.g., Austin, 1993; Gadberry, 1980; Robinson, Wilde, Navracruz, Haydel, & Varady, 2001; Strasburger & Donnerstein, 1999). Active parental involvement, such as rules limiting media use and active mediation (both positive encouragement to watch "positive" media and discouragement of "negative" messages) can be effective in influencing children's viewing, understanding, reactions to, and imitation of program content (Dorr & Rabin, 1995; Lin & Atkin, 1989). When parents are asked how often they put limits on the amount of time their children may play video or computer games, 55 percent say "always" or "often," and 40 percent say they "always" or "often" check the video game ratings before allowing their children to buy or rent video games (Gentile & Walsh, 2002). However, parents may overestimate the amount of monitoring they do. In one study of eighth and ninth grade children, only 13 percent say their parents "always" or "often" put limits on time, and 43 percent say they "never" do (Gentile et al., in press). Similarly, only 15 percent say their parents "always" or "often" check the ratings, and over half (53 percent) say they "never" do. Yet, parental limits on both time and content of video games are significantly related to lower levels of youths' aggressive behavior.

In sum, although there appear to be general effects of playing violent video games (Anderson & Bushman, 2001), we believe the effects are not likely to be identical for all children. The characteristics that are most likely to emerge as significant risk factors for the negative effects of exposure to violent video games are: younger ages, poor social problem-solving skills, low parental monitoring, male sex, hostile personality, and a history of aggression and violence. Yet, this does not mean that violent video games are likely to affect only children who possess these other risk factors. Exposure to video game violence is a significant predictor of physical fights, even when children's sex, hostility level, and amount of video game playing are controlled statistically (Gentile et al., in press). If hostility were a necessary risk factor, then only hostile children would tend to get into fights, and children with the lowest hostility scores would not get into physical fights regardless of their video game habits. Figure 7.3 shows the percentages of eighth and ninth grade students who report being involved in physical fights within the previous year. Children with the lowest hostility scores are almost 10 times more likely to have been involved in physical fights if they play a lot of violent video games than if they do not play violent games (38 percent compared to 4 percent). In fact, the *least* hostile children who play a lot of violent video games are *more* likely to be involved in fights than the *most* hostile children if those children do not play violent video games.

Figure 7.3
Percentages of Eighth and Ninth Graders Involved in Physical Fights, Split by Hostility and Violent Video Game Exposure

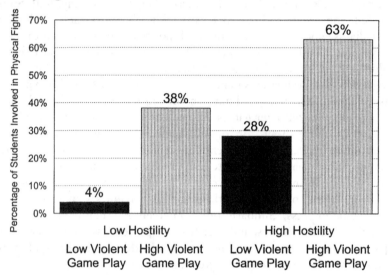

Playing Violent Video Games Makes a Difference

Note: The low and high hostility bars represent children in the bottom and top quartiles on a measure of trait hostility, respectively. The low and high violent video game play bars represent children in the bottom and top quartiles on a measure of exposure to violent video games. Data are extracted from Gentile, Lynch, Linder, & Walsh, in press. Total N = 607.

VIDEO GAMES AS TEACHING TOOLS

Video games are excellent teaching tools. For example, video games have been created to teach children healthy skills for the self-care of asthma and diabetes (Lieberman, 1997). Video games were used as the teaching method in these programs because (1) they are so successful at getting children's attention, (2) children participate actively rather than passively, (3) they train children in all the steps necessary to be successful (rehearse the whole sequence of behaviors), (4) they are motivating for children, (5) they provide many opportunities for practice, (6) they provide immediate feedback and reinforcement, (7) they enhance perceived mastery and self-efficacy, and (8) they teach attitudes necessary for successful behaviors. Research showed that the video games were successful at teaching children the attitudes, skills, and behaviors that the games were designed to teach (Lieberman, 1997). If health video games can successfully teach health behaviors, and flight-simulator video games can teach people how to fly, then what should we expect violent, murder-simulating games to teach?

Lieutenant Colonel David Grossman has argued that violent video games can train people to kill in much the same manner that the U.S. Army trains people to kill (1996, 1998). Grossman, a former Army Ranger and teacher of psychology, has noted that almost all people have a natural aversion to the killing of other people. In the army, this aversion is considered to be a problem. Historically, only 15 to 20 percent of infantrymen were willing to shoot at an exposed enemy soldier in World War II. This was unacceptable to the army, so new training regimens were created to "improve" upon this, and by the Vietnam War, the percentage had risen to over 90 percent. Grossman argues that the army uses four steps to systematically reduce the aversion to killing: (1) desensitization, (2) observation and imitation, (3) classical conditioning, and (4) operant conditioning. He argues that all four of these can be shown to be at work in violent media.

CRITIQUES OF THE VIDEO GAME RESEARCH LITERATURE

Any new research domain has strengths and weaknesses. If all goes well, over time the researchers identify the weaknesses and address them in a variety of ways. When the new research domain appears to threaten the profits of some large industry, there is a tendency for that industry to deny the threatening research and to mount campaigns designed to highlight the weaknesses, obfuscate the legitimate findings, and cast doubt on the quality of the research. The history of the tobacco industry's attempt to ridicule, deny, and obfuscate research linking smoking to lung cancer is the prototype of such efforts. The TV and movie industries have had considerable success in their 40-year campaign against the media violence research community. The same type of effort has now been mounted by the video game industry. We do not claim that there are no weaknesses in the video game research literature. Indeed, we have highlighted some of them in our own prior writings. In this final section, we focus on two types of criticisms, legitimate ones (usually raised by researchers) and illegitimate ones (usually raised by the video game industry and their supporters in the scholarly community).

Illegitimate Criticisms

1. *There are too few studies to warrant any conclusions about possible negative effects.*

This can be a legitimate concern if the small number of studies yields a lack of power to detect small effects. However, it is an illegitimate argument when it is used to claim that the current set of video game studies do not warrant serious concern about exposure to violent video games. If anything, it is remarkable that such reliable effects have emerged from such a relatively small number of studies (compared to TV and movie violence studies), and that the studies that vary so much in method, sample population, and video game stimuli.

2. *There are problems with the external validity of lab experiments due to demand characteristics, participant suspicion and compliance problems, trivial measures, artificial settings, and unrepresentative participants.*

These old arguments against laboratory studies in the behavioral sciences have been successfully debunked many times, in many contexts, and in several different ways. Both logical and empirical analyses of such broad-based attacks on lab experiments have found little cause for concern (Anderson, Lindsay, & Bushman, 1999; Banaji & Crowder, 1989; Kruglanski, 1975; Mook, 1983). Furthermore, more specific examination of these issues in the aggression domain have consistently found evidence of high external validity, and have done so in several very different ways (Anderson & Bushman, 1997; Berkowitz & Donnerstein, 1982; Carlson, Marcus-Newhall, & Miller, 1989; Giancola & Chermack, 1998).

3. *Complete dismissal of correlational studies: "Correlation is not causation."*

This is an overly simplistic view of how modern science is conducted. Psychology instructors teach this mantra to introductory psychology students, and hope that they will gain a much more sophisticated view of methods and scientific inference by the time they are seniors. Whole fields of science are based on correlational data (e.g., astronomy). Correlational studies are used to test causal theories, and thus provide falsification opportunities. A well-conducted correlational design, one which attempts to control for likely "third variable" factors, can provide much useful information. To be sure, correlational studies are generally (but not always) less informative about causality than experimental ones. What is most important is the whole pattern of results across studies that differ in design, procedure, and measures. And the existing research on violent video games yields consistent results (Anderson & Bushman, 2001).

4. *Arousal accounts for all video game effects on aggressive behavior.*

Physiological arousal dissipates fairly quickly (Cantor, Zillman, & Bryant, 1975). Therefore, the arousal claim does not apply to studies that measure aggressive behavior more than 30 minutes after game play has occurred, or studies in which aggression is measured by a retrospective report. For example, this criticism generally doesn't apply to correlational studies, but correlational studies show a significant link between violent video game exposure and aggression (Anderson & Bushman, 2001). Furthermore, there are a few experimental studies in which the violent and nonviolent game conditions were equated on arousal, and significant violent-content effects still occurred (e.g., Anderson & Dill, 2000, Study 2).

5. *There are no studies linking violent video game play to "serious" or actual aggression.*

This criticism is simply not true. A number of correlational studies have linked repeated violent video game play to serious aggression. For example,

Anderson and Dill (2000, Study 1) showed that college-student reports of violent video game play in prior years were positively related to aggression that would be considered criminal (e.g., assault, robbery) if known to police. Similarly, Gentile et al. (2003) found significant links between violent game play and physical fights.

6. *Violent media affect only a few who are already disturbed.*

As discussed earlier, there are reasons (some theoretical, some empirical) to believe that some populations will be more negatively affected than others. However, no totally "immune" population has ever been identified, and populations sometimes thought to be at low risk have nonetheless yielded significant violent video game exposure effects (e.g., Anderson & Dill, 2000; Gentile et al., in press).

7. *Effects of media violence are trivially small.*

Once again, this is simply not true. Violent video game effects are bigger than: (a) effects of passive tobacco smoke and lung cancer; (b) exposure to lead and IQ scores in children; (c) calcium intake and bone mass (for more comparisons, see Anderson & Bushman, 2001; Bushman & Anderson, 2001).

Note that the critics use these seven illegitimate criticisms to basically dismiss all research on violent video games. Once one has dismissed all correlational studies (number 3, above) and all experiments that use laboratory or other "trivial" measures of aggression (number 2, above), the only potential type of study left is clearly unethical: an experimental field study in which violent crime is the measure of aggression. Such a study would require randomly assigning children to high versus low video game violence conditions for a period of years and then following up on their rates of violent criminal activity over the course of their lives. It is not an accident that all ethically feasible types of studies are dismissed by the industry and its supporters.

Legitimate Criticisms

1. *Sample sizes tend to be too small in many studies.*

If the average effect size is about r = 0.20 (Anderson & Bushman, 2001), then N (the number of study participants) should be at least 200 for 0.80 power (power is the likelihood of being able to find a legitimate difference between groups). When N is too small, individual studies will *appear* inconsistent even if they are all accurate samples of the true r = 0.20 effect. For this reason, the best way of summarizing the results of a set of too-small studies is to combine the results via meta-analysis, rather than using the more traditional narrative review. When this is done, we see that the video game studies yield consistent results (Anderson & Bushman, 2001).

2. *Some studies do not have "violent" and "nonviolent" games that are sufficiently different in actual violent content.*

This problem was noted earlier in this chapter in the discussion of how early studies might find weaker effects because the "violent" video games in the early years were not very violent by contemporary standards. Figures 7.1 and 7.2, described earlier, confirm this problem. Future studies need to do a better job of assessing the violent content of the video games being compared.

3. *Some experimental studies have used a "control" or "nonviolent game" condition that was more boring, annoying, or frustrating than the violent game.*

The obvious solution for future studies is to do more pilot testing or manipulation checks on such aggression-relevant dimensions. In trying to summarize past research, one can sometimes find a more appropriate comparison condition within the same experiment.

4. *Some studies did not report sufficient results to enable calculation of an effect size for participants who actually played a video game.*

This problem arose in several cases in which half of the participants played a video game while the other half merely observed. Reported means then collapsed across this play versus observe dimension. Future reports should include the individual means.

5. *Some studies that purportedly study aggressive behavior have used dependent variables that are not true aggressive behavior.*

A surprising number of past studies have used trait or personality aggression scales as measures of aggressive behavior in short-term experiments. This is a problem because there is no way that a short-term manipulation of exposure to violent versus nonviolent video games (e.g., 20 minutes) can influence one's past frequency of aggression. In this short-term context, such a trait measure might possibly be conceived as a measure of cognitive priming, but clearly it is not a measure of aggressive behavior.

A related problem is that some studies have included hitting an inanimate object as a measure of aggressive behavior. Most modern definitions of aggression restrict its application to behaviors that are intended to harm another person (Anderson & Bushman, 2002a; Anderson & Huesmann, in press; Geen, 2001).

The obvious solution for future studies is to use better measures of aggression. In the analysis of past research one can sometimes disaggregate the reported composite measure to get a cleaner measure of aggression.

6. *There are no longitudinal studies.*

This is true. Major funding is needed to conduct a large-scale longitudinal study of video game effects. To date, such funding has not been forthcoming. Thus, one must rely on longitudinal studies in the TV/movie violence domain to get a reasonable guess as to the likely long-term effects.

Best Studies

What happens to the meta-analytic estimates of the effects of exposure to violent video games when only the "best" studies are used (as outlined in the preceding section on legitimate criticisms)? Figure 7.4 displays the results for several breakdowns of results for aggressive behavior. Interestingly, each effect size estimate is above 0.20 and is statistically significant, regardless of whether it came from experimental or nonexperimental studies, children or adult studies, or studies that measured more or less extreme forms of aggression.

SUMMARY

Although there is less research on the effects of violent video games than there is on television and movies, the preponderance of evidence looks very similar to the research on violent television. In particular, violent video games appear to increase aggressive thoughts and feelings, physiological arousal, and aggressive behaviors, as well as to decrease prosocial behaviors. There are many theoretical reasons why one would expect violent video games to have a greater effect than violent television, and most of the reasons why one would expect them to have a lesser effect are no longer true because violent video games have become so realistic, particularly since the late 1990s.

Figure 7.4
Effect of Exposure to Violent Video Games on Aggressive Behavior as a Function of Study Type

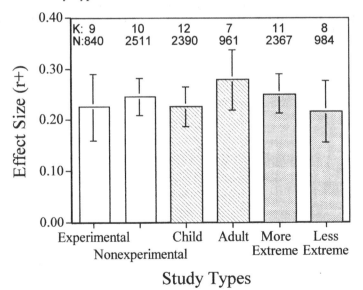

Study Types

Note: "More extreme" and "less extreme" refer to the severity of the aggressive behavior measured. K = number of independent tests. N = number of participants.

APPENDIX A: LETTER TO PARENTS—HOW CAN YOU TELL IF A VIDEO GAME IS POTENTIALLY HARMFUL?

1. Play the game, or have someone else demonstrate it for you.
2. Ask yourself the following six questions:
   - Does the game involve some characters trying to harm others?
   - Does this happen frequently, more than once or twice in 30 minutes?
   - Is the harm rewarded in any way?
   - Is the harm portrayed as humorous?
   - Are nonviolent solutions absent or less "fun" than the violent ones?
   - Are realistic consequences of violence absent from the game?
3. If two or more answers are "yes," think very carefully about the lessons being taught before allowing your child access to the game.[3]

NOTES

1. The authors are grateful for substantial help writing this section from Dr. Paul Lynch.

2. All effect sizes reported in the chapter are scaled as correlation coefficients, regardless of whether the study was experimental or correlational in design. See Comstock and Scharrer (this volume) for a discussion of how to interpret effect sizes.

3. From *Video Game Suggestions* from Dr. Craig A. Anderson, April 23, 2002. Copyright by Craig A. Anderson. The entire document can be found at: http://www.psychology.iastate.edu/faculty/caa/VG_Recommend.pdf.

CHAPTER 8

The Effects of Violent Music on Children and Adolescents

Donald F. Roberts, Peter G. Christenson, and Douglas A. Gentile

The best music . . . is essentially there to provide you something to face the world with.

—Bruce Springsteen

Music can change the world.

—Ludwig van Beethoven

Music is spiritual. The music business is not.

—Van Morrison

Although much of the debate about the effects of media on youth revolves around television, music is very important to children and adolescents. Try to change the radio station in the car after your child has set it, and you will quickly see that they have very clear and deeply held opinions. In a survey of junior and senior high school students in northern California (Roberts & Henriksen, 1990), students were asked what media they would choose to take with them if they were stranded on a desert island. They were allowed to nominate a first, second, and third choice from a list including: TV set, books, video games, computer, newspapers, VCR and videotapes, magazines, radio, and music recordings and the means to play them. Because radio is almost exclusively a music medium for adolescents, radio and recordings were combined into a single "music" category. As Table 8.1 displays, at all grade levels, music media were preferred over television (which placed second overall), and this preference increased with age. Over 80 percent of the total sample nominated music as one of their first three choices. By eleventh grade, music was selected first by a margin of two to one.

Table 8.1
Which Medium Would Adolescents Take to a Desert Isle?

	Seventh Grade (%)		Ninth Grade (%)		Eleventh Grade (%)	
	TV	Music	TV	Music	TV	Music
First choice	26	40	29	44	26	52
First two choices	43	66	49	73	43	80
First three choices	57	82	65	86	61	90

Note: Figures are rounded to the nearest percentage
Source: Adapted from Roberts, D. F., & Henriksen, L. (1990, June). *Music listening vs. television viewing among older adolescents.* Paper presented at the annual meeting of the International Communication Association, Dublin, Ireland.

Music's importance to youth can also be measured by the amount of time they spend listening to it. One sample of Southeastern junior high school students spent an average of three hours per day listening to music and over four hours watching television (Brown, Campbell, & Fischer, 1986). More recent studies have shown similar high numbers for music. In a study of over 600 eighth and ninth graders from public and private schools in Minnesota (Gentile, Lynch, Linder, & Walsh, in press), children reported spending an average of almost 21 hours per week listening to music, compared to 25 hours per week watching television (Table 8.2). This pattern can also be seen across larger age ranges, although the amount of time spent with music increases with age (e.g., Roberts, Foehr, Rideout, & Brodie, 1999). However, it is likely that most studies underestimate the amount of time children and adolescents may listen to music, because music is so often a secondary background activity for many other activities, such as reading, studying, talking, driving, and doing housework. Music's tendency to slip between foreground and background raises questions about what kind of "listening" should be counted as true *exposure.* We believe background listening ought to be included, and for those who might disagree we offer this challenge: Simply turn off the "background" music when youth are studying, chatting, or doing chores and observe their responses.

Research that addresses *all* listening, whether from radio or other sources and whether background or foreground, finds levels of exposure to music at least as high as to TV in late grade school and considerably *higher* in adolescence. For example, one survey required sixth and tenth graders to report how much time they had spent the previous day watching television, listening to

Table 8.2
Average Amounts of Media Use by Eighth and Ninth Grade Students (Hours/ Week)

	Boys and Girls		Boys		Girls	
	M	SD	M	SD	M	SD
Playing Video Games	9.0	11.9	12.9[c]	13.3	4.9[c]	8.6
Watching TV	25.3	15.4	27.4[b]	16.4	23.2[b]	14.0
Listening to Music	20.7	24.4	18.6	23.3	21.9	23.0
Reading for Pleasure	3.4	4.3	3.0[a]	4.2	3.8[a]	4.4

Note: M = mean, SD = standard deviation
[a]Means significantly different from each other at $p < 0.05$.
[b]Means significantly different from each other at $p < 0.01$.
[c]Means significantly different from each other at $p < 0.001$.
Source: Adapted from Gentile, D. A., Lynch, P. J., Linder, J. R., & Walsh, D. A. (in press). The effects of violent video game habits on adolescent hostility, aggressive behaviors, and school performance. *Journal of Adolescence.*

the radio, and listening to audio recordings (Greenberg, Ku, & Li, 1989). Sixth graders reported 4.1 hours of TV viewing and 3.8 hours of combined music listening; tenth graders reported 3.9 hours of TV viewing compared to 4.9 hours of music listening.

Amount of listening is not uniform across all groups of youth. First, age makes a big difference: adolescents devote more time to music than school-age children, and older adolescents devote more time to music than younger adolescents. Although many children begin listening to popular music early in the grade-school years (Christenson, DeBenedittis, & Lindlof, 1985), television consumes a much greater amount of time for younger children than does music. About the beginning of junior high school, however, this pattern begins to change. The early teen years mark a sharp increase in the amount of time kids devote to popular music, and the trend toward higher levels of music consumption continues through the end of high school.

Girls also tend to listen more than boys, at least once adolescence is reached. Although research on grade schoolers finds no significant sex-correlated differences in amount of listening (Christenson & DeBenedittis, 1986; Lyle & Hoffman, 1972), this picture begins to change about the time children enter middle school. By high school, girls listen substantially more than boys do (Greenberg et al., 1989; Roberts & Foehr, in press; Roberts & Henriksen, 1990), and African American youth tend to listen more than whites (Brown, Childers, Bauman, & Koch, 1990).

USES AND GRATIFICATIONS OF POPULAR MUSIC

At the simplest, most global level, people of all ages listen to music because it provides pleasure. For adolescents especially, the pleasure can be intense and tends to be associated with the most intense, "peak" experiences of life. Lull (1992, p. 1) has stated, "Music promotes experiences of the extreme for its makers and listeners, turning the perilous emotional edges, vulnerabilities, triumphs, celebrations, and antagonisms of life into hypnotic, reflective tempos that can be experienced privately or shared with others." Given the importance of music and its central role in adolescence, it is clear that it has a number of important effects. Yet although there has been concern for decades about possible deleterious effects of popular music, for most children, the effects are not deleterious. While this chapter cannot describe in detail the uses of music, we will describe briefly three major uses: affective uses, social uses, and the uses of lyrics (for a detailed review, see Christenson & Roberts, 1998). It also should be noted that the research on music videos appears to show different effects from music alone; thus music videos will be discussed later in this chapter.

Affective Uses

The major difference between popular music and other media lies in music's ability to enhance or modify mood. In a study of Swedish adolescents, Roe (1985) presented possible reasons for listening to music and asked students to indicate how often each applied to their listening. Factor analyses revealed three general trends: (1) atmosphere creation and mood control, (2) silence-filling and passing the time, and (3) attention to lyrics. Of the three types of uses, atmosphere creation and mood control emerged as the most important, with time-filling second and attention to lyrics a distant third. Summarizing the research on adolescent uses of music, Christenson & Roberts (1998, p. 48) suggested a principle they labeled "the primacy of affect." For most young people, music use is driven primarily by the motivation to control mood and enhance emotional states. Music's ability to communicate emotion and influence mood has been widely noted. Even preschoolers and infants as young as eight months can reliably discriminate "happy" and "sad" music (Gentile & Pick, under review; Gentile, Pick, Flom, & Campos, 1994; Gentile, Stoerzinger, Finney, & Pick, 1996; Sullivan, Gentile, & Pick, 1998). Studies of mood induction often use music in order to change people's moods (e.g., Kenealy, 1988; Pignatiello, Camp, Elder, & Rasar, 1989; Pignatiello, Camp, & Rasar, 1986). Because of the affective efficacy of music, when adolescents want to be in a certain mood, when they seek reinforcement for a certain mood, when they feel lonely, or when they seek distraction from their troubles, music tends to be the medium of choice to accomplish the task.

While both males and females report using music to affirm or manage their moods, there are some consistent differences in their goals. Research shows that males are more likely than females to use music as a tool to increase their energy level and seek stimulation—that is, to get "pumped up." In contrast, females are more likely than males to listen to lift their spirits when they're sad or lonely, or even to dwell on a somber mood (Arnett, 1991a; Larson, Kubey, & Colletti, 1989; Roe, 1985; Wells, 1990). Although they do so less commonly than females, males will also match music with their negative moods. In the same way that girls often listen to sad songs when they are sad, many heavy metal fans say they listen to angry music when they are angry. In one study, a typical heavy metal fan said he sought out "full-blown thrashing metal" when he was "mad at the world" (Arnett, 1991a, p. 82).

Social Uses

Some have suggested that while the emotional uses of popular music are important, the social uses and meanings provide the real key to understanding its niche in the lives of youth (Frith, 1981; Lull, 1987; Roe, 1984, 1985). For this discussion, we suggest two divisions within the broad category of social uses: "*quasi-social*" uses and "*socializing*" uses. By *quasi-social*, we mean listening that occurs alone but still serves goals and needs related to social relationships. Perhaps the best example of this is when music replaces or invokes the presence of absent peers in order to relieve feelings of loneliness. For example, in a study of college students, two-thirds reported listening either "somewhat frequently" or "very frequently" to "make me feel less alone when I'm by myself" (Gantz, Gartenberg, Pearson, & Schiller, 1978). This and other studies suggest that this quasi-social use is more common for girls than for boys (Larson et al., 1989; Roe, 1984). Solitary music listening may also perform a number of "delayed" social uses (Lull, 1987), by preparing youth for future peer interactions and relationships. There is a strong connection between interest in popular music and peer orientation. To a large extent, those who know nothing about pop culture or current music trends are relegated to the periphery of youth culture. Conversely, adolescent pop music "experts" tend to have more friends and enjoy enhanced status in the adolescent social structure (Adoni, 1978; Brown & O'Leary, 1971; Dominick, 1974).

By *socializing* uses, we mean two broad types of uses: (1) those that occur within the context of a social occasion, and (2) those that help to define social boundaries (Christenson & Roberts, 1998). Social occasions may take various forms (Lull, 1987). In romantic dyads, music is used to accompany courtship and sexual behavior. In friendships, music often provides a basis for the initial bond, and often helps to maintain the relationship. In larger gatherings, such as parties, dances, or clubs, music reduces inhibitions, attracts attention and approval, provides topics for conversation, and encourages dancing.

Music also works at a more diffuse social level to define the important subgroups in adolescent culture and to identify who belongs to them. Al-

though it is far from the only cue about group membership—school performance, extracurricular interests, social background, clothing, and other
elements of personal style figure in too—an adolescent's music affiliation says
much about his or her social affiliation. Popular music at once expresses,
creates, and perpetuates the essential "us-them" distinctions that develop between groups. The most typically discussed us-them distinction is between
youth and adults, although this is not likely to be the most important one.
For many youth, the type of music one listens to helps to define oneself and
one's in-group. *Music style*, defined as the selection of a certain type of music
and a personal style to go with it, is one of the most powerful identifying
markers in the school crowd structure. Within any high school it is usually
easy to classify many subgroups of adolescents according to their music preferences (e.g., "metalheads," "goths," "alternatives," "hip-hop," "punkers,"
"rastas," etc.). These labels may change as music changes, but the underlying
processes of adolescent subcultures are likely to remain the same.

The social uses of music make a great deal of sense when considered with
reference to the developmental tasks at different ages (for details see Gentile
& Sesma, chapter 2, this volume). In middle childhood, especially after age
eight, children begin to become more interested in popular music. As we have
seen, this interest increases through adolescence. Two of the key developmental tasks of middle childhood are (1) to learn how to be accepted by peers
and to build loyal friendships, and (2) to consolidate the self-concept (especially in terms of "which group do I belong to?"). Popular music serves these
goals very well. As has been mentioned, popular music often can serve as the
initial basis for friendships, and is important for peer acceptance (e.g., Adoni,
1978; Brown & O'Leary, 1971). In adolescence, two key developmental tasks
are (1) to learn to build intimate relationships (both same-sex and cross-sex),
and (2) to develop a personal identity (in terms of "how am I different from
others?"). Popular music continues to serve these goals well, by becoming
part of the social backdrop for exploring feelings of intimacy and by defining
in-groups and out-groups along lines of musical preferences.

The Uses of Music Lyrics

When asked why they like to listen to music, youth rarely list the lyrics as
the main reason. Usually it is something about the "sound" of the music that
attracts them. However, lyrics are far from irrelevant—they are mentioned as
a primary gratification by a significant number of youth and a secondary gratification by most (Gantz et al., 1978; Roe, 1985). In one study (Rouner, 1990),
high school students were asked to rank music against several other possible
sources of moral and social guidance, including parents, teachers, friends,
church leaders, and coworkers. Sixteen percent ranked music among the top
three sources of moral guidance, and 24 percent placed music in the top three

for information on social interaction. For better or worse, then, lyrics are often attended to, processed, discussed, memorized, and even taken to heart.

Given the controversy surrounding antisocial themes that are sometimes present in heavy metal and rap lyrics, it is important to note that heavy metal and rap fans report much higher levels of interest and attention to lyrics than do teens in general (Arnett, 1991a; Kuwahara, 1992). Two general patterns seem to emerge from the research on attention to lyrics: First, the more *important* music is to an adolescent, the more importance he or she places on lyrics relative to other elements of music gratification. Second, attention to lyrics is highest among fans of *oppositional* or controversial music (whether it be 1960s protest folk or rock or the heavy metal and rap of today). In other words, the more defiant, alienated, and threatening to the mainstream a music type is, the more closely its fans follow the words (Christenson & Roberts, 1998).

THE EFFECTS OF VIOLENT MUSIC ON YOUTH

Most of the criticism aimed at current popular music stems from the assumption that "content" (i.e., the attitudes, values, and behaviors portrayed in lyrics) may influence how young listeners think and act. Not surprisingly, it is a concern that emphasizes the negatives, such as violence, misogyny, racism, suicide, Satanism, and substance abuse (Carey, 1969; Christenson & Roberts, 1998; Fedler, Hall, & Tanzi, 1982; Roberts, Henriksen, & Christenson, 1999). Articles have even been written with headlines like "Hard rock music creates killer mice!" based on high school science-fair experiments in which groups of mice were trained to run mazes. Groups of mice listened to classical music, hard rock, or no music. The classical mice became faster in running the maze, whereas the hard rock mice became slower. The student performing the study stated, "I had to cut my project short because all the hard-rock mice killed each other. . . . None of the classical mice did that" (Eaton, 1997; Health, Wealth, & Happiness, n.d.).

Regardless of the merits of such alarmist reports, it is difficult to deny that music has become more aggressive and edgy over the decades. In 1958, the Everly Brothers sang, "When I want you in my arms, all I have to do is dream." Twenty-eight years later, the message had been simplified to, "Hey, we want some pussy" (2 Live Crew, 1986). Claims that popular song lyrics pose a danger implicitly assume that young people interpret songs in much the same way that adult critics do. That is, for violent lyrics to promote youth violence or for substance use portrayals to encourage experimentation with illicit drugs, young audiences presumably must find violent or substance-related messages in the songs. Indeed, to be truly "influenced," young people may need to go a step farther and connect such messages to their own lives. The problem with such assumptions is that several decades of communication research shows quite clearly that lyric interpretation is as much a process of construction as of recognition or discovery. Thus, what young people make of popular songs depends not only on what the lyric brings to them, but also on what they bring to the lyric.

Given the rhetoric that controversies often breed, it is perhaps not surprising that many people assume that the idea of media effects is synonymous with the idea of "massive and uniform" effects. That is, many people assume that if media have an effect, the effect would be seen by showing that media messages influence large numbers of people in the same ways. The music literature does not support this conception of media effects, but this may not be the most productive way to conceptualize media effects. A focus on massive, uniform effects confuses "massive" and "uniform" with "important." Effects do not need to affect large numbers of people to be important. Effects may vary for different people, but still be important. Research has found that different subgroups interpret music lyrics in different ways. Yet, this does not necessarily make the effects unimportant. Many studies seek to find a 10 percent effect on a full population (massive, uniform effects). Yet those that seek to find a 100 percent effect on a specifiable subgroup that may only comprise 10 percent of the population (conditional effects; Chaffee, 1977) can also document subjectively important media effects. Our approach to media effects presumes that important effects need not and probably do not extend to a large proportion of the total audience. Rather, listeners respond in terms of various social, psychological, and physical conditions that influence how they use music, how they interpret messages, and whether, when, and how they act on what they have learned. This approach also can fit within a risk factor approach (Gentile & Sesma, chapter 2, this volume), in which children who are already at risk for suicide or violence may increase their risk by heavy use of music extolling those themes. However, for children without preexisting risk factors, or for those who have a number of protective factors, music with themes of suicide or violence is likely to have little short-term effect. There certainly could be long-term, cumulative effects (such as desensitization), but more research is needed to look for these types of long-term effects.

Heavy Metal Music

A number of correlational studies report positive associations between exposure to heavy metal music and a variety of troublesome attitudes and behaviors. Heavy metal music in particular has a high proportion of violent, sexual, and misogynistic themes. Fans of heavy metal music do tend to possess different characteristics from other youth. With regard to school, heavy metal fans report more conflict with teachers and other school authorities and perform less well academically than those whose tastes run more to the mainstream (Christenson & van Nouhuys, 1995; Hakanen & Wells, 1993). They tend to be distant from their families (Martin, Clarke, & Pearce, 1993) and are often at odds with their parents. When relationships with parents are described as satisfactory, it is usually because the parents let the children go their own way (Arnett, 1991a). At the same time, there is no evidence that heavy metal fans see themselves as socially isolated. They are just as satisfied with the quality of their peer relationships as nonfans are (Arnett, 1991a). If anything, the peer group exerts a more powerful influence on heavy metal fans than on most other adolescents (Gordon, Hakanen, & Wells, 1992).

According to Arnett (1991a, 1991b), hard-core heavy metal fans tend to be driven by a generalized tendency to seek sensation and thrills and a need to engage in a variety of risky behaviors, more or less "to see what it would be like." In accord with this thesis, he reports differences between heavy metal fans and nonfans not only in their expression of sensation-seeking motivations generally but also in their self-reports of specific reckless behaviors, including drunk driving, casual sex, and marijuana and cocaine use. Other research has found a similar connection between risky, reckless attitudes and behavior and the choice of heavy metal music (Martin et al., 1993). Youth in juvenile detention were three times as likely as regular high school students to be metal fans (Wass, Miller, & Reditt, 1991).

Hansen and Hansen (1991) found that the amount of time college students listened to heavy metal was correlated with a "macho" personality. Specifically, exposure to heavy metal correlated positively with "male hypersexuality" (as indicated by the level of agreement with the idea that "young men need sex even if some coercion of females is required to get it") and negatively with general respect for women. Christenson and van Nouhuys (1995) report a connection between heavy metal and interest in other-sex contact as early as age 11.

Concern has also been expressed over the potential impact of heavy metal music's often dismal, depressed view of the world and its depiction of depression and suicide. Arnett (1991a) writes:

One can hear an echo in [heavy metal themes] of concerns with social issues from the music of the 1960's, but with this difference: the songs of the sixties often lamented the state of the world but promised a brighter future if we would mend our ways; heavy metal songs often lament the state of the world but do not provide even a hint of hope for the future. Hopelessness and cynicism pervade the songs. (p. 93)

Martin's and his colleagues' data (1993) from more than 200 Australian high school students showed that those who preferred heavy metal or hard rock music reported feelings of depression, suicidal thoughts, and deliberate infliction of self-harm more frequently than others in the sample. For instance, 20 percent of the male and more than 60 percent of the female heavy metal/hard rock fans reported having deliberately tried to kill or hurt themselves in the last six months, compared with only 8 percent and 14 percent, respectively, of the pop music fans.

Do these various findings support the notion of a "heavy metal syndrome," that is, of a constellation of related traits with heavy metal as the focal point? Probably not. If there is a "syndrome" at work here, it is a "troubled youth syndrome," not a heavy metal syndrome. Leaving aside for now the question of whether popular music exercises any influence on adolescents' values and behavior, assuredly the consumption of heavy metal is not what brings together the various "at-risk" characteristics with which heavy metal fandom is associated. The best way to phrase the relation is to say that white adolescents who are troubled or at risk gravitate strongly toward the style of music that provides the most support for their view of the world and meets their particular needs: namely, heavy metal.

The point can be further clarified, perhaps, by juxtaposing these statements: (1) Most heavy metal fans are not particularly troubled or at risk, but (a) those youths who are troubled or at risk tend overwhelmingly to embrace heavy metal. In other words, whatever percentage one uses to estimate the proportion of heavy metal fans in the total adolescent population, they surely number in the tens of millions. Most of these young people are not on drugs, not in jail, not failing in school, not depressed, perhaps not even particularly at odds with their parents (except maybe when it comes to music). Arguing the other way, however, if we know a youth is white, male, 15 years old, drug involved, and in trouble with the law, then the odds are *very high* indeed that his music of choice will be some form of hard rock or heavy metal.

Our rejection of the idea of a true heavy metal syndrome should not be taken to imply that heavy metal music plays only a peripheral role in the lives of its devotees. Heavy metal fans are an especially committed, devoted audience. Those who love the genre are highly absorbed in their musical identity, in terms of both listening time (Wass, Miller, & Stevenson, 1989) and a variety of other music-related behavior. Arnett (1991a) reports that high school students describing themselves as "metalheads" spent more than twice as much money on albums, concerts, and music equipment as a comparison group of nonmetal fans. They also tended to express very high levels of personal identification with their favorite performers, were more likely to say lyrics are important to them, claimed a deeper understanding of lyrics, and were more likely than other youth to adopt their favorite musicians as role models. As Arnett points out, heavy metal plays a crucial role in the lives of the alienated and disaffected youths who seek it out; for many such youths, listening to heavy metal is what matters to them most. As has been noted in other chapters in this volume, the question of "initial causality" is probably not the important question. That is, whether heavy metal music is the thing that starts children becoming more troubled, or whether alienated youth start to like heavy metal (which is what research suggests), is probably not the best question to ask. A better question might be how will music with antisocial themes affect children who are already at risk for antisocial behaviors? It does not matter whether music started the cycle; it matters that the themes encountered in the music may help to perpetuate it. That is, the music may reinforce aggressive and antisocial thoughts and feelings, and thus make those thoughts and feelings more likely to occur in the future. Heavy metal music may thus be a risk factor, affecting most those who are already most at risk.

Violent Music Lyrics

As shown above, a number of correlational studies suggest a connection between the types of music youth listen to and a wide range of troublesome attitudes and behaviors. Some of these studies focus on aggressive and violent attitudes. For example, college students who prefer rap and heavy metal music report more hostile attitudes than students who prefer other styles of music, such as country, alternative, dance/soul, or adult contemporary (Rubin, West, & Mitchell, 2001). Fans of rap music tend to be more distrustful than fans of other styles, and heavy metal fans tend to hold more negative attitudes toward women.

There have been few experimental studies of the effects of violent music lyrics on listeners. Some have found no effects of lyric content on aggression-related variables (Ballard & Coates, 1995; St. Lawrence & Joyner, 1991; Wanamaker & Reznikoff, 1989). Some of these studies have had methodological problems with indecipherable lyrics or confounds with general arousal. However, contrary to suggesting that music has no effect, these studies have provided evidence that the effects may be more subtle than we typically expect. For example, St. Lawrence and Joyner (1991) set out to test whether listening to sexually violent heavy metal would increase acceptance of gender-role stereotypes and sexually violent behavior. Groups of undergraduate males heard either sexually violent heavy metal rock, Christian heavy metal rock, or easy-listening classical music. A month before and immediately after listening, the students answered a questionnaire measuring gender-role stereotyping, adversarial sexual beliefs, acceptance of interpersonal violence, rape myth acceptance (the idea that women invite and/or enjoy rape), and self-reported sexual arousal. The somewhat surprising result was that it did not matter whether participants heard sexually violent heavy metal or Christian heavy metal. Relative to classical music, exposure to either type of music produced more negative attitudes toward women. In other words, the lyrics did not make a difference, but the heavy metal musical form did. While there is reason to wonder whether the students really "heard" the lyrics, the larger issue may be that the sound of the music carries a great deal of information independent of lyrical content. "Angry-sounding" music may increase aggressive thoughts and feelings, regardless of the specific lyrical content. Christenson and Roberts (1998) argue that the "sound" of heavy metal serves to cue more aggressive schemata, and thus increase the likelihood of aggressive responses.

Others studies have shown lyric-specific effects with a variety of types of measures (e.g., Anderson, Carnagey, & Eubanks, 2003; Barongan & Hall, 1995; Wester, Crown, Quatman, & Heesacker, 1997). Barongan & Hall

(1995) had male college students listen to misogynous or neutral rap music and subsequently view three vignettes (neutral, sexual-violent, or assaultive). They then chose one of the three vignettes to be shown to a female confederate. Students who had listened to the misogynous rap music chose to have the female view the assaultive vignette significantly more frequently than students who listened to neutral music did. Students who showed the violent vignettes reported that the women had been more upset by them than did students who showed the neutral vignettes (although the confederates had been trained not to react to the vignettes). This pattern of results suggests that music with misogynous lyrics may facilitate sexually aggressive behavior. Wester et al. (1997) exposed male undergraduates to one of the following: (1) sexually violent rap music and lyrics, (2) the same music without lyrics, (3) sexually violent lyrics without music, or (4) a no-music control condition. While there were no differences in the general amount of negative attitudes toward women among the four groups, the students exposed to violent lyrics (groups one and three) were significantly more likely to view their relationships with women as more adversarial.

Anderson and his colleagues (2003), using the theoretical framework of the General Aggression Model (described in chapter 5), hypothesized that violent lyrics would be most likely to show short-term effects on aggressive emotions and aggressive thoughts. These hypotheses were confirmed in a series of five studies with undergraduate students (both males and females). The songs were matched for style but varied in terms of violent content (e.g., violent versus nonviolent songs from the same rock group, humorous violent versus humorous nonviolent songs). Across the studies, violent song lyrics were associated with increases in aggressive thoughts. Aggressive thoughts were measured in a number of manners that are typical when studying aggressive cognition. In one experiment, students who heard the violent song read aggressive words faster than they read nonaggressive words, thus showing priming of aggressive concepts. In two more experiments, students who heard the violent song were more likely to complete word fragments as aggressive words than as nonaggressive words (e.g., completing KI_ _ as "kill" rather than as "kiss"). Across the studies, violent song lyrics were associated with increases in hostile and aggressive feelings. These effects were shown across a variety of songs and, importantly, were not attributable to differences in arousal. As the authors note, however, the types of hostile thoughts and feelings that were primed by violent lyrics are likely to be a short-term effect, and may be easily disrupted if some other nonviolent event occurs.

Suicides and Shootings

It is a huge leap from the short-term outcomes demonstrated in the research on the effects of popular music to the claims often made in public discussions about music's role in teenage suicides and recent school shootings.

Yet certain facts surrounding these tragic events have led to charges that popular music—and other elements of popular culture such as violent movies and video games—are at least partially to blame (Christenson & Roberts, 1998; Egan, 1998; Litman & Farberow, 1994; "Rock on Trial," 1988; *Vance v. Judas Priest*, 1990). A few comments on the issue are in order here. It is true that a number of adolescent suicide victims have spent the hours immediately prior to taking their lives immersed in heavy metal music. It is also true that several of the young people involved in recent school shootings have been avid fans of Marilyn Manson and other "goth rock" performers. However, that exposure to popular music can operate as "the" cause of such drastic behaviors is unlikely. Millions of heavy metal and "gangsta rap" fans spend hours with their chosen music genres and never threaten others or themselves. Moreover, most researchers concerned with the causes of suicide and violence point to a broad array of risk factors unrelated to popular culture (e.g., depression, access to guns, substance abuse, etc.) that seem to be precursors of such drastic acts. Indeed, these conditions have characterized most or all of the incidents at issue in the recent debate (Berman & Jobes, 1991; Egan, 1998; Levy & Deykin, 1989).

This is not, however, to absolve popular music from a role in at least some suicides and violent incidents. Recall earlier points about the uses of music and about heavy metal fans in particular. First, one of the more important functions of popular music for adolescents is what we have called the "primacy of affect" (Christenson & Roberts, 1998). Teens (and most age groups) frequently use music as a tool to maintain or change particular moods, and they readily admit that music has direct, profound effects on their emotions. Moreover, some of the research on music's impact on mood suggests what might be called an "amplification effect," a strong tendency for music to heighten whatever emotional state a listener brings to a listening situation—including anger and depression (Gordon et al., 1992; Wells, 1990). As noted earlier, although it is not legitimate to assume that all fans of extreme music are "troubled," kids who *are* troubled are very likely to be fans of extreme music. There is substantial evidence that adolescents who are depressed, angry, alienated, experiencing suicidal thoughts, having family problems, abusing drugs or alcohol, or having difficulty at school constitute a group that is particularly drawn to the sort of angry, nihilistic music that celebrates these "troubled" states and traits. These factors, when coupled with the high levels of identification with the music and its performers, seem at the very least cause for reason to be concerned.

To immerse oneself in angry, desperate, depressing music is a poor strategy for coping with anger, despair, and depression. Neuroscience suggests that "brooding," or dwelling on one's current emotional state, is more likely to deepen the state rather than to alleviate it (Goleman, 1995). Litman and Farberow (1994) contend that "addictive and antisocial behaviors" are at first adopted as *alternatives* to suicide, but, when they fail, and if conditions worsen, such behaviors may actually function as *contributory causes* of suicide. Similarly, if a preoccupation with heavy metal music is carried to an extreme, it too may become an addictive, antisocial behavior—a form of "media delinquency" (Roe, 1995)—and ultimately a contributor to the problem rather than a solution. For the small minority of kids who are already alienated and disturbed, extreme music may be another risk factor for violence or suicide.

Summary

Taken together, these studies suggest that the main effects of music may be carried by the emotional "sound" of the music rather than by the lyrics. The effects of violent music lyrics do not appear to be nearly as powerful as the effects of other, more visual, violent media. In fact, this may be because lyric content may be difficult to understand, may be interpreted differently by different people, or because visual images may be a more direct and powerful communicator. As is discussed by Comstock & Scharrer (chapter 11, this volume), visual images of violence or danger appear to be more primary in terms of their ability to elicit fear reactions than verbal or cognitive descriptions of violence or danger. These considerations make it necessary to question whether violent music videos have a greater effect on viewers than violent music alone has on listeners. In short, the answer is yes, violent music videos appear to have a much more powerful effect.

MUSIC VIDEOS

Although music has been paired with visual displays for hundreds of years, the form that we call the music video was launched in 1981 with the beginning of the MTV network. Music videos began as commercial advertisements to help record sales, but they are now a commercial item in themselves and are an increasingly popular item for sale and rental at home video outlets. The vast majority of preadolescents and adolescents watch music videos. Three-quarters of 9- to 12-year-olds (Christenson, 1992a) and 80 percent of 12- to 14-year-olds report watching music videos at least occasionally. In a national random sample of parents of 2- to 17-year-olds, two-thirds (65 percent) of parents reported that their children at least occasionally watched music videos on TV (Gentile & Walsh, 1999). Despite these statistics, music video viewing occupies relatively little time compared with music listening. Most published reports set the average amount of viewing between 15 and 30 minutes a day (Christenson, 1992a; Kubey & Larson, 1989; Leming, 1987; Wartella, Heintz, Aidman, & Mazzarella, 1990). Interest in music videos appears to peak early in adolescence, and drop off into the high school years, even as overall interest in music continues to rise.

When asked about their reasons for watching music videos, the "music" is the most frequently mentioned gratification (Christenson, 1992a; Sun & Lull,

1986). However, adolescents offer many different uses and gratifications beyond appreciation of the music itself. Brown and her colleagues (1986) presented adolescents with 19 separate reasons for watching music videos. The students used a three-point scale (from "a lot" to "not at all") to indicate how much each reason applied to them. The original 19 were reduced statistically to a list including diversion, attention to lyrics, trend surveillance (e.g., fashion, dance), "make me wish I were like some of the characters," and so forth. In general, the results suggested that personal diversion and interpretation of lyrics are more important than either social uses or the seeking of information and guidance.

Over half (53 percent) of music videos include violent portrayals (NTVS, 1998). There are a number of reasons to expect that violent music videos may have a greater effect than violent music (with no visual component). The most obvious reason, of course, is the presence of visual information. The visual images and narratives of music videos clearly have more potential to form attitudes, values, or perceptions of social reality than does the music alone because they add additional information and rely less on imagination. Second, even though less time is spent watching music videos than listening to music, the fact that the time is spent watching and not merely listening means that music video viewing is more likely a foreground than a background activity. If the eyes are directed to a screen, less attention can be given to accompanying activities such as reading, studying, working, or socializing. Third, while studies of music lyrics have shown that lyric intelligibility and interpretation can vary across different listeners, much less interpretation is needed to understand a violent image. Even if the "story" in a video is inscrutable, it is difficult to miss such visual standbys as threatening displays of weapons or fighting. Fourth, the "meaning" of the song as shown in the video can become self-reinforcing—if viewers listen to the song after seeing the video, they are likely to "flash back" to the visual images from the video (Took & Weiss, 1994). Finally, we should not forget that the small average amount of time spent with music videos conceals the range of responses. Although adolescents average less than 30 minutes a day viewing music videos, surveys regularly reveal a segment of 5 percent to 15 percent who watch them for several hours a day. These highly absorbed viewers obviously stand a much greater chance of being influenced.

Although research on the effects of violent music videos is still in the early stages, the findings to date seem to parallel the effects of violent television. There appear to be effects on aggressive emotions, attitudes, and behaviors. Hansen and Hansen (1990a) showed college students a set of videos with varying levels of sex and violence and found that higher levels of violence not only produced more negative responses to the video and song, but stimulated a host of intense negative emotions. As violence went up, students said they felt less happy, more fearful, and more anxious and aggressive.

Videos with many violent images have been shown to increase aggressive attitudes, including antagonism toward women and acceptability of violence both for themselves and in others (Greeson & Williams, 1986; Hansen & Hansen, 1990b; Johnson, Jackson, & Gatto, 1995; Peterson & Pfost, 1989). In a study of seventh and tenth graders, those who viewed 30 minutes of music videos with high concentrations of sex, violence, and antiestablishment themes showed higher approval of premarital sex than did similar participants who viewed 30 minutes of videos randomly taped off of the air. Among tenth graders, these videos also reduced disapproval of violence (Greeson & Williams, 1986). Peterson and Pfost (1989) showed undergraduate males collections of music videos that varied in both eroticism and violence, resulting in four stimulus types: erotic/violent, erotic/nonviolent, nonerotic/violent, and nonerotic/nonviolent. Of the four types of content, only the violent images had much of an effect: Males who watched violent videos scored higher than other groups on measures of negative affect and "antagonistic orientation toward women."

These studies could be criticized for not disguising the intent of the study, therefore perhaps influencing the results. However, studies that have disguised the intent more carefully show similar results. For example, Johnson et al. (1995) showed identical groups of 11- through 16-year-old lower-income African American boys either eight violent rap videos or eight nonviolent rap videos, ostensibly as part of a memory test. After completing the "memory study," participants moved on to a second study of "decision-making skills" in which they answered questions about two brief stories. One story described an incident in which a young man physically attacks both his girlfriend and an old male friend of hers after seeing the two exchange a friendly hug and kiss. The second scenario involved an exchange between two old high school friends, one of whom is now working hard attending college, the other of whom drives a BMW and wears nice clothes and jewelry, with no indication of how he can afford such nice things. The results indicated an effect of videos on both approval of violence and academic aspirations. Those who had viewed the violent videos were more likely than those in either the nonviolent video group or the no-video control group to condone the attack against the girl's old friend and to say that they would have done the same thing. Boys who watched either violent or nonviolent rap videos were less likely than those in the control group to want to be like the young man who was attending college or to believe that he would ever finish school.

Other studies using this sort of two-phase experimental design have also found that music video content can alter viewers' subsequent assessments of other people and other people's behavior. Hansen and Hansen (1990b) gave university students the impression that they were to evaluate two applicants for a job hosting a TV show about rock music. While waiting for the job interview to begin, groups of students killed time by watching either three antisocial or three neutral videos. Next, the students "accidentally observed" what they (incorrectly) believed to be a real event in which one job applicant, while telling a joke to the other, was brusquely warned to "settle down" by an authority figure, who then left the room. Half the students in the violent video condition and half in the neutral condition then saw the rebuked "job applicant" make an obscene gesture toward the retreating authority figure; the other half saw him merely adjust his clothing. Subsequently, all students saw a taped interview—which they thought was live—of the two job applicants, then completed a questionnaire indicating the degree to which each applicant was someone they would like personally, and evaluated each applicant on a number of adjectives (e.g., honest/dishonest, polite/impolite, etc.).

Students who saw the neutral videos liked the job applicant less and ascribed fewer positive traits to him if they had seen him make an obscene gesture as opposed to simply adjusting his clothing. For those who watched the antisocial videos, however, evaluations of the job applicant were the same regardless of whether he had made the gesture; that is, the students liked him no less when he made the gesture than when he did not. In other words, a relatively brief exposure to antisocial videos essentially cancelled out (desensitized) the natural tendency to dislike those who exhibit rude, defiant behavior.

In a study of third through fifth grade children (Gentile, Linder, & Walsh, 2003), children who report watching MTV more regularly also report getting into more physical fights than children who do not watch MTV regularly. More importantly, peers and teachers also report differences in the children's observed behaviors at school. Children who watch MTV more regularly are rated by their peers as significantly more verbally aggressive, more relationally aggressive, and more physically aggressive than children who do not watch regularly. They are also rated by their teachers as significantly more relationally aggressive, more physically aggressive, and less prosocial (helpful). These ratings are significant because it is unlikely that peers and teachers would know how regularly others watch MTV.

CODA: A NOTE TO PARENTS

> Music is the shorthand of emotion.
>
> —Leo Tolstoy

Does all this mean that the booming bass and screeching guitars that parents hear behind their children's bedroom doors or the green-haired, leathered, and pierced dervish whirling across the music video screen are turning young people into monsters? Generally not. Even violent music does not seem to have the same effect as violent television and video games. Violent music videos, in contrast, may have an effect of similar size to that of violent television (chapters 4 and 11, this volume), although there is much less research on the effects of violent music and music videos than there is on violent TV, movies, and video games.

When we are asked by concerned parents whether they should be worried about the music their children are listening to, we respond with the following questions. Are your child's grades good, or have they been slipping? Is your child's mood generally angry or depressed? Do you like your child's friends? If you like your child's friends and his/her grades are fine, then there's probably very little to worry about from the lyric content of the songs he/she likes. However, it is perhaps worth remembering that the main power of music may be the power to change or maintain emotional moods. Thus, if your child is listening to angry-sounding music for three hours each day, that may signal a reason for concern. It may be likely that your child is angry about something and is dwelling on those feelings. At the least, all that angry music is not likely to make him/her less angry.

That said, for most kids, most of the time, music is a source of pleasure (even angry music!). They listen not to analyze lyrics and learn about the world, not to sort out emotions and feelings, not to facilitate social interaction, but because they like it. To be sure, popular music does teach them things, does help them to sort out emotions and feelings, does facilitate social interaction. It is, as we have noted, the medium that matters most to adolescents, and not least because it addresses issues that are central to their developmental stage—love, sex, loyalty, independence, friendship, authority—with a directness they often do not get from adults. Although many teenagers will discuss sensitive personal issues with the significant adults in their lives, just as many will avoid such discussions, opting instead for what they perceive as more legitimate sources—other youth, but also the culture of youth. For most adolescents, popular music functions not just as equipment for living, but as *essential* equipment for living.

Children's and Adolescents' Exposure to Different Kinds of Media Violence: Recurring Choices and Recurring Themes

Jennifer A. Kotler and Sandra L. Calvert[1]

For over 40 years, parents, scholars, and policymakers have raised concerns about the impact of children's exposure to violent media content. Social scientists have extensively documented the detrimental effects of exposure to violent television content on children (Murray, 1995) while the content makers deny those effects (Valenti, 2000). Regardless of the debate or the findings, American children continue to be exposed to a steady stream of violent media images from both older and newer media (Calvert, 1999).

Two areas are included in this chapter that move beyond the effects issue. The first area involves our decisions as a society to use violent media. Why do we buy it? Why do we expose our children to it? If we didn't use it, it would cease to exist for lack of a market. The second area involves the kinds of content where violence is most likely to be found, how that content then travels to, and is transformed by, our newer media, and whether there are any different effects after exposure in older and newer media or after exposure to different kinds of programs containing violent content.

WHAT IS AGGRESSION?

The definition of aggression is one that researchers have grappled with over time. Does one, for example, focus only on the consequences of an action, or does one emphasize the motivations and intentions of the person committing the "aggressive" act? In courts of law, motive is a major discriminating factor in determining justice. Accidental aggression, even if it results in mayhem, is treated with a reduced punishment compared to aggression that is done on purpose. There are also disagreements about when aggression is an acceptable behavior and when it is not (Fraczek, 1985). Conflict is a reality of life. For some, aggression is never an acceptable response whereas for others there are times when aggression is justified. For example, some parents believe that children should stand up for themselves, protect younger siblings, and protect other weaker children from bullies (Osterweil & Nagano-Nakamura, 1992). The intent in the latter situation is to protect, not to harm another person. That kind of aggression is also part of heroism. Children understand these messages. For instance, elementary school aged children are more likely to accept aggression if used in self-defense than if it is not (Ginzler, 1998).

Two forms of aggression are often cited in the literature: hostile and instrumental. In hostile aggression, the intent is to inflict injury or to harm another person, whereas instrumental aggression occurs in the quest of some object, often a toy when children are involved (Bushman & Anderson, 2001). Young children typically aggress for instrumental purposes. With development, however, children are more likely to aggress with the intent to hurt or harm (Coie & Dodge, 1998). However, as they grow even older, preadolescents and adolescents come to understand that revenge is not the right moral path, even though they may grapple with their own yearnings for revenge. Only children who have weak social ties and few friends endorse revenge as a way of solving conflicts (Rose & Asher, 1999).

With development, children make finer discriminations about violence. For example, Krcmar and Cooke (2001) found that younger, four- to seven-year-old children thought that unpunished violence was more acceptable than punished violence. Older children, by contrast, were more likely to assess an act of violence as justified if the act was provoked rather than unprovoked, which is a more subtle distinction than punished versus unpunished violence. In other words, to older children, there are subtle distinctions as to when violence is acceptable and when it is not.

The difference between physical and verbal aggression is another developmental milestone. Young children tend to hit; older children tend to fight with words (Coie & Dodge, 1998). The developmental change to verbal aggression is one that children increasingly employ. For instance, older children switch to name-calling rather than hitting a peer.

Similar struggles to understand the definition of violence occur in film, television, video games, and online presentations. Those arguing that the relationship between exposure to violent media and children's aggressive behavior is unclear often point to research definitions of aggression that lack the most important characteristics of violence: motives and context (Smith, 2002). Although different researchers have used different definitions of violence in their studies, a great deal of violent behavior is found on television regardless of the specific definition used. The most comprehensive study of television violence, the National Television Violence Study (NTVS, 1997), found extensive levels of violence even when the context, motivation, and the type of portrayal was included. This study also found that children's television programs were particularly high in violent content.

In media portrayals, aggression is concentrated in certain kinds of programs (Wilson et al., 2002). In television and film, for example, the hero fights against the villain for justice. The evening news is filled with depictions of the dark deeds committed by people, with the long arm of justice in active pursuit. Even our comedies have a dark side: we laugh at the expense and humiliation of others. These same formulas appear in our new media as well. The heroic tale travels to video as well as to online games. The news is available online as well as on television. Yet new forms of violent expression also take place in the new media. Hate speech occurs online. Adolescents, who are often anonymous online, can and sometimes do engage in the character assassination of others users (Greenfield, 2000). In this chapter, we examine these different kinds of aggressive media content and their respective impact on children.

CHILDREN'S ATTRACTION TO AGGRESSIVE CONTENT AND ITS IMPACT ON BEHAVIOR

In the aggression literature, media research has concentrated on the effects side of the equation. That is, what are the effects or the outcomes of exposure to media violence on children? Social cognitive theory, which emphasizes modeling and imitation, and arousal theory, which emphasizes physiological responses to violent material, are the two main paradigms used to demonstrate the harmful effects of violent media on children. With few exceptions, there are negative outcomes for children who view or interact with aggressive content, particularly for younger children, for boys, and for those who are strongly predisposed to aggressive behavior (Calvert, 1999). These effects include imitation and disinhibition of aggressive responses (Bandura, 1997) as well as desensitization to aggressive content (Bryant & Zillmann, 1991).

Little research, however, has been devoted to why children view or interact with violent content in the first place. Uses and gratification theory, which examines the needs of the viewer in relation to content, is one approach for understanding why we are drawn to aggressive portrayals. Psychoanalytic theory, an approach that deals with the underlying drives of human beings, is another approach. The concepts of Carl Jung (1954, 1959, 1968), who modified and extended psychoanalytic theory, are well known and used by those who create film and television programs (e.g., Voytilla, 1999), yet academic researchers have virtually ignored their importance.

USES AND GRATIFICATION THEORY

In uses and gratification theory, users come to media with certain needs, and they fulfill them by using certain media (Rubin, 1994). In the area of aggression, one might speculate that children view and interact with media containing aggressive content because they are in search of interesting stories or because they are bored and looking for stimulation. One kind of program that fills this need and that contains high levels of violent content and action is the heroic tale. Children also look to media for role models who can serve as guides for their own actions. Heroic tales are again the most noticeable program type that fills that need.

Another need that media fill for children is one of entertainment (Rubin, 1994). Children use television, film, and video games for their pleasure, and some of these programs, such as heroic tales and humorous cartoons, contain violent content. Funk (2002) argues that children who are at risk for low self-esteem, such as bullies and victims, may fill their needs for mastery and power, in part, by playing violent video games. Another need that media fill is one for information (Rubin, 1994). While not the most intentionally sought-after program by youth, there is still considerable exposure to news programming, much of which is violent. The news is also real rather than fictional, a quality that children increasingly understand with development.

In our discussion below we examine children's use of and attraction to heroic tales, and also the effects that heroic tales, humorous cartoons, and the news have on children's aggression. We also enter into the newer domain of online Internet interactions, focusing on hate speech. For those who are antisocial, the Internet forum provides an anonymous vehicle to fulfill one's desires to hurt and harm another person.

Heroic Tales

If one accepts the thesis that children come to media in search of stimulating and interesting stories, then the realm of myth has much to offer us in understanding children's viewing and play choices with old and new media. In myth, we capture the long-held values and beliefs about what is important to us.

Myths rely on the collective unconscious and archetypes. Building on psychoanalytic theory, Carl Jung (1954, 1959, 1968) created the idea of the collective unconscious, the repository of the shared collective images of the human species. Within the collective unconscious, we have inherited the archetypes, prototypical images that are passed on anew to each new generation. These images, according to Jung (1954, 1959, 1968), exist in the collective unconscious as primitive images that are then developed by our individual and cultural experiences. These archetypes include the persona (our external presentation of self to the world), the anima (the feminine side of the male psyche), the animus (the masculine side of the female psyche), the shadow (the life-preserving, yet potentially destructive facet of the personality), the self, the wizard, the hero, the crone, animals such as wolves howling, symbols of nature such as the full moon, and religious symbols such as birth and rebirth

(Hall & Nordby, 1973). Of particular interest to our discussion are those archetypes most closely associated with aggression: the hero and the shadow (Calvert, Kondla, Ertel, & Meisel, 2001).

In mythic tales that existed long before the appearance of a movie or television screen, the hero pursued a quest, faced obstacles, and eventually triumphed over them to be reborn as a new and more fully integrated person (Campbell, 1949). The travels of Odysseus after the Trojan War are one such quest, eventually resulting in his return to his homeland. But even there, Odysseus had to fight to regain his wife from those who thought him dead and who had pursued Penelope as their own wife. The trial of stringing his own bow and shooting an arrow straight through the sockets of twelve ax heads in a row, a task that had kept his wife's many suitors at bay, led to victory over his enemies and the restoration of his home and family. The heroic formula, built upon myths such as these, continues to appear in our culture as movie after movie and program after program reenact the personal struggles and triumphs that we all face in life. As these types of stories and myths are universal themes, children can relate to these tales (Poling, 2001).

The hero uses aggression in an instrumental way, not a hostile way. His goal is to restore order, to fight for justice, to defeat evil and tyranny. While his (or more recently her) actions are aggressive, the motive is to protect, and the outcome is just. The moral intent of the hero raises an interesting question: if aggression involves hostile intent to hurt or harm others, is the hero aggressive? When do children understand the motives of the hero, making intent an important criterion for imitation? In what circumstances do children imitate the aggressive actions of heroes without the moral concern to protect others, and when does that understanding come to moderate aggressive effects?

In the hero's tale, there is also a dark force, the villain. It is that villain, or in Jung's conception the dark side of the shadow, that provides the countervailing force of the hero. So the white knight fights against dark evil forces (Calvert, 1999). In fiction, particularly children's television programs, the lines of good and evil are clearly marked. The good guys are good; the bad guys are evil. These plot lines simplify the plot comprehension skills that children must acquire to get the message. In adult programs, however, frequent commercial interruptions, particularly between the violent action and consequences, can impede children's understanding that the villain is punished for his dark deeds (Collins, 1973).

More recent depictions portray the hero as one who fights his or her own internal battle with their own shadow rather than the more simple external battle with the evil villain. Xena the Warrior Princess and Batman are two such heroes who fight with their own internal demons (Calvert et al., 2001; Zehnder, 2002). This more complex internal struggle, while more accurate, is also more difficult to understand. College students, for example, are more likely to advocate compassion and using your head before your sword as qualities of heroes, particularly for those characters who are perceived to be role models (Calvert et al., 2001; Zehnder, 2002). However, even high-school-aged adolescents struggle to understand why revenge is not an acceptable solution when a hero is dealt a major blow, such as the murder of his parents. In film and television depictions, true heroes never kill for revenge; to do so would take them into the dark realm of the destructive side of their shadow. It is the moral strength to walk away from revenge that uplifts the hero and that make him or her worthy as a role model.

Unlike television and film, aggressive video, computer, and online games focus little on plot or the moral struggles of the hero. The action is conveyed visually with almost no verbal or written dialogue, and when dialogue does appear, many children just click through it.

When the heroic tale is applied to video games, it is virtually stripped of any moral tone (Calvert, 1999). The story consists of beating, or even being, the bad guys. The movie *Crouching Tiger, Hidden Dragon*, for example, depicts a complex struggle that characters face between being heroes and falling prey to the dark side of their shadows; heroic characters use their minds and compassion, not brute force (Calvert et al., 2001). By contrast, in the video game based on this movie, all characters seek revenge against Jade Fox through sword play and other martial arts fighting skills (Connell, 2002), a direction that violates the richness of the original story theme and moral message.

At best, games are often amoral or retain a passing reference to the hero trying to save a damsel in distress. The focus on aggressive action, with little reference to motive beyond winning the game, probably undermines the potentially constructive parts of the mythic story that the game is based on: that good triumphs over evil. It is notable that video games now surpass movies as moneymakers in American culture (Ashdown, 2002), and that children's favorite games, particularly those of boys, are often violent action adventure games (Buchman & Funk, 1996; Children Now, 2001; Funk, Germann, & Buchman, 1997; Gailey, 1996; Gentile & Anderson, chapter 7, this volume).

In summary, the universal nature of the archetypes and the mythic tales associated with the tension between the hero and the shadow is one under-researched area that can help explain our fascination with action-adventure, heroic programs. There are clear developmental differences in children's skills at understanding the motives of the hero and the qualities that make a person a hero. There are also clear differences in how children understand the duality of human nature, our ongoing conflict to do the right thing rather than give in to our dark side. For Jung (1968), an important developmental task was to integrate our shadow into our personalities in constructive ways, as the shadow provides direction for a full-bodied life. This human struggle resonates with the audience: we want the hero to win just as we want ourselves to win over our darker impulses. The reduction of this formula to simple fight scenes, common in video games, encourages the aggressive action without the nuances of motive and internal struggle. It also provides a direct outlet for children to practice aggression, eliminating the step between observation and imitation (Calvert & Tan, 1994). Potential role models are provided to children, increasing the possibility that they will act aggressively, but how that aggression is manifested will depend on child characteristics, qualities that are also mediated by their level of cognitive development. For example, girls are less likely to imitate aggression than are boys (Lemish, 1988), and those who are old enough to understand the intent of the hero are less likely to imitate the aggression than are younger children (e.g., Liss, Reinhardt, & Fredriksen, 1983).

Heroic tales: Role models for children

The exciting and often engaging stories that children see in entertainment media provide numerous potential role models that can influence children's behavior. The concern with children's exposure to violent media is that they will be more likely to imitate the actions, be more tolerant of aggression and violence in their own lives, and see violence as a venue for solving problems (Murray, 1995).

Social cognitive theory provides the best fit for explaining why children become aggressive after viewing heroic, aggressive models, and why those effects are attenuated as they grow older. In social cognitive theory, attractive role models demonstrate power and nurturance (Bandura, 1997), the qualities of a hero (Calvert et al., 2001). Indeed, television violence has a greater impact on children's behavior when it is exhibited by heroes rather than by villains (Vooijs & van der Voort, 1993). Children do not usually admire the villain; they admire the hero.

Even young children can figure out who the hero and the villain are, in part by relying on visual features depicting the characters. For example, young children are able to understand who the "bad guys" are in cartoons by their crooked, jagged features (Acuff, 1997).

Because superheroes are the "good people" who fight the "bad people," it is not surprising that children and adolescents identify with them and tend to emulate their actions. In an experimental field study, Stein and Friedrich (1972) found that preschool children who were exposed to the *Batman* and *Superman* cartoons and not the prosocial program *Mister Rogers' Neighborhood* were found to be more physically active, both in the classroom and on the playground. They were also more likely to get into fights and scrapes with each other. They played roughly with toys, broke toys, snatched toys from others, and got into little altercations. Similarly, elementary-school-aged children who viewed *Mighty Morphin' Power Rangers* committed seven times more aggressive acts in a subsequent two-minute play period than did a control group (Boyatzis, Matillo, & Nesbitt, 1995).

The arousing aspects of aggressive heroic stories can lead to aggression compared to arousing aspects of competition. Molitor and Hirsch (1994), for example, showed fourth and fifth graders a clip of the *Karate Kid* versus an

Olympic competition scene (both were considered to be highly arousing). Children who viewed the *Karate Kid* took more time to intervene when they saw a video with two children, who were presumably in another room, becoming more aggressive with each other. Perhaps if the movie was shown in its entirety, rather than solely as an aggressive clip, children would understand the antiviolence message in the theme.

There is evidence, for example, that as children get older, they are able to understand the prosocial message in heroic portrayals even when it is combined with aggression. For example, Liss, Reinhardt, and Fredriksen (1983) found that kindergarteners who viewed an episode of *Superfriends* that contained prosocial acts combined with aggression were more hurtful than helpful in a subsequent game than were those who saw a prosocial program or a strictly aggressive program. To understand the effect of cognitive development on this finding, the authors then showed kindergarten, second grade, and fourth grade children either the prosocial program or the mixed message program. The kindergarteners were still more likely to hurt than to help, and they showed the least comprehension of the program content. However, the second and fourth grade boys exposed to the mixed prosocial/aggressive episode were more helpful than hurtful. Furthermore, the more the boys understood the story, the more helpful they were. This highlights the importance of story comprehension and understanding of intent as a mediator of children's tendencies toward aggression after viewing televised violence (Calvert, 1999). That is, while older children are less aggressive because they can understand the program content, the younger children are more aggressive because they don't understand the program message, perhaps imitating the aggressive heroic role models.

The social impact of game play on aggression, by contrast, may be more consistent across developmental periods because there is no moral plot to moderate the aggression. Preschoolers, for example, became more physically aggressive after playing *Space Invaders* or karate games (Schutte, Malouff, Post-Garden, & Rodasta, 1988; Silvern & Williamson, 1987). Similarly, adolescent college students who played a virtual reality game, *Dactyl Nightmare*, were more aroused and had more aggressive thoughts than did game observers or a control group who only simulated nonaggressive game movements (Calvert & Tan, 1994). Meta-analyses conducted on video game play supports the thesis that aggressive game play increases aggressive behavior, aggressive thoughts, aggressive affect, and physiological arousal for both adults and children (Anderson, 2002; Anderson & Bushman, 2001).

Slapstick Violence: Animated Cartoons

According to uses and gratification theory, a central reason that children use media is to be entertained (Rubin, 1994). Children consider humor to be one of the most important elements in successful television programming designed for them (Valkenburg & Janssen, 1999).

Humor is often paired with violent and antisocial content in children's television programs, particularly children's cartoons. Humor/slapstick types of programs, which focus on visual humor such as slipping on a banana peel and falling, contain approximately 29 acts of violence per hour, with almost 30 percent of the total program time devoted to physical aggression (Wilson et al., 2002). Slapstick comedies are dominated by anthropomorphized perpetrators. Such programs contain unrealistic portrayals of harm with the victim getting up and going on as if nothing has happened.

Humor has been conceptualized in a few different ways by communication scholars, but one of the most common definitions describes humor as occurring in situations where we are made to feel superior to others because of some display of inadequacy or ineptitude on the part of another (McGhee & Lloyd, 1981). According to Zillmann (2000), contemporary media humor often occurs in the presence of put-downs, insults, and downright humiliations. Humor, therefore, is present in situations where someone is debased. This type of humor is generally known as *superiority or dispositional humor* (McGhee & Lloyd, 1981) and it is antisocial by nature.

According to Freud, however, people become amused when innocuous displays are paired with dispositional or hostile type of displays. It is not socially acceptable to find purely hostile acts or statements funny. The innocuous aspect of the humorous display masks some of the aggressive aspects of the situation and allows people to feel free to laugh and find merriment (Zillman, 2000). Freud also suggests that as people become aware of the socially unacceptable themes that underlie the humor, they find such humor less funny. Guilt is aroused if they find themselves laughing at something that is truly hostile, but much of the time people do not fully know exactly why they are laughing (Gollob & Levine, 1967).

Young children, in particular, do not understand dispositional humor, as it relies heavily on verbal skills and abstract thinking skills. Preschool children, for example, have difficulty understanding joke resolutions and verbal ambiguities (Schultz & Horibe, 1974; Schultz & Pilon, 1973; Spector, 1996). Because young children are attracted to the visually salient aspects of humor, slapstick humor may have the most impact on them. Slapstick humor often contains visual depictions of aggression that children can imitate (e.g., poking someone in the eyes or bonking them on the head). As children age, however, they perceive humor more as a psychological characteristic than as a behavioral one (Warnars-Kleverlann, Oppenheimer, & Sherman, 1996).

There are also gender differences in children's reactions to humor. Humorous elements disrupted third to fifth grade boys' understanding of main story themes, but no such effect was found for girls of the same age (Weiss

& Wilson, 1998). This implies that the boys may focus on humorous elements of programs more than girls do. Interestingly, boys' assessments of the funniness of dispositional humor is higher when the victim is a person the child does not like or feels unrelated to. This is not consistently found with girls (McGhee & Lloyd, 1981). When both boys and girls were asked to think about the victims' feelings in a violent cartoon portrayal, they found the cartoon to be less funny than did those who were not asked to think about the victim (Nathanson & Cantor, 2000). These findings point to the incompatibility of cruelty and empathy, making empathy an important moderator of potentially aggressive media outcomes.

While some argue that the cathartic nature of humor would diffuse concurrent aggression, the evidence indicates that aggressive humor does lead to aggressive tendencies more so than neutral humor (Berkowitz, 1970). Perhaps because the violent portrayals in slapstick types of programs seem like they are all in good fun, violence may not be perceived as harmful because nothing truly bad happens to the characters. Indeed, there is often a gap between what the research community has considered "violent" and, hence, worrisome and what public perception considers violent. Potter (1999; also chapter 13, this volume) notes that there is a definitional discrepancy that often leads to lesser acceptance by the general public of researchers' concern over the portrayals of certain kinds of violence. Despite the fact that there are disagreements over definitions of violence, humorous aggression does influence children's behavior. Preschool children who were exposed to a violent slapstick *Road Runner* cartoon, for example, became more aggressive afterward compared to those who had not been exposed to the cartoon (Silvern & Williamson, 1987).

Slapstick humor remains amusing to children, even at older ages. For example, second through sixth grade boys developed greater pro-violence attitudes after viewing a *Woody Woodpecker* cartoon compared to children who had not been exposed to the cartoon (Nathanson & Cantor, 2000).

One popular type of program that elementary-school-aged children view is professional wrestling. Although wrestling may not be considered slapstick in the same sense as humorous cartoons, it contains characters doing outrageous and silly things to each other. Lemish (1998) interviewed children in Israel about their viewing of the World Wrestling Federation (WWF) programs. Ten percent of the girls said that they imitated WWF fights frequently or occasionally during the current year, whereas 23 percent of the boys reported having done so. Boys' descriptions of the type of wrestling behaviors they performed at school were detailed and vivid. Girls hardly ever mentioned fighting at school, but some of them told stories of how they acted out wrestling behaviors at home. Because aggression is rewarded for boys more so than girls, the findings are consistent with the modeling and imitation effects of social cognitive theory.

Real Violence: The News

Studies utilizing uses and gratification theory as a framework also document that we seek informational needs through media exposure. At no stage during childhood or adolescence, however, does the news become a favorite content-type of children. However, children are greatly exposed to the news, probably due to secondary exposure when their parents are viewing it. For example, in a national poll (Children Now, 1994), 65 percent of the adolescents surveyed said that they had viewed television news the day before. Even very young children, who probably do not understand much of the content, are routinely exposed to the news. Smith (2002) found that almost one-third of the kindergartners through sixth graders she interviewed reported watching television news "every day" or "most days" of the week.

Developmental differences have been found in children's reaction to local stories compared to more distal news stories (Smith & Wilson, 2002). Older children exposed to local versions of crime stories reported more worry than those who were exposed to nonlocal versions of the same stories. Furthermore, older more than younger children exhibited more facial fear during the local as opposed to nonlocal version of crime stories. The results show that older children are more likely to understand, as well as be frightened by, television news than are younger children, probably because they are more likely to understand that the events are real and presumably can happen to them since the violence occurred near them.

Children are also exposed to, and sometimes seriously disturbed by, national tragedies via the news. Pfefferbaum et al. (2001) found that middle-school children's viewing of bomb-related television in the aftermath of the Oklahoma City disaster was extensive. Approximately two-thirds of the sample said most or all of their television viewing in the aftermath of the bombing was bomb related. Children's television exposure to the events was associated with post-traumatic stress seven weeks after the attack. Among children with no direct physical or emotional exposure, the degree of television exposure was directly related to post-traumatic stress symptomatology. Traumatic memories may persist in an active state because of the intrusion of distressing memories about the events and the arousal engendered by thinking about that negative experience (Pynoos & Nader, 1989). Other studies of media exposure to disasters, such as the explosion of the Challenger shuttle (Wright, Kunkel, Pinon, & Huston, 1989), and the 1979 radiation warning, industrial disasters, and earthquakes (Breton, Valla, & Lambert, 1993; Handford et al. 1986) all suggest that post-traumatic stress symptoms and other types of psychological disturbances are common among children, even if they are not directly affected by the traumatic event (Nader, Pynoos, Fairbanks, Al-Ajeel, & Al-Asfour, 1993). The implication is that television viewing may cultivate and maintain stressful states in children even when other forms of exposure are absent.

In light of the events of September 11 and the world events that have followed, we expect that children and adolescents were exposed to a tremendous amount of footage containing violent imagery, particularly the destruction of the World Trade Center and the Pentagon. Children's emotional responses to television programs suggest that young children are most affected by visual portrayals while older children are most affected by psychological factors (Valkenburg, Cantor, & Peeters, 2000). Because war and destruction images are highly visually salient, war and attacks are then expected to shock and scare children. Many children were seriously traumatized after viewing the September 11 attack, just as adults were (Gershoff, Aber, & Kotler, 2003).

Interestingly, much of the war against terrorism is depicted as a war pitting good against evil, with the president using political rhetoric such as the "evil-doers" and the "axis of evil" in his speeches (Poling, 2001; Schneider, 2002). In so doing, he calls up archetypal images of the hero and the shadow in the audience.

We also know that adolescents use the Internet to read the news and to learn about local events (Subramanyam, Greenfield, Kraut, & Gross, 2001). However, little is currently known about how this online exposure affects them.

Online Hate Speech

A final need that media can provide for people is an opportunity to express their darkest feelings. The Internet provides the opportunity for anonymous interactions with others, some of which are potentially destructive (Wallace, 1999). Finkelhor, Mitchell, and Wolak (2000) found that about one out of five 10- to 17-year-olds who use the Internet regularly were exposed to unwanted solicitations or approaches, mostly in the form of sexual advances. Approximately 25 percent of those who were exposed to such advances were highly disturbed by them.

Another example of a new violent outlet that has emerged is online hate speech. Examples of online racial bigotry and hate speech have been documented (Greenfield, 2000), disproving the prediction that the Internet would remove racial adversity because of the lack of embodied persons. Similarly, some people attack other characters online with little consequences to them for their antisocial actions. Cyber-rape has been reported online (Wallace, 1999). For example, one online character took control of another person's character and raped her (Turkle, 1995). What kind of consequences can prevent such violent acts when the actor can simply disappear and return as a different online character, thereby escaping punishment for antisocial actions?

Some children have worked through their aggressive altercations with the support of their collective groups. For example, Cassell (2002) brought children together in an online forum and an online argument ensued, with hateful speech taking place between an Israeli child and a Palestinian child. Other group members eventually intervened, resulting in more mutual understanding between the two children. Others, however, may not fare nearly as well, particularly when they are in anonymous, unsupervised settings.

CONCLUSIONS

Justice restoration, humor, and information seeking seem to be the underlying themes of the programs containing violence that children view the most. Such themes may also be the reasons that children are drawn to programs that contain violence. Underlying each of these themes is the idea that children want good things to happen to good people and for the bad people to get their just desserts. It is the struggle of the hero versus the shadow that seems to be pervasive in programs for children and that reflects children's own struggle to form their own identities.

Children's skills at understanding these messages, however, develop over time. For young and immature children, particularly those with little conscience, the temptation to imitate effective aggressive strategies may result in antisocial activity. However, older and emotionally mature children who have developed a sense of empathy are less affected by the dark portrayals. Instead, they look for compassionate, heroic role models who have a sense of conscience, suggesting that they are able to moderate aggressive effects. Based on the literature, we think that 9- to 10-year-olds initially begin to understand the motives and intents of characters reasonably well, thereby potentially moderating the effects of aggressive television exposure. These same cognitive skills, however, bring with them an appreciation of humorous messages that demean and humiliate others, a popular kind of content among developing youth, and they can be frightened by news messages that bring violent current events into their homes and that they now understand are real rather than fictional.

Newer media, particularly violent video games, strip the moral message from heroic television or film content. Playing with aggressive video game content poses potentially harmful effects on children due to its interactive nature, where actions can be directly incorporated into the behavioral repertoire. For children who are at risk, game play can undermine the development of empathy and moral development (Funk, 2002). In particular, acting in antisocial, aggressive ways in game play can impede empathic skill development where children take the perspective of another, a potential moderator of real-life aggressive actions. Playing video games where children can assume the identity of the villain poses a special threat to the developing character of our youth. Online forums provide yet another avenue for people to act with impunity on their dark impulses via hate speech and antisocial symbolic actions.

The struggle of good over evil is a recurring media theme, one that touches the very hearts and souls of all human beings because it is a struggle that we all face. Helping children to construct images and themes in ways that encourage heroic, compassionate youth are goals worthy of pursuit, ones that a free society cannot ignore. Many heroes stepped forward to rescue and protect our people after the attack on America on September 11, 2001. The internal struggles that our youth face to make the right moral decisions should be supported by our society and by our media. The main task, as we perceive it, is to be sensitive to how children of different ages perceive and understand these messages, and to begin to emphasize the compassionate and thinking aspects of heroism rather than the aggression.

NOTE

1. Sandra Calvert thanks the National Science Foundation (Sponsor Award #BCS-0126014) for their financial support of the Children's Digital Media Center.

CHAPTER 10

Media and Fear in Children and Adolescents

Joanne Cantor

> When I was seven years old, I watched (although it felt like I witnessed) *Friday the Thirteenth, Part 2*. My family didn't have cable television or any movie channels but my friend Mark's family did. One day, just he and I watched Jason Voorhees chop up and mutilate a camp full of oversexed teenagers. I hadn't seen an R-rated movie before this gruesome experience. It blew me away. I stayed for the entirety of the film because I didn't want Mark to think I was a "wussy," and I was also morbidly fascinated by something I'd never been exposed to. After viewing the film, I had nightmares for weeks. I would even lie awake at night (with all the lights on) wondering how long it would take Jason and his twenty-inch blade to find me!
>
> (Cantor, 1998, pp. 34–35)

The preceding quote is from a first-person report by a college student,[1] and it is typical of responses that children and adolescents commonly experience from watching media violence. Yet, media-induced fear and its attendant lingering effects have not received nearly the public attention that the aggression-promoting effects of media violence have. This is not because it is a newly discovered problem. As early as 1917, the following observations appeared in a report of the Cinema Commission of Inquiry established by the National Council of Public Morals in London, England:

> My chief objection to the films is that they make children, whose thoughts should be happy and wholesome, familiar with ideas of death by exhibiting shootings, stabbings, and the like. Nor are these death scenes merely brief incidents in the stories, for where a character is represented to be mortally wounded[,] the story pauses while the children

are shown an enlarged view of the victim's features during the death and agony. Owing to this deliberate emphasis of the repulsiveness of such situations, it is difficult to see how the child's nerves can maintain their tone; we should look for a want of balance in children subjected repeatedly to these ordeals, and thence delinquency would not be unlikely. At any rate, such exhibitions are highly objectionable for children, whether they lead to delinquency or not. (Leeson, 1917, p. 187)

By the 1930s in the United States, researchers had begun to look at media-induced fear systematically. Blumer (1933) reported that 93 percent of the children in a study he conducted said they had been frightened or horrified by a motion picture. Other researchers in the 1930s and 1940s also noted the prevalence of children's fright reactions to movies and to radio crime dramas (Eisenberg, 1936; Preston, 1941). But as television took hold in the 1950s and 1960s, more attention was paid to the role this new medium might be playing in the increasing levels of violence in society than in its stimulation of children's fears.

Interest in media and fear seems to have reemerged in the 1970s, as highly popular movies were becoming increasingly graphic and full of horror. For example, *The Exorcist* (1973), a supernatural thriller about the demonic possession of a young girl, was reported to be causing *even men* (!) to faint or vomit, and *Jaws* (1975), a blockbuster movie about a killer shark, was reported to have ruined many vacations at the seashore. Adults were considered to be on their own, but there was increasing concern about children's responses. In the mid-1980s, the reactions of children (and angry parents) to intense scenes in *Indiana Jones and the Temple of Doom* (1984), a violent action-adventure movie, and *Gremlins* (1984), a comic horror story about adorable pets that transform into vicious killers, led the Motion Picture Association of America to add PG-13 ("Parents Strongly Cautioned") to its rating system (Zoglin, 1984).

Psychiatric case studies of acute and disabling anxiety states precipitated by movies have been reported sporadically over the years (Buzzuto, 1975; Mathai, 1983; Simons & Silveira, 1994), but researchers again began systematically studying fright reactions to media in the 1980s. Johnson (1980) asked a random sample of adults whether they had ever seen a motion picture that had disturbed them "a great deal." Forty percent said they had, and the median length of the reported disturbance was three days. Respondents also reported on the type, intensity, and duration of symptoms such as nervousness, depression, fear of specific things, and recurring thoughts and images. Based on these reports, Johnson judged that 48 percent of these respondents (19 percent of the total sample) had experienced what he termed a "significant stress reaction" for at least two days as the result of watching a movie. Johnson argued, "It is one thing to walk away from a frightening or disturbing event with mild residue of the images and quite another thing to ruminate about it, feel anxious or depressed for days, and/or to avoid anything that might create the same unpleasant experience" (Johnson, 1980, p. 786). On the basis of his data, Johnson concluded that fright reactions were more prevalent and more severe than had previously been assumed.

In the mid-1980s, Barbara J. Wilson and her associates (Wilson, Hoffner, & Cantor, 1987) surveyed preschool and elementary school children in Wisconsin and Pennsylvania and noted that 75 percent of the children questioned reported having been scared by something they had seen on TV or in a movie. In the 1990s, Cantor and Nathanson (1996) conducted a random survey of parents of elementary school children in Madison, Wisconsin, and reported that 43 percent of the sample said that their child had experienced enduring TV-induced fright. Gentile and Walsh (2002) conducted the first national random survey on this topic and noted that 62 percent of parents reported that their child had become scared by something he or she had seen on television or in a movie.

Recent correlational studies have shown that watching television is related to the occurrence of both anxiety and sleep disturbances. A survey of elementary and middle school children reported that the more television a child watched, the more likely he or she was to report the symptoms of anxiety, depression, and post-traumatic stress (Singer, Slovak, Frierson, & York, 1998). Similarly, a survey of elementary school children reported that the more television a child watched (especially at bedtime), the higher the rate of reported sleep disturbances, such as nightmares, difficulty falling asleep, and the inability to sleep through the night (Owens et al., 1999).

Research involving retrospective reports by college students provides powerful evidence of the prevalence and severity of the problem of media-induced fear. Harrison and Cantor (1999) offered college students at two universities extra course credit for filling out a questionnaire. The initial question read as follows: "Have you ever seen a television show or movie that frightened or disturbed you so much that the emotional effect endured after the program or movie was over?" Respondents could reply "yes" or "no." If they said "no," that's all they had to do. But if they said "yes," they were required to write a paper about the experience and to fill out a three-page questionnaire. Either way, respondents received the same amount of extra credit.

In spite of the fact that the procedure made it a great deal easier to say "no" than "yes," 90 percent of the respondents said "yes," and most went on to describe intensely negative emotional experiences, similar to the one that was described in the excerpt at the beginning of this chapter. More than half of the respondents (52 percent) reported disturbances in eating or sleeping, 35 percent said they had become anxious about or avoided situations similar to those depicted in the program or movie, and 22 percent reported difficulty getting the images or events they had seen off their mind. The most striking findings relate to the duration of these responses: 35 percent of the respondents said that these effects had endured a year or more, and 26 percent said that these responses were still with them at the time the survey was taken.

Given that the average age at exposure was 14 and the average age of the respondents was close to 21, these effects had been lingering for an average of more than six years. The following excerpt of one student's account from this study is typical of these enduring responses:

After the movie [*Jaws*], I had nightmares for a week straight. Always the same one. I'm in a room filled with water with ducts in the walls. They would suddenly open and dozens of sharks would swim out. I felt trapped with no place to go. I would usually wake up in a sweat. Occasionally I'll still have that exact same dream. The movie didn't just affect me at night. To this day I'm afraid to go into the ocean, sometimes even a lake. I'm afraid there will be a shark even if I know deep down that's impossible. (Cantor, 1998, pp. 9–10)

Richard J. Harris and his associates also conducted a series of retrospective studies and reported similar results regarding the prevalence and intensity of media-induced fright reactions (Harris et al., 2000; Hoekstra, Harris, & Helmick, 1999). In these studies, intense reactions and lingering effects, such as general anxiety, "wild imagination," and fear of sleeping alone, were commonly observed.

In summary, research shows that media-induced fright reactions are quite common. A substantial proportion of children experience lingering effects that disturb their sleep and interfere with a variety of normal, healthy activities.

WHAT TYPES OF MEDIA IMAGES INDUCE FRIGHT REACTIONS?

It should come as no surprise that violence or the threat of violence is the most prominent feature of television programs and movies that produce fear (Cantor & Wilson, 1988). In fact, it is difficult to conceive of a horror movie that does not focus on the threat of violence. As has been argued elsewhere (Cantor, 2002), fear is the natural response to perceived physical threat, and it is reasonable to expect that viewers respond with fear to threats depicted in the media through a process of stimulus generalization (see Pavlov, 1927). In other words, events that would produce fear if encountered in the real world produce similar but less intense reactions if encountered in the media. Two categories of real-world stimuli that typically cause fear and that are prominent in fear-evoking media are the display of dangers and injuries and the depiction of fearful or endangered people (see Cantor, 2002, for a more extensive discussion). Violent encounters and other things that are considered dangerous, such as vicious animals, natural disasters, and ghastly diseases, naturally cause fear. The sight of injuries or other people who are in danger or fearful should also be frightening because the presence of others who are injured or in danger often suggests that those in the vicinity are in danger as well. Even when viewers know they are not in immediate danger, the mediated depiction of these images is often frightening.

A third category of fear-evoking stimuli has been termed *distortions of natural forms* (see Cantor, 2002). These consist of injuries and mutilations as well as bodily distortions that occur in nature, as in dwarves, giants, hunchbacks, and mutants. Injured and deformed realistic characters are prominent in scary movies and television shows, as are weird-looking supernatural and fantasy creatures, like monsters, witches, vampires, and ghosts. Often in television programs and movies, distorted creatures are depicted as evil and violent. However, as will be seen in the next section, even when such creatures are kind and benevolent, they often produce fear anyway, especially in young children. It is possible that certain types of physical distortions implicitly convey a sense of danger or impending threat (Cantor, 1998).

What frightens a particular child is no doubt a function of many individual factors, including temperament, real-world experience, and concurrent events in the child's life. In addition to these idiosyncratic factors, research has determined that the viewer's chronological age and, to a lesser extent, biological gender are important determinants of the source and intensity of media-induced fears. The next two sections summarize the major findings related to age and gender differences in fright responses to media. (See Table 10.1.)

Developmental Differences in What Frightens Children in the Media

Children of different ages tend to fear different things (see Cantor, Wilson, & Hoffner, 1986, for a review). According to a variety of studies of fears in general, children up to eight years of age are frightened primarily by animals; the dark; supernatural beings, such as ghosts, monsters, and witches; and by anything that looks strange or moves suddenly. The fears of 9- to 12-year-olds are more often related to personal injury and physical destruction and the injury and death of family members. Adolescents continue to fear personal injury and physical destruction, but school fears and social fears arise at this age, as do fears regarding political, economic, and global issues.

A large body of research has examined the types of mass media stimuli and events that frighten children at different ages. Experiments and surveys have been conducted to test expectations based on theories and findings in cognitive development. The experiments have the advantage of testing rigorously controlled variations in program content and viewing conditions, using a combination of self-reports, physiological responses, the coding of facial expressions of emotion, and behavioral measures. For ethical reasons, only small excerpts of relatively mild television shows and movies are used in experiments. In contrast, the surveys investigate the responses of children who have been exposed to a particular mass media offering in their natural environment, without any researcher intervention. Although less tightly controlled, the

Table 10.1
Developmental Differences in Media Stimuli That Frighten Children

Approximate Age Group Characteristics	Typically Frightening Stimuli
Up to 8 Years: Perceptual dependence; inability to fully grasp fantasy-reality distinction	- Threatening visual images, real or not, including vicious animals and grotesque, mutilated, or deformed characters (can be cartoon or live-action images) -Physical transformations of characters -Natural disasters, shown vividly - Visual images of devastation or traumatized victims - Sudden loud or eerie noises
8–12 Years: Grasp of fantasy-reality distinction; limited capabilities for abstract thought	- Realistic threats and dangers, especially things that can happen to children -Violence or the threat of violence -Victimization of children
13 Years and Older: Grasp of fantasy-reality distinction and abstract reasoning; awareness of world issues; ambiguity about supernatural forces	- Realistic physical harm or threats of intense harm - Molestation, sexual assault, and stalking - Threats from aliens, demonic possession, or supernatural powers - Global threats

surveys permit the study of responses to much more intensely frightening media fare and can involve explorations of effects of longer duration.

The findings regarding the media stimuli that frighten children at different ages are consistent with observed changes in children's fears in general. This section summarizes broad generalizations and supportive findings.

The importance of appearance

Research on cognitive development indicates that, in general, very young children react to stimuli predominantly in terms of their perceptible characteristics and that with increasing maturity, they respond more and more to the conceptual aspects of stimuli (see Flavell, 1963; Melkman, Tversky, & Baratz, 1981). Research findings support the generalization that the impact of appearance in frightening media decreases as the child's age increases. In other words, preschool children (up to the age of about six years) are more likely to be frightened by something that looks scary but is actually harmless than by something that looks attractive but is actually harmful; for older elementary school children (approximately 9 to 11 years), appearance carries much less weight, relative to the behavior or destructive potential of a character, animal, or object.

This generalization is supported by a survey conducted in 1981 (Cantor & Sparks, 1984), in which parents were asked to name the programs and movies that had frightened their children the most. In this survey, parents of preschool children most often mentioned offerings with grotesque-looking characters, such as the television series *The Incredible Hulk* and the feature film *The Wizard of Oz;* parents of older elementary school children more often mentioned programs or movies (like *The Amityville Horror*) that involved threats without a strong visual component, and that required imagination to comprehend. Sparks (1986) replicated this study, using children's self-reports rather than parents' observations, and obtained similar findings. Both surveys included controls for possible differences in exposure patterns in the different age groups.

Another study supporting a similar conclusion explored children's reactions to excerpts from *The Incredible Hulk* (Sparks & Cantor, 1986). (Although this program, about a man who transforms into a grotesque superhero to perform good deeds, was not intended to be scary, Cantor and Sparks's (1984) survey reported that it was named by 40 percent of the parents of preschoolers as a show that had scared their child.) When children were shown a shortened episode of the *Hulk* program and were asked how they had felt during different scenes, preschool children reported the most fear after the attractive, mild-mannered hero had transformed into the monstrous-looking Hulk. Older elementary school children, in contrast, reported the least fear at this time, because they understood that the Hulk was really the benevolent hero in another physical form, and that he was using his superhuman powers to rescue a character who was in danger. Preschool children's unexpectedly intense reactions to this program seem to have been partially due to their overresponse to the visual image of the Hulk character and their inability to look beyond his appearance and appreciate his benevolent behavior.

Hoffner and Cantor (1985) tested the effect of appearance more directly, by creating a story in four versions, so that a major character was either attractive and grandmotherly looking or ugly and grotesque. The character's appearance was factorially varied with her behavior—she was depicted as behaving either kindly or cruelly. Figure 10.1 illustrates this manipulation, using one frame from the same moment in each of the four versions. In judging how nice or mean the character was and in predicting what she would do in the subsequent scene, preschool children were more influenced than older children (6–7 and 9–10 years) by the character's looks and less influenced by her kind or cruel behavior. As the age of the child increased, the character's looks became less important and her behavior carried increasing weight. A follow-up experiment revealed that in the absence of information about the

Figure 10.1
Illustration of Manipulation of Character's Appearance and Behavior—Conditions Are (clockwise from upper left): Attractive Kind; Ugly Kind; Ugly Cruel; Attractive Cruel

Source: Reprinted from Hoffner, C., & Cantor, J. (1985). Developmental differences in responses to a television character's appearance and behavior. *Developmental Psychology, 21,* 1065–1074. Copyright American Psychological Association.

character's behavior, children in all age groups engaged in physical-appearance stereotyping, that is, they thought that the ugly woman would be mean and the attractive woman would be nice.

Harrison and Cantor's (1999) retrospective study of fright responses to media also provided evidence of the diminishing influence of appearance. When students' descriptions of the program or movie that had frightened them were categorized as to whether they involved immediately perceptible stimuli (e.g., monstrous-looking characters, eerie noises), the percentage of respondents whose described scene fell into this category declined as the student's age at the time of the incident increased.

Responses to fantasy content

The data on trends in children's fears in general suggest that very young children are more likely than older children and adolescents to fear things that are not real, in the sense that their occurrence in the real world is impossible (e.g., monsters). The development of more "mature" fears seems to require the acquisition of knowledge regarding the objective dangers posed by different situations. One important component of this knowledge includes an understanding of the distinction between reality and fantasy, a competence that develops only gradually throughout childhood (see Flavell, 1963; Kelly, 1981; Morison & Gardner, 1978).

Research shows that as children mature cognitively, they become less responsive to fantastic dangers and more responsive to realistic threats depicted in the media. In Cantor and Sparks's (1984) survey of what had frightened children, the parent's tendency to name fantasy offerings, depicting events that could not possibly occur in the real world, decreased as the child's age increased, and the tendency to mention fictional offerings, depicting events that could possibly occur, increased. Sparks (1986) replicated these findings using children's self-reports. Further support comes from a study of children's fright responses to television news (Cantor & Nathanson, 1996). A survey of parents of children in kindergarten and second, fourth, and sixth grades in Wisconsin showed that the percentage of children frightened by fantasy programs decreased as the child's grade increased, whereas the percentage frightened by news stories increased with age. Valkenburg, Cantor, and Peeters (2000), in a random survey of children in the Netherlands, also found a decrease between the ages of 7 and 12 in fright responses to fantasy content. The following anecdote is typical of young children's responses to blatantly unrealistic content:

An example that I will never forget is when I watched the movie *Pinocchio*. I saw this movie with my mother when I was about four or five years old. I really thought that what was happening in the movie was real. In the movie, if a child misbehaved, he or she was turned into a donkey. Also, if a child lied, their nose would grow. I really believed that this would happen to me if I was bad. I remember being extremely scared even a few weeks after I had seen the movie because I thought that the same thing would happen to me if I misbehaved. (Cantor, 1998, p. 89)

Although fright reactions to overtly fantastic content decline with age, retrospective reports reveal that certain types of fantasy stories—those that involve the supernatural—retain their ability to frighten viewers through the teen years and beyond (see Cantor, 1998). Supernatural themes seem to occupy an ambiguous border between fantasy and realistic fiction. Even when people become aware of the difference between what is real and what is make-believe, they often have ambivalent feelings about the veracity of stories involving demonic possession (e.g., *The Exorcist*) or attacks by alien invaders or individuals with supernatural powers (e.g., *Alien, Nightmare on Elm Street, The Blair Witch Project*). The mass media often amplify this ambiguity by featuring purportedly true instances of supernatural forces and demonic possession. The following student's experience illustrates this process:

The film I viewed was *The Exorcist*. It contained graphic scenes of a young girl possessed by the devil. I was approximately 12 years old at the time and was in a slumber-party situation. I vividly remember the stress this film caused me. I was not only extremely afraid of the devil and evil, but I became obsessed with the possibility of becoming possessed myself. To make matters worse, later on in the same week I came home from school and turned on some afternoon talk show with the subject matter consisting of "real" stories of "real" people who were at one time possessed. That program and the movie were enough to keep me from sleeping for two nights straight and finally when I did fall asleep I had terrible nightmares. I slept with my parents for the next few weeks. (Cantor, 1998, pp. 109–110)

Responses to abstract threats

Theories and findings in cognitive development show that the ability to think abstractly emerges relatively late in cognitive development (e.g., Flavell, 1963). This generalization is consistent with the general sources of children's fears, cited earlier. Similarly, as children mature, they become frightened by media depictions involving increasingly abstract concepts.

Data supporting this generalization come from a survey of children's responses to the television movie *The Day After* (Cantor, Wilson, & Hoffner, 1986). Although many people were concerned about young children's reactions to this movie, which depicted the devastation of a Kansas community by a nuclear attack (Schofield & Pavelchak, 1985), developmental considerations led to the prediction that the youngest children would be the least affected by it. In a random telephone survey of parents, conducted the night after the broadcast of this movie, children under 12 were reportedly much less disturbed by the film than were teenagers, and parents were the most disturbed. The very youngest children were the least frightened. The findings seem to be due to the fact that the emotional impact of the film comes from the contemplation of the potential annihilation of the earth as we know it— a concept that is beyond the grasp of the young child. The visual depictions of injury in the movie were quite mild compared to the enormity of the consequences implied by the plot.

Gender Differences in Media-Induced Fright Responses

Although research on developmental differences has focused on the stimuli that evoke fear at different ages, research on gender differences has explored whether females are more frightened by media than males in general, independent of the media content. There is a common stereotype that girls are more easily frightened than boys (Birnbaum & Croll, 1984; Cantor, Stutman, & Duran, 1996), and indeed that females in general are more emotional than males (e.g., Fabes & Martin, 1991; Grossman & Wood, 1993). A good deal of research would seem to support this contention with regard to responses to scary media, although the gender differences may be weaker than they appear at first glance. Moreover, the observed differences seem to be partially attributable to socialization pressures on girls to express their fears and on boys to inhibit them.

Peck (1999) conducted a meta-analysis of the studies of media-induced fear that were produced between 1987 and 1996. Her analysis, which included 59 studies that permitted a comparison between males and females, reported a moderate gender-difference effect size ($d = 0.41$), with females exhibiting more fear than males. Females' responses were more intense than those of males for all dependent measures. However, the effect sizes were largest for self-report and behavioral measures (those that are arguably under the most conscious control) and smallest for heart rate and facial expressions. In addition, the effect size for gender differences increased with age, consistent with the notion that gender-role pressures mount as children get older (e.g., Crouter, Manke, & McHale, 1995).

Peck (1999) also conducted an experiment in which male and female college students were exposed to two movie scenes from the *Nightmare on Elm Street* series, one featuring a male victim and the other featuring a female victim. She found that women's self-reports of fear were more intense than those of males, especially when the victim was female. However, when the victim was male, some of the physiological responses (pulse amplitude and hemispheric asymmetry) suggested that men were experiencing more intense physiological reactions than women.

More research is needed to explore the extent of gender differences in media-induced fear and the factors that contribute to them. However, these findings suggest that the size of the gender difference may be partially a function of social pressures to conform to gender-appropriate behavior.

FRIGHT RESPONSES TO NEWS COVERAGE

Although research shows that fear reactions to the news generally increase with age (Cantor & Nathanson, 1996; Smith & Wilson, 2002), no one at any age is immune to the effects of horrific news stories. For young children, who are not adept at distinguishing fantasy from reality, news reports are no more likely to be frightening than reports of things that cannot possibly happen. Young children may be less frequently frightened by the news because news stories are usually not as visually spectacular as fantasy stories. But certain types of news stories do frighten young children, especially if they vividly depict dangers, injuries, and terrorized victims. For example, Cantor and Nathanson's (1996) survey reported that 58 percent of the kindergarteners whose parents said they were frightened by a news report were scared by coverage of natural disasters. Among sixth graders, this proportion was only 7 percent. Older children who were frightened by the news were more likely to be frightened by violent crime (55 percent versus 11 percent of kindergarteners). Smith and Wilson (2002) reported similar developmental differences when interviewing children directly. Although images of ongoing disasters are frequently shown on the news, interpersonal crimes of violence are less frequently caught on camera and are more likely to be described verbally than to be shown visually.

A study of children's reactions to television coverage of the war in the Persian Gulf showed that children of all ages may be affected by intense news stories, but that different ages typically react to different elements of the coverage (Cantor, Mares, & Oliver, 1993). A random survey of parents of children in public school in Madison, Wisconsin, conducted shortly after the Gulf War, reported that 45 percent of children were observed to have been frightened by television coverage of the war, and there were no significant differences between first, fourth, seventh, and eleventh graders in the prevalence or intensity of negative emotional reactions. However, children in different grades were upset by different aspects of the coverage. In their descriptions of the elements that had disturbed their child the most, parents of younger children, but not of adolescents, stressed the visual aspects of the coverage and the direct, concrete consequences of combat (e.g., the missiles exploding). As the child's age increased, the more abstract, conceptual aspects of the coverage (e.g., the possibility of the conflict spreading) were cited by parents as the most disturbing.

The terrorist hijacking-murders of September 11, 2001, frightened and upset people of all ages (see Schuster et al., 2001), and recent research shows that the degree of exposure to 9/11 (e.g., proximity to attack sites, contact with someone in the buildings, watching the events live on TV) was a strong predictor of emotional distress (Silver, 2002). Although research on the effects of 9/11 news coverage on children is only beginning to appear, there is little doubt that many children were profoundly affected by exposure to the coverage of these events.

Stacy Smith and her collaborators (Smith, Moyer, Boyson, & Pieper, 2002) conducted a random survey of parents of children between the ages of 5 and 17 in Ingham County, Michigan, during the week following the attacks (September 13–18, 2001). These researchers reported that almost all of the children (87 percent) were exposed to news coverage of the events of September 11 on that day and the days immediately afterward. Moreover, 60 percent of the children were said to have experienced fear and 25 percent were said to exhibit "behavioral upsets" (sleep disturbances, nightmares, eating difficulties, or anxiety attacks). As expected from prior research on developmental differences, both exposure to the news and the prevalence and intensity of fear increased as the age of the child increased. Although a child's amount of news exposure did not correlate with the parent's report of the child's level of fear per se, exposure to the news in the days following September 11 did predict children's concerns for their own personal safety and their worries about flying in airplanes. These relationships held even after statistical controls for age and gender were applied.

A study of the longer-term responses of children in New York City schools (Applied Research and Consulting et al., 2002) reported a broad range of mental health problems six months after the 9/11 attacks, including agoraphobia (15 percent), separation anxiety (12 percent), and post-traumatic stress disorder (11 percent). Although children in New York learned about these events from a variety of sources, including, in some cases, direct eyewitness exposure, the survey showed that 62 percent of the children said they had spent "a lot" of time learning about the attack from TV. Moreover, children who reported heavy exposure to the news coverage had higher rates of post-traumatic stress disorder than children with less television exposure. This was true for children living near "ground zero" as well as for those inhabiting the rest of New York City.

The intense reactions of children to coverage of catastrophic news events may have surprised some parents. Many parents do not think of the news when they worry about the effects of the media on their children. However, it is clear that children are often affected by the news, even if they do not seem to be watching it.

WHAT TYPES OF STRATEGIES ARE USEFUL IN ALLEVIATING FEAR?

No matter how sensitive parents are to the emotional vulnerabilities of their children, children are likely to be frightened at one time or another by what they see on television or in a movie. The choice of an effective coping strategy is not always obvious, however. Research shows that there are consistent age and gender differences in the strategies that typically work in alleviating media-induced fear. The next sections summarize the findings of this research.

Developmental Differences in the Use and Effectiveness of Coping Strategies

Developmental differences in children's information-processing abilities yield differences in the effectiveness of strategies to prevent or reduce their media-induced fears (Cantor & Wilson, 1988). The findings of research on coping strategies can be summarized as follows: In general, preschool children benefit more from noncognitive than from cognitive strategies whereas cognitive strategies tend to be more effective for older elementary school children.

Noncognitive strategies

Noncognitive (or nonverbal) strategies are those that do not involve the processing of verbal information and that appear to be relatively automatic. The most heavily tested noncognitive strategy is desensitization, or gradual exposure to threatening images in a nonthreatening context. This strategy has been shown to be effective for both preschool and older elementary school children. Studies have used prior exposure to filmed snakes, live lizards, still photographs of worms, and rubber replicas of spiders to reduce the emotional impact of frightening movie scenes involving similar creatures (Weiss, Imrich, & Wilson, 1993; Wilson, 1987, 1989a; Wilson & Cantor, 1987). In addition, fear reactions to the Hulk character in *The Incredible Hulk* were shown to be reduced by exposure to footage of Lou Ferrigno, the actor who plays the character, having his makeup applied so that he gradually took on the menacing appearance of the character (Cantor, Sparks, & Hoffner, 1988). None of these experiments revealed developmental differences in the effectiveness of desensitization.

Other noncognitive strategies involve physical activities, such as clinging to a loved one or an attachment object, having something to eat or drink, or leaving the situation and becoming involved in another activity. Although these techniques can be used by viewers of all ages, there is reason to believe they are more effective for younger than for older children. First, it has been argued that the effectiveness of such techniques is likely to diminish as the infant's tendency to grasp and suck objects for comfort decreases (Bowlby, 1973). Second, it seems likely that the effectiveness of such techniques is partially attributable to distraction, and distraction techniques should be more effective in younger children, who have greater difficulty allocating cognitive processing to two simultaneous activities (e.g., Manis, Keating, & Morison, 1980).

Children seem to be intuitively aware that physical techniques work better for younger than for older children. In a study asking children to evaluate the effectiveness of various strategies for coping with media-induced fright, preschool children's ratings of "holding onto a blanket or a toy" and "getting something to eat or drink" were significantly higher than those of older elementary school children (Wilson, Hoffner, & Cantor, 1987). Similarly, Harrison and Cantor's (1999) retrospective study showed that the percentage of respondents who reported having used a "behavioral" (noncognitive) coping strategy to deal with their media-induced fear declined as the respondent's age at exposure to the frightening fare increased.

Another noncognitive strategy that has been shown to have more appeal and more effectiveness for younger than for older children is covering one's eyes during frightening portions of a presentation. In an experiment by Wilson (1989b), when covering their eyes was suggested as an option, younger children used this strategy more often than older children. Moreover, the suggestion of this option reduced the fear of younger children, but actually increased the fear of older children. Wilson noted that the older children recognized the limited effectiveness of covering their eyes (while still being exposed to the audio features of the program) and that they may have reacted by feeling *less* in control, and therefore more vulnerable, when this strategy was offered to them.

Cognitive strategies

In contrast to noncognitive strategies, cognitive (or verbal) strategies involve verbal information that is used to cast the threat in a different light. These strategies involve relatively complex cognitive operations, and research consistently finds such strategies to be more effective for older than for younger children.

When dealing with fantasy depictions, the most typical cognitive strategy seems to be to provide an explanation focusing on the unreality of the situation. This strategy should be especially difficult for preschool children, who do not have a full grasp of the implications of the fantasy-reality distinction. In an experiment by Cantor and Wilson (1984), older elementary school children who were told to remember that what they were seeing in *The Wizard of Oz* was not real showed less fear than their classmates who received no instructions. The same instructions did not help preschoolers, however. A more recent study (Wilson & Weiss, 1991) showed similar developmental differences in the effectiveness of reality-related strategies.

Children's beliefs about the effectiveness of focusing on the unreality of a media offering have been shown to be consistent with these experimental findings. In the study of perceptions of fear-reducing techniques (Wilson et al., 1987), preschool children's ranking of the effectiveness of "tell yourself it's not real" was significantly lower than that of older elementary school children. In contrast to both preschool and elementary school children, who apparently view this strategy accurately, parents do not seem to appreciate the inadequacy of this technique for young children. Eighty percent of the parents of both the preschool and elementary school children who participated in another study (Wilson & Cantor, 1987) reported that they employed a "tell them it's not real" coping strategy to reduce their child's media-induced fear. The following anecdote illustrates this misunderstanding and the ineffectiveness of cognitive strategies for young children:

My mom claims that one calm warm summer night, she and my father felt like watching a scary film, *Creature from the Black Lagoon*. I must have been about four to five years old, and they figured I would have no problem watching because I was with them. Their rationale was, "Hey, he's with us, so we can explain to him that none of this is real." After maybe the first five minutes of the film, when the creature pops out of the pond, I maniacally began to cry my eyes out, and would not stop until my father turned off the television. Mother tells me that no matter how much they tried to explain to me that what was on TV was make-believe, I was still shaking. Her only option was to stay up with me all night, touching me and singing to me softly. (Cantor, 1998, p. 131)

To reduce fright reactions to media depictions involving realistic threats, the most prevalent cognitive strategy seems to be to provide an explanation that minimizes the perceived severity of the depicted danger. This type of strategy is not only more effective with older children than with younger ones, in certain situations it has been shown to have a fear-enhancing rather than anxiety-reducing effect with younger children. In an experiment involving the frightening snake-pit scene from *Raiders of the Lost Ark* (Wilson & Cantor, 1987), children were first exposed to an educational film involving the presence or absence of reassuring information about snakes (including, for example, the statement that most snakes are not poisonous). Although this information tended to reduce the fear of older elementary school children while watching the snake-pit scene, kindergarten and first grade children seem to have only partially understood the information, responding to the word "poisonous" more intensely than to the word "not." For them, negative emotional reactions were more prevalent if they had heard the supposedly reassuring information than if they had not heard it.

Data also indicate that older children use cognitive coping strategies more frequently than preschool children do. In the survey of reactions to *The Day After* (Cantor et al., 1986), parents' reports that their child had discussed the movie with them after viewing it increased with the age of the child. In a laboratory experiment involving exposure to a scary scene (Hoffner & Cantor, 1990), significantly more 9- to 11-year-olds than 5- to 7-year-olds reported that they had spontaneously employed cognitive coping strategies (thinking about the expected happy outcome or thinking about the fact that what was happening was not real). Similarly, Harrison and Cantor's (1999) retrospective study showed that the tendency to employ a cognitive strategy to cope with media-induced fear increased with the respondent's age at the time of the incident.

Studies have also shown that the effectiveness of cognitive strategies for young children can be improved by providing visual demonstrations of verbal explanations (Cantor, Sparks, & Hoffner, 1988), and by encouraging repeated rehearsal of simplified, reassuring information (Wilson, 1987). In addition, research has explored some of the specific reasons for the inability of young children to profit from verbal explanations, such as those involving relative quantifiers (e.g., "some are dangerous, but most are not," Badzinski, Cantor, & Hoffner, 1989) and probabilistic terms (e.g., "this probably will not happen to you," Hoffner, Cantor, & Badzinski, 1990). It is clear from these studies that it is a challenging task to explain away threats that have induced fear in a child, particularly when there is a strong perceptual component to the threatening stimulus, and when the reassurance can only be partial or probabilistic, rather than absolute (see Cantor & Hoffner, 1990).

Gender Differences in the Use of Coping Strategies

Few studies have explored gender differences in strategies for coping with scary media. Hoffner (1995) found that adolescent girls reported using more noncognitive coping strategies than boys did, but that there were no gender differences in the use of cognitive strategies. Similarly Valkenburg et al. (2000) found that among 7- to 12-year-old children, girls reported resorting to social support, physical intervention, and escape more often than boys did, but that there was no gender difference in the use of cognitive reassurance as a coping strategy. Both of these findings are consistent with Hoffner's (1995) explanation that these differences may reflect gender-socialization pressures. Because boys are less willing to show their emotions than girls are, they perhaps avoid noncognitive strategies, whose use can usually be observed by others. In contrast, the two genders employ cognitive strategies with equal frequency because these strategies are less readily observable.

IMPLICATIONS FOR PROMOTING CHILDREN'S MENTAL HEALTH

A recent meta-analysis (Twenge, 2000) revealed a striking linear increase in the levels of anxiety reported by young people in the decades since the 1950s. This analysis, including 170 samples of college students and 99 samples of children, yielded a surprisingly large effect size ($d = 0.98$) between average anxiety scores in 1952 versus 1993. According to Twenge's analysis, the average anxiety score in the 1990s (i.e., the fiftieth percentile) would fall near the high end (the eighty-fourth percentile) of a distribution of self-reports of anxiety in the 1950s. Twenge's data suggest that increasing divorce rates and crime rates may play a role in this increase. Although Twenge did not test the possible role of the media, the data presented at the beginning of this chapter suggest that the increasing prominence of the media in children's lives may be contributing to this increase as well.

The research on fright reactions suggests that media content can have substantial negative effects on children's emotional well-being, and that these effects can endure for long periods of time. Moreover, unhealthy effects on a child can be physical as well as emotional, such as when children are suddenly reluctant to sleep alone (or to sleep at all) or to engage in everyday activities that remind them of the fear-provoking television show or movie (see Cantor & Omdahl, 1991). These findings highlight the importance of taking the child's media exposure seriously and of trying to prevent severe emotional disturbances to the extent possible.

There are a variety of things we can do to reduce the likelihood that children will experience unduly intense fear responses to media (Cantor, 1998). Parents are the first line of defense. They can monitor their children's media exposure and be aware of the content of the television and movies their children see. They can do this by watching programs and movies beforehand, by acquiring whatever information is available from television and movie ratings, by reading reviews and program descriptions, or by watching programs with their children. An awareness of developmental trends in the media images and events that frighten children can help parents choose the programming that their children of different ages are likely to view without problems.

Because the presence of television in the home makes it easy for children to encounter frightening media, parents should be aware that their children may be affected by what other family members (themselves included) are viewing, even if the children don't seem to be paying attention. They should also avoid placing a television in a child's bedroom, where it is easy to view without parental knowledge and where television viewing at bedtime is likely. Parents should also consider using blocking technologies, such as the V-chip. Although nothing, including blocking, can replace parental guidance (especially because television news is not rated, and TV ratings may not reflect what is likely to be scary), parents can use blocking to screen out some of the more obviously inappropriate shows at times when they can't be present. In addition, by understanding the types of coping strategies for dealing with media-induced fears that are effective for children of different ages, parents can help their children reduce their fears once they have been aroused. Parents should be aware that their children (especially boys) may be unwilling to admit their fears, but they may nevertheless be in need of parental reassurance.

Schools, childcare providers, and teachers can also help reduce the risk that children will experience traumatic reactions to media. They can use an understanding of developmental differences to make sound choices of audiovisual stimuli for their classes, as well as of movies they choose for students' entertainment. They can also make sensible, age-appropriate decisions regarding which news stories to bring into the classroom, and they can be prepared to help their students cope with the unsettling issues that confront them in the media. This information is sorely needed as evidenced by the fact that many teachers exposed their students to live news coverage of the September 11 attacks and subsequent events without anticipating the consequences and without being prepared to help their students manage their anxieties. Although it is appropriate for students to be aware of what is going on in the world around them, live television news is often not the age-appropriate way to keep them informed.

The media could make it easier to shield children from content that they are not yet able to handle effectively. This means television programmers could endeavor to make access to frightening content at least predictable from the viewer's standpoint. Stations and channels should be pressured to refrain from airing ads with scary images and promos for intensely violent or frightening movies and TV shows during programs with a sizeable child audience. They should be encouraged to rate and label media offerings in a way that warns parents of potentially threatening content. And they should be urged to avoid showing threatening visual images in newscasts in the early evening— or to at least give viewers advance warning that horrific images are upcoming.

Finally, government can play a role. If the media industries' rating systems aren't working to inform parents, lawmakers can promote a universal, readily understandable rating system that's based on sound criteria, including an awareness of which stimuli are likely to traumatize children. Any effective system would make program raters accountable to input from parents and child development experts.

NOTE

1. All of the personal accounts in this chapter are excerpts of reports by individuals. They are either from questionnaire responses of research participants or from papers written by students in classes that had not covered the effects of frightening media. The only modifications from the original texts involve changing names to protect privacy and correcting mistakes in grammar or spelling.

CHAPTER 11

Meta-Analyzing the Controversy over Television Violence and Aggression

George Comstock and Erica Scharrer

The meaningfulness of scientific inquiry rests on two factors. The first is the quality and veracity of evidence, which is assessed by the various applications of the concepts of reliability and validity (Cook & Campbell, 1979). The second is the inevitably somewhat subjective interpretation of these findings. Both are well served by meta-analysis, which provides estimates of relationships among variables based on all retrievable studies and can confine inferences to data from studies of the highest quality and greatest conformity to real-life circumstances (Hunt, 1997).[1]

In the case of television and film violence and aggressive and antisocial behavior, there is a substantial array of data—there have been seven meta-analyses that have studied outcomes that overlap in their coverage but are far from identical. Meta-analysis, because it provides estimates of the magnitude of the relationships among variables that are more reliable and valid than those produced by a single study, assists enormously in addressing five important questions:

1. Is there a statistically significant relationship between the independent and dependent variables of primary interest (in this case, exposure to television or film violence and aggressive or antisocial behavior)?

2. Does the pattern of outcomes favor a causal inference (how we explain a significant relationship)?

3. What are the circumstances that facilitate or inhibit a relationship (the attributes of the portrayal, viewer, or situation that make a difference)?

4. How robust is the relationship in the face of methodological challenges (the stability of outcomes when criteria such as ecological validity and study quality are applied[2])?

5. What is the magnitude of the relationship (in meta-analytic jargon, the "effect size")?

IN THE LAP OF THE ANALYST

The strength of meta-analysis is that it addresses these questions by pooling all retrievable data, thereby easily surpassing the informativeness of any single study. Any single study has particular strengths and weaknesses. These might reside in the measures, procedures, or samples. Other studies have different strengths and weaknesses. Multiple studies in effect compensate for each other's weaknesses. Thus, a strength of meta-analysis is that by combining studies, the weaknesses of specific individual studies are overcome. Nevertheless, meta-analysis is no substitute for interpretation.

This interpretation occurs on two levels. At the first, the very outcomes that are quantitatively aggregated must be assigned some meaning. Experimental findings that clearly document causation within the circumstances of experimental data collection may not generalize to other circumstances. Positive correlation coefficients within a survey may or may not imply causation. Adjudication is required. At the second level, individual studies may produce data that challenge or lead to the qualification of an explanation offered for the outcomes aggregated by meta-analysis. Adjustment of perspective may be necessary. Thus, meta-analysis is a nifty machine that supplies superior data but stubbornly leaves scientific meaning in the lap of the analyst.

In a pioneering effort, Andison (1977) simply categorized the outcomes of 67 experiments and surveys as to the direction and size of the relationship between violence viewing and aggressive or antisocial behavior. He was followed by Hearold (1986), who was the first to apply the now widely accepted meta-analytic practice of using the statistical measure of variance, the standard deviation, as a criterion of effect size to the literature on media and behavior. She was a student of Eugene Glass at the University of Colorado, who is credited with developing meta-analysis in the 1970s in an attempt to quantitatively discredit H. J. Eysenck's claims that psychotherapy was ineffective.[3] In an ambitiously comprehensive undertaking, she examined more than 1,000 relationships drawn from 168 studies between exposure to antisocial and prosocial portrayals and antisocial and prosocial behavior. In stark contrast, Wood, Wong, and Cachere (1991) focused only on manipulations that clearly permitted causal inference and spontaneous antisocial behavior, examining 23 experiments in and out of the laboratory in which the dependent variable was "unconstrained interpersonal aggression" among children and teenagers, thereby strengthening ecological validity. Allen, D'Alessio, and Brezgel (1995) were similarly focused, aggregating the data from 33 laboratory-type experiments in which the independent variable was exposure to video or film erotica and the dependent variable was aggression. Hogben (1998) chose a very different focus, assessing only studies measuring everyday viewing. He also chose to include outcomes that varied widely, including aggressive behavior, hostile attitudes, personality variables, and in one instance (Cairns, Hunter, & Herring, 1980) the inventing by children of imagined news stories. Bushman and Anderson (2001) produced a time series representing the correlations between exposure to violent portrayals and aggressive behavior by 5-year intervals over 25 years beginning in 1975. Paik and Comstock (1994), in a comprehensive updating of Hearold's assessment of the relationship between exposure to television violence and aggressive and antisocial behavior, included 82 new studies for a total of 217 that produced 1,142 coefficients between the independent and dependent variables.[4]

This is a vast accumulation of data representing the behavior of many thousands of persons of all ages, a wide range of independent and dependent variables, and an array of methods (Table 11.1). These are all typically positive features of meta-analyses, which reflect the characteristics of their topic areas in contrast to the narrow profile of a single study.

ASSOCIATION AND CAUSATION

These seven analyses listed above make it irrefutably clear that children and teenagers who view greater amounts of violent television and movie portrayals are more likely to behave in an aggressive or antisocial manner (Table 11.1). This holds for the data from both of the basic designs, experiments (where the effects of a treatment are assessed and causality can be inferred), and surveys (where everyday behavior is reflected). Interpretation nevertheless shoulders a heavy burden, because experimental findings may lack external validity and correlation is not synonymous with causation.

What should be made of this association? The case for causation rests on (a) the consistency of the outcomes for the experimental designs and (b) the confirmation by the outcomes of the survey designs that the condition necessary for real-life causation exists—an everyday positive correlation between violence viewing and aggressive or antisocial behavior. Across the experimental designs, exposure to violent portrayals is regularly followed by increases in aggressive or antisocial behavior. Across the survey designs, there is consistently an association between violence viewing and behavior not readily explainable without some contribution by exposure to violent portrayals.

The "reverse hypothesis" (Belson, 1978), which holds that the association in everyday life is attributable to the seeking out of violent entertainment by those particularly likely to engage in such behavior, fares particularly badly. The most striking evidence comes from Kang's (1990) reanalysis of the NBC panel data (Milavsky, Kessler, Stipp, & Rubens, 1982) on elementary school children.[5] Most survey data must be confined to claims of association (and thus, failure to decidedly rule out the reverse hypothesis) rather than causation because variables are measured at only one point in time, thereby obscuring the issue of which variable caused a change in the other. Kang (1990) overcame

Table 11.1
Selected Effect Sizes from Seven Meta-Analyses of Media Violence and Aggression

AUTHOR	INDEPENDENT VARIABLE	DEPENDENT VARIABLE	N*	EFFECT SIZE ($r =$)
Andison, 1977	Television violence	Aggressive behavior	67	.28**
Hearold, 1986	Antisocial portrayals	Antisocial behavior	528	.30
Wood, Wong, and Cachere, 1991	Aggressive portrayals	Unconstrained interpersonal aggression	12	.20
Allen, D'Alessio, and Brezgel, 1995	Pornography	Aggressive behavior	7	.13
Hogben, 1998	Violent programming	Aggression-related responses	56	.11
Bushman and Anderson, 2001	Television violence	Aggressive behavior	202	.15**
Paik and Comstock, 1994	Television violence	Aggressive behavior	1142	.31

* Number of coefficients represented by effect size.
** Calculated from the distribution of coefficients by size of effect.
Note: In some cases, Cohen's *d* converted to *r* by Table 2.3 (Rosenthal, Rosnow, & Rubin, 2000, p. 16). All *r*'s are statistically significant; for example, the Paik and Comstock *p* is less than .0000.

this methodological obstacle by using data from a survey design in which questionnaires were administered at multiple points in time, allowing for the establishment of time order that is necessary to claim causation. He found twice as many significant coefficients, 8 versus 4, for a viewing-to-behavior effect than for a behavior-to-viewing outcome out of a total of 15 waves of earlier and later measurement, with only one instance of reciprocal association. Belson (1978) similarly found in his survey of about 1,600 London teenage males that the data did not support the reverse hypothesis as the explanation for a positive association between violence viewing and the committing of seriously harmful acts (such as attempted rape; use of a tire iron, razor, knife, or gun in a fight; falsely reporting a bomb threat) among a sub-population with a high likelihood of delinquent behavior (violence viewing predicted a substantial difference in antisocial behavior, while aggressive propensity predicted only a minute difference in violence viewing). There is also the very widely cited finding of Lefkowitz, Eron, Walder, and Huesmann (1977), in an upstate New York sample of about 200 males, that the amount of violent television viewing at age 8 predicted aggressive behavior at age 19 ($r = 0.31$) but aggressive behavior at age 8 did not predict the viewing of violent television at age 19 ($r = 0.01$).

CIRCUMSTANCES AND ROBUSTNESS

Gender

Both females and males are affected by media violence. In the meta-analysis of Paik and Comstock (1994), effect sizes are similar for the two genders in surveys (females, $r = 0.19$; males, $r = 0.18$), the method that most closely represents real-life, everyday associations, and it is only in the experiments that effect sizes are somewhat greater for males (females, $r = 0.39$; males, $r = 0.44$). This is a pattern whose recognition is owed to meta-analysis, and is quite different from the impression given (and often repeated in textbooks) by the early experiments with nursery school children of Bandura and colleagues (Bandura, Ross, & Ross, 1963a, 1963b) in which effects were greater among males.

Age

Somewhat surprisingly, age fails to offer the mitigation that one might expect from enhanced ability to comprehend, analyze, and react critically to what is seen on the screen. In the Paik and Comstock (1994) meta-analysis, effect sizes in experiments do decrease between the preschool and adult years but they increase among those of college age, and in surveys, which most accurately reflect everyday events, the effect size for adults is greater than for any other age group except those of preschool age. Our conclusion is that effects cannot be said to disappear as people grow older, although they are particularly pronounced among the very young.

Time

The likelihood of an effect among children and adolescents increases with the passage of time. This conclusion rests on four different aspects of the NBC panel data.

In the original analysis by Milavsky, Kessler, Stipp, and Rubens (1982), the coefficients among the elementary school sample became larger as the span of time between measurements grew longer. In the same analysis, the coefficients among the same sample are somewhat larger when there are no statistical controls to eliminate the influence of earlier viewing. In the further reanalysis of the NBC panel data by Cook, Kendzierski, and Thomas (1983), there is evidence throughout of increasing coefficients among both the elementary and teenage samples with the passage of time, and for a variety of alternate measures of aggression. And finally, Kang (1990) found among his eight significant viewing-to-behavior coefficients that five were clustered among the longest time spans (while among his four significant behavior-to-viewing coefficients, three were clustered among the shortest time spans), thereby providing additional evidence that effects on behavior increase with the passage of time and any behavior-to-viewing effects are largely confined to the short term.

These studies taken together show an important pattern of results. The Milavsky et al. (1982) study above suggests a longitudinal effect. It also shows a cumulative effect. The Cook et al. (1983) analysis shows either a longitudinal or cumulative effect. And the Kang (1990) study shows the apparently decisive role of the passage of time in behavioral effects. Earlier viewing appears to affect later behavior, presumably because the young viewer becomes better prepared or more motivated to emulate in some fashion what has been observed, and this phenomenon is enhanced when greater amounts of violence viewing continue between the dates when earlier viewing and later behavior are measured.

SOCIOECONOMIC STATUS

Milavsky and colleagues (1982) argued that socioeconomic status (SES) spuriously contributed to any signs of positive coefficients in their data (with those of lower SES watching more television, and therefore more television violence, and also as a consequence of lower SES behaving more aggressively). As an inferential escape this proves to be a dead end. Cook, Kendzierski, and Thomas (1983) reanalyzed the NBC data to show that middle-class girls, when examined separately, displayed the same pattern of increasing coefficients with greater time spans that was visible for males, and nowhere has there been convincing evidence that socioeconomic status fully explains the positive associations between violence viewing and aggressive or antisocial behavior (Belson, 1978; Chaffee, 1972; Comstock & Scharrer, 1999).

Exacerbating Conditions

The effects of media violence exposure are exacerbated by low socioeconomic status, poor parenting skills, unsatisfactory social relationships, low psychological well-being, and a predisposition toward aggressive and antisocial behavior. These factors function either through increasing the frequency of exposure to violent portrayals or the likelihood of engaging in antisocial behavior (Comstock & Scharrer, 1999; U.S. Department of Health and Human Services, 2001). Socioeconomic status is inversely associated with exposure to television and television violence (i.e., lower SES groups tend to be exposed to higher amounts of TV violence; Comstock & Scharrer, 1999), although, as mentioned above, the role of socioeconomic status is certainly not powerful enough to account fully for the relationship between exposure to television violence and aggression. An emphasis within the family on constructive, open communication among parents and children also is inversely associated with exposure to television programming in general as well as to violent television entertainment (Chaffee, McLeod, & Atkin, 1971; McLeod, Atkin, & Chaffee, 1972). Parental interest in children's whereabouts is inversely associated with a wide range of delinquent behavior (Thornton & Voigt, 1984). Social conflicts and psychological stress similarly increase the likelihood of viewing greater amounts of television, and thereby greater amounts of violence (Comstock & Scharrer, 1999). There is certainly plenty of evidence that those with a predisposition for aggressive or antisocial behavior are particularly likely to be affected. By predisposition, we mean higher levels of antisocial behavior or attributes that are correlates of antisocial behavior. For example, in two survey designs, correlations with violence are particularly pronounced or limited to those already committing delinquent acts or earlier displaying aggression (Belson, 1978; Robinson & Bachman, 1972). In experiments, effects sometimes have been limited to those scoring higher in earlier aggressiveness (Celozzi, Kazelskis, & Gutsch, 1981; Josephson, 1987). And Paik (1991), in her meta-analytic dissertation, found a larger effect size for those scoring higher on measures of aggressive predisposition. We are somewhat hesitant, however, to conclude that predisposition is a necessary condition. Our basis is the consistency of results for surveys of samples with no known biases and for experiments with subjects randomly assigned to conditions. This consistency indicates that the association between exposure and behavior is common among the general population. If it is necessary, then it is also very common (and thereby no reason to expect that effects will be rare). Thus, those most at risk in regard to the behavioral effects of television violence are those facing the greatest challenges in coping with life (for a discussion of risk factors, see Gentile & Sesma, chapter 2, this volume).

Sex versus Violence

Two of the meta-analyses produced effect sizes for exposure to explicitly sexual treatments. Both Allen, D'Alessio, and Brezgel (1995), who examined only sexually explicit portrayals, and Paik and Comstock (1994), who examined sexually explicit as well as violent portrayals, report effect sizes for violent erotica that are among the largest they recorded.

Allen and colleagues (1995) reported an overall effect size for exposure to all types of pornography (with nudity, nonviolent sexual behavior, and violent sexual behavior pooled) that was modest ($r = 0.13$), although it achieved statistical significance. However, the picture changed somewhat when they confined the analyses to erotica without violence ($r = 0.17$) and violent erotica ($r = 0.22$). Paik and Comstock (1994) reported an effect size for violent erotica (versus all other treatments with which violent erotica was compared) that was substantial ($r = 0.60$). Their comparable effect size for erotica without violence was smaller but still substantial ($r = 0.46$). Both well exceed the Paik and Comstock overall effect size for exposure to television and film violence ($r = 0.31$).

There has been considerable debate over whether the "sex" is a major factor contributing to aggressive or antisocial outcomes (Weaver, 1991) or whether the contributing factor is primarily the "violence" (Donnerstein, Linz, & Penrod, 1987). The answer appears to be "both." Effect sizes for erotica with violence are consistently higher than they are for erotica without violence. However, coefficients for the latter are consistently positive. In both cases, exposure to the sexually explicit portrayals can be considered the cause of the aggressive or antisocial behavior because all the studies employed experimental designs. Thus, a strong claim can be made for an effect on aggressive and antisocial behavior of erotica without violence.

Allen and colleagues (1995) provide additional important data. They followed the schema developed by the 1986 Attorney General's Commission on Pornography and divided their independent variables into an ascending scale representing the treatment of females as objects of sexual domination. There were three categories: portrayals of nudity without sex, erotica without violence, and violent erotica. For portrayals of nudity they found an inverse effect size (i.e., greater exposure was associated with lower levels of aggressive or antisocial behavior; $r = -0.14$). For erotica without violence and violent erotica, effect sizes, as just discussed, were positive and increased with the shift from the former to the latter. Violent portrayals alone, as the evidence clearly attests, can have an effect without an erotica element. Erotica can have an effect without violence. The two in combination, however, apparently become a powerful joint stimulus.

Our interpretation is that the inverse effect size in the data of Allen and colleagues for nudity and the weaker effect size for erotica are attributable to the comparative absence of cues that would encourage aggression, including the depiction of the female participants as meriting abuse, derision, or contempt. This factor would be at a maximum for violent erotica, reduced for erotica, and largely absent for nudity. We are constrained from invoking a logical alternative, lower levels of induced arousal, by Allen and colleague's finding that self-reported arousal was inversely associated to a modest degree with aggressive and antisocial outcomes.

Ecological Validity and Study Quality

One of the features of meta-analysis is that it permits objectively testing whether confining the analysis to studies that were particularly high in ecological validity or methodological quality would alter the conclusions (e.g., better sampling, better controls, etc.). The sole requirement is that the studies be rated on these two characteristics. Neither Hearold (1986) nor Paik and Comstock (1994), who both rated the studies they collected on both dimensions, found any evidence that the conclusion that exposure to violent portrayals predicts aggressive and antisocial behavior would be altered by focusing only on studies high either in ecological validity or methodological quality. However, Hearold, who examined prosocial as well as antisocial portrayals and outcomes, did uncover an interesting symmetry when examining only the studies higher in methodological quality. Exposure to antisocial portrayals predicted heightened aggressive or antisocial behavior and lowered prosocial behavior. Exposure to prosocial portrayals predicted lowered aggressive or antisocial behavior and heightened prosocial behavior. Hearold (1986) concluded, " [W]hen the analysis is confined to studies of higher quality, antisocial and pro-social treatments are symmetrical in their association with behavior, and the data become entirely consistent with the view that the former encourages antisocial and inhibits pro-social behavior and the latter encourages pro-social and inhibits antisocial behavior" (p. 99).

Evidence and Media Coverage

Two parallel analyses were conducted by Bushman and Anderson (2001). In one, they examined the correlations between exposure to violent portrayals and aggressive behavior in both experimental and nonexperimental designs by five-year intervals beginning in 1975. In the other, they examined news coverage of the television violence and aggression controversy beginning in 1950.

In the first, they found statistically significant positive associations for experimental designs that were essentially stable across the 25 years and statistically significant positive associations for nonexperimental designs that increased in magnitude over the same period. The net result was an increase in the estimated size of the relation between exposure to violent portrayals and aggressive behavior. In the second, the dependent variable was the scientifically accurate report that exposure to media violence is positively correlated with aggressive behavior. They found that the evidence and media coverage diverged. The former had become stronger since 1975 while the accurate representation of the scientific record since 1950, after rising in frequency between 1950 and 1980, had actually become less frequent (see Figure 11.1). Thus, the curve representing the correlations sweeps upward while the curve representing the accuracy of coverage languishes with a visible (if less dramatic) decline. In fact, for the six data points since 1975 they record a large negative correlation of $r = -0.68$ between effect sizes and the accuracy ratings of news stories. Bushman and Anderson conclude that the behavior of the news media "is disheartening at best" and observe that "it has been decades since one could reasonably claim that there is little reason for concern about media violence effects" (2001, p. 485).

EFFECT SIZE

There are four ways to interpret meta-analytic effect sizes. The first essentially employs the kind of labeling that we use so frequently in everyday life—established criteria for what should be considered large, medium, small, or

Figure 11.1
Effect of Media Violence on Aggression: Comparing News Reports with Scientific Studies

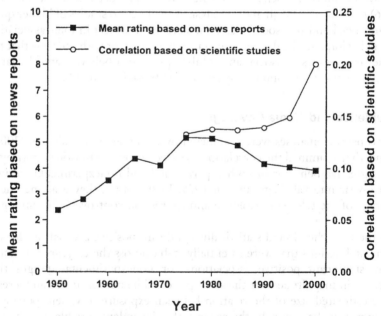

Note: Ratings based on news reports are positive if the article said that exposure to media violence is positively related to aggression. Correlations based on scientific studies are positive if media violence was positively related to aggression.

Source: From B. J. Bushman and C. A. Anderson (2001). Media violence and the American public. *American Psychologist, 56,* 447–489. Copyright © 2001 by the American Psychological Association. Reprinted with permission.

null. The second introduces the seriousness of the purported outcome to weight the size of the effect (the analogy is fear, with fear increasing not only with the probability of an undesirable event but also with the direness of its consequences). The third is a comparison with effect sizes in other realms to provide some context as to what might be expected and what should be judged as substantial. The fourth is the predictability of the fate of the individual implied by the effect size.

Established Criteria

The most widely employed guidelines are those developed by Cohen (1988). By his criteria, $r = 0.10$ should be considered "small"; $r = 0.30$, "medium"; and, $r = 0.50$, "large"(Rosenthal, Rosnow, & Rubin, 2000). His grounds were essentially pragmatic. The frequency of statistically significant correlation coefficients, an accepted measure of effect size, in the social and behavioral sciences is inversely related to their size. As size increases, coefficients become increasingly scarce. More stringent criteria would sweep many at the bottom from notice while leaving few—perhaps to an embarrassing degree—with compelling magnitude. The thresholds at which null crosses into small territory, or other borders are violated, remains open to judgment [Hemphill (2003) argues that 0.30 is large when considered empirically].

By these criteria the effect sizes for interpersonal aggression in the Paik and Comstock (1994) meta-analysis, the most comprehensive in regard to violent portrayals and a wide range of aggressive behavior, approach the threshold for medium ($r = 0.24$ for physical aggression and $r = 0.27$ for verbal aggression). We use the plural, "effect sizes," because they differ for each category of aggression, and within each category of aggression vary depending on method, program characteristics, and age and gender of respondents or subjects. The approach of the medium range in this instance is quite important. Interpersonal aggression is the real-life (and thereby, ecologically valid) outcome that has been studied most often, and it clearly possesses an unpleasant and definitely-to-be-avoided experience for the victim—stealing, hitting, name-calling. Thus, it combines extensive data with personal discomfort and thus social significance. In the same Paik and Comstock meta-analysis, coefficients for both simulated aggression (such as aggressive inclination measured by questionnaire or performance on an aggression machine) and minor aggression (such as violence done to an object or aggression against a person that ordinarily would not come to the attention of a law enforcement agency)[6] usually approach or achieve the medium range by Cohen's criteria, although sometimes they are in the large range.

Seriousness

If a focus on more perilous or decidedly illegal behavior is demanded, the Paik and Comstock meta-analysis produces effect sizes that are decidedly smaller than for interpersonal aggression but are statistically significant. These types of behaviors represent greater harm than stealing, hitting, or name-calling, and the corresponding effect sizes almost always achieve the small and sometimes achieve the medium range in magnitude. For seriously hurtful or illegal activities, the omnibus effect for all observations is $r = 0.17$. As the seriousness of the offense increases, effect sizes become smaller. Even so, violence against a person registers an effect size of $r = 0.10$, achieves statistical significance, and produces a fail-safe number of almost 3,000.[7]

Examples from individual studies certainly support the view that sizable effects are not limited to interpersonal aggression. Belson (1978), in his large London probability sample of teenage males, found that among delinquents the very low rate of committing seriously hurtful (and decidedly criminal) acts increased by 50 percent among those who viewed greater amounts of violent television entertainment, and he presents a good case for attributing this difference to the contribution of viewing violence. In a second noteworthy instance, a group led by the methodologist Thomas Cook (Hennigan et al., 1982) took advantage of the Federal Communications Commission's (FCC) freeze on television station licenses in the late 1940s to conduct a quasi-experimental time series with switching replications (Cook & Campbell, 1979). They found that at two points in time (the early and late introduction of television) and in two samples (cities and states, with the frequency of set ownership used to distinguish those that were early and late adoption sites), the arrival of the medium was accompanied by a significant increase in larceny theft. This outcome has been variously attributed to relative deprivation traceable to the materialistic emphasis of the medium (Hennigan et al., 1982) and the emulation of television's antisocial portrayals at a level where apprehension would be unlikely and sanctions minimal (Comstock, 1991). Whatever the underlying dynamics, the increases of about 6 to about 17 percent across the four coefficients represented a sizable change. One can imagine the huge headlines that would follow similar percentage increases in national crime rates or the prevalence nationally of a serious disease such as cancer. These increases constitute a socially substantial effect. And in their widely publicized longitudinal study of 707 individuals that appeared in *Science*, Johnson, Cohen, Smailes, Kasen, and Brook (2002) found that "assault or physical fights resulting in injury" as well as "any aggressive act against another person" were more frequent among males at ages 16 or 22 who viewed greater amounts of television (and presumably, therefore, greater amounts of violence) at the age of 14. The fact that the statistically significant results remain after controlling for five important covariates (or predictors) of both television viewing and aggression—childhood neglect, growing up in an unsafe neighborhood, low family income, low parental education, and psychiatric disorder (p. 2469)— suggest that television contributed causally as well as possibly reinforcing the effects of these enemies of well-being.

Finally, drawing on Paik and Comstock (1994), the Surgeon General's recent report on youth violence (U.S. Department of Health and Human Services, 2001) identifies exposure to television violence as one of about 20 early—between the ages of 6 and 11—risk factors (including individual, family, school, and peer variables) for the committing of seriously harmful criminal violence between the age of 15 and 18 (p. 58, Box 4–1). The effect size of $r = 0.13$ was classified as small. However, effects were said to be similarly small for three-fourths of the variables identified as early risk factors (Figure 11.2).

Other Effect Sizes

Bushman and Anderson (2001) supply a very recent catalogue of effect sizes from other realms (Figure 11.3). There exist, of course, effect sizes that are much grander than those presented. For example, the effect sizes for gender on height and for a year of additional school on the ability of a child to read are far larger (Hearold, 1986). However, these represent substantial associations occurring in the natural order of things—physical differences between males and females, and the consequences among children of study and maturation for the acquisition of a cognitive skill. When we confine ourselves to interventions that are outside such basic human phenomena, the effect sizes for exposure to television or film violence and aggressive or antisocial behavior are respectable. Quite a few effect sizes whose importance socially or statistically are hard to deny fall into the small range—exposure to lead and IQ scores among children, nicotine patch adoption and smoking cessation, calcium intake and bone mass, homework and academic achievement, exposure to asbestos and laryngeal cancer, and self-examination and extent of breast cancer. All of these match the smaller television violence effect sizes for more serious aggressive and antisocial outcomes, and fall distinctly below the larger effect sizes for media violence and aggression in general represented here by $r = 0.31$.

Predictability

The criterion of predictability extends the comparison of effect sizes as a means of estimating the importance that should be attached to a particular size of effect to a narrower focus on what an effect size implies for the individual. We step from the effect size as our outcome of interest to its informativeness about what would be expected, given a particular effect size, once a score or standing on the independent variable is known.

Rosenthal and colleagues have been at the forefront in the development of this approach, offering both an analysis of the behavioral research on media violence and aggression (Rosenthal, 1986) and a very recent, more general treatment of effect sizes in social research (Rosenthal, Rosnow, & Rubin, 2000). The key in these analyses is the "binomial effect size display" (BESD) initially introduced as a way of displaying the magnitude of effects demon-

Figure 11.2
Effect Sizes of Factors Constituting Early Risks (Ages 6–11) for Serious Violence at Ages 15–18

General offenses	.38 ///////////////////////
Substance use	.30 //////////////////
Being male	.26 ///////////////
Low SES/poverty	.24 //////////////
Antisocial parents	.23 ////////////
Male aggression	.22 ///////////
Psychological condition	.15 ////////
Hyperactivity	.13 //////
Poor parent-child relations	.15 ////////
Harsh, lax, or inconsistent discipline	.13 //////
Weak social ties	.15 ////////
Problem behavior (antisocial)	.13 //////
Exposure to television violence	.13 //////
Poor attitude toward performance in school	.13 //////
Low IQ	.12 /////
Other family conditions	.12 /////
Broken home	.09 ////
Separation from parents	.09 ////
Antisocial attitudes, beliefs	
Dishonesty (males only)	.12 /////
Abusive parents	.07 ///
Neglect	.07 ///
Antisocial peers	.04 //

-02 –01 0 0.1 0.2 0.3 0.4

Sources: Meta-analysis by Hawkins et al. (1998); Lipsey and Derzon (1998); and Paik and Comstock (1994); or, pooling of outcomes from two or more longitudinal studies of general population samples. Specific factors listed when data permits. Adapted from U.S. Department of Health and Human Services (2001, p. 60, Table 4–1).

Figure 11.3
Selected Effect Sizes versus the Meta-Analytic Television Violence Effect Size of $r = 0.31$

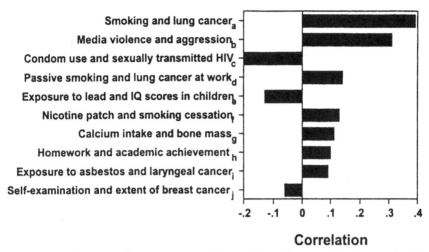

Note: A correlation coefficient can range from –1 (a perfect negative linear relation) to + 1 (a perfect positive linear relation), with 0 indicating no linear relation.

Sources: (a) The effect of smoking tobacco on lung cancer was estimated by pooling the data from Figures 1 and 3 in Wynder and Graham's (1950) classic article. The remaining effects were estimated from meta-analyses: (b) Paik and Comstock (1994); (c) Weller (1993); (d) Wells (1998); (e) Needleman and Gatsonis (1990); (f) Fiore, Smith, Jorenby, and Baker (1994); (g) Welten, Kemper, Post, and van Staveren (1995); (h) Cooper (1989); (i) Smith, Handley, and Wood (1990); (j) Hill, White, Jolley, and Mapperson (1988). Adapted from Bushman and Anderson (2001).

strated experimentally (Rosenthal & Rubin, 1982). The question asked is, "What should we expect in regard to an individual's standing on the dependent variable given a particular effect size and exposure to the treatment?" In practice in our case, the predictor becomes belonging to the treatment or control group in an experiment or falling above or below the median in exposure in a survey. The BESD is a crude measure, but it has two important properties: (a) it conveys a sense of how much an effect size improves knowledge about the outcome, and (b) it permits an estimate of how many persons will be affected.

This is a matter in this case of translating the "r" into a contingency table with the rows representing the independent variable and the columns the dependent variable, with both treated as dichotomous. Rosenthal, Rosnow, and Rubin (2000) present a general example using $r = 0.32$ as an effect size with equal Ns, with interesting results (Table 11.2). The effect size was chosen because it was one reported by Glass (1976) for psychotherapy in what was

Table 11.2
Binomial Effect Size Display

| | Outcome | | |
Condition	Improved	Not Improved	Totals
Treatment	66	34	100
(Psychotherapy)			
Control	34	66	100
Totals	100	100	200

Note: r = 0.32
Source: Adapted from Rosenthal, Rosnow, and Rubin (2000).

the public unveiling of what has become known as meta-analysis. The effect size ensures a success rate—modestly represented in this case by some degree of improvement—of 66 percent for those experiencing the treatment (in this case, some form of psychotherapy) in contrast with a rate of 34 percent for those not experiencing the treatment. In other words, a more desirable state of affairs is achieved for two-thirds instead of one-third of the population. Construed in this way, an effect size of this magnitude has important social implications if the dependent variable has social importance.

The reader undoubtedly will have noticed that the Paik and Comstock effect size of $r = 0.31$ for the media exposure and aggression in general is almost identical. Bushman and Huesmann (2001) performed the necessary calculations:

The 0.31 correlation is equivalent to aggressive behavior being exhibited by 65.5 percent of those above the median in exposure . . . but only by 34.4 percent of those below the median. (p. 234)

In symmetry with the outcome for psychotherapy, the peril rate (those who behaved more aggressively) was increased from slightly more than one-third to two-thirds of the population by the treatment of exposure to television or film violence.

Rosenthal, Rosnow, and Rubin present three examples from biomedical research that compellingly identify very small effect sizes as important when the effect is of consequence. Effect sizes of small $r = 0.03$, 0.04, and 0.07 obtained from large samples (22,071 male physicians, 2,108 heart patients, and 4,462 army veterans, respectively) produced BESDs indicating that 3.4 percent fewer of the physicians would have suffered from a heart attack, 4 percent fewer of the patients would have suffered from a new attack, and

7 percent more veterans suffered from alcohol abuse or dependence if they had served in Vietnam rather than some other place. In the first two instances, the results were judged so important that the placebo trials were halted on the grounds that it was unethical to deprive the control population (and everyone else) of the benefits; in the second, Rosenthal, Rosnow, and Rubin (2000, p. 27) remark with glee (because of the dramatic support for their advocacy of the importance of small effect sizes) that the r^2 began with a double zero (which means that less than one percent of the variance in total attacks was explained by or associated with the independent variable despite the undeniable social—and personal—benefit of reducing attacks by 4 percent).

We are led to three conclusions. First, effect sizes in the realm of media violence and aggressive or antisocial behavior handily satisfy each of the four criteria. Second, they are not trivial, and in each case represent a socially substantial impact. Third, size inevitably must be weighted by the risk or benefit implied. Ascription of substantial social impact thus rests on the unwelcome and undesirable character of the outcome—minor aggressive behavior, with a medium effect size, and hurtful and illegal acts, with a smaller effect size (in the Paik and Comstock meta-analysis, $r = 0.31$ and 0.17, respectively).

BEYOND META-ANALYSIS

Meta-analysis, as should now be apparent, does not substitute for individual studies but complements them. Meta-analysis has the strength of determining whether there is an effect and estimating its strength. Sometimes, however, individual studies are particularly useful for indicating how an effect occurs or whether a particular independent or dependent variable is involved. Often, individual studies will provide information not found in a meta-analysis because that particular issue has not been investigated often enough to appear in a meta-analysis or because a particular study has unusual strengths. An example of the latter occurs with Belson's (1978) sample of about 1,600 London male teenagers. The sample was extremely large, and is the only probability sample among the surveys undertaken specifically to investigate the television violence and aggression issue (and thus the only survey that statistically can be said to represent a larger population). Procedures were high in quality, with respondents personally interviewed for three-and-one-half hours in a physician-like clinical setting by a conservatively attired male. Thus, the data appear to us as highly credible in representing real-world patterns of behavior.

The surprise in the Belson data is that there is no evidence of an effect of viewing on dispositions—attitudes, norms, and values. Exposure to violence failed to predict antisocial attitudes, approval of violence, hostile personality traits, willingness to commit violence, and social contagion (engaging in aggressive and antisocial acts while in the company of other boys). The first four represent the direct measurement of attitudes, norms, and values; the fifth represents those implied by the expressed beliefs and behavior of associates. Thus, neither directly nor indirectly was there evidence of some influence of viewing on dispositions, and thus no evidence of a dispositional linkage between viewing and behavior. Thus, the Belson data unequivocally indicate that attitudes, norms, and values are not consistently a necessary link in the causal chain between exposure to violent portrayals and behavior. This raises the possibility that one route by which violent portrayals may affect behavior is by making the behavioral responses in question more accessible in the repertoires of viewers (Comstock, 2003).

EVALUATING THE META-ANALYSES

The seven meta-analyses provide a strong and impressive body of data linking exposure to violent television and film portrayals with subsequent aggressive or antisocial behavior. Regardless of the vagaries and variety in the independent and dependent variables, each one produces positive and statistically significant effect sizes. This means that many types of violent portrayals are implicated in any effects on behavior. Those who view greater amounts of violent television and film portrayals of many kinds engage in higher levels of aggressive and antisocial behavior. This is an outcome that holds for all ages, both genders (except for experiments employing sexually explicit treatments, where subjects usually are males), and occurs across both experimental designs, where causation can be inferred, and nonexperimental survey designs, which produce data describing everyday occurrences. Thus, the meta-analyses not only confirm a correlation between exposure to portrayals and behavior but point to the portrayals as a causal factor (because of the data from the experimental designs), and one that operates in real life (because of the evidence from the nonexperimental designs). Four criteria were advanced to evaluate the meta-analytic effect sizes—accepted scientific guidelines for assessing magnitude, social seriousness of the outcomes, comparisons with effect sizes in other areas where health and safety are of concern, and the degree to which the likelihood of an individual engaging in the behavior is increased and can be predicted. In each case, the effect sizes met the criterion.

By Cohen's guidelines, the overall effect size in the Paik and Comstock meta-analysis is of medium magnitude ($r = 0.31$). Similar effect sizes were registered by two (out of three) other meta-analyses that were comprehensive in the measures of exposure and behavior included (Andison, 1977; Hearold, 1986). This implies that television violence in general—again, a wide range of types of violent portrayals—is implicated in any effects. Many of the analyses report effect sizes for portions of the data that are larger and sometimes substantially so than their overall effect size. For example, Allen, D'Alessio and Brezgel (1995) report $r = 0.22$ for violent erotica (compared to their overall effect size of $r = 0.13$, which was depressed by the negative association for portrayals of nudity); Hearold (1986) reports $r = 0.62$ for human or real versus cartoon violence and $r = 0.44$ for justified versus unjustified violence (compared to her overall $r = 0.30$); and Paik and Comstock (1994) report $r = 0.60$ for violent erotica and $r = 0.46$ for erotica without violence (compared to their overall $r = 0.31$). This means that some types of portrayals are particularly problematic. Of course, by the very nature of arithmetic, effect sizes for some types of portrayals would be smaller than average, but the overall effect sizes of medium magnitude indicate a substantial social impact for television and film violence in general.

The criterion of sufficient seriousness also is met. Wood, Wong, and Cachere (1991) examined only experimental designs, so causation could be inferred, and unconstrained interpersonal aggression, so that their outcome represents real, observable conflict. Their effect size was $r = 0.20$. Paik and Comstock (1994) reported $r = 0.17$ for illegal activities, although a much smaller figure for violent illegal activities. These effect sizes, which fall between small and medium by Cohen's guidelines, are buttressed by the outcomes of several individual studies that document an association between exposure to television violence and criminal behavior. For example, Belson (1978), the group led by Cook (Hennigan et al., 1982), and Johnson, Cohen, Smailes, Kasen, and Brook (2002) all present such data ranging from larceny theft to rape and physical injury, and each presents an analysis that makes a good case for causation. In addition, the Surgeon General's recent report on youth violence (U.S. Department of Health and Human Services, 2001) specifies television violence viewing between the ages of 6 and 11 as a risk factor for criminal violence between the ages of 15 and 18, with an effect size that is about the same as that for 15 of the 20 conditions identified as risk factors (Figure 11.2). Thus, the outcomes of exposure to television and film violence cannot be dismissed as inconsequential.

Comparison with effect sizes for other threats to health and safety documents that the media effect sizes are comparable and often larger in size. These other effect sizes include the effects of passive smoking, exposure to asbestos, and exposure to lead (Figure 11.1). Conversely, the (social and individual) positive effect sizes for homework and scholastic achievement, calcium intake and bone mass, and self-examination and extent of breast cancer are actually *smaller* than the effect size for the adverse association of aggressive and antisocial behavior with exposure to violent television and film portrayals. Thus, the media effect sizes stand up quite well when compared with those for other effects, whether the focus is on undesired or desirable outcomes.

The criterion of predictive power also is handily met. The effect sizes for media violence lead to the conclusion that in the absence of violence viewing substantially greater numbers of people would fall below the median presently observed for aggressive and antisocial behavior. Comparable effect sizes, and for that matter much smaller ones, from the field of public health indicate that the differences for individual welfare are substantial. This criterion also leads to an important observation. Effect size must be weighted by the risk or benefit implied. A large effect size is of scant importance if the outcome involved is of no significance. Conversely, even a very small effect size is of great social and individual significance, as exemplified by the data presented by Rosenthal, Rosnow, and Rubin (2000) indicating that a minute correlation between a remedy and the arrest of a disorder means that its application can save hundreds of thousands of lives. Thus, the evaluation of the meta-analyses in the end rests on a judgment about the seriousness of the behavior represented—hitting, fighting, and engaging in illegal activities.

Meta-analyses have made it clear to the scientific and public health communities that the effects of media violence on aggressive and antisocial behavior are real and important. Two apparent puzzles have made it difficult for the public to accept this. One is the occasion when an individual's behavior seems to deviate from his or her attitudes, norms, and values—the main means, in the minds of many, by which the media influence people. Our response is that there are multiple routes to behavior, and media sometimes may affect behavior by making certain kinds of acts more accessible in the behavioral repertoires of viewers without affecting dispositions. The second puzzle is when the enormity of a violent act seems to exceed any imaginable contribution of the media. Our response is that the role of the media in the complex processes governing behavior may be comparatively modest when the act is severe and dramatic. It may be confined to gatekeeping, in the sense that the media contribute to the options that individuals perceive as open to them. In that respect, the modest contribution may be crucial by increasing the likelihood of behavior made more prominent and often seemingly endorsed by the media. Thus, the evidence asserts that violent television and film portrayals contribute to acts of extreme violence as well as to the comparatively minor but nonetheless frequently socially disruptive behavior represented by interpersonal aggression.

NOTES

1. Meta-analysis estimates the size of the relationship between two variables using all retrievable data. An attempt is made to gather all existing studies on a particular topic for the purpose of making inferences about them in the collective. It addresses the "file drawer problem" (publication bias favoring statistically significant relationships) by including all locatable unpublished studies. The key concept is effect size. The prototypic calculation is represented by the ratio of the difference between treatment and control means and an estimate of the standard deviation:

$$\text{Effect Size} = \frac{\text{Mean}_t - \text{Mean}_c}{\text{ESD}}$$

where t = treatment, c = control, and ESD = estimate of the standard deviation. Because the standard deviation bears the same relationship to all normal distributions regardless of the particular metric, the resulting effect sizes can be averaged. This calculation obviously fits the data offered by experimental designs. However, over the years statistical maneuvers have made it possible to estimate comparable effect sizes for surveys and other designs. In addition, it has become possible to calculate statistical significance for the average effect size, and also "fail-safe numbers" (the quantity of nonsignificant findings necessary to reduce an effect size to the null range). In this process, studies are treated as if they were respondents in a survey with every conceivable attribute open to coding. A single study with multiple measures can generate more than one effect size; this has become the preferred practice in order to extract as much information as possible about the performance of different variables. Thus, analyses can be as narrow and theoretically focused as the investigator wishes, although most meta-analyses begin with a broad and inclusive treatment of the independent and dependent variables. The three strengths of meta-analysis are: (a) the unrelenting search for all available data; (b) estimates using the total number of cases studied; and (c) the ability to focus on questions of theoretical interest or data possessing particular qualities.

2. Ecological validity refers to the degree to which the conditions of a study match the everyday circumstances in which the phenomenon under observation occurs. Generally speaking, the greater the ecological validity, the more generalizable the results to everyday life. The exception is when a study, by whatever means, induces a response that also would influence behavior in everyday life; generalizability here is advanced regardless of the degree of ecological validity. For example, we need ecological validity to understand the conditions that lead to frustration, but we don't need ecological validity to conclude that frustration, however induced, enhances the likelihood of aggression. Study quality refers to attributes that facilitate valid inference. These include (depending on the analyst) a corroborating measure for a dependent variable, random assignment of subjects in an experiment, or high scores on scales of internal or external (ecological) validity.

3. Glass is foremost among the pioneers of the meta-analytic paradigm, because its public unveiling occurred in 1976 in his presidential address at the annual meeting of the American Educational Research Association in San Francisco (Glass, 1976). However, Robert Rosenthal at Harvard was working on a similar scheme (Rosenthal and Rubin, 1978), and neither Glass nor Rosenthal knew of the other's work.

4. Although aggressive portrayals and aggressive behavior comprised the largest number of independent and dependent variables examined by Hearold (1986), she included all possible combinations of antisocial and prosocial portrayals and behavior. Among the antisocial outcomes she included such putatively undesirable responses as stereotyping, passivity, reduced social interaction, and feelings of powerlessness. However, she did not include erotica with or without violence as an independent variable. Paik and Comstock (1994) took a narrower approach in regard to their dependent variables. They confined themselves to aggressive outcomes but included erotica with and without violence among their independent variables.

5. NBC collected the data over a three-and-a-half-year period from panels of elementary and high school students in a midwestern and a southwestern city. Measures of viewing and behavior were collected at six points in time, leading to 15 wave pairs (I-II, I-III, etc.) of earlier and later measurement. The time lags varied from three months to three-and-a-half years. The Ns varied from 497 for the shortest period to

112 for the longest period, and progressively declined as time lags grew longer because of attrition.

6. Please note that "minor aggression" may still be quite serious from the perspective of the victim, especially if the victim is a child.

7. As pointed out in an earlier footnote, fail-safe numbers are the quantity of non-significant findings necessary to reduce an effect size to the null range. A small fail-safe number indicates that only a few new studies with null results would be necessary to do so. A large fail-safe number, as is the case in the present instance, indicates that a very great many such studies would be necessary to do so.

CHAPTER 12

The Road to the V-Chip: Television Violence and Public Policy

Dale Kunkel

In his 1996 State of the Union address, President Bill Clinton called on Congress to adopt legislation to establish the V-chip as a means of helping parents limit their children's exposure to television violence. After roughly 50 years of controversy and debate about media violence, the president of the United States had decided to play a central role in addressing the issue. Clinton's initiative soon proved to be effective, as Congress quickly added a V-chip provision to the Telecommunications Act of 1996, which became law just three months following the president's speech.

How did the topic of media violence become part of the president's agenda? What developments, both scientific and political, led to this particular policy outcome as opposed to other alternatives? How viable is the V-chip as a means of resolving societal concern about the harmful effects of television violence on children? These and other related questions are the focus of this chapter on media violence and public policy. To address these topics, we will consider the historical development of both research and policy in this realm, as well as the interplay that has occurred across these two arenas over the many years of debate and controversy surrounding this issue.

THE ROOTS OF CONCERN ABOUT TELEVISION VIOLENCE

Concern about media violence predates the advent of television, which entered most American households during the 1950s. Research regarding the effects of violent media images on young people had focused initially on the movies. An elaborate series of projects known as the Payne Fund studies conducted in the 1930s included research examining the impact of motion picture crime and violence. The findings of the study by Blumer and Hauser (1933), entitled *Movies, Delinquency, and Crime*, read much like the conclusions from contemporary research on television violence, indicating that effects are contingent upon the age of the child, their personal characteristics, and the nature of the violent depiction involved. Nonetheless, this study, along with other Payne Fund reports (Charters, 1933; Dysinger & Ruckmick, 1933; Holaday & Stoddard, 1933; Peterson & Thurstone, 1933), established that there were widespread effects of the movies on children, fueling public concern about children's vulnerability to media influence (Wartella & Reeves, 1985).

Following the introduction of television, the public discussion about children and media violence quickly shifted focus from film to TV. Congress held its first hearings on the topic of television violence in the early 1950s, before even a single empirical study assessing the effects of television violence on children had been published (Cooper, 1996: Rowland, 1983). Despite that vacuum, members of the U.S. Senate Subcommittee on Juvenile Delinquency nonetheless concluded that television violence could be harmful to young viewers (U.S. Senate, Committee on the Judiciary, 1956).

While the debate about television violence was initially engaged in the 1950s, little more than heated discussion of the issue occurred prior to the 1960s, as politicians called for restraint from the television industry and network officials began to offer promises to take steps to address the problem (Cole & Oettinger, 1978). During the decade of the 1960s, public attention was further directed to the topic of TV violence as a result of popular press coverage of the work of Albert Bandura, a Stanford University psychologist who was in the early stages of developing his theory of observational learning. Television was a natural choice for Bandura to study given that his theory posited that children could learn to imitate or model behaviors they observed whether the behavior was live or "mediated," such as that shown on television or film.

Bandura's famous Bobo doll studies indicated that children who watched violent material were more likely to hit the doll following their viewing of violence that was not immediately punished. The effect remained whether they watched a human model on the screen or a woman dressed as an animal, such as might be found in a children's program of that era (Bandura, Ross, & Ross, 1963). Follow-up investigation by other researchers showed that children could replicate novel aggressive behaviors learned from television viewing as much as six to eight months later (Hicks, 1965, 1968).

These findings received prominent attention in the press (Bandura, 1963; "Picture of violence," 1964), and policymakers began to pay greater attention to the topic. In response to societal violence, including assassinations and riots in the 1960s, President Lyndon Johnson appointed a National Commission on the Causes and Prevention of Violence. Chaired by Dr. Milton Eisenhower, the group came to be known as the Eisenhower Commission. Its charter was to examine violence in society broadly, with the question of media influence only one of many factors within its purview. The Commission did not undertake any major new media research but rather surveyed all of the existing evidence before issuing a strong conclusion about the effects of televised violence:

We believe it is reasonable to conclude that a constant diet of violent behavior on television has an adverse effect on human character and attitudes. Violence on television encourages violent forms of behavior, and fosters moral and social values about violence in daily life which are unacceptable in a civilized society. (National Commission on the Causes and Prevention of Violence, 1969, p. 199)

If that conclusion was meant as an indictment, it was not intended to stimulate any formal government regulation. Indeed, in a separate volume prepared by the Eisenhower Commission's Media Task Force, the staff report observed:

The public has tremendous powers to bring about changes in mass media content that are held by no governmental agency. The source of the public's power derives directly from the fact that modern mass media organizations are economic in nature and orientation, and are directly dependent upon the public for their economic welfare. (Baker & Ball, 1969, p. 381)

Clearly, the suggestion was that viewers should turn away from violent programming, and that once they did, the industry would be forced to provide alternative approaches to entertainment that would attract larger audiences and thus greater advertising revenues. This perspective was consistent with that offered a few years earlier by Senator John Pastore, the chair of the U.S. Senate Subcommittee on Communications. In an address to the National Association of Broadcasters, Pastore observed that there was increasing evidence about the harmful effects of televised violence on children. Yet even so, he declared in 1962:

There is no one more than I, myself, who would resist interference with freedom of expression. On the other hand, it is well to remember that there is one distinguishing factor that separates the broadcasting system from almost every business in the United States—that is, a condition that the broadcaster must operate in the public interest. . . . I would urge the entire broadcast industry to take a new, long, hard look at itself and its practices, particularly in programming. (quoted in Cater & Strickland, 1975, pp. 15–16)

Again, the threat of any formal regulation was avoided at the same time that the industry was asked to take voluntary steps to address the concerns about violent programming. This pattern of policymakers using a "raised eyebrow" approach to address the issue of TV violence, which first surfaced in the 1950s, was becoming a regular theme.

Oversight for regulation of the broadcast industry fell squarely within Pastore's jurisdiction in the Senate. He was anxious to tackle the issue but felt it prudent to wait for the Eisenhower Commission to first conclude its work. Yet even before the Commission issued its report, Pastore dispatched a senior staffer to interview social scientists who were studying the issue to help him decide how he should proceed. Their advice was that further research was needed to establish more definitively the relationship between viewing televised violence and subsequent aggression (Cater & Strickland, 1975). Thus, in 1969, Pastore formally requested that the Surgeon General conduct a study of the effects of televised violence, "which will establish scientifically insofar as possible what harmful effects, if any, these programs have on children" (quoted in Cater & Strickland, 1975).

Some have suggested that Pastore's request was honored rather quickly because of resistance to the Eisenhower Commission's conclusion that TV violence was causing adverse effects on society (Ball-Rokeach, 2000). Regardless of the rationale, President Nixon gave his personal endorsement to Pastore's request, writing in a letter to the senator:

I want you to know that I join you in supporting the proposed one-year study of the possible relationship between . . . violence on television and anti-social behavior among young people. . . . I share your deep concern and strongly applaud your vigorous criticism of what you regard as a misuse of this great medium. (quoted in Cater & Strickland, 1975, pp. 19–20)

THE SURGEON GENERAL'S REPORT ON TV VIOLENCE

Working with unusual speed, the Surgeon General commissioned a large number of new empirical studies on the effects of televised violence on children, which were conducted by prominent scholars in psychology, communication, and the related social sciences. But the evidence produced by these studies was interpreted by an advisory board overseeing the projects, which was as much a political as a scientific body. Indeed, the Surgeon General had granted to the television industry veto power to object to the appointment of any particular social scientist, and many leading scholars such as Albert Bandura, Leonard Berkowitz, and Percy Tannenbaum were secretly blackballed from the group (Cater & Strickland, 1975; Liebert & Sprafkin, 1988). This fact was subsequently brought to public attention by the American Association for the Advancement of Science (AAAS) in its flagship publication, *Science* (Boffey & Walsh, 1970), raising a tempest within the scientific community.

The research projects commissioned by the Surgeon General encompassed a range of different methodologies and aspects of the issue. Some were experiments, others were surveys. Some were conducted in the field, others in the lab. Differing approaches were employed for defining and measuring violent behavior. From a scientific perspective, these differences were considered a critical strength because researchers feel most confident in drawing conclusions across studies when they have approached an issue from many diverse perspectives and can still produce convergent findings.

When the Surgeon General's Scientific Advisory Committee began to sift through the research that had been produced, it faced a formidable challenge. There were more than 20 independent research projects and 60 technical documents that had to be reviewed, digested, and integrated into an overall conclusion. Given that 5 of the 12 committee members had direct links to the television industry (as either current or former employees), there was significant debate about the need for qualifications before a final report could be issued (Cater & Strickland, 1975). Although cautious, the bottom line conveyed by the report still indicated clearly that television violence was contributing to harmful effects for some children.

Thus, the two sets of findings [experimental and survey] converge in three respects: a preliminary and tentative indication of a causal relation between viewing violence on television and aggressive behavior; an indication that such causal relation operates only on some children (who are predisposed to be aggressive); and an indication that it operates only in some environmental contexts. Such tentative and limited conclusions are not very satisfying. They represent substantially more knowledge than we had two years ago, but they leave many questions unanswered. (Surgeon General's Scientific Advisory Committee on Television and Social Behavior, 1972, pp. 18–19)

Twelve days after the final report was first delivered to the Surgeon General's office, and well before any public release of its findings was contemplated, the *New York Times* published a front-page story written by its television critic, who had obtained a leaked copy of the document (Gould, 1972). The headline, "TV Violence Held Unharmful to Youth," captures the essence of the journalist's fundamental misunderstanding of the report. Written by an individual sympathetic to the industry who was apparently overwhelmed by the technical language and scientific qualifications that had been carefully crafted by the committee, the story essentially absolved television of any responsibility for harmful effects. While the actual report stated that those affected by viewing TV violence might be either "a small portion or a substantial portion of the total population of young television viewers," the *Times*'s story opened with the following claim:

The office of the United States Surgeon General has found that violence in television programming does not have an adverse effect on the majority of the nation's youth but may influence small groups of youngsters predisposed by many factors to aggressive behavior. (Gould, 1972, p. 1)

The Surgeon General was caught flat-footed by the leak, and the *New York Times* story was so widely distributed that a major opportunity to convey the evidence about TV violence accurately to the public was clearly lost. In retrospect, this turn of events may well have set back efforts to ameliorate the harms of televised violence for at least a decade or two by fueling the public misconception that research on the topic was equivocal or inconclusive.

Pastore conducted hearings subsequent to the release of the Surgeon General's report in an effort to correct the record. At the outset of those hearings, Surgeon General Jesse Steinfeld testified:

While the committee report is carefully phrased and qualified in language acceptable to social scientists, it is clear to me that the causal relationship between televised violence and anti-social behavior is sufficient to warrant appropriate and immediate remedial action. (U.S. Senate Subcommittee on Communications, 1972, p. 73)

Seeking to underscore the clarity of the Surgeon General's conclusion, Senator Pastore pursued the following exchange with his star witness:

Pastore: You, Dr. Steinfeld, as the chief health officer of the United States of America, have said, " . . . There comes a time when the data are sufficient to justify action. That time has come." Is that your unequivocal opinion?

Steinfeld: Yes, sir.

Pastore: And you reached that opinion from this report?

Steinfeld: From this report, the five volumes [of research findings], and other reading and attendance at a number of meetings. (quoted in Cater & Strickland, 1975, pp. 86)

According to most observers, the hearings adjourned in a spirit of high concern if somewhat vague purpose (Cater & Strickland, 1975). If the public record had been corrected, the press was paying much less attention than when the report was initially leaked. Thus, the impact of the hearings on public opinion was muted.

NO EASY SOLUTIONS ON THE HORIZON

As one means of acting on the research findings, Pastore suggested an ongoing monitoring project that would report on the levels of violence on television from year to year. The idea was to force accountability for the industry's public pronouncements that it would seek to reduce and/or present more responsibly any violent depictions in its programming. Although conducted largely without any governmental support, such an effort was pursued in subsequent years on an intermittent basis by George Gerbner and his colleagues at the Annenberg School of Communications at the University of Pennsylvania (Gerbner & Gross, 1976; Gerbner, Gross, Morgan, & Signorielli, 1986). Gerbner's reports received substantial attention in the press but had little impact on industry practices, as they were constantly criticized by television executives on various grounds, such as for including cartoon or comedic violence in the tallies.

Pastore also pressured the Federal Communications Commission (FCC) to take action to reduce violence on television, and in 1975 FCC Chair Richard Wiley took a fateful step as he sought to address the issue. Wiley summoned the heads of each of the major commercial broadcast networks to his office in Washington, and he issued an ultimatum that led them to "voluntarily" adopt a self-regulatory policy known as the "Family Viewing Hour." Under the policy, the first hour of prime time on each network (8:00–9:00 P.M. on the East and West Coasts; 7:00–8:00 P.M. in the Midwest) would be devoted exclusively to programming without any violence and thus would presumably be appropriate for viewing by all members of the family regardless of age. Although the Family Hour policy was adopted solely as industry self-regulation, it was ultimately overturned in the courts as a First Amendment violation because of the coercion applied by the FCC chair to instigate it (Cowan, 1979).

With the dawning of the decade of the 1980s, a significant shift occurred in the extent to which the FCC was willing to regulate the broadcast industry (Derthick & Quirk, 1985; Horwitz, 1989). The growth of cable television was burgeoning and beginning to threaten the broadcasters' domination of the television audience. Broadcasters complained that it was unfair to saddle them with any further "public interest obligations" when their new competitors faced no such constraints. Given the Reagan administration's general reliance on marketplace competition rather than governmental regulation to promote the public interest, the FCC soon began to issue rulings rescinding many of its long-standing rules. With the regulatory climate clearly shifting, and the threat of any formal governmental intervention more improbable than ever, there was little to be gained by policymakers conveying any further "raised eyebrow" concern about TV violence.

Not surprisingly, then, the issue of TV violence was largely ignored by politicians for a time, although more research evidence continued to accrue (Potter, 1999). In 1982, the National Institutes of Mental Health (NIMH) issued a "ten-year update" summarizing the new empirical evidence that had been produced since the original Surgeon General's report in 1972 (Pearl, Bouthilet, & Lazar, 1982). The growth in knowledge had been substantial, with many more published studies on the topic having appeared in academic journals. With a stronger base of findings upon which to draw, the NIMH report concluded much more strongly than had the Surgeon General that viewing televised violence was causally related to aggressive attitudes and behaviors, desensitization, and fear effects in children. Indeed, the report sought to move the debate forward by emphasizing in its executive summary: "The research question has moved from asking whether or not there is an effect to seeking explanations for that effect" (National Institutes of Mental Health, 1982, p. 6).

Unlike the 1970s, when broadcast executives responded contritely to most policymakers' complaints about televised violence, in the 1980s the industry shifted to a more contentious stance. Emboldened by the favorable shift in the political climate they now enjoyed, industry leaders began to openly question the validity of the conclusion that television violence was harmful for children. The ABC network prepared an elaborate response to the 1982 NIMH report, offering a detailed critique of the methodological shortcomings of many of the major studies cited in the document and suggesting that their findings simply could not be trusted. Then, benefiting from a fortuitous development in academic circles, the National Association of Broadcasters (NAB) distributed to every member of Congress a copy of a literature review published by Jonathan Freedman (1984), a psychologist at the University of Toronto, that sternly refuted the conclusion that violence on television causes any negative effects for children.

Like the ABC report, Freedman criticized in painstaking detail methodological limitations that in his view rendered all of the existing evidence on the topic of little value. To those unfamiliar with social science, and its reliance on the convergence of evidence across many imperfect studies to draw meaningful conclusions, Freedman's criticism may have seemed compelling (for further discussion see Huesmann & Taylor, chapter 6, this volume). His arguments certainly received significant attention from television critics and reporters sympathetic to the industry who often harbored their own personal doubts about the harmful effects of media violence. Although Freedman remained virtually a lone dissenter among social scientists, he received disproportionate coverage from reporters trained to cover "both sides" of every story, further contributing to the public's misperception that researchers remained divided about the effects of TV violence.

One final development transpired in the 1980s that further loosened restrictions on the portrayal of violence on television. The NAB had long maintained an industrywide, self-regulatory code (known as the NAB Code) that included a broad range of stipulations, from limits on the amount of advertising that could be aired to the ways in which violence could be depicted. Given that the NAB Code was originally crafted as a means to respond to governmental concerns in the 1940s and 1950s, it was ironic that in the 1980s the Reagan administration's Justice Department challenged the Code as an antitrust violation. The industry was only too happy to abandon its self-regulatory Code and agreed to a consent decree to do so in 1983 before the case even went to trial (Maddox & Zanot, 1984; MacCarthy, 1995). Without the industrywide Code, it was now up to the discretion of each network or station regarding what limits if any to place on depictions of violence (Wurtzel & Lometti, 1984). In an era when broadcasters were facing increased competition from unedited movies shown on cable, pressure began to mount to "push the envelope" in defining the limits of acceptable content for broadcast television. While it is impossible to disentangle all of these factors, the confluence of a reduced threat of governmental involvement coupled with relaxed self-regulation led many observers to conclude that television violence increased in intensity if not frequency during the 1980s (Murray, 1995).

A RENEWAL OF CONCERN, AND FINALLY SOME ACTION

While attention to the issue of television violence generally waned in the 1980s, an unlikely champion for the cause emerged in the latter part of that decade. Senator Paul Simon of Illinois, a Democrat who was a strong free-speech advocate, took a personal interest in the topic after viewing a particularly gruesome scene of violence on television that troubled him, causing him to worry about its impact on children. Simon quickly became a student of the topic, reviewing all of the previous studies and reports on the issue. Convinced by the evidence that portrayals of violence led to harmful effects on children, yet uncomfortable with the prospect of any governmental censorship of program content, Simon sought an alternative path to address the problem. Like Senator Pastore before him, Senator Simon called upon television industry leaders to exercise self-restraint in their presentation of violence, reducing "excessive" or "gratuitous" depictions. While this stance alone might not have garnered much attention, Simon offered a novel proposal by also introducing legislation to help facilitate his request.

Aware that the courts had ruled that the old industrywide, self-regulatory guidelines, the NAB Code, represented an antitrust violation, Simon introduced a new legislative proposal to grant the industry an exemption from antitrust law for the purpose of collective discussions across networks about how to reduce violence on television. Technically speaking, the legislation required nothing of the industry. It simply created the opportunity for television executives to meet and consider ways to respond to the problem should they choose to do so without fear of antitrust litigation, which they had often argued prohibited such action in the past. Simon's proposal, known as the Television Program Improvement Act of 1990, was approved by Congress, granting a three-year period during which the antitrust exemption would apply (Schlegel, 1993).

For most of that three-year period, the television industry declined to take any action in response to Senator Simon's initiative. During that time, however, other events were unfolding that increased the political pressure on the industry (Windhausen, 1994). In particular, the level of consensus within the scientific community about the effects of televised violence began to consolidate in important ways. Such organizations as the American Medical Association (1996), the American Psychological Association (1993), the Centers for Disease Control (1991), and the National Academy of Sciences (Reiss &

Roth, 1993) all issued reports drawing the same strong conclusion: viewing televised violence poses a risk of harmful effects on children. Public opinion followed right in step with these conclusions, with a strong majority holding the view that media violence is harmful to children and that there was too much violence on television (Guttman, 1994; Times Mirror Center for People and the Press, 1993; Welkos, 1995).

Sensing the shift in the political climate, the industry finally agreed in 1993 to a formal response to Simon's initiative, pledging both to treat violence more responsibly in programs and to commission independent academic studies to hold them accountable for their promise (National Television Violence Study, 1997, 1998a, 1998b; UCLA Center for Communication Policy, 1995, 1996, 1998). To the industry's surprise, however, these actions proved to be "too little, too late" to avoid further government intervention.

In a political context shaped by strong scientific consensus about the harms of violent portrayals, and perhaps even stronger public opinion against media violence, a new proposal known as the V-chip started to gain significant support. Initially championed by U.S. Representative Edward Markey, and then boosted immeasurably by President Clinton's endorsement in his State of the Union address, V-chip legislation was approved as part of the Telecommunications Act of 1996. The television industry was clearly caught off guard by the speed of these developments. After decades of experiencing idle threats but never any formal action from policymakers, the V-chip was now the second piece of legislation to be approved by Congress in the 1990s on the topic of television violence.

THE BIRTH OF THE V-CHIP

The technology of the V-chip is relatively simple. It is an electronic filtering device that parents can use to block the reception of sensitive or potentially harmful programming they do not want their children to see, presuming that television sets are equipped with V-chip filters and programs are categorized in some fashion that can facilitate blocking decisions.

Under the law passed by Congress, the television industry was given one year to devise its own system to categorize programs for violence and other sensitive material (including sex and offensive language), and to then submit this system to the FCC for its approval. If the television industry failed to act, or if its system was not deemed "acceptable," then the FCC would be required to appoint an advisory committee to design a model V-chip rating system. Oddly enough, however, the industry would not be bound to actually employ such a system designed by the FCC, or for that matter, any system at all. The only firm requirement in the law was that all television sets sold in the United States must be equipped with a V-chip device that would facilitate program-blocking capabilities.

Clearly this law is strongly coercive, although technically it is true that the industry's decision to employ V-chip ratings was a voluntary one. This provision has led most legal scholars to conclude that the V-chip policy adopted by Congress is not a violation of the First Amendment (Minsky, 1997; Price, 1998; Spitzer, 1998), although no court has yet been asked to rule on that question.

Once the V-chip law was adopted, the television industry faced the task of devising a system of ratings to categorize programs for potential blocking by parents. The industry could hardly afford to refuse; to do so would leave it in an extraordinarily awkward position. With TV sets soon to include the technology to filter out the most violent programs, refusing to label those programs in some way would almost certainly yield the industry a public relations nightmare.

Longtime Motion Picture Association of America (MPAA) President Jack Valenti led the industrywide effort to create a rating system for use with the V-chip technology, bringing together both broadcast and cable networks. The initial rating system, first implemented in early 1997, employed an age-based advisory framework virtually identical to that used in the MPAA's film rating system. The MPAA ratings, introduced in 1968 and also devised by Valenti, have been criticized for ignoring scientific evidence about the impact of media on children while emphasizing parents' concerns about the "offensiveness" of the content (Cantor, 1998a; Wilson, Linz, & Randall, 1990). Like the MPAA system, the new V-chip ratings provided a single prescriptive judgment about the appropriateness of the content for children of a particular age range, without conveying any specific, descriptive content information. This meant that parents who wanted to simply block out all violent programming would be stymied, as the new V-chip ratings offered no means to identify programs that contained violence. Congressman Markey quipped that Mr. Valenti had taken the "V" out of the V-chip.

Almost as soon as they were unveiled, the V-chip program ratings came under attack from academic experts, parents, and child advocacy groups (Cooper, 2000; Gruenwald, 1997). Concern was raised about the risk of a boomerang effect from the age-based advisories, whereby younger children might be more attracted to a show that was rated as intended for older children. Research documenting this "forbidden fruit" effect had just been published, demonstrating that simple descriptive content labels (e.g., contains violent content) did not increase children's interest in programs, whereas age-based advisories (e.g., parental discretion advised for children under a certain age) did (Bushman & Stack, 1996; Cantor & Harrison, 1997; Hofschire, 2001). Subsequent studies have confirmed that some children do indeed "misuse" the ratings to identify programs for viewing simply because they are rated more restrictively (Greenberg, Rampoldi-Hnilo, & Hofschire, 2001; Foehr, Rideout, & Miller, 2001a).

Criticism was also fueled by the findings from survey research indicating that most parents preferred straightforward descriptive information about the levels of violence in a given show, unfiltered by the television industry's judgment about the age at which children should be allowed to view a program (Cantor, Stutman, & Duran, 1997; Mifflin, 1997). Complaints from the child advocacy community quickly reached a fever pitch, generating significant controversy about the V-chip ratings initially devised by the industry (Cantor, 1998b; Cooper, 2000). Frequent front-page coverage was devoted to the story in most newspapers, and a congressional hearing soon focused the debate (U.S. Senate Committee on Commerce, Science, & Transportation, 1997).

Shortly thereafter, and less than a year after the V-chip ratings were first introduced, the industry agreed to amend the ratings framework to incorporate content-specific categories that would complement the age-based advisory labels (Farhi, 1997). Programs would receive a "V" to designate violence, an "S" for sexual behavior, a "D" for sexual dialogue, and an "L" for adult language (see Table 12.1). Finally, instead of applying a standard "V" to label the violence found in children's cartoon shows, an "FV" designation was devised to identify what the industry termed "fantasy violence." All of these new ratings were applied as a complement to the basic age-based rating framework that remained in effect.

HOW WELL IS THE V-CHIP WORKING?

By the end of 1997, most networks—both broadcast and cable—were applying all aspects of the V-chip ratings to their qualifying programming, although NBC was (and still is) a lone dissenter in refusing to add the content descriptors to the basic age-based advisory framework. Under the system guidelines, sports and news are exempt and thus all such programs go unrated, as do all advertisements and program promotions, regardless of whether or not they contain any violence. It was not until several years later, in January 2000, that all television receivers (13″ or larger) sold in the United States actually included the V-chip capability. Thus, during these early years it was impossible for most parents to employ the V-chip technology's blocking capabilities, although the information about each program's rating, which appears on-screen and in many program-listing services, could be used by parents who actively supervise their children's television diet. Since 2000, any family with a new TV set can now use the V-chip as a filtering device.

From the outset, support for the concept of the V-chip system was very strong among parents. In one nationally representative survey, 84 percent of parents said they strongly favor or somewhat favor the V-chip, and 72 percent said they would use it often or once in awhile (Stanger & Gridina, 1999). Only 11 percent said they would never use it. Another nationally representative survey of parents in 1998 found that 54 percent reported they often or sometimes used the program ratings to help guide their children's viewing

Table 12.1
V-Chip Rating Category Descriptions

The TV Rating Guidelines		
The following categories apply to programs designed solely for children:		
TVY	All Children	This program is designed to be appropriate for all children. Whether animated or live-action, the themes and elements in this program are specifically designed for a very young audience, including children from ages 2 to 6. This program is not expected to frighten younger children.
TVY7	Directed to Older Children	This program is designed for children age 7 and above. It may be more appropriate for children who have acquired the developmental skills needed to distinguish between make-believe and reality. Themes and elements in this program may include mild fantasy violence or comedic violence, or may frighten children under the age of 7. Therefore, parents may wish to consider the suitability of this program for their very young children.
TV-Y7-FV	Directed to Older Children Fantasy Violence	For those programs where fantasy violence may be more intense or more combative than other programs in this category, such programs will be designated TV-Y7-FV.
The following categories apply to programs designed for the entire audience:		
TVG	General Audience	Most parents would find this program suitable for all ages. Although this rating does not signify a program designed specifically for children, most parents may let younger children watch this program unattended. It contains little or no violence, no strong language and little or no sexual dialogue or situations.
TVPG	Parental Guidance Suggested	This program contains material that parents may find unsuitable for younger children. Many parents may want to watch it with their younger children. The theme itself may call for parental guidance and/or the program contains one or more of the following: moderate violence (V), some sexual situations (S), infrequent coarse language (L), or some suggestive dialogue (D).
TV14	Parents Strongly Cautioned	This program contains some material that many parents would find unsuitable for children under 14 years of age. Parents are strongly urged to exercise greater care in monitoring this program and are cautioned against letting children under the age of 14 watch unattended. This program contains one or more of the following: intense violence (V), intense sexual situations (S), strong coarse language (L), or intensely suggestive dialogue (D).
TVMA	Mature Audience Only	This program is specifically designed to be viewed by adults and therefore may be unsuitable for children under 17. This program contains one or more of the following: graphic violence (V), explicit sexual activity (S), or crude indecent language (L).

Source: http://www.tvguidelines.org.

(Foehr, Rideout, & Miller, 2001b). More recently, a national survey conducted in 2000–2001 found that 16 percent of parents said they always use the ratings, 10 percent said they often use them, and 7 percent said they sometimes use them (Krcmar, Pulaski, & Curtis, 2001). Although differences in question phrasing may account for some of the variation across studies, it seems clear that there is a substantial group of parents who use the V-chip ratings, but that many still do not (Greenberg & Rampoldi-Hnilo, 2001).

Several factors probably account for this response. First of all, large numbers of parents simply don't know about the V-chip. One study found that roughly one of every five parents are not aware of the V-chip rating system (Foehr, Rideout, & Miller, 2001b), while another indicated that more than half (53 percent) of parents who own a television set equipped with a V-chip device are unaware of that capability (Kaiser Family Foundation, 2001). Given the roughly 10-year life expectancy for most television receivers, it will be quite some time before more than a small minority of families actually have a TV set with the V-chip technology in it. Those that do, and who have tried to use the V-chip capability, report that the user interface is poorly designed and that activating the blocking feature is difficult and complicated (Woodard et al., 2002). And even if a parent has a V-chip in their television and desperately wishes to activate it, there is no easy source of help for a parent who is having difficulty doing so. Unlike almost any other new technology, there is no sponsor associated with this device who either markets, publicizes, or supports its use. All of these factors have clearly posed obstacles to the widespread adoption of the V-chip.

Another possibility may also be contributing to the apparent gap between the strong support voiced for the concept of the V-chip and the lukewarm reception it has subsequently experienced. In surveying public opinion about the impact of television on children, numerous studies have identified a common pattern known as the "third-person effect" (Hoffner & Buchanan, 2002; Hoffner et al., 1999, 2001). This phenomenon refers to parents who believe that television violence has a harmful effect on children in general, but either less so or not at all on their own child. Given the frequency with which this belief pattern occurs, it may well be that most parents feel society needs a V-chip, but that they don't necessarily need to use it to protect their children, whom they consider to be less vulnerable than the average child to such influence.

Besides these factors, other issues perhaps best characterized as "growing pains" have also limited the utility of the system for parents so far. One study indicates that the content-based ratings are not applied accurately, resulting in the vast majority of violent programming not receiving a "V" label (Kunkel et al., 2002). Another finds that the rating listed for a program in the *TV Guide* does not always match with the rating assigned to the same program when it is actually aired (Greenberg, Eastin, & Mastro, 2001). And a third study documents that parents would rate programs more restrictively than the V-chip ratings typically applied to programs by the television industry (Walsh & Gentile, 2001). Clearly, parents who might be potential adopters of the system but who encounter any or all of these shortcomings may be discouraged from bothering with it at all (Greenberg & Rampoldi-Hnilo, 2001). Thus, given the limited number of families with access to the technology and the many complications that still surround its use, it is too soon to reasonably pass judgment on the extent to which the V-chip will ultimately prove useful as a means of resolving concern about television violence.

To be sure, many of the problems with the current television ratings are not specific to the V-chip system. Other ratings systems face similar issues, such as parents questioning the validity of media-rating judgments. For example, Walsh and Gentile (2001) asked parents to assign ratings for TV shows, video games, and movies, and then compared the parents' judgments with the industry-provided ratings for the same content. Across all three media, the industry-provided ratings were consistently more lenient than the ratings assigned by parents. Another common concern involves the confusion that parents experience when forced to deal with different rating systems that vary substantially from one medium to the next. To address this concern, some have suggested the creation of a universal system of media ratings that would employ a consistent ratings framework across all of the media commonly used by children (Walsh & Gentile, 2001; Walsh, Gentile, & van Brederode, 2002), and Congress has already begun to show some interest in this possibility (U.S. Senate Committee on Governmental Affairs, 2001).

ALTERNATIVE APPROACHES FOR ADDRESSING CONCERN ABOUT TV VIOLENCE

It remains unclear whether the V-chip and ratings will stand as the principal policy response to concerns about television violence, or if other options might be pursued in the future. Certainly there are policymakers who believe further steps are necessary, and several new legislative proposals have been introduced in Congress in recent years. Among these are bills that would either facilitate or mandate greater industry self-regulation, as well as restrict the times at which violent programming could be aired. It is this latter proposal that is most intriguing because of its parallel to the current regulation of broadcast indecency, a policy that has withstood repeated legal challenge over the years.

The policy to protect children from broadcast indecency is radically different from the regulatory approach used for violent portrayals. Material considered indecent includes both sexually explicit content and certain forms of offensive language (Milagros-Rivera, 1995; Milagros-Rivera & Ballard, 1998). Under long-standing FCC rules, indecent content may not be broadcast at times when children are likely to be in the audience, which is presently considered to be between 6:00 A.M. and 10:00 P.M. This policy has been challenged repeatedly in the courts on First Amendment grounds, yet consistently upheld as constitutional (*Action for Children's Television v. FCC*, 1995; *FCC v. Pacifica Foundation*, 1978), largely because of the unique aspects of the broadcast medium. The airwaves belong to the public, and are a scarce resource that cannot function effectively without government regulation controlling who uses each frequency. Consequently, those granted the privilege of broadcasting on the public airwaves must comply with public interest obligations, such as the FCC's restriction on indecent material.

Since 1993, Senator Ernest Hollings has sponsored legislation in every session of Congress that would regulate television violence in essentially the same fashion as broadcast indecency. That is, violent programming would be subject to a "safe harbor" time restriction, whereby it could not be aired until late evening hours when children are either not watching or are expected to be supervised by an adult. Hollings has persisted with his support for this proposal even following the adoption of the V-chip. He argues that the children at greatest risk of harmful influence from viewing TV violence are from families least likely to use the V-chip (i.e., latch-key children, children with inattentive parents), a premise already corroborated by research (Abelman, 1999, 2001). While the V-chip allows each parent to decide the level of exposure to violent programming that they deem appropriate for their child, it also allows parents to decide on no limits at all. From a public health perspective, that outcome would do nothing to stem the contribution of media violence to societal violence, thus rendering the V-chip at best only a partial solution to the problems posed by children who view TV violence.

From a legal perspective, the social science evidence documenting the risk of negative effects from children's viewing of televised violence constitutes a "compelling governmental interest," which may therefore legitimize regulatory intrusions on otherwise protected speech. Courts employ a balancing test, which weighs the degree of harm at risk with the extent of freedoms that are sacrificed by adoption of a given law. When Hollings initially introduced his proposal, then–U.S. Attorney General Janet Reno (1993) formally endorsed the constitutionality of the "safe harbor" approach to regulating TV violence at a congressional hearing, just as have some other legal scholars (Saunders, 1996), though not all who have addressed the topic (Edwards & Berman, 1995). Hollings's proposal has gained serious attention, receiving the Senate Commerce Committee's formal approval in the 106th Congress in 2000 before expiring at the end of the session without further consideration.

In sum, restricting the times at which television violence may be shown remains a potential policy strategy, although it suffers several serious limitations. It generates strong opposition from free-speech advocates who are troubled by its strong degree of government censorship; there is no clear legal consensus that the policy would indeed be considered constitutional by the courts; it treats all portrayals of violence the same, grouping together those depictions with a relatively high risk of harmful effects on child viewers with those judged more benign; and, to be effective, the policy would have to be applied to cable as well as broadcast television, which would pose even greater legal challenges to the law's constitutionality. It is well established that non-broadcast media such as cable qualify for greater First Amendment protection than do broadcast media (Carter, Franklin, & Wright, 1999).

PROSPECTS FOR THE FUTURE

Economist Jay Hamilton (1998) observes that the high frequency of violence on television is the product of rational, self-interested decisions by television programmers, who know well that such content succeeds in attracting large audiences. Hamilton offers the novel argument that the harms of television violence are, from a public policy perspective, much like the harms associated with environmental pollution.

Television violence generates negative externalities, which economists define as costs that are borne by individuals other than those involved in the production activity. Environmental pollution is a familiar example of an externality, since a firm that generates hazardous wastes may not incorporate the full costs to society of its production decisions if it is not led to consider the damage to the environment from its wastes. Similarly, broadcasters attempting to deliver audiences to advertisers . . . may not fully incorporate the costs to society of their violent programming if these costs include such factors as increased levels of crime and aggression. The parallel to pollution is important, since in the United States the remedies proposed to deal with violent programming such as zoning provisions (e.g., restricting violent broadcasts to certain times) and information provision (e.g., reporting on the violent content of programming . . .) are similar to policies already adopted to deal with environmental pollution. (Hamilton, 1998, p. 3)

The harms of television violence have also been linked metaphorically with those of cigarette smoking, most recently by Bushman and Anderson (2001).

First, not everyone who smokes gets lung cancer, and not everyone who gets lung cancer is a smoker. Similarly, not everyone who watches violent media becomes aggressive, and not everyone who is aggressive watches violent media. Second, smoking is not the only factor that causes lung cancer, but it is an important factor. Similarly, watching violent media is not the only factor that causes aggression, but it is an important one. . . . One cigarette has little impact on lung cancer. However, repeated exposure to tobacco smoke . . . seriously increases the likelihood of a person contracting lung cancer. Similarly, watching one violent TV show has little impact on the likelihood of a child becoming a habitual violent offender, but the empirical evidence now shows that repeated exposure to violent media . . . causes a serious increase in the likelihood of a person becoming a habitually aggressive person and occasionally a violent offender. (Bushman & Anderson, 2001, p. 481)

There is one further parallel that links the problems associated with television violence to each of the issues of environmental pollution and cigarette smoking, and that is the posture adopted by the affected industries in which they contest the legitimacy of the science that documents the societal ills to which they contribute. In the realm of television violence, that campaign continues today. Consider the following examples. In an effort to clarify the state of the scientific evidence, four leading public health organizations (American Academy of Pediatrics, American Academy of Child and Adolescent Psychiatry, American Psychological Association, and American Medical Association) recently issued a "Joint Statement on the Impact of Entertainment Violence on Children" (2000) at a Congressional Public Health Summit. The statement concluded that studies "point overwhelmingly to a causal connection between media violence and aggressive behavior in some children" (p. 1). Shortly thereafter, the leaders of each of these organizations received the following letter from the Motion Picture Association of America (MPAA):

I read with interest the "Joint Statement on the Impact of Entertainment Violence on Children" released on July 26th of this year. In the statement and at the Congressional Public Health Summit, your organization stated that studies exist that prove a causal connection between violent entertainment and aggressive behavior in children. . . . I am not aware of any studies that show such a "causal connection." I would very much appreciate your sending me copies of, or at least citations to, the studies that your members conducted or relied upon that proved this "causal connection" between media violence and aggression in children.

Sincerely yours,

Fritz Attaway

Senior Vice-President for Government Relations

Washington General Counsel

At almost the same time, the MPAA commissioned Jonathan Freedman to update his 1984 review in which he concluded that all of the evidence supporting the link between viewing violence and subsequent aggressive behavior is flawed. Freedman (2002) has now parlayed that report into a new book making the same arguments. Concurrently, a children's television writer, Gerard Jones (2002), has published a popular press book entitled *Killing Monsters: Why Children Need Fantasy, Super-Heroes, and Make-Believe Violence*, endorsing the catharsis hypothesis (i.e., viewing violence purges the need for children to act aggressively), which has been consistently and unequivocally rebutted by empirical research. And finally, newspapers such as the *New York Times* continue to publish Op-Ed columns from media industry figures criticizing the scientific finding that viewing televised violence poses a risk of harmful effects for children (Rhodes, 2000) and then refuse to print rebuttals from leading social scientists who attempt to set the record straight (Bushman & Anderson, 2001).

Given this context, it is understandable that the public may become confused about the state of the evidence documenting the harmfulness of television violence. Unlike most other aspects of science, the study of television viewing involves an area in which everyone has direct experience, and virtually everyone seems to have a personal opinion regarding the impact of media violence on human behavior. Consequently, reporters who cover the topic can easily obtain a contrasting perspective, and their journalistic training may be prompting them to provide "balance" to the scientific claims (Hoffner, 1998). Today, however, the two sides of this issue are hardly in equilibrium.

On one side is the U.S. Surgeon General, the U.S. Centers for Disease Control and Prevention, the National Institutes of Mental Health, the American Medical Association, the American Psychological Association, and a host of other public health, professional, and scientific agencies. They all concur that viewing televised violence poses a risk of harmful effects on children. On the other side is the media entertainment industry and a handful of academic dissenters such as Freedman who criticize the empirical research of others but perform none of their own to buttress their viewpoints. Indeed, not a single scholar among those few who dissent from the overwhelming scientific consensus has published a study in a peer-reviewed journal to provide any new data consistent with their claim over the last quarter-century. Rather, the counterpoint they offer to the scientific consensus is quite simply a collection of contrarian arguments—that the measures in the studies are flawed, that the sample of subjects is too small, that one can't extrapolate experiments to the real world, and so on. All of these reservations have been carefully considered and dismissed as invalid by a legion of the most prestigious public health and social scientific organizations in the country (see Huesmann & Taylor, chapter 6, this volume). Yet astonishingly, most news coverage of the topic of television violence still gives substantial emphasis to the "contrasting viewpoint," leaving the clear impression that there are two equal sides to this story (Bushman & Anderson, 2001; Hoffner, 1998).

Two ingredients are essential if there are to be any new policies that address the ongoing concerns about television violence. The first is that there must be compelling scientific evidence documenting the risks posed by children's exposure to violent depictions. That criterion has already been met. But there must also be a public consensus that new policies are needed to address the concerns. Thus, the future battles about television violence policy may well be focused more on public opinion than on scientific evidence. Given that context, it is essential that scientists and child advocates play an active role in communicating their knowledge to the public-at-large about the effects of television violence on children. It is an interesting paradox that such efforts necessarily involve the television industry itself to deliver the message.

CHAPTER 13

The Frontiers of Media Research

W. James Potter

The purpose of all media violence research is, in essence, to contribute to our understanding about risks of exposure. In moving us toward this goal, each media violence study can be categorized as advancing our understanding along one of three paths. One path includes those studies that were designed to determine if particular effects could occur as a result of exposure to violence in the media; this is the "effects" path. A second group of studies seeks to determine which factors—in the portrayals, in the viewers, and in the exposure environments—are associated with which effects; this is the "influence" path. A third line of research has analyzed media content to determine how much violence was being presented, where it was being displayed, and the nature of those portrayals; this is the "content" path. Increases in our understanding of risk depend on researchers generating high-quality findings along all three paths of inquiry.

In this chapter, I will briefly show how far we have come along each of these three paths, thus defining the frontier of our understanding. Then I will argue that there are certain steps we desperately need to take so that we can use our resources most efficiently and generate findings that have the greatest chance of increasing our understanding about the nature of these effects and how we can control risks.

EFFECTS PATH

For more than seven decades, social critics have been speculating on the variety of changes the media have been bringing about in our lives. Social scientists have been conducting studies to document which of those effects actually do occur. This formal research began in the late 1920s with a set of a dozen investigations—called the Payne Studies—of the effect of movies on children (Charters, 1933). Other notable studies during this early period of media research were *The Invasion from Mars: A Study in the Psychology of Panic* by Hadley Cantril (1940) and *Television in the Lives of Our Children* (Schramm, Lyle, & Parker, 1961). The findings of these studies indicated that exposure to media violence can cause fear effects and it can influence some to behave aggressively.

At the end of the 1960s, Congress funded *The Surgeon General's Report: Television and Growing Up* in order to generate a range of social science studies to determine clearly and convincingly whether media violence was exerting an effect on the public. The social scientists involved with the project concluded that there was strong evidence that exposure to violent messages on television can often lead to the lowering of an individual's natural inhibitions toward behaving aggressively. This conclusion, however, was muddled in the political process surrounding the release of the report.

Since that time, researchers have continued to look for evidence of many more effects from exposure to violence in the media. Scholars reviewing this continually growing body of research are in substantial agreement that exposure to media violence can lead people to learn how to behave aggressively and that exposure can furthermore disinhibit them (see Table 13.1). Beyond these few well-documented effects, there are many others that are mentioned as possible effects, but scholars differ in their interpretations about which effects have been documented well.

This lack of agreement illuminates the frontier of media effects research. While there is a consensus around a few effects, there appears to be some confusion about how many effects there are and what they should be named. For example, "learning" seems to be used by scholars to refer to more than one effect. The National Television Violence Study (NTVS) (1996, 1997) used the term "learning" to apply to a range of effects including what some reviewers split into disinhibition and imitation (Comstock, Chaffee, Katzman, McCombs, & Roberts, 1978; Condry, 1989; Gunter, 1994; Liebert & Schwartzberg, 1977) or into observational learning and disinhibition (Signorielli, 1990). Also, Gunter (1994) separates arousal and desensitization, while Condry (1989) lumps them together as one effect. Donnerstein, Slaby, and Eron (1994) refer to an "aggressor effect" but what they seem to be doing is including the effects of observational learning, imitation, triggering, and disinhibition into one effect.

Just as it has been important for researchers to reach a consensus that there are effects from exposure to violence in the media (see Huesmann & Taylor, chapter 6, this volume), it is now important for researchers to reach a consensus about what those effects are. It is not sufficient to stop at the current agreement that there are disinhibition and fear effects. It is now important that we recognize that there is already evidence for several more effects and

Table 13.1
How Many Effects of Media Violence Are There?

- Liebert and Schwartzberg (1977) see two primary effects: direct imitation and disinhibition.

- Hearold (1986) sees three: learning, incitement of violent acts, and catharsis.

- NTVS (1996, 1997) perceives three: learning, desensitization, and fear.

- Comstock, Chaffee, Katzman, McCombs, and Roberts (1978) see four major effects: imitation, disinhibition, desensitization, and catharsis.

- Josephson (1995) lists four for children: imitation, disinhibition, triggering, and "displacing of activities, such as socializing with other children and interacting with adults, that would teach children nonviolent ways to solve conflicts" (p. 9), although she says that none of the effects is specific to a certain age.

- Condry (1989) observes four: cultivation, imitation, disinhibition, and arousal/desensitization. He says he considers arousal and desensitization together because they are part of the same process or mechanism, and aggression is positively related to both.

- Donnerstein, Slaby, and Eron (1994) claim there are four: aggressor effect, victim effect, bystander effect, and appetite effect.

- Signorielli (1991) sees five: catharsis, observational learning, disinhibition, arousal, and cultivation.

- Gunter (1994) lists seven: catharsis, arousal, disinhibition, imitation, desensitization, cultivation, and fear.

---

furthermore that there may be a much larger number of effects than we have previously imagined.

In order to take a broader view on identifying possible effects from exposure to media violence, I suggest we: (1) consider more the long-term as well as immediate effects, (2) consider more nonbehavioral effects as well as behavioral effects, (3) consider more the effects on society as well as on individuals, (4) consider more the effects from media other than television and film, and (5) consider more the positive effects as well as the negative ones.

Long-Term Effects

There have been some notable studies of long-term effects, such as the longitudinal study conducted by Huesmann and Eron (1986) in which they followed the behavior of their participants over a 10-year period. They were able to find that degree of exposure to violent media messages early in life was associated with increased aggressive activity later.

Designing studies that would be able to identify long-term effects is a very difficult task, as MacBeth points out in chapter 3 (this volume). This is one of the major reasons why we do not have more tests of long-term effects. However, the difficulty of the task should not continue to be a barrier for us to explore long-term effects now that we have a good deal of guidance from the current research. For example, cultivation is a long-term effect, which has yet to be tested in a longitudinal manner. There is a fair-sized body of cross-sectional research studies that give us indications that people who watch more television on average are more likely to hold real-world beliefs that are associated with the television world. This evidence warrants the expense of a longitudinal study to determine whether heavy viewing leads to cultivated beliefs or whether holding certain beliefs makes one look for reinforcement of those beliefs in the habit of heavy viewing. Until such a study is conducted we will not know whether heavy viewing causes cultivated beliefs, whether beliefs cause the heavy viewing, or whether the two instead simply represent a spurious relationship.

It is indeed a major shortcoming of our literature that there are not more studies to determine if there are long-term effects from exposure to violence in the media. It is likely that once more longitudinal studies are conducted we will find evidence of many more long-term effects, and furthermore we may find evidence that these long-term effects will be more serious than are the immediate effects.

Nonbehavioral Effects

The strongest contribution of research on the effects path is to document that there are behavioral effects, especially disinhibition, imitation, triggering, and fear. Most of that research has limited its search for a manifestation to high-profile behaviors, and this limitation tends to provide us with evidence that underestimates the magnitude of the effect. Gentile and Sesma provide a good illustration of this in chapter 2 (this volume), where they show that if we think of violence in schools purely in terms of numbers of deaths we would, of course, be horrified to learn that there were 35 deaths due to violence in schools in 1998. But this greatly underestimates the problem of aggression in schools. When we consider just four other behavioral manifestations of violence, the number of instances in 1998 explodes to well over 20 million acts.

Researchers need to expand their view on what should be considered behavioral outcomes that result from exposure to violence in the media. Perhaps the constant media portrayals of violence show up in other behavioral effects, such as higher rates of highway aggression (e.g., "road rage"), lower rates of volunteerism, or higher levels of voting for authoritarian law-and-order political candidates. Perhaps the level of civility in society has changed, thus allowing (or even encouraging) higher rates of aggression that can be seen in competitiveness (in career and sports participation) and in politeness (being treated unjustly by sales clerks).

We need to think more about nonbehavioral types of effects to help us consider a wider range of possible effects. This research path has found several nonbehavioral effects, such as changes in cognition (observational learning), attitudes (cultivation), emotions (desensitization), and physiology (arousal). However, there are likely to be many more. Thinking about effects as being cognitive, attitudinal, emotional, physiological, or behavioral gives us more insight into the nature of effects, and it can help expand our perspective concerning the number of effects possible.

Effects on Institutions and Society

Almost all of the research in this effects path has looked for effects on individuals; few have attempted to look for effects on society or its institutions. Because there are many documented effects on individuals, it is likely that those changes in individuals manifest themselves on a broader scale in society. For example, if many more people are behaving aggressively, then the criminal justice system cannot help but be influenced. If much of that aggression is highly violent in nature, then the medical community will be affected. Many public schools now have metal detectors at the doors and a lowering of students' privacy as a result of massacres in a handful of schools.

Tannis MacBeth (chapter 3, this volume) displays the key studies that have been conducted to examine effects on the macro level. As will be clear from reading her chapter, there is reason to believe that society has been affected by media violence. But the number of studies examining those macro effects is much smaller than the number of studies on individuals. This is a serious shortcoming, especially considering the importance of these macro effects.

Additional Media

Almost all of the research on media violence has been conducted on either television or film. This largely ignores other types of media that are not both visual and aural and therefore rely on exposure experiences that might lead to a different dynamic of influence. First there are print media. It is likely that when people expose themselves to violence in print media, different effects may result than if they had exposed themselves to violence in a movie. For example, it is likely that when people read about a violent occurrence in a magazine, they would be more likely to have a cognitive effect (with exposure to more information at their own pace) and less likely to have a physiological effect of arousal compared to experiencing that occurrence dramatized on television.

Second, media researchers have not done much work documenting effects accruing from exposure to aural media, especially the violent lyrics in music transmitted through radio or CDs. Earlier in this book, Roberts, Christenson, and Gentile argued that the "effects of violent music lyrics do not appear to be nearly as powerful as the effects of other, more visual, violent media" (chapter 8). They speculate that this might be the case because "lyric content may be difficult to understand, may be interpreted differently by different people, or because visual images may be a more direct and powerful communicator." These appear to all be good reasons, but there may be another—that is, listening to music is a mundane activity. It serves as background for other things. This means that the violent lyrics are likely entering a person's unconsciousness and may exert their effect totally outside the person's awareness. Thus when researchers ask people about their exposure to music and especially violent messages, they may have no way to access that information. Thus we may not have a list of effects from the aural media, not because those effects do not exist, but because we do not yet have enough experience in looking for them.

The third, and perhaps most pressing need for future effects research is with the increasingly popular interactive media. As Gentile and Anderson (chapter 7, this volume) point out, compared to television, video games may be exerting a stronger effect on people. This is because video games allow for players to practice sequences of violent behaviors repeatedly and with immediate reinforcement. Also, the Internet affords the chance to talk to others about violent actions and hate speech, thus reinforcing that there are similar thinkers out there. Kotler and Calvert (chapter 9, this volume) warn of incidences of cyber-rape and attacks on other people without any negative consequences because it is anonymous.

Prosocial Effects

We need to consider that some effects may be positive; they need not all be negative. It is ironic that despite the fact that prosocial effects of the media may be stronger than antisocial effects, researchers have been much more likely to focus on negative effects, but more scholars are pointing out that violence can also have a prosocial effect (e.g., leading to increased helping behaviors or decreased aggressive behaviors) if presented in the right context (for example, see Strasburger & Wilson, chapter 4, this volume). Hearold (1986) conducted a meta-analysis on 230 studies published before 1978 concerning television's effect on social behavior. She compared the average effect sizes of the antisocial effects with those of the prosocial effects and found the prosocial effects to be stronger—twice as strong. Subsequent meta-analysis has concluded that the effect size of prosocial effects is about the same as those of antisocial effects (Mares & Woodward, 2001; Paik & Comstock, 1994).

Mares and Woodward (2001) conducted a follow-up to Hearold's study—they did meta-analysis of prosocial effects of television on children and found 34 studies. Interestingly, only six of these studies were published after 1981 and none since 1989. This led the authors to conclude among other things that "few studies of prosocial effects were conducted in the 1990s, despite the fact that many questions remain about how best to achieve prosocial outcomes of viewing" (p. 187). They also say that "research on prosocial effects has largely languished since the 1970s. This would be justified only if it were clear that prosocial effects seldom occur and should be considered a lost cause or if research had already answered all the important questions about how to design effective prosocial messages" (p. 199). They observe that neither of those conditions is true.

In summary, research has come a long way in terms of expanding the list of documented negative effects from exposure to violence in the media. However, there is evidence to suggest that the list of negative effects may be much longer than we have believed. We need to expand our perspective on effects to include long-term as well as immediate, nontelevision as well as television, effects on society as well as on individuals, more examination of nonbehavioral manifestations, and prosocial as well as antisocial effects. When we do so, it is possible to read the research literature and see that there is some evidence for a much larger number of effects from exposure to violence in the media (see Table 13.2). There is a need to shift our resources and conduct more examinations of these little-researched effects. When we do so, it is possible that we may identify a much greater number of effects than we now believe to exist. It is also possible that some of these newly documented effects—especially long-term ones—may be more prevalent than the effects we currently consider to be the most serious ones.

INFLUENCE PATH

Since the 1960s, influence path research has been especially prevalent and fruitful. Many factors have been tested, and most have been found to be associated to some extent with a negative effect. For a summary of these, see Table 13.3. While we have identified many factors, we are far from understanding the process of that influence. Until we understand this process well, we cannot devise good estimates of risk. This is the frontier of this line of research. To move forward on this path, we need to concentrate on three tasks. First, we need to shift our attention more onto active factors. Second, we need to determine the relative importance among factors. Third, we need to develop the calculus for arranging these factors in a single scale to predict risk.

Active Factors

Returning to the list of factors in Table 13.3, notice that some of the factors are active and some are grouping variables. For example, a person's age is a grouping variable, where all people (say, at age 7) are assumed to be the same. In contrast, cognitive developmental level is an active variable, because it

Table 13.2
Overview of Media Effects

Type	Immediate	Long Term
Physiological	Fight/Flight Reaction	Physiological Habituation
Emotional	Temporary Fear	Emotional Habituation
Cognitive	Learning Specific Acts and Lessons	Generalizing Patterns (Cultivation of Estimates)
		Acquiring Social Norms (Prosocial and Antisocial)
Attitudinal	Opinion Creation/Change	Reinforcement
		Cultivation of Beliefs
Behavioral	Imitation/Copying	Generalizing Novel Behaviors
	Disinhibition	
	Triggering/Activation	
	Attraction (Avoidance)	
Societal		Shifting Norms
		Changing Institutions

Source: Adapted from Potter, 1999.

identifies a condition in people that makes them especially vulnerable to a media effect. Research using grouping variables has documented that older children are influenced differently than younger children and that males are influenced differently than are females. Age, gender, and other demographic variables have been useful in categorizing research participants and examining if there are differences across groups. But their usefulness is less in defining what makes people vulnerable and more in providing indications about where the active forces are.

We need to move beyond grouping variables and shift the research focus from attribute variables to active variables; that is, we need to look more at the psychological and sociological processes that can better account for whether a person is affected by media violence or not. What is it about age differences that can account for the differences in influence? Is it cognitive development? If so, then we need good measures of cognitive development, and we need to use them rather than age as predictors of influence. Age is a surrogate for something more active and important as a predictor. Not all five-year-olds are affected the same, because not all five-year-olds are at the

Table 13.3
Factors Associated with Negative Effects from Exposure to Media Violence

Factors about the Media Portrayals of Violence
    Consequences in plot
        Rewards and punishments for perpetrators of violence
        Pain and harm to victims of violence
    Justification for the violent action
    Realism
        Animation or real action
        Settings and characters resembling viewer's life
        Potential applicability of actions in one's own life
    Presence of weapons as cue value
    Production techniques
        Graphicness and explicitness to elicit arousal
        Enhancing comprehension
    Humor
    Eroticism
    Frequency of violent actions
        Rates per hour
        Time on screen
    Consistency across portrayals over time

Factors about People Exposed to the Portrayals of Violence
    Demographics
        Age
        Gender
        Socioeconomic Status
        Ethnicity
    Traits
        Developmental level (cognitive, emotional, moral)
        Socialization against behaving aggressively
        Intelligence
        Personality
        Depression
        Cognitive processing style
        Ability to use coping strategies
    States
        Arousal
        Emotions (especially anger and frustration)
        Identification with characters and situations
    Prior experience
        Abused as child
        Witness to violence and aggression in real life
        History of use of violence and aggression
    Motivations for exposure

Factors about the Environment
    Presence of cues in the real-life situation
    Absence of sanctions against antisocial behavior

Source: Adapted from Potter, 1999.

same level of cognitive development; therefore age will be a less powerful predictor than cognitive score. For example, when using cognitive development in our research designs, we should not use age as a substitute for a true measure of cognitive development. Researchers need to test for cognitive development and, for example, distinguish among those children who are in the stage of concrete operations from those who are in the stage of formal operations (e.g., Ginsburg & Opper, 1988). Doing this is better than using age, but still the stages are grouping variables; all we have done is better grouping. We need to measure the more active factors, such as field dependency, locus of control, conceptual differentiation, and the like (Potter, 1999).

In shifting our attention much more toward active-type variables, we are likely to find other variables to add to our list of factors. For example, it is likely that other forms of human development—such as emotional development and moral development—will become promising factors. Our reactions to portrayals have an important emotional component; if people vary in their degree of awareness of these emotions and their ability to control those emotions, then there will be important differences in how violence affects them. Our reactions to portrayals of violence involve making moral judgments about the action; if people vary in their abilities to work through problems of morality, then there will be important differences in how violence affects them. A person's development cognitively, emotionally, and morally are all interrelated. This full spectrum of development is likely to be a major explanatory factor of why certain people are more affected by media violence than are others. Our reactions to portrayals of violence require cognitive processing; if adults vary in the degree they perceive and process contextual cues, then there will be important differences in how violence affects them.

Relative Importance of Factors

While we have developed a fairly extensive list of factors that belong in our examination of the effects process, we do not as yet have a good idea of their relative importance as far as degree of influence. In the past, experiments have been limited to dealing with only two or three factors at a time, and then the focus was more on determining whether particular factors were statistically significant in treatment differences rather than on how strong an effect they exerted. There have been some good meta-analyses to try to address this concern. An excellent example of this is Comstock and Scharrer (chapter 11, this volume). In their Figure 11.2, it is clear that while exposure to television violence is not the major factor in predicting aggressive behavior, it does make a contribution at a fairly important level—much more important than having abusive parents or antisocial peers.

Calculus

Once we have identified the active factors in the process of influence, we need to assemble them into a formula of risk. This is the task of figuring out the calculus. The simplest thing to do would be to weight each factor by its relative importance, then sum across factors. The resulting number would be degree of risk, with the higher the number the greater the degree of risk. While this would be an elegant solution, it is likely to be too simple, because the world is more complex than that. I'll address three of these "complexities" for the calculus: interactions, asymmetry, and thresholds.

Interactions

To explain this, I'll use a real-world type of example. Let's say you have two friends whom you like to spend time with. When you are alone with Harry, you always have a good time, and when you are alone with Joan, you always have a good time. Does it then follow that you will have a truly great time if you spend time with Harry and Joan together? Not necessarily. It may be the case that the chemistry among the three of you is even better than it is between any pair of you, so that the best times are had when all three of you are together (a positive interactive effect). But what if Harry and Joan hate each other? If so, then bringing the three of you together would destroy the chance for a good time you would have with either of them alone.

Factors interact like friends in the example above. However, researchers have little idea at this time which of the factors interact in a positive way, which interact in a negative way, and which do not interact at all.

Asymmetric relationships

Most tests of relationships among variables assume a symmetric association. So a finding of a weak or non-relationship does not necessarily mean that there is no type of relationship, only that there is no symmetric relationship. There are few documented asymmetric relationships in media effects research (for example see Potter, 1991a). This should not be interpreted to mean that asymmetric relationships are rare; instead it is an indication that rarely do researchers test for them.

Thresholds

As for thresholds, there are some effects that do not show up until the amount of media exposure passes a certain point. For example, viewing television generally does not have a negative influence on children's academic performance until it reaches a point of about 30 hours per week, when it really begins cutting into study time (Potter, 1987). So a student who increases her television viewing time from 10 hours to 20 hours per week is not likely to show a decrease in academic performance. But a student who increases his viewing from 30 to 35 hours per week is very likely to show a drop in grades.

With media violence, it is likely that exposure does not begin to have an observable influence until a person has reached a certain threshold, but this type of research has not yet been conducted. For example with the testing of immediate effects, researchers could vary the amount, duration, and/or intensity of violence across their experimental treatments to document the point at which disinhibition effects begin to become prevalent. Until this type of research is conducted, we cannot know if the existing experimental literature has relied on treatments with violence below the threshold—in which case this set of research reflects an underestimation of the disinhibition influence of media violence.

When we consider all of these issues, the resulting model is likely to be very complex. But the influence process itself is very complex. This is a huge challenge methodologically. We need to design effects studies that take into account large numbers of these factors simultaneously. We need to see how the factors work together in altering levels of risk. Until we have such research completed, we will be limited to guessing what the calculus should be, such as a simple additive formula (NTVS, 1997). It matters how we do this (Potter, 1996). For example, I took the same factors and used them in four formulas to predict which television network presented programs that would present the greatest degree of risk of a disinhibition effect. The rank orders of those networks were different across all four models.

CONTENT PATH

There are many challenges in analyzing media content for violence. By far the most significant of those challenges is the conceptual one of defining "violence." The way this concept is defined makes a huge difference in terms of how many acts of it will be found when various programs are analyzed.

The term is usually treated as if it has one definition that is shared by everyone. But violence is a construct that must be carefully defined by researchers when they design analyses of violent content in the media, and that process of definition requires the making of decisions on at least eight key issues (see Table 13.4). While there is fairly high degree of agreement on some of these issues, there is little agreement on most of them (see Table 13.5). This variation in definitions makes it essential that we not merely report results when comparing across studies but that we also examine how those results are influenced by the definitions used. For example, a study using a very narrow definition (such as answering no to all eight questions in Table 13.4) would likely result in a content analysis finding about one act of violence per hour on American television, while a broad definition (such as answering yes to all eight questions in Table 13.4) would yield about 40 acts per hour when examining the same content (Potter, 1999).

To avoid the problems generated by a variety of definitions, I recommend that content analysts answer yes to all eight issues and thus craft a broad definition and use it consistently. This would allow them to make a more complete count of the incidence of violence and its various types. Another advantage of using a broad definition that catalogs types of violence is that it provides effects researchers with some guidance. For example, there is evidence of a shift in type of violent act from the 1970s to the 1990s (Potter &

Table 13.4
Key Elements in Definitions of Violence

1. Does the act have to be directed toward a person? Gang members swing baseball bats at a car and totally destroy it. Is this violence?

2. Does the act have to be committed by a person? A mudslide levels a town and kills 20 people. Do acts of nature count? Remember that nature does not write the scripts or produce the programming.

3. Does the act have to be intentional? A bank robber drives a fast car in a getaway chase. As he speeds around a corner he hits a pedestrian (or destroys a mailbox). Do accidents count?

4. Does the act result in harm? Tom shoots a gun at Jerry, but the bullet misses. Is this violence? Or what if Tom and Jerry are cartoon characters and Tom drops an anvil on Jerry who is momentarily flattened like a pancake. A second later Jerry pops back to his original shape and appears fine.

5. What about violence we don't see? If a bad guy fires a gun at a character off-screen and we hear a scream and a body fall, is this violence even though we do not see it?

6. Does the act have to be physical (such as assaults) or can it be verbal (such as insults)? What if Tom viciously insults Jerry who is shown through the rest of the program experiencing deep psychological and emotional pain as a result? What if Tom embarrasses Jerry who then runs from the room, trips, and breaks his arm?

7. What about fantasy? If 100 fighting men "morph" into a giant creature the size of a 10-story building, which then stomps out their enemies, does this count as violence?

8. What about humorous portrayals? When the Three Stooges hit each other with hammers, is this violence?

Vaughan, 1997) with more serious acts of violence (such as killings) disappearing and lesser forms of violence (such as insults) increasing. If content analyses use narrow definitions that focus only on the more serious acts, they will be able to observe only half of this trend and their findings will be misleading. A broad definition is needed so that content analysts can keep the focus on trends in the big picture.

The ignoring of verbal violence in many content analyses of television is also puzzling, because experiments in the effects path of research have not ignored verbal violence. Verbal violence is often a prominent part of the media participants are exposed to (Geen, 1975; Thomas & Drabman, 1975; Thomas & Tell, 1974). In these studies there were arguments with insults and intimidation leading up to a fistfight. Sometimes only verbal aggression is used. In one study, viewers were shown a brief film showing a businessman and his secretary in a hostile verbal interaction (Carver, Ganellan, Froming, & Chambers, 1983). Also, Berkowitz (1970) had women listen to a tape-recording of either a hostile comedy routine by Don Rickles or a nonaggressive routine by George Carlin.

Table 13.5
Comparing Definitions of Violence/Aggression

Study	Are These Elements Included in the Counting?							
	Acts of Nature	Non-Int. Accidents	No Harm	Nonphys	Off-Screen	Nonhuman Target	Fantasy	Humor
Gerbner & colleagues	Yes	Yes	Yes	No	No	Yes	Some	Some
Gunter & Harrison	No	Some	Yes	No	No	Yes	?	?
Center for M.&P.A.	No	No	Yes	No	No	No	?	?
NTVS	Some	Some	Yes	No	Yes	Yes	Yes	Yes
NCTV	No	No	?	No	?	No	?	?
ABC	Yes	Yes	Yes	No	?	Yes	?	?
Mustonen & Pulkkinen	Yes	Yes	Yes	Yes	?	Yes	?	?
Williams, Zabrack, & Joy	?	?	No	Yes	?	?	?	?
Potter, Vaughan, Warren, Howley, Land & Hagemeyer	Yes	Yes	Yes	Yes	Yes	Yes	Yes	Yes
Oliver	No	Yes	Yes	Yes	No	Yes	?	?
Sommers-Flanagan	No	No	Yes	Yes	Yes	No	?	?
Potter & Ware	Yes	Yes	Yes	Yes	No	Yes	Yes	Yes
Greenberg & colleagues	No	Yes	Yes	Yes	No	Yes	?	?

Note: The definition used by ABC is included in this analysis for purposes of compar-ison. No results of content analyses have been published by ABC; instead this com-mercial broadcast network uses this definition for internal monitoring of prospective programs and episodes by its Broadcast Standards and Practices Department.

Sometimes verbal violence appears as a treatment variable (serving to anger participants) in addition to the media exposure treatment. While most of these studies used electric shocks to produce anger in their participants, some had an experimenter insult the participants to make them angry (Baron, 1977; Berkowitz, 1974; Berkowitz & Rawlings, 1963; Donnerstein & Berkowitz, 1981; Goranson, 1969; Leyens & Picus, 1973; Turner & Berkowitz, 1972).

And finally, verbal violence is sometimes included as a dependent variable. Hapkiewicz and Stone (1974) used a variety of measures of aggression in their experimental participants, and one of these was their verbal aggression. Berkowitz and Alioto (1973) had their participants evaluate another participant in the study, and this retaliation was not physical (such as administering electric shocks) but symbolic (ratings on a form).

To date, the reporting of results from these studies does not make it possible to draw conclusions about the relative contributions of different kinds of violence on viewers' disinhibitions. It is time for experimental researchers to bring all types of violence more prominently into their designs so that they can assess the relative influence of different kinds of violence. Perhaps, it is the less serious forms of violence that pose the greatest risk to viewers. Perhaps because the inhibitions preventing viewers from imitating insults and lies are much lower than the inhibitions that prevent them from imitating assaults, a small reduction in a person's inhibition would be more likely to show up as a behavioral effect with the less serious forms of violence. This is an important issue that needs to be addressed by experimenters before we can make an accurate assessment of viewer risk.

Another problem with defining violence is that the set of definitions that scholars use seem to be at variance with the set of definitions used by the public. There are profound differences between how social scientists conceptualize violence and how the public sees it. From a scientific point of view, cartoons such as the *Road Runner* and *Bugs Bunny* are very violent—in fact, researchers consistently find cartoons to be the most violent of all program genres on television (Gerbner et al., 1980; Greenberg et al., 1980; NTVS, 1996). The characters in these shows are continuously getting stabbed, shot, hit with heavy objects, blown up, rocketed into the sky, and flattened into the ground.

Social scientists who make strong statements about the harmfulness of viewing *Tom and Jerry* and *Road Runner* cartoons, the *Three Stooges*, and *America's Home Videos* put themselves in danger of being regarded as fuzzy-headed academics wasting their time with silly research. Most viewers would not regard any of these programs as violent (Howitt & Cumberbatch, 1975). Critics (such as Morrison, 1993) look at this situation and conclude that social scientists must use poor definitions of violence. Yet, it is not that scientific content analyses use "poor" definitions. Instead, the definitions used by scientists and the public are based on different concerns. The public is primarily concerned with being shocked by severe harm to victims. Social scientists are primarily concerned with harm to viewers.

Viewers' judgments of the degree of violence are not based on the actual number of violent acts in the program. Instead, it appears that viewers are most concerned with the degree of graphicness and explicitness (Potter et al., 2002). Viewers are more likely to regard a movie as being violent if it has one highly graphic act of violence than if it had dozens of sanitized acts of violence.

Also, children have been found to rate the frequency of violence in particular programs as lower than the frequency found in content analysis (Van der Voort, 1986). In addition, it appears that shows with many acts of violence are not regarded as being violent if the context of the show is fantasy or humor (Potter & Warren, 1998).

In contrast, scientists are less concerned with the harm to characters than they are concerned with the potential harm to viewers. A social scientist who watches a cartoon such as *Tom and Jerry* sees a large number of violent actions that are in a sanitized (low reality, high humor, no harm) contextual pattern and knows this increases the likelihood that viewers will become desensitized. Social scientists also see the high justification as a contributing agent to a disinhibition effect. This show would be considered very violent by content analysts and not violent at all by the public.

The differences in definitions lead to an apparent problem of ecological validity. The definitions used by social scientists appear too abstract and out of touch with real people. We could close the definitional gap by simply accepting the public's definition of violence. But given what we know about effects, that would be unethical. We would then become part of this public health problem rather than using our knowledge to effect a solution. The definitional gap, of course, needs to be closed.

On this definitional issue, both sides need more education. Social scientists need to attend more to receiver definitions of violence and focus on how the salient and interruptive characteristics of violence contribute to or reduce the risk for a negative effect. The public needs to attend more to the case being made by social scientists who document types of violent portrayals.

CONCLUSIONS

Researchers have generated a great deal of insight into the risks we incur from exposure to violence in the media. This research has proceeded down three paths: documenting effects, determining which factors influence risk, and examining content of media for evidence of violence.

Once researchers can move beyond the current frontiers and provide a better understanding of the variety of effects and a better conceptualization of what violence is, then they can test the influence of various forms of violence and how those content influences interact with factors in a person's life. This will put scholars in a position to braid the findings from the three lines of research together in a more systematic, complete manner and thus generate the insights we need to understand risk well enough to control it.

References

INTRODUCTION

Leland, J. (2000, September 25). Family's guidance can blunt the effect of video violence. *New York Times.* Accessed September 25, 2000, at http://www.nytimes.com/2000/09/25/technology/25TEEN.html.

CHAPTER 1

Adler, R., Friedlander, B., Lesser, G., Meringoff, L., Robertson, T., Rossiter, J., & Ward, S. (1977). *Research on the effects of television advertising to children: A review of the literature and recommendations for future research.* Washington, DC: U.S. Government Printing Office.

Andersen, R. E., Crespo, C. J., Bartlett, S. J., Cheskin, L. J., & Pratt, M. (1998). Relationship of physical activity and television watching with body weight and level of fatness among children. *Journal of the American Medical Association, 279,* 938–942.

Anderson, C. A., Benjamin, A. J., Jr., & Bartholow, B. D. (1998). Does the gun pull the trigger? Automatic priming effects of weapon pictures and weapon names. *Psychological Science, 9,* 308–314.

Anderson, C. A., & Bushman, B. J. (2001). Effects of violent video games on aggressive behavior, aggressive cognition, aggressive affect, physiological arousal, and prosocial behavior: A meta-analytic review of the scientific literature. *Psychological Science, 12,* 353–359.

Anderson, C. A., & Bushman, B. J. (2002). The effects of media violence on society. *Science, 295,* 2377–2379.

Bandura, A. (1973). *Aggression: A social learning analysis.* Englewood Cliffs, NJ: Prentice-Hall.

Bandura, A. (1983). Psychological mechanisms of aggression. In R. G. Geen & E. I. Donnerstein (Eds.), *Aggression: Theoretical and empirical reviews: Vol. 1* (pp. 1–40). New York: Academic Press.

Bartholow, B. D., & Anderson, C. A. (2002). Effects of violent video games on aggressive behavior: Potential sex differences. *Journal of Experimental Social Psychology, 38*, 283–290.

Bartholow, B. D., Anderson, C. A., Carnagey, N. L., & Benjamin, A. J., Jr. (in press). Interactive effects of life experience and situational cues on aggression: The weapons priming effect in hunters and nonhunters. *Journal of Experimental Social Psychology*.

Berkowitz, L. (1993). *Aggression: Its causes, consequences, and control.* Philadelphia, PA: Temple University Press.

Berkowitz, L., & LePage, A. (1967). Weapons as aggression-eliciting stimuli. *Journal of Personality and Social Psychology, 7*, 202–207.

Buchman, D. D., & Funk, J. B. (1996). Video and computer games in the '90s: Children's time commitment and game preference. *Children Today, 24*, 12–16.

Bushman, B. J. (1998). Effects of television violence on memory of commercial messages. *Journal of Experimental Psychology: Applied, 4*, 291–307.

Bushman, B. J., & Anderson, C. A. (2001). Media violence and the American public: Scientific facts versus media misinformation. *American Psychologist, 56*, 477–489.

Bushman, B. J., & Bonacci, A. M. (2002). Violence and sex impair memory for television ads. *Journal of Applied Psychology, 87*, 557–564.

Bushman, B. J., & Huesmann, L. R. (2001). Effects of televised violence on aggression. In D. G. Singer & J. L. Singer (Eds.), *Handbook of children and the media.* Thousand Oaks, CA.: Sage Publications.

Bushman, B. J., & Phillips, C. M. (2001). If the television program bleeds, memory for the advertisement recedes. *Current Directions in Psychological Science, 10*, 44–47.

Cantor, J. (1998). *"Mommy, I'm scared": How TV and movies frighten children and what we can do to protect them.* San Diego, CA: Harvest/Harcourt.

Cantor, J. (2001). The media and children's fears, anxieties, and perceptions of danger. In D. G. Singer & J. L. Singer (Eds.), *Handbook of children and the media* (pp. 207–221). Thousand Oaks, CA: Sage Publications.

Carnagey, N. L., Bushman, B. J., & Anderson, C. A. (under review, manuscript submitted for publication). *Video game violence desensitizes players to real world violence.*

Center for Media and Public Affairs (1999, June). Merchandising mayhem: Violence in popular entertainment. Available at http://www.cmpa.com/archive/viol98.htm.

Cialdini, R. B. (2001). *Influence: science and practice* (4th ed.). Boston, MA: Allyn and Bacon.

Cline, V. B., Croft, R. G., & Courrier, S. (1973). Desensitization of children to television violence. *Journal of Personality and Social Psychology, 27*, 360–365.

Communications Subcommittee. (1972). *Hearings on the Surgeon General's Report by the Scientific Advisory Committee on Television and Social Behavior.* Serial No. 92–52. Washington, DC: U.S. Government Printing Office.

Comstock, G. A., & Scharrer, E. (1999). *Television: What's on, who's watching, and what it means.* San Diego, CA: Academic Press.

Congressional Record (1988). Floor debate on the Television Violence Act (H.R. 3848).

Cooperative Institutional Research Program (1999). *Cooperative Institutional Research Program survey results*. Ames, IA: Office of Institutional Research.

Crespo, C. J., Smith, E., Toiano, R. P., Bartlett, S. J., Macera, C. A., & Andersen, R. E. (2001). Television watching, energy intake, and obesity in U.S. children. *Archives of Pediatric and Adolescent Medicine, 155*, 360–365.

Dennison, B. A., Erb, T. A., & Jenkins, P. L. (2002). Television viewing and television in bedroom associated with overweight risk among low-income preschool children. *Pediatrics, 109*, 1028–1035.

Dietz, T. L. (1998). An examination of violence and gender role portrayals in video games: Implications for gender socialization and aggressive behavior. *Sex Roles, 38*, 425–442.

Dietz, W. H., & Gortmaker, S. L. (1985). Do we fatten our children at the television set? Obesity and television viewing in children and adolescents. *Pediatrics, 75*, 807–812.

Dill, K. E., Gentile, D. A., Richter, W. A., & Dill, J. C. (2001, August). *Violence, race, sex and age in video games: A content analysis.* Paper presented at the annual meeting of the American Psychological Association, San Francisco, CA.

Durant, R. H., Rich, M., Emans, S. J., Rome, B. S., Alfred, E., & Woods, B. R. (1997). Violence and weapon carrying in music videos: A content analysis. *Archives of Pediatrics and Adolescent Medicine, 151*, 443–448.

Elmer-Dewitt, P. (1993, September). The amazing video game boom. *Time*, 66–73.

Fox, R. F. (2002, Summer). Hucksters hook captive youngsters. *Mizzou: The Magazine of the MU Alumni Association, 90*, 22–27. Available from the University of Missouri Alumni Association, 123 Donald W. Reynolds Alumni and Visitor Center, Columbia, MO 65211.

Funk, J. B. (1993). Reevaluation of the impact of violent video games. *Clinical Pediatrics, 32*, 86–90.

Funk, J. B., Flores, G., Buchman, D. D., & Germann, J. N. (1999). Rating electronic games: Violence is in the eye of the beholder. *Youth & Society, 30*, 283–312.

Gentile, D. A., Lynch, P. J., Linder, J. R., & Walsh, D. A. (in press). The effects of violent video game habits on adolescent aggressive attitudes and behaviors. *Journal of Adolescence*.

Gentile, D. A., & Walsh, D. A. (2002). A normative study of family media habits. *Applied Developmental Psychology, 23*, 157–178.

Gerbner, G. (1994a, January 27). *Highlights of the Television Violence Profile No. 16.* Remarks prepared for the National Association of Television Executives Annual Conference, Miami Beach, FL.

Gerbner, G. (1994b). Making a killing. *Psychology Today, 27*, 18.

Gerbner, G. (1999). The stories we tell. *Peace Review, 11*, 9–16.

Gerbner, G., Gross, L., Morgan, M., & Signorielli, N. (1994). Growing up with television: The cultivation perspective. In J. Bryant & D. Zillmann (Eds.), *Media effects: Advances in theory and research* (pp. 17–41). Hillsdale, NJ: Lawrence Erlbaum.

Griffiths, M. D., & Shuckford, G.L.J. (1989). Desensitization to television violence: A new model. *New Ideas in Psychology, 7*, 85–89.

Grossman, D., & Degaetano, G. (1999). *Stop teaching our kids to kill: A call to action against TV, movie and video game violence.* New York: Random House.

Groebel, J. (2001). Media violence in cross-cultural perspective: A global study on children's media behavior and some educational implications. In D. G. Singer & J. L. Singer (Eds.), *Handbook of children and the media* (pp. 255–268). Thousand Oaks, CA.: Sage Publications.

Hamilton, J. T. (1998). *Channeling violence: The economic market for violent television programming.* Princeton, NJ: Princeton University Press.

Harrison, K., & Cantor, J. (1999). Tales from the screen: Enduring fright reactions to scary media. *Media Psychology, 1,* 97–116.

Hettrick, S. (1995, May 11). Video games on target for $22 billion. *Hollywood Reporter.*

Jhally, S. (Executive Producer/Director) (1994). *The Killing Screens* [Video recording]. Available from Media Education Foundation, 26 Center Street, Northampton, MA 01060.

Joint statement on the impact of entertainment violence on children: Congressional Public Health Summit. (2000, July 26). Retrieved December 19, 2000, from: http://www.senate.gov/~brownback/violence.pdf.

Kent, S. L. (2001). *The ultimate history of video games.* Roseville, CA: Prima Publishing.

Kubey, R., & Csikszentmihalyi, M. (February 23, 2002). Television addiction is no mere metaphor. *Scientific American, 286,* 74–83.

Kunkel, D. (2001). Children and television advertising. In D. G. Singer & J. L. Singer (Eds.), *Handbook of children and the media* (pp. 375–393). Thousand Oaks, CA: Sage Publications.

Kunkel, D., & Gantz, W. (1992). Children's television advertising in the multi-channel environment. *Journal of Communication, 42,* 134–152.

Lazarus, R. S., Speisman, M., Mordkoff, A. M., & Davison, L. A. (1962). A laboratory study of psychological stress produced by a motion picture film. *Psychological Monographs: General and Applied, 76*(34), Whole No. 553.

Levin, S., Petros, T., & Petrella, F. (1982). Preschoolers' awareness of television advertising. *Child Development, 53,* 933–937.

Linz, D., Donnerstein, E., & Adams, S. M. (1989). Physiological desensitization and judgments about female victims of violence. *Human Communication Research, 15,* 509–522.

Looney, G. (1971, October). *Television and the child: What can be done?* Paper presented at the meeting of the American Academy of Pediatrics, Chicago, IL.

Markoff, J. (2002, May 24). Recession? Don't tell the video game industry. *New York Times.* Retrieved June 20, 2002, from http://www.nytimes.com/2002/05/24/technology/24GAME.html?ex=1023256208&ei=1&en=b044bbd10bda69d2.

Medved, M. (1995, October). Hollywood's 3 big lies. *Reader's Digest, 147*(882), 155–159.

Moore, J. W. (1993, December 18). Lights! Camera! It's gun control time. *National Journal,* 3007.

National Cable Television Association. (1993, January). *Industry policy statement regarding violence.* Washington, DC: Author.

National Institute on Media and the Family. (n.d.). *Jolts and tricks: How the media hook kids* [Video recording]. Available from the National Institute on Media and the Family, 606 24th Avenue South, Suite 606, Minneapolis, MN 55454.

National Television Violence Study. (1998). *National Television Violence Study: Vol. 3.*

Santa Barbara: University of California, Santa Barbara, Center for Communication and Social Policy.

Network Television Association. (1992, December). *Standards for depiction of violence in television programs.* New York: Author.

Nielsen Media Research (1998). *Galaxy explorer.* New York: Author.

Oliver, M. B. (1994). Portrayals of crime, race, and aggression in "reality based" police shows: A content analysis. *Journal of Broadcasting and Electronic Media, 38,* 179–192.

Parents Television Council. (1999, August 31). *The family hour: Worse than ever and headed for new lows.* Retrieved June 11, 2002, from http://www.parentstv.org/main/publications/reports/famhrstudy99/main.asp.

Poll says games are safe. (1999, May 27). Retrieved February 1, 2000, from http://pc.ign.com/articles/068/068231p1.html.

Potter, W. J. (1999). *On media violence.* Thousand Oaks, CA: Sage Publications.

Provenzo, E. F. (1991). *Video kids: Making sense of Nintendo.* Cambridge, MA: Harvard University Press.

Roberts, D. F., Foehr, U. G., Rideout, V. G., & Brodie, M. (1999). *Kids & the media @ the new millennium: Executive summary.* Menlo Park, CA: Kaiser Family Foundation.

Robinson, T. M. (1999). Reducing children's television viewing to prevent obesity: A randomized controlled trial. *Journal of the American Medical Association, 282,* 1561–1567.

Rule, B. G., & Ferguson, T. J. (1986). The effects of media violence on attitudes, emotions, and cognitions. *Journal of Social Issues, 42,* 29–50.

Signorielli, N., Gerbner, G., & Morgan, M. (1995). Violence on television: The cultural indicators project. *Journal of Broadcasting and Electronic Media, 39,* 278–283.

Smith, S. L., & Boyson, A. R. (2002). Violence in music videos: Examining the prevalence and context of physical aggression. *Journal of Communication, 52,* 61–83.

Smith, S. L., & Donnerstein, E. (1998). Harmful effects of exposure to media violence: Learning of aggression, desensitization, and fear. In R. G. Geen & E. Donnerstein (Eds.), *Human aggression: Theories, research, and implications for social policy* (pp. 167–202). San Diego, CA: Academic Press.

Strasburger, V. C. (2001). Children and TV advertising: Nowhere to run, nowhere to hide. *Journal of Developmental & Behavioral Pediatrics, 22,* 185.

Strasburger, V. C., & Wilson, B. J. (2002). *Children, adolescents, and the media.* Thousand Oaks, CA: Sage Publications.

Thomas, M. H. (1982). Physiological arousal, exposure to a relatively lengthy aggressive film, and aggressive behavior. *Journal of Research in Personality, 16,* 72–81.

Thomas, M. H., Horton, R. W., Lippincott, E. C., & Drabman, R. S. (1977). Desensitization to portrayals of real-life aggression as a function of exposure to television violence. *Journal of Personality and Social Psychology, 35,* 450–458.

Time Warner (Producer). (2000, May 12). CNN: The world today. Atlanta, GA: CNN.

Trotta, L. (2001). Children's advocacy groups. In D. G. Singer & J. L. Singer (Eds.), *Handbook of children and the media.* Thousand Oaks, CA.: Sage Publications.

TV Turnoff Network. (n.d.). TV facts and figures: TV undermines family life. Retrieved September 4, 2002, from http://www.tvturnoff.org/factsheets.htm.

Violence bill debated in Washington. (1990, February 5). *Broadcasting, 118*(6), 77–78.

Walsh, D. A. (1994). *Selling out America's children: How America puts profits before values—and what parents can do.* Minneapolis, MN: Fairview Press.

Walsh, D. A. (2001a). *Doctor Dave's cyberhood.* New York: Simon & Schuster.

Walsh, D. A. (2001b). *Sixth annual video and computer game report card.* [On-line]. National Institute on Media and the Family. Retrieved September 5, 2002, from http://www.mediafamily.org/research/vgrc/2001-2.shtml.

Walsh, D. A., & Gentile, D. A. (2001). A validity test of movie, television, and video-game ratings. *Pediatrics, 107,* 1302–1308.

Ward, S., Reale, G., & Levinson, D. (1972). Children's perceptions, explanations, and judgments of television advertising. A further exploration. In G. Comstock & E. Rubinstein (Eds.), *Television and social behavior: Vol. 4.* Washington, DC: U.S. Government Printing Office.

Wolpe, J. (1982). *The practice of behavior therapy* (3rd ed.). New York: Pergamon Press.

CHAPTER 2

Anthony, E. J. (1974). The syndrome of the psychologically invulnerable child. In E. Anthony & C. Koupernick (Eds.), *The child in his family: Vol 3. Children at psychiatric risk* (pp. 529–544). New York: John Wiley & Sons.

Aber, J. L., & Jones, S. J. (1997). Indicators of positive development in early childhood: Improving concepts and measures. In R. M. Hauser, B. V. Brown, & W. R. Prosser (Eds.), *Indicators of children's well-being* (pp. 395–408). New York: Sage Foundation.

Belsky, J., & Fearon, R.M.P. (2002). Infant-mother attachment security, contextual risk, and early development: A moderational analysis. *Development and Psychopathology, 14,* 293–310.

Brachear, M. (2002, July 19). Copycat stunt injures youth. *Dallas Morning News.* Retrieved July 19, 2002, from http://www.dallasnews.com/latestnews/stories/071902dntexstunt.811a0.html.

Bushman, B. J., & Anderson, C. A. (2001). Media violence and the American public. *American Psychologist, 56,* 477–489.

Centerwall, B. S. (1989). Exposure to television as a risk factor for violence. *American Journal of Epidemiology, 129,* 643–652.

Cicchetti, D., & Toth, S. L. (1998). The development of depression in children and adolescents. *American Psychologist, 53,* 221–241.

Crick, N. R. (1995). Relational aggression: The role of intent attributions, feelings of distress, and provocation type. *Development and Psychopathology, 7,* 313–321.

Crick, N. R., & Dodge, K. A. (1996). Social information-processing mechanisms in reactive and proactive aggression. *Child Development, 67,* 993–1002.

Donnerstein, E., Slaby, R. G., & Eron, L. D. (1994). The mass media and youth aggression. In L. D. Eron, J. H. Gentry, & P. Schlegel (Eds.), *Reason to hope: A psychosocial perspective on violence and youth* (pp. 219–250). Washington, DC: American Psychological Association.

Erikson, E. H. (1963). *Childhood and society* (2nd ed.). New York: Norton.

Freedman, J. L. (2002). *Media violence and its effect on aggression.* Toronto, Canada: University of Toronto Press.

Ferguson, C. J. (2002). Media violence: Miscast causality. *American Psychologist, 57,* 446–447.

Gentile, D. A., Walsh, D. A., Bloomgren, B. W., Atti, J. A., & Norman, J. A. (2001, April). *Frogs sell beer: The effects of beer advertisements on adolescent drinking knowledge, attitudes, and behaviors.* Paper presented at the Biennial Conference of the Society for Research in Child Development, Minneapolis, MN.

Gibbs, N., & Roche, T. (1999, December 20). The Columbine tapes. *Time,* 40–50.

Glantz, M. D., & Johnson, J. L. (Eds.) (1999). *Resilience and development: Positive life adaptations.* New York: Kluwer.

Greene, V. S. (1999). *Television viewing, perceptions of advertising's influence and appearance-related concerns.* Unpublished manuscript, University of Massachusetts, Amherst.

Grossman, D. (1996). *On killing.* Boston, MA: Little, Brown & Co.

Grossman, D. (1998, August 10). Trained to kill. *Christianity Today,* 31–39.

Hemphill, J. F. (2003). Interpreting the magnitudes of correlation coefficients. *American Psychologist, 58,* 78–79.

Keller, W. (2002, August 10). *Wrestling's state of business is taking more knocks then [sic] deserved.* Retrieved November 1, 2002, from http://www.pwtorch.com/artman/publish/printer_163.shtml.

Masten, A. S. (2001). Ordinary magic: Resilience processes in development. *American Psychologist, 56,* 227–238.

Masten, A. S., & Braswell, L. (1991). Developmental psychopathology: An integrative framework. In P. R. Martin (Ed.), *Handbook of behavior therapy and psychological science: An integrative approach* (pp. 35–56). New York: Pergamon Press.

Masten, A. S., & Coatsworth, J. D. (1998). The development of competence in favorable and unfavorable environments: Lessons from research on successful children. *American Psychologist, 53,* 205–220.

Masten, A. S., Hubbard, J. J., Gest, S. D., Tellegen, A., Garmezy, N., & Ramirez, M. (1999). Competence in the context of adversity: Pathways to resilience and maladaptation from childhood to late adolescence. *Development and Psychopathology, 11,* 143–169.

Masten, A. S., Miliotis, D., Graham-Bermann, S. A., Ramirez, M., & Neemann, J. (1993). Children in homeless families: Risks to mental health and development. *Journal of Consulting and Clinical Psychology, 61,* 335–343.

Masten, A. S., & Reed, M.G.J. (2002). Resilience in development. In S. R. Snyder & S. J. Lopez (Eds.), *The handbook of positive psychology* (pp. 74–88). New York: Oxford University Press.

Masten, A. S., & Wright, M. O. (1998). Cumulative risk and protective models of child maltreatment. In B.B.R. Rossman & M. S. Rosenberg (Eds.), *Multiple victimization of children: Conceptual, developmental, research, and treatment issues* (pp. 7–30). Binghamton, NY: Haworth.

Means Coleman, R. R. (2002). In R. R. Means Coleman (Ed.), *Say it loud* (pp. 249–284). New York: Routledge.

Modzeleski, W. (2002, May). *Threat assessment in schools.* Training materials for U.S. Secret Service and U.S. Department of Education.

Paik, H., & Comstock, G. (1994). The effects of television violence on antisocial behavior: A meta-analysis. *Communication Research, 21*(4), 516–546.

Potter, W. J. (1999). *On media violence.* Thousand Oaks, CA: Sage Publications.

Rutter, M. (2000). Resilience reconsidered: Conceptual considerations, empirical findings, and policy implications. In J. P. Shonkoff & S. J. Meisels (Eds.), *Handbook of early childhood invention* (2nd ed.) (pp. 651–682). Cambridge, UK: Cambridge University Press.

Rutter, M., Maughan, B., Meyer, J., Pickles, A., Silberg, J., Simonoff, E., & Taylor, E. (1997). Heterogeneity of antisocial behavior: Causes, continuities, and consequences. In R. Dienstbier (Series Ed.) & D. W. Osgood (Vol. Ed.), *Nebraska symposium on motivation: Vol. 44. Motivation and delinquency* (pp. 45–118). Lincoln, NE: University of Nebraska Press.

Sameroff, A. J., & Fiese, B. H. (2000). Transactional regulation: The developmental ecology of early intervention. In J. P. Shonkoff & S. J. Meisels (Eds.), *Handbook of early childhood intervention* (2nd ed.) (pp. 135–159). Cambridge, UK: Cambridge University Press.

Sameroff, A. J., Seifer, R., & Bartko, W. T. (1997). Environmental perspectives on adaptation during childhood and adolescence. In S. S. Luthar, J. A. Burack, D. Ciccetti, & J. R. Weisz (Eds.), *Developmental psychopathology: Perspectives on adjustment, risk, and disorder* (pp. 507–526). New York: Cambridge Press.

Sroufe, L. A. (1979). The coherence of individual development: Early care, attachment, and subsequent developmental issues. *American Psychologist, 34,* 834–841.

Sroufe, L. A. (1995). *Emotional development: The organization of emotional life in the early years.* New York: Cambridge Press.

Sroufe, L. A. (1997). Psychopathology as an outcome of development. *Development and Psychopathology, 9,* 251–268.

Sroufe, L. A., Cooper, R. G., & DeHart, G. B. (1996). *Child development: Its nature and course* (3rd ed.). New York: McGraw-Hill.

Sroufe, L. A., Egeland, B., & Carlson, E. A. (1999). One social world: The integrated development of parent-child and peer relationships. In W. A. Collins & B. Laursen (Eds.), *Relationships as developmental context: The 30th Minnesota symposium on child psychology.* Hillsdale, NJ: Erlbaum.

Stiff sentence—14-year-old gets life in prison for wrestling death. (2001, March 9). Retrieved July 19, 2002, from http://abcnews.go.com/sections/us/DailyNews/tate-sentence010309.html.

Texas talkback. (n.d.). Retrieved November 1, 2002, from http://www.txcn.com/cgi-bin/survey.cgi?survey = 1104&step = View%20comments.

Walsh, D. A. (2001). *Dr. Dave's cyberhood.* New York: Fireside.

Woodward, G. C., & Denton, R. E. (2000). *Persuasion & influence in American life* (4th ed.). Prospect Heights, IL: Waveland Press.

Zigler, E., & Styfco, S. J. (2001). Can early childhood intervention prevent delinquency? A real possibility. In A. C. Bohart & D. J. Stipek (Eds.), *Constructive and destructive behavior: Implications for family, school, & society* (pp. 231–248). Washington, DC: APA.

CHAPTER 3

Anderson, D. R., Huston, A. C., Smith, K. L., Linebarger, D. L., & Wright, J. C. (2001). Adolescent outcomes associated with early childhood television viewing: The Recontact Study. *Monographs of the Society for Research in Child Development.*

Armstrong, G. B., Neuendorf, K. A., & Brentar, J. E. (1992). TV entertainment, news, and racial perceptions of college students. *Journal of Communication, 42*(3), 153–176.

Bandura, A. (1977). *Social learning theory.* Englewood Cliffs, NJ: Prentice Hall.

Bandura, A. (1994). Social cognitive theory of mass communication. In J. Bryant & D. Zillmann (Eds.), *Media effects: Advances in theory and research* (pp. 61–90). Hillsdale, NJ: Lawrence Erlbaum.

Bandura, A., Ross, D., & Ross, S. A. (1963). Vicarious reinforcement and imitative learning. *Journal of Abnormal and Social Psychology, 67,* 601–607.

Becker, A. E., Burwell, R. A., Herzog, D. B., Hamburg, P., & Gilman, S. E. (2002). Eating behaviours and attitudes following prolonged exposure to television among ethnic Fijian adolescent girls. *British Journal of Psychiatry, 180,* 509–514.

Bosch, Y. (2000). Fat is out in Fiji. (Sidebar). *Journal of the American Medical Association, 283*(11), 1409.

Brown, W. J., & Cody, M. J. (1991). Effects of a prosocial television soap opera in promoting women's status. *Human Communication Research, 18*(1), 114–142.

Bushman, B. J. (1995). Moderating role of trait aggressiveness in the effects of violent media on aggression. *Journal of Personality and Social Psychology, 69,* 950–960.

Gerbner, G., Gross, L., Morgan, M., & Signorielli, N. (1994). Growing up with television: The cultivation perspective. In J. Bryant & D. Zillmann (Eds.), *Media effects: Advances in theory and research* (pp. 17–41). Hillsdale, NJ: Lawrence Erlbaum.

Greenberg, B. S. (1988). Some uncommon television images and the drench hypothesis. In S. Oskamp (Ed.), *Applied Social Psychology Annual: Television as a social issue: Vol. 8.* Newbury Park, CA: Sage.

Grossman, Lt. Col. D. (1998). Television's virus of violence: Medium is mayhem. Toronto, ON: *The Globe and Mail,* Ideas, Saturday, May 23.

Himmelweit, H. T., Oppenheim, A. N., & Vince, P. (1958). *Television and the child.* London: Oxford University Press.

Horton, D., & Wohl, R. R. (1956). Mass communication and para-social interaction: Observations on intimacy at a distance. *Psychiatry, 19,* 215–229.

Jönsson, A. (1986). TV: A threat or a complement to school? *Journal of Educational Television, 12*(1), 29–38.

Joy, L. A., Kimball, M. M., & Zabrack, M. L. (1986). Television and children's aggressive behavior. In T. M. Williams (Ed.), *The impact of television: A natural experiment in three communities* (pp. 303–360). NY: Academic Press.

Katz, E., & Wedell, G. (1977). *Broadcasting in the Third World: Promise and performance.* Cambridge, MA: Harvard University Press.

Katz, E., Haas, H., & Gurevitch, M. (1997). 26 years of television in Israel: Are true long-run effects on values, social connectedness, and cultural practices? *Journal of Communication, 47*(2), 3–20.

Kottak, C. P. (1991). Television's impact on values and local life in Brazil. *Journal of Communication, 41*(1), 70–87.

MacBeth, T. M. (2001). The impact of television: A Canadian natural experiment. In C. McKie & B. D. Singer (Eds.), *Communications in Canadian society* (pp. 196–213). Toronto: Thompson Educational Publishing.

MacBeth, T. M. (1996a). Indirect effects of television. In T. M. MacBeth (Ed.), *Tuning in to young viewers: Social science perspectives on television* (pp. 149–219). Thousand Oaks, CA: Sage Publications.

MacBeth, T. M. (1996b). Introduction. In T. M. MacBeth (Ed.), *Tuning in to young viewers: Social science perspectives on television* (pp. 1–35). Thousand Oaks, CA: Sage Publications.

Meyrowitz, J. (1985). *No sense of place: The impact of electronic media on social behavior.* New York: Oxford University Press.

Mitra, S. (1986, January 15). "Hum Log": The final flourish. *India Today,* pp. 142–143.

Murray, J. P. (1998). Studying television violence: A research agenda for the 21st century. In J. K. Asamen & G. L. Berry (Eds.), *Research paradigms, television, and social behavior* (pp. 369–410). Thousand Oaks, CA: Sage Publications.

Murray, J. P., & Kippax, S. (1977). Television diffusion and social behavior in three communities: A field experiment. *Australian Journal of Psychology, 29*(1), 31–43.

Murray, J. P., & Kippax, S. (1978). Children's social behavior in three towns with differing television experience. *Journal of Communication, 28,* 19–29.

Nariman, H. N. (1993). *Soap operas for social change: Toward a methodology for entertainment—education television.* Westport, CT: Praeger.

National Institute of Mental Health. (1972). *Report from the Surgeon General's Scientific Advisory Committee on Television and Social Behavior: Vols. 1–5.* Rockville, MD: U.S. Government Printing Office.

Phillips, D. P. (1985). The found experiment: A new technique for assessing the impact of mass media violence on real world aggressive behavior. *Public Communication and Behavior, 1,* 260–307.

Rosengren, K. E., & Windahl, S. (1989). *Media matter: TV use in childhood and adolescence.* Norwood, NJ: Ablex.

Ryerson, W. N. (1994). Population communications international: Its role in family planning soap operas. *Population and environment, 15,* 255–264.

Sabido, M. (1981). *Towards a social use of soap operas.* Paper presented at the International Institute of Communication, Strassbourg, France.

Schramm, W., Lyle, J., & Parker, E. B. (1961). *Television in the lives of our children.* Stanford, CA: Stanford University Press.

Singhal, A., & Rogers, E. M. (1988). Television soap operas for development in India. *Gazette, 41,* 109–126.

Snyder, L., Roser, C., & Chaffee, S. (1991). Foreign media and the desire to emigrate from Belize. *Journal of Communication, 41*(1), 117–132.

Stein, A. H., & Friedrich, L. K. (1972). Television content and young children's behavior. In J. P. Murray, E. A. Rubenstein, & G. A. Comstock (Eds.), *Television and social behavior: Television and social learning: Vol. 2* (pp. 207–317). Washington, DC: Government Printing Office.

Tate, E., & Trach, L. (1980). The effects of United States television programs upon Canadian beliefs about legal procedure. *Canadian Journal of Communication, 6*(4), 1–16.

Vidmar, N., & Rokeach, M. (1974). Archie Bunker's bigotry: A study in selective perception and exposure. *Journal of Communication, 24*(1), 36–47.

Williams, T. M. (1986). *The impact of television: A natural experiment in three communities.* New York: Academic Press (Harcourt Brace Jovanovich).

Winter, J., & Goldman, I. (1995). Mass media and Canadian identity. In B. D. Singer (Ed.), *Communications in Canadian society* 4th ed. (pp. 201–220). Toronto: Nelson.

CHAPTER 4

Abelson, R. P. (1976). Script processing in attitude formation and decision-making. In J. Carroll & J. Payne (Eds.), *Cognition and social behavior.* Hillsdale, NJ: Lawrence Erlbaum.

American Academy of Pediatrics. (2001). Media violence. *Pediatrics, 108,* 1222–1226.

American Medical Association. (1996). *Physician guide to media violence.* Chicago, IL: Author.

American Psychological Association. (1993). *Violence and youth: Psychology's response.* Washington, DC: Author.

Anderson, C. A., & Bushman, B. J. (2002). Human aggression. *Annual Review of Psychology, 53,* 27–51.

Anderson, C. A., & Bushman, B. J. (2002). The effects of media violence on society. *Science, 295,* 2377–2378.

Andison, F. S. (1977). TV violence and viewer aggressiveness: A cumulation of study results. *Public Opinion Quarterly, 41,* 314–331.

Archer, D. (1994). American violence: How high and why? *Law Studies, 19,* 12–20.

Auletta, K. (1993, May 17). Annals of communication: What won't they do. *The New Yorker, 69,* 45–53.

Bai, M. (1999, May 3). Anatomy of a massacre. *Newsweek, 133,* 25–31.

Bandura, A. (1965). Influence of models' reinforcement contingencies on the acquisition of imitative response. *Journal of Personality and Social Psychology, 1,* 589–595.

Bandura, A. (1977). *Social learning theory.* New York: Prentice-Hall.

Bandura, A. (1986). *Social foundations of thought and action: A social cognitive theory.* Englewood Cliffs, NJ: Prentice Hall.

Bandura, A., Ross, D., & Ross, S. A. (1961). Transmission of aggression through imitation of aggressive models. *Journal of Abnormal and Social Psychology, 63,* 575–582.

Bandura, A., Ross, D., & Ross, S. A. (1963a). Imitation of film-mediated aggressive models. *Journal of Abnormal and Social Psychology, 66,* 3–11.

Bandura, A., Ross, D., & Ross, S. A. (1963b). Various reinforcement and imitative learning. *Journal of Abnormal and Social Psychology, 67,* 601–607.

Belson, W. A. (1978). *Television violence and the adolescent boy.* Westmead, UK: Teakfield.

Berkowitz, L., & Rawlings, E. (1963). Effects of film violence on inhibitions against subsequent aggression. *Journal of Abnormal and Social Psychology, 66,* 405–412.

Berkowitz, L. (1984). Some effects of thoughts on anti- and prosocial influences of media events: A cognitive-neoassociation analysis. *American Psychologist, 45,* 494–503.

Berkowitz, L. (1990). On the formation and regulation of anger and aggression: A cognitive neoassociationistic analysis. *American Psychologist, 45,* 494–503.

Boyatzis, J., Matillo, G. M., & Nesbitt, K. M. (1995). Effects of the "Mighty Morphin

Power Rangers" on children's aggression with peers. *Child Study Journal, 25,* 45–55.

Bryant, J., Carveth, R. A., & Brown, D. (1981). Television viewing and anxiety: An experimental examination. *Journal of Communication, 31*(1), 106–109.

Buka, S. L., Stichick, T. L., Birdthistle, I., & Earls, F. J. (2001). Youth exposure to violence: Prevalence, risks, and consequences. *American Journal of Orthopsychiatry, 71,* 298–310.

Bushman, B. J., & Anderson, C. A. (2001). Media violence and the American public: Scientific facts versus media misinformation. *American Psychologist, 56,* 477–489.

Bushman, B. J., & Huesmann, L. R. (2001). Effects of televised violence on aggression. In D. G. Singer & J. L. Singer (Eds.), *Handbook of children and the media* (pp. 223–254). Thousand Oaks, CA: Sage Publications.

Carlson, M., Marcus-Newhall, A., & Miller, N. (1990). Effects of situational aggression cues: A quantitative review. *Journal of Personality & Social Psychology, 58,* 622–633.

Centers for Disease Control. (1997, February 7). Rates of homicide, suicide, and firearm-related death among children: 26 industrialized countries. *Morbidity & Mortality Weekly Report, 46,* 101–105.

Centerwall, B. S. (1992). Television and violence: The scale of the problem and where to go from here. *Journal of the American Medical Association, 267,* 22–25.

Clary, M. (2001, January 25). Defense pulls pro-wrestling into murder trial; Today a Florida jury begins to consider whether a 12-year-old was simply imitating TV heroes when he killed his playmate, 6; The boy faces life in prison. *Los Angeles Times,* pp. A1, A5.

Cline, V. B., Croft, R. G., & Courrier, S. (1973). Desensitization of children to television violence. *Journal of Personality and Social Psychology, 35,* 450–458.

Comstock, G. (1991). *Television and the American child.* San Diego, CA: Academic Press.

Comstock, G., & Strasburger, V. C. (1990). Deceptive appearances: Television violence and aggressive behavior. *Journal of Adolescent Health Care, 11,* 31–44.

Comstock, G., & Strasburger, V. C. (1993). Media violence: Q & A. *Adolescent Medicine: State of the Art Reviews, 4,* 495–509.

Dominick, J. R., & Greenberg, B. S. (1972). Attitudes toward violence: The interaction of television exposure, family attitudes, and social class. In G. A. Comstock & E. A. Rubinstein (Eds.), *Television and social behavior: Television and adolescent aggressiveness: Vol. 3* (pp. 314–335). Washington, DC: Government Printing Office.

Donnerstein, E., Slaby, R. G., & Eron, L. D. (1994). The mass media and youth aggression. In L. D. Eron, J. H. Gentry, & P. Schlegel (Eds.), *A reason to hope: A psychological perspective on youth & violence* (pp. 219–250). Washington, DC: American Psychological Association.

Donnerstein, E., & Smith, S. (2001). Sex in the media. In D. G. Singer & J. L. Singer (Eds.), *Handbook of children and the media* (pp. 289–307). Thousand Oaks, CA: Sage Publications.

Drabman, R. S., & Thomas, M. H. (1974). Does media violence increase children's toleration of real-life aggression? *Developmental Psychology, 10,* 418–421.

Elliott, D., Hatot, N. J., Sirovatka, P., & Potter, B. B. (Eds.). (2001). *Youth violence: A report of the Surgeon General.* Rockville, MD: Office of the Surgeon General.

Retrieved on May 14, 2002, from http://www.surgeongeneral.gov/library/youthviolence/report.html.

Eron, L. D. (1997). The development of antisocial behavior from a learning perspective. In D. M. Stoff, J. Breiling, & J. D. Maser (Eds.), *Handbook of antisocial behavior* (pp. 140–147). New York: Wiley & Sons.

Federal Trade Commission. (2000). *Marketing violent entertainment to children: A review of self-regulation and industry practices in the motion picture, music recording & electronic game industries.* Retrieved on May 14, 2002 from http://www.ftc.gov/reports/violence/vioreport.pdf.

Feshbach, S. (1955). The drive-reducing function of fantasy behavior. *Journal of Abnormal and Social Psychology, 50,* 3–11.

Feshbach, S. (1961). The stimulating versus cathartic effects of a vicarious aggressive activity. *Journal of Abnormal and Social Psychology, 63,* 381–385.

Feshbach, S., & Singer, R. (1971). *Television and aggression.* San Francisco: Jossey-Bass.

Fessenden, F. (2000, April 9). They threaten, seethe and unhinge, then kill in quantity. *New York Times,* p. A1.

Forum on Child and Family Statistics. (1999). *America's children: Key national indicators of child well-being, 1999.* Washington, DC: Government Printing Office.

Fowles, J. (1999). *The case for television violence.* Thousand Oaks, CA: Sage Publications.

Freedman, J. L. (1984). Effect of television violence on aggressiveness. *Psychological Bulletin, 96,* 227–246.

Freedman, J. L. (1986). Television violence and aggression: A rejoinder. *Psychological Bulletin, 100,* 372–373.

Geen, R. G. (1994). Television and aggression: Recent developments in research and theory. In D. Zillmann, J. Bryant, & A. C. Huston (Eds.), *Media, children, and the family: Social, scientific, psychodynamic, and clinical perspectives* (pp. 151–162). Hillsdale, NJ: Lawrence Erlbaum.

Gerbner, G., Gross, L., Morgan, M., & Signorielli, N. (1980). The "mainstreaming" of America: Violence profile no. 11. *Journal of Communication, 30*(3), 10–29.

Gerbner, G., Gross, L., Morgan, M., & Signorielli, N. (1994). Growing up with television: The cultivation perspective. In J. Bryant & D. Zillmann (Eds.), *Media effects: Advances in theory and research* (pp. 17–41). Hillsdale, NJ: Lawrence Erlbaum.

Ginsburg, M. (2001, March 24). An "ethic of violence" fostered, Ashcroft says; Attorney general urges the media and gamemakers to curb violence and cultivate a "culture of responsibility." *The San Francisco Chronicle,* p. A1.

Grossman, D., & DeGaetano, G. (1999). *Stop teaching our kids to kill: A call to action against TV, movie and video game violence.* New York: Crown.

Guerra, N. G., Huesmann, L. R., Tolan, P. H., Van Acker, R., & Eron, L. D. (1995). Stressful events and individual beliefs as correlates of economic disadvantage and aggression among urban children. *Journal of Consulting & Clinical Psychology, 63,* 518–528.

Hanratty, M. A., O'Neal, E., & Sulzer, J. L. (1972). Effect of frustration upon imitation of aggression. *Journal of Personality & Social Psychology, 21,* 30–34.

Harrison, K., & Cantor, J. (1999). Tales from the screen: Enduring fright reactions to scary media. *Media Psychology, 1,* 97–116.

Hawkins, R. P., & Pingree, S. (1981). Uniform messages and habitual viewing: Unnecessary assumptions in social reality effects. *Human Communication Research,* 7, 291–301.

Hearold, S. (1986). A synthesis of 1,045 effects of television on social behavior. In G. Comstock (Ed.), *Public communication and behavior: Vol. 1* (pp. 65–133). New York: Academic Press.

Hemphill, J. F. (2003). Interpreting the magnitudes of correlation coefficients. *American Psychologist, 58,* 78–79.

Hogben, M. (1998). Factors moderating the effect of televised aggression on viewer behavior. *Communication Research, 25,* 220–247.

Huesmann, L. R. (1986). Psychological processes promoting the relation between exposure to media violence and aggressive behavior by the viewer. *Journal of Social Issues, 42,* 125–139.

Huesmann, L. R. (1988). An information processing model for the development of aggression. *Aggressive Behavior, 14,* 13–24.

Huesmann, L. R. (1998). The role of social information processing and cognitive schemas in the acquisition and maintenance of habitual aggressive behavior. In R. G. Geen & E. Donnerstein (Eds.), *Human aggression: Theories, research, and implications for social policy* (pp. 1120–1134). San Diego, CA: Academic Press.

Huesmann, L. R., & Eron, L. D. (1986). *Television and the aggressive child: A cross national comparison.* Hillsdale, NJ: Lawrence Erlbaum.

Huesmann, L. R., & Miller, L. S. (1994). Long-term effects of repeated exposure to media violence in childhood. In L. R. Huesmann (Ed.), *Aggressive behavior: Current perspectives.* (pp. 153–186). New York: Plenum Press.

Huesmann, L. R., Eron, L. D., Klein, R., Brice, P., & Fischer, P. (1983). Mitigating the imitation of aggressive behaviors by changing children's attitudes about media violence. *Journal of Personality & Social Psychology, 44,* 899–910.

Huesmann, L. R., Lagerspetz, K., & Eron, L. D. (1984). Intervening variables in the TV violence-aggression relation: Evidence from two countries. *Developmental Psychology, 20,* 746–775.

Hughes, M. (1980). The fruits of cultivation analysis: A re-examination of television in fear of victimization, alienation, and approval of violence. *Public Opinion Quarterly, 44,* 287–302.

Huston, A. C., Donnerstein, E., Fairchild, H. H., Feshbach, N. D., Katz, P. A., Murray, J. P., Rubinstein, E. A., Wilcox, B. L., & Zuckerman, D. (1992). *Big world, small screen: The role of television in American society.* Lincoln, NE: University of Nebraska Press.

Jo, E., & Berkowitz, L. (1994). A priming effect analysis of media influences: An update. In J. Bryant & D. Zillmann (Eds.), *Media effects: Advances in theory and research* (pp. 43–60). Hillsdale, NJ: Lawrence Erlbaum.

Johnson, J. G., Cohen, P., Smailes, E. M., Kasen, S., & Brook, J. S. (2002). Television viewing and aggressive behavior during adolescence and adulthood. *Science, 295,* 2468–2471.

Joy, L. A., Kimball, M. M., & Zabrack, M. L. (1986). Television and children's aggressive behavior. In T. M. Williams (Ed.), *The impact of television: A natural experiment in three communities* (pp. 303–360). New York: Academic Press.

Kenny, D. A. (1984). The NBC study and television violence: A review. *Journal of Communication, 34*(1), 176–188.

Lazarus, R. S., & Alfert, E. (1964). Short-circuiting of threat by experimentally altering cognitive appraisal. *Journal of Abnormal & Social Psychology, 69,* 195–205.

Lefkowitz, M. M., Eron, L. D., Walder, L. O., & Huesmann, L. R. (1972). Television violence and child aggression: A follow-up study. In G. A. Comstock & E. A. Rubinstein (Eds.), *Television and social behavior: Television and adolescent aggressiveness: Vol. 3* (pp. 33–135). Washington, DC: Government Printing Office.

Liebert, R. M., & Sprafkin, J. (1988). *The early window: Effects of television on children and youth* (3rd ed.). Elmsford, NY: Pergamon Press.

Linz, D., Donnerstein, E., & Penrod, S. (1984). The effects of multiple exposures to filmed violence against women. *Journal of Communication, 34*(3), 130–147.

Liss, M. B., Reinhardt, L. C., & Fredriksen, S. (1983). TV heroes: The impact of rhetoric and deeds. *Journal of Applied Developmental Psychology, 4,* 175–187.

Mares, M.-L., & Woodard, E. H. (2001). Prosocial effects on children's social interactions. In D. G. Singer & J. L. Singer (Eds.), *Handbook of children and the media* (pp. 183–205). Thousand Oaks, CA: Sage Publications.

Mares, M.-L. (1996). The role of source confusions in television's cultivation of social reality judgments. *Human Communication Research, 23,* 278–297.

McIntyre, J. J., & Teevan, J. J., Jr. (1972). Television violence and deviant behavior. In G. A. Comstock & E. A. Rubinstein (Eds.), *Television and social behavior: Television and adolescent aggressiveness: Vol. 3* (pp. 173–238). Washington, DC: Government Printing Office.

McKenna, M. W., & Ossoff, E. P. (1998). Age differences in children's comprehension of a popular television program. *Child Study Journal, 28,* 53–68.

McLeod, J. M., Atkin, C. K., & Chaffee, S. H. (1972). Adolescents, parents, and television use: Adolescent self-report measures from Maryland and Wisconsin samples. In G. A. Comstock & E. A. Rubinstein (Eds.), *Television and social behavior: Television and adolescent aggressiveness: Vol. 3* (pp. 173–238). Washington, DC: Government Printing Office.

Milavsky, J. R., Kessler, R., Stipp, H. H., & Rubens, W. S. (1982). *Television and aggression: A panel study.* New York: Academic Press.

Molitor, F., & Hirsch, K. W. (1994). Children's toleration of real-life aggression after exposure to media violence: A replication of the Drabman and Thomas studies. *Child Study Journal, 24,* 191–207.

Morgan, M., & Shanahan, J. (1996). Two decades of cultivation analysis: An appraisal and a meta-analysis. In B. Burleson (Ed.), *Communication yearbook: Vol. 20* (pp. 1–45). Thousand Oaks, CA: Sage Publications.

Mullin, C. R., & Linz, D. (1995). Desensitization and resensitization to violence against women: Effects of exposure to sexually violent films on judgments of domestic violence victims. *Journal of Personality & Social Psychology, 69,* 449–459.

Naisbitt, J., Naisbitt, N., & Philips, D. (1999). *High tech, high touch: Technology and our search for meaning.* New York: Broadway.

Nathanson, A. I. (1999). Identifying and explaining the relationship between parental mediation and children's aggression. *Communication Research, 26,* 124–143.

National Center for Injury Prevention and Control (2000). Youth violence in the United States. Atlanta, GA: Author. Retrieved January 23, 2001, from www.cdc.gov.ncipc/factsheets/yvfacts.htm.

Nationline. (1997, October 3). Teen accused in killings wrote note, officials say. *USA Today*, p. 3A.

Ogles, R. M., & Hoffner, C. (1987). Film violence and perceptions of crime: The cultivation effect. In M. L. Mclaughlin (Ed.), *Communication yearbook: Vol. 10* (pp. 384–394). Newbury Park, CA: Sage Publications.

O'Keefe, D. J. (2002). *Persuasion: Theory and research* (2nd ed.). Thousand Oaks, CA: Sage Publications.

Paik, H. J., & Comstock, G. (1994). The effects of television violence on antisocial behavior: A meta-analysis. *Communication Research, 21,* 516–546.

Pearl, D., Bouthilet, L., & Lazar, J. (Eds.). (1982). *Television and behavior: Ten years of scientific progress and implications for the eighties: Technical reviews: Vol. 2.* Rockville, MD: National Institute of Mental Health.

Pelletier, A. R., Quinlan, K. P., Sacks, J. J., Van Gilder, T. J., Gulchrist, J., & Ahluwalia, H. K. (1999). Firearm use in G- and PG-rated movies. *Journal of the American Medical Association, 282,* 428.

Perloff, R. (2002). The third-person effect. In J. Bryant & D. Zillmann (Eds.), *Media effects: Advances in theory and research* (2nd ed., pp. 489–506). Mahwah, NJ: Elbaum.

Plagens, P., Miller, M., Foote, D., & Yoffe, E. (1991, April 1). Violence in our culture. *Newsweek, 117* (U.S. ed.), 46–52.

Potter, W. J. (1993). Cultivation theory and research: A conceptual critique. *Human Communication Research, 19,* 564–601.

Potter, W. J. (1999). *On media violence.* Thousand Oaks, CA: Sage Publications.

Purugganan, O. H., Stein, R.E.K., Silver, E. J., & Benenson, B. S. (2000). Exposure to violence among urban school-aged children: Is it only on television? *Pediatrics, 106,* 949–953.

Raine, A. (1997). Antisocial behavior and psychophysiology: A biosocial perspective and a prefrontal dysfunction hypothesis. In D. M. Stoff, J. Breiling, & J. D. Maser (Eds.), *Handbook of antisocial behavior* (pp. 289–304). New York: Wiley & Sons.

Robinson, J. P., & Bachman, J. G. (1972). Television viewing habits and aggression. In G. A. Comstock & E. A. Rubinstein (Eds.), *Television and social behavior: Television and adolescent aggressiveness: Vol. 3* (pp. 173–238). Washington, DC: Government Printing Office.

Rothenberg, M. B. (1975). Effect of television violence on children and youth. *Journal of the American Medical Association, 234,* 1043–1046.

Shaw, D. S., & Winslow, E. B. (1997). Precursors and correlates of antisocial behavior from infancy to preschool. In D. M. Stoff, J. Breiling, & J. D. Maser (Eds.), *Handbook of antisocial behavior* (pp. 148–158). New York: Wiley & Sons.

Shrum, L. J. (2001). Processing strategy moderates the cultivation effect. *Human Communication Research, 27,* 94–120.

Signorielli, N., & Morgan, M. (1990). *Cultivation analysis: New directions in media effects research.* Newbury Park, CA: Sage Publications.

Singer, J. L., & Singer, D. G. (1981). *Television, imagination, and aggression: A study of preschoolers' play.* Hillsdale, NJ: Lawrence Erlbaum.

Singer, J. L., Singer, D. G., & Rapaczynski, W. (1984). Family patterns and television viewing as predictors of children's beliefs and aggression. *Journal of Communication, 34*(2), 73–89.

Singer, M. I., Miller, D. B., Guo, S., Flannery, D. J., Frierson, T., & Slovak, K. (1999). Contributors to violent behavior among elementary and middle school children. *Pediatrics, 104,* 878–884.

Smith, S. L., & Boyson, A. R. (2002). Violence in music videos: Examining the prevalence and context of physical aggression. *Journal of Communication, 52*(1), 61–83.

Smith, S. L., & Donnerstein, E. (1998). Harmful effects of exposure to media violence: Learning of aggression, emotional desensitization, and fear. In R. G. Geen & E. Donnerstein (Eds.), *Human aggression: Theories, research, and implications for social policy* (pp. 167–202). San Diego, CA: Academic Press.

Smith, S. L., Wilson, B. J., Kunkel, D., Linz, D., Potter, W. J., Colvin, C., & Donnerstein, E. (1998). Violence in television programming overall: University of California, Santa Barbara study. In *National television violence study: Vol. 3* (pp. 5–200). Newbury Park, CA: Sage Publications.

Snyder, H. N., & Sickmund, M. (1999). *Juvenile offenders and victims: 1999 national report* (NCJ 178257). Washington, DC: U.S. Department of Justice, Office of Juvenile Justice and Delinquency Prevention.

Steuer, F. B., Applefield, J. M., & Smith, R. (1971). Televised aggression and interpersonal aggression of preschool children. *Journal of Experimental Child Psychology, 11,* 442–447.

Strasburger, V. C. (1995). *Adolescents and the media: Medical and psychological impact.* Thousand Oaks, CA: Sage Publications.

Strasburger, V. C., & Grossman, D. (2001). How many more Columbines? What can pediatricians do about school and media violence? *Pediatric Annals, 30,* 87–94.

Strasburger, V. C., & Wilson, B. J. (2002). *Children, adolescents, and the media.* Thousand Oaks, CA: Sage Publications.

Thomas, M. H., & Drabman, R. S. (1975). Toleration of real-life aggression as a function of exposure to televised violence and age of subject. *Merrill-Palmer Quarterly, 21,* 227–232.

Thomas, M. H., Horton, R. W., Lippincott, E. C., & Drabman, R. S. (1977). Desensitization to portrayals of real-life aggression as a function of exposure to television violence. *Journal of Personality & Social Psychology, 35,* 450–458.

Williams, T. B. (Ed.). (1986). *The impact of television: A natural experiment in three communities.* New York: Academic Press.

Wilson, B. J., Kunkel, D., Linz, D., Potter, W. J., Donnerstein, E., Smith, S. L., Blumenthal, E., & Berry, M. (1998). Violence in television programming overall: University of California, Santa Barbara study. In *National television violence study: Vol. 2* (pp. 3–204). Thousand Oaks, CA: Sage Publications.

Wilson, B. J., Kunkel, D., Linz, D., Potter, W. J., Donnerstein, E., Smith, S. L., Blumenthal, E., & Gray, T. (1997). Violence in television programming overall: University of California, Santa Barbara study. In *National television violence study: Vol. 1* (pp. 3–268). Thousand Oaks, CA: Sage Publications.

Wilson, B. J., Linz, D., Federman, J., Smith, S., Paul, B., Nathanson, A., Donnerstein, E., & Lingsweiler, R. (1999). *The choices and consequences evaluation: A study of Court TV's anti-violence curriculum.* Santa Barbara, CA: Center for Communication and Social Policy, University of California.

Wilson, B. J., Smith, S. L., Potter, W. J., Kunkel, D., Linz, D., Colvin, C. M., & Donnerstein, E. (2002). Violence in children's television programming: Assessing the risks. *Journal of Communication, 52*(1), 5–35.

Wood, W., Wong, F., & Chachere, J. G. (1991). Effects of media violence on viewers' aggression in unconstrained social interaction. *Psychological Bulletin, 109,* 371–383.

Zillmann, D. (1971). Excitation transfer in communication-mediated aggressive behavior. *Journal of Experimental Social Psychology, 7,* 419–434.

Zillmann, D. (1991). Television viewing and physiological arousal. In J. Bryant & D. Zillmann (Eds.), *Responding to the screen: Reception and reaction processes* (pp. 103–133). Hillsdale, NJ: Lawrence Erlbaum.

Zillmann, D., & Johnson, R. C. (1973). Motivated aggressiveness perpetuated by exposure to aggressive films and reduced by exposure to nonaggressive films. *Journal of Research in Personality, 7,* 261–276.

CHAPTER 5

Abelson, R. P. (1981). Psychological status of the script concept. *American Psychologist, 36,* 715–729.

Anderson, C. A. (1997). Effects of violent movies and trait irritability on hostile feelings and aggressive thoughts. *Aggressive Behavior, 23,* 161–178.

Anderson, C. A., Anderson, K. B., & Deuser, W. E. (1996). Examining an affective aggression framework: Weapon and temperature effects on aggressive thoughts, affect, and attitudes. *Personality and Social Psychology Bulletin, 22,* 366–376.

Anderson, C. A., & Arnoult, L. H. (1985). Attributional models of depression, loneliness, and shyness. In J. Harvey & G. Weary (Eds.), *Attribution: Basic issues and applications* (pp. 235–279). New York: Academic Press.

Anderson, C. A., Benjamin, A. J., & Bartholow, B. D. (1998). Does the gun pull the trigger? Automatic priming effects of weapon pictures and weapon names. *Psychological Science, 9,* 308–314.

Anderson, C. A., & Bushman, B. J. (2001). Effects of violent video games on aggressive behavior, aggressive cognition, aggressive affect, physiological arousal, and prosocial behavior: A meta-analytic review of the scientific literature. *Psychological Science, 12,* 353–359.

Anderson, C. A., & Bushman, B. J. (2002). Human aggression. *Annual Review of Psychology, 53,* 27–51.

Anderson, C. A., & Dill, K. E. (2000). Video games and aggressive thoughts, feelings, and behavior in the laboratory and in life. *Journal of Personality and Social Psychology, 78,* 772–790.

Anderson, C. A., & Huesmann, L. R. (in press). Human aggression: A social-cognitive view. In M. A. Hogg & J. Cooper (Eds.), *Handbook of Social Psychology.*

Anderson, C. A., & Sechler, E. S. (1986). Effects of explanation and counterexplanation on the development and use of social theories. *Journal of Personality and Social Psychology, 50,* 24–34.

Anderson, K. B., Anderson, C. A., Dill, K. E., & Deuser, W. E. (1998). The interactive relations between trait hostility, pain, and aggressive thoughts. *Aggressive Behavior, 24,* 161–171.

Bandura, A. (1965). Influence of models' reinforcement contingencies on the acquisition of imitative responses. *Journal of Personality and Social Psychology, 6*, 589–595.

Bandura, A. (1971). Psychotherapy based upon modeling principles. In A. E. Bergin and S. L. Garfield (Eds.), *Handbook of psychotherapy and behavior change.* New York: Wiley.

Bandura, A. (1973). *Aggression: A social learning theory analysis.* Englewood Cliffs, NJ: Prentice-Hall.

Bandura, A. (1983). Psychological mechanism of aggression. In R. G. Geen & E. I. Donnerstein (Eds.), *Aggression: Theoretical and empirical reviews: Vol. 1* (pp. 1–40). New York: Academic Press.

Bandura A., Ross, D., & Ross, S. A. (1961). Transmission of aggression through imitation of aggressive models. *Journal of Abnormal & Social Psychology, 63*, 575–582.

Bandura, A., Ross, D. & Ross, S. A. (1963). Imitation of film-mediated aggressive models. *Journal of Abnormal and Social Psychology, 66*, 3–11.

Bargh, J. A., Lombardi, W. J., & Higgins, E. T. (1988). Automaticity of chronically accessible constructs in person X situation effects on person perception: It's just a matter of time. *Journal of Personality and Social Psychology, 55*, 599–605.

Berkowitz, L. (1984). Some effects of thoughts on anti- and prosocial influences of media events: A cognitive-neoassociation analysis. *Psychological Bulletin, 95*(3), 410–427.

Berkowitz, L. (1989). Frustration-aggression hypothesis: Examination and reformulation. *Psychological Bulletin, 106*, 59–73.

Berkowitz, L. (1990). On the formation and regulation of anger and aggression: A cognitive-neoassociationistic analysis. *American Psychologist, 45*(4), 494–503.

Berkowitz, L. (1993). Pain and aggression: Some findings and implications. *Motivation and Emotion, 17*, 277–293.

Berkowitz, L., & Geen, R. G. (1967). Stimulus qualities of the target of aggression: A further study. *Journal of Personality and Social Psychology, 5*, 364–368.

Bower G. (1981). Mood and memory. *American Psychologist, 36*, 129–48.

Bryant, J., Carveth, R. A., & Brown, D. (1981). Television viewing and anxiety: An experimental examination. *Journal of Communication, 31*, 106–119.

Bryant, J., & Zillmann, D. (1979). Effect of intensification of annoyance through unrelated residual excitation on substantially delayed hostile behavior. *Journal of Experimental Social Psychology, 15*, 470–480.

Bushman, B. J. (2002). Does venting anger feed or extinguish the flame? Catharsis, rumination, distraction, anger, and aggressive responding. *Personality and Social Psychology Bulletin, 28*, 724–731.

Bushman, B. J. (1995). Moderating role of trait aggressiveness in the effects of violent media on aggression. *Journal of Personality and Social Psychology, 69*, 950–960.

Bushman, B. J., & Anderson, C. A. (2002). Violent video games and hostile expectations: A test of the general aggression model. *Personality and Social Psychology Bulletin, 28*, 1679–1686.

Bushman, B. J., & Bonacci, A. M. (2002). Violence and sex impair memory for television ads. *Journal of Applied Psychology, 87*, 557–564.

Bushman, B. J., & Geen, R. G. (1990). Role of cognitive-emotional mediators and individual differences in the effects of media violence on aggression. *Journal of Personality and Social Psychology, 58*, 156–163.

Bushman, B. J., & Phillips, C. M. (2001). If the television program bleeds, memory for the advertisement recedes. *Current Directions in Psychological Science, 10,* 44–47.

Cantor, J. (1994). Fright reactions to mass media. In J. Bryant & D. Zillmann (Eds.), *Media effects: Advances in theory and research* (pp. 213–245). Hillsdale, NJ: Erlbaum.

Cantor, J. (1998). *"Mommy, I'm scared": How TV and movies frighten children and what we can do to protect them.* San Diego, CA: Harvest/Harcourt.

Cantor, J. (2001). The media and children's fears, anxieties, and perceptions of danger. In D. G. Singer & J. L. Singer (Eds.), *Handbook of children and the media* (pp. 207–221). Thousand Oaks, CA: Sage.

Cantor, J., & Sparks, G. G. (1984). Children's fear responses to mass media: Testing some Piagetian predictions. *Journal of Communication, 34,* 90–103.

Cantor, J., & Wilson, B. J. (1984). Modifying responses to mass media in preschool and elementary school children. *Journal of Broadcasting, 28,* 431–443.

Cantor, J., Wilson, B. J., & Hoffner, C. (1986). Emotional responses to a televised nuclear holocaust film. *Communication Research, 13,* 257–277.

Carnagey, N. L., Bushman, B. J., & Anderson, C. A. (under review). Video game violence desensitizes players to real world violence.

Cline, V. B., Croft, R. G., & Courrier, S. (1973). Desensitization of children to television violence. *Journal of Personality and Social Psychology, 27,* 360–365.

Collins, A. M., & Loftus, E. F. (1975). A spreading activation theory of semantic processing. *Psychological Review, 82,* 407–428.

Crick, N. R., & Dodge, K. A. (1994). A review and reformulation of social information processing mechanisms in children's adjustment. *Psychological Bulletin, 115,* 74–101.

Dexter, H. R., Penrod, S., Linz, D., & Saunders, D. (1997). Attributing responsibility to female victims after exposure to sexually violent films. *Journal of Applied Social Psychology, 27,* 2149–2171.

Dill, J., & Anderson, C.A. (1995). Effects of justified and unjustified frustration on aggression. *Aggressive Behavior, 21,* 359–369.

Dill, K. E., Anderson, C. A., Anderson, K. B., & Deuser, W. E. (1997). Effects of aggressive personality on social expectations and social perceptions. *Journal of Research in Personality, 31,* 272–292.

Dodge, K. A, & Crick, N. R. (1990). Social information-processing bases of aggressive behavior in children. *Personality and Social Psychology Bulletin, 16,* 8–22.

Dollard, J., Doob, L., Miller, N., Mowrer, O., & Sears, R. (1939). *Frustration and aggression.* New Haven, CT: Yale University Press.

Forgas, J. P. (1992). Affect in social judgments and decisions: A multiprocess model. *Advances in Experimental Social Psychology, 25,* 227–275.

Freud, S. (1909/1961). *Analysis of a phobia in a five-year-old boy* (standard ed.). London: Norton.

Freud, S. (1920/1961). *Beyond the pleasure principle* (standard ed.). London: Norton.

Geen, R. G. (1990). *Human aggression.* Pacific Grove, CA: McGraw Hill.

Geen, R. G., & Berkowitz, L. (1966). Name-mediated aggressive cue properties. *Journal of Personality, 34,* 456–465.

Geen, R. G., & O'Neal, E. C. (1969). Activation of cue-elicited aggression by general arousal. *Journal of Personality and Social Psychology, 11,* 289–292.

Geen, R. G., & Quanty, M. B. (1977). The catharsis of aggression: An evaluation of a hypothesis. In L. Berkowitz (Ed.), *Advances in Experimental Social Psychology, Vol. 10* (pp. 1–37). New York: Academic Press.

Gerbner, G., Gross, L., Jackson-Beeck, M., Jeffries-Fox, S., & Signorielli, N. (1978). Cultural indicators: Violence profile no. 9. *Journal of Communication, 28,* 176–207.

Gerbner, G., Gross, L., Morgan, M., & Signorielli, N. (1982). Charting the mainstreaming: Television's contributions to political orientations. *Journal of Communication, 32,* 100–127.

Gerbner, G., Gross, L., Morgan, M., & Signorielli, N. (1980). The "mainstreaming" of America: Violence profile no. 11. *Journal of Communication, 30,* 10–29.

Gilovich, T. (1991). *How we know what isn't so: The fallibility of human reason in everyday life.* New York: Free Press.

Gunter, B., & Furnham, A. (1984). Perceptions of television violence: Effects of programme genre and type of violence on viewers' judgments of violent portrayals. *British Journal of Social Psychology, 23,* 155–164.

Hansen, C. H., & Hansen, R. D. (1990). The influence of sex and violence on the appeal of rock music videos. *Communication Research, 17,* 212–234.

Harrison, K., & Cantor, J. (1999). Tales from the screen: Enduring fright reactions to scary media. *Media Psychology, 1*(2), 97–116.

Hilgard, E. R., & Bower, G. H. (1975). *Theories of learning.* Englewood Cliffs, NJ: Prentice-Hall.

Huesmann, L. R. (1998). The role of social information processing and cognitive schema in the acquisition and maintenance of habitual aggressive behavior. In R. Geen & E. Donnerstein (Eds.), *Human aggression: Theories, research and implications for policy* (pp. 73–109). New York: Academic Press.

Huesmann, L. R. (1986). Psychological processes promoting the relation between exposure to media violence and aggressive behavior by the viewer. *Journal of Social Issues, 42*(3), 125–139.

Huesmann, L. R., & Miller, L. S. (1994). Long-term effects of repeated exposure to media violence in childhood. In L. R. Huesmann (Ed.), *Aggressive behavior: Current perspectives* (pp. 153–186). New York: Plenum Press.

James, W. (1890). *Principles of psychology.* New York: Holt.

Janis, I. L., & Mann, L. (1977). Decision making: A psychological analysis of conflict, choice, and commitment. New York: Free Press.

Kirsh, S. J. (1998). Seeing the world through Mortal Kombat–colored glasses: Violent video games and the development of a short-term hostile attribution bias. *Childhood, 5,* 177–184.

Krull, D. S. (1993). Does the grist change the mill?: The effect of perceiver's goal on the process of social inference. *Personality and Social Psychology Bulletin, 19,* 340–348.

Krull, D. S., & Dill, J. C. (1996). On thinking first and responding fast: Flexibility in social inference processes. *Personality and Social Psychology Bulletin, 22,* 949–959.

Lazarus, R. S., Speisman, M., Mordkoff, A. M., & Davison, L. A. (1962). A laboratory study of psychological stress produced by a motion picture film. *Psychological Monographs: General and Applied, 34,* Whole No. 553.

Lewin, K. (1951). Problems of research in social psychology. In D. Cartwright (Ed.), *Field theory in social science,* (pp. 155–169). New York: Harper & Row.

Linz, D. G., Donnerstein, E., & Penrod, S. (1988). Effects of long-term exposure to violent and sexually degrading depictions of women. *Journal of Personality and Social Psychology, 55,* 758–768.

Lorenz, K. (1966). *On aggression.* New York: Bantam.

Miller, N. E. (1941). The frustration-aggression hypothesis. *Psychological Review, 48,* 337–342.

Mischel, W. (1973). Toward a cognitive social learning reconceptualization of personality. *Psychological Review, 80,* 252–283.

Mischel, W., & Shoda, Y. (1995). A cognitive-affective system theory of personality: Reconceptualizing situations, dispositions, dynamics, and invariance in personality structure. *Psychological Review, 102,* 246–268.

Osborn, D. K., & Endsley, R. C. (1971). Emotional reactions of young children to TV violence. *Child Development, 42,* 321–331.

Owens, J., Maxim, R., McGuinn, M., Nobile, C., Msall, M., & Alario, A. (1999). Television-viewing habits and sleep disturbance in school children. *Pediatrics, 104*(3), 552. (Abstract).

Potter, W. J. (1999). *On media violence.* Thousand Oaks, CA: Sage Publications.

Schacter, D. L. (2000). Memory systems. In A. E. Kazdin (Ed.), *Encyclopedia of psychology: Vol. 5* (pp. 169–172). New York and Washington, DC: Oxford University Press and the American Psychological Association.

Schachter, S., & Singer, J. (1962). Cognitive, social, and physiological determinants of emotional state. *Psychological Review, 69,* 379–399.

Schank, R.C., & Abelson, R. P. (1977). *Scripts, plans, goals and understanding: An inquiry into human knowledge structures.* Hillsdale, NJ: Lawrence Erlbaum.

Schwarz, N., & Clore, G. L. (1996). Feelings and phenomenal experiences. In E. Higgins & A. Kruglanski (Eds.), *Social psychology: Handbook of basic principles* (pp. 433–465). New York: Guilford.

Sedikides, C., & Skowronski, J. J. (1990). Towards reconciling personality and social psychology: A construct accessibility approach. *Journal of Social Behavior and Personality, 5,* 531–546.

Shaw, M. E., & Costanzo, P. R. (1982). *Theories of Social Psychology* (pp. 3–18). New York: McGraw-Hill.

Singer, M. I., Slovak, K., Frierson, T., & York, P. (1998). Viewing preferences, symptoms of psychological trauma, and violent behaviors among children who watch television. *Journal of the American Academy of Child and Adolescent Psychiatry, 37*(10), 1041–1048.

Smith, S. L., & Donnerstein, E. (1998). Harmful effects of exposure to media violence: Learning of aggression emotional desensitization, and fear. In R. G. Geen & E. Donnerstein (Eds.), *Human aggression: Theories, research, and implications for social policy* (pp. 167–202). New York: Academic Press.

Sparks, G. G., & Cantor, J. (1986). Developmental differences in fright responses to a television program depicting a character transformation. *Journal of Broadcasting and Electronic Media, 30,* 309–323.

Steyer, J. P. (2002). *The other parent: The inside story of the media's effect on our children.* New York: Atria Books.

Surbeck, E. (1975). Young children's emotional reactions to TV violence: The effect of children's perceptions of reality. *Dissertation Abstracts International, 35,* 5139–A.

Thomas, M. H. (1982). Physiological arousal, exposure to a relatively lengthy aggressive film, and aggressive behavior. *Journal of Research in Personality, 16*, 72–81.

Thomas, M. H., Horton, R. W., Lippincott, E. C., & Drabman, R. S. (1977). Desensitization to portrayals of real life aggression as a function of television violence. *Journal of Personality and Social Psychology, 35*, 450–458.

Thorndike, E. L. (1898). Animal intelligence: An experimental study of the associative processes in animals. *Psychological Monographs, 2*, Whole No. 8.

Uleman, J. S. (1987). Consciousness and control: The case of spontaneous trait inferences. *Personality and Social Psychology Bulletin, 13*, 337–354.

Wilson, B. J., Kunkel, D., Linz, D., Potter, J., Donnerstein, E., Smith, S. L., Blumenthal, E., & Gray, T. (1997). Violence in television programming overall: University of California, Santa Barbara study. In M. Seawall, (Ed.), *National television violence study: Vol. 1*. Thousand Oaks, CA: Sage Publications.

Wilson, B. J., Kunkel, D., Linz, D., Potter, J., Donnerstein, E., Smith, S. L., Blumenthal, E., & Gray, T. (1998). Violence in television programming overall: University of California, Santa Barbara study. In M. Seawall, (Ed.), *National television violence study: Vol. 2*. Thousand Oaks, CA: Sage Publications.

Wolpe, J. (1958). *Psychotherapy by reciprocal inhibition*. Stanford, CA: Stanford University Press.

Zillmann, D. (1971). Excitation transfer in communication-mediated aggressive behavior. *Journal of Experimental Social Psychology, 7*, 419–434.

Zillmann, D. (1983). Arousal and aggression. In R. Geen & E. Donnerstein (Eds.), *Aggression: Theoretical and empirical reviews: Vol. 1* (pp. 75–102). New York: Academic Press.

CHAPTER 6

Abelson, R. P., Aronson, E., McGuire, W. J., Newcomb, T. M., Rosenberg, M. J., & Tannenbaum, P. H. (Eds.) (1968). *Theories of cognitive consistency*. Chicago: Rand McNally.

Anderson, C. A., & Bushman, B. J. (1997). External validity of "trivial" experiments: The case of laboratory aggression. *Review of General Psychology, 1*, 19–41.

Anderson, C. A., & Huesmann, L. R. (in press). Human aggression. In M. A. Hogg & J. Cooper (Eds.), *Sage handbook of social psychology*. London: Sage Publications.

Bandura, A. (1977). *Social learning theory*. Englewood Cliffs, NJ: Prentice Hall.

Bandura, A. (1986). *Social foundations of thought and action: A social-cognitive theory*. Englewood Cliffs, NJ: Prentice-Hall.

Bandura, A. (1994). Social cognitive theory of mass communication. In J. Bryant & D. Zillmann (Eds.), *Media effects: Advances in theory and research* (pp. 61–90). Hillsdale, NJ: Erlbaum.

Bandura, A., Ross, D., & Ross, S. A. (1963). Imitation of aggression through imitation of film-mediated aggressive models. *Journal of Abnormal and Social Psychology, 66*, 3–11.

Baran, S. J. (1976). Sex on TV and adolescent sexual self-image. *Journal of Broadcasting, 20*(1), 61–68.

Bargh, J. A. (1982). Attention and automaticity in the processing of self-relevant information. *Journal of Personality and Social Psychology, 43*(3), 425–436.

BBC Panorama. (1997). *The killing screens* [videotape]. London: John Claxton Associates.

Berkowitz, L. (1993). *Aggression: Its causes, consequences, and control.* New York: Mc-Graw-Hill.

Berkowitz, L., & Donnerstein, E. (1982). External validity is more than skin deep: Some answers to criticism of laboratory experiments. *American Psychologist, 37,* 245–257.

Berkowitz, L., & LePage, A. (1967). Weapons as aggression-eliciting stimuli. *Journal of Personality and Social Psychology, 7,* 202–207.

Bjorkqvist, K. (1985). *Violent films, anxiety and aggression.* Helsinki: Finnish Society of Sciences and Letters.

Boyatzis, C. J., Matillo, G. M., & Nesbitt, K. M. (1995). Effects of the "Mighty Morphin Power Rangers" on children's aggression with peers. *Child Study Journal, 25*(1), 45–55.

Brehm, S. S., & Brehm, J. W. (1981). *Psychological reactance: A theory of freedom and control.* New York: Academic Press.

Bryant, J., & Rockwell, S. C. (1994). Effects of massive exposure to sexually oriented prime-time television programming on adolescents' moral judgment. In D. Zillmann, J. Bryant, & A. C. Huston (Eds.), *Media, children, and the family* (pp. 183–195). Hillsdale, NJ: Lawrence Erlbaum.

Buerkel-Rothfuss, N. L., & Buerkel, R. A. (2001). Family mediation. In *Television and the American family* (pp. 355–376). Mahwah, NJ: Lawrence Erlbaum.

Bushman, B. J. (2002). Does venting anger feed or extinguish the flame? Catharsis, rumination, distraction, anger, and aggressive responding. *Personality and Social Psychology Bulletin, 28*(6), 724–731.

Bushman, B. J., & Anderson, C. A. (2001). Media violence and the American public: Scientific facts versus media misinformation. *American Psychologist, 56*(6/7), 477–489.

Bushman, B. J., & Huesmann, L. R. (2000). Effects of televised violence on aggression. In D. Singer & J. Singer (Eds.), *Handbook of children and the media* (pp. 223–254). Thousand Oaks, CA: Sage Publications.

Bushman, B. J., Baumeister, R. F., & Stack, A. D. (1999). Catharsis, aggression, and persuasive influence: Self-fulfilling or self-defeating prophecies? *Journal of Personality and Social Psychology, 76*(3), 367–376.

Butterworth, G. (1999). Neonatal imitation: Existence, mechanisms, and motives. In J. Nadel & G. Butterworth (Eds.), *Imitation in infancy* (pp. 63–88). Cambridge: Cambridge University Press.

Cantor, J., & Nathanson, A. I. (1997). Predictors of children's interest in violent television programs. *Journal of Broadcasting & Electronic Media, 41,* 155–167.

Carnagey, N. L., & Anderson, C. A. (this volume). The role of theory in the study of media violence: The general aggression model. In D. Gentile (Ed.), *Media Violence and Children.* Westport, CT: Praeger.

Chaiken, S. (1980). Heuristic versus systematic information processing and the use of source versus message cues in persuasion. *Journal of Personality & Social Psychology, 39*(5), 752–766.

Cline, V. B., Croft, R. G., & Courrier, S. (1973). Desensitization of children to television violence. *Journal of Personality & Social Psychology, 27,* 360–365.

Cumberbatch, G. (1989). *A Measure of uncertainty: The effects of the mass media.* London: John Libbey.

Davison, W. P. (1983). The third-person effect in communication. *Public Opinion Quarterly, 47,* 1–15.

Dodge, K. A. (1980). Social cognition and children's aggressive behavior. *Child Development, 51,* 620–635.

Dodge, K. A. (1985). Attributional bias in aggressive children. In P. C. Kendall (Ed.), *Advances in cognitive and behavioral research and therapy.* New York: Academic Press.

Dodge, K. A., Pettit, G. S., Bates, J. E., & Valente, E. (1995). Social information-processing patterns partially mediate the effect of early physical abuse on later conduct problems. *Journal of Abnormal Psychology, 104,* 632–643.

Doob, A. N., & Wood, L. E. (1972). Catharsis and aggression: Effects of annoyance and retaliation on aggressive behavior. *Journal of Personality and Social Psychology, 22*(2), 156–162.

Eron, L. D., Huesmann, L. R., Lefkowitz, M. M., & Walder, L. O. (1972). Does television violence cause aggression? *American Psychologist, 27,* 253–263.

Feshbach, S., & Singer, R. D. (1971). *Television and aggression: An experimental field study.* San Francisco: Jossey-Bass.

Fowles, J. (1999). *The case for television violence.* Thousand Oaks, CA: Sage Publications.

Freedman, J. (1984). Effects of television violence on aggressiveness. *Psychological Bulletin, 96,* 227–246.

Freedman, J. L. (2002). *Media violence and its effects on aggression: Assessing the scientific evidence.* Toronto: University of Toronto Press.

Geen, R. G., & O'Neal, E. C. (1969). Activation of cue-elicited aggression by general arousal. *Journal of Personality and Social Psychology, 11,* 289–292.

Geen, R. G., & Thomas, S. L. (1986). The immediate effects of media violence on behavior, *Journal of Social Issues, 42,* 7–28.

Gerbner, G., Gross, L., Morgan, M., & Signorielli, N. (1994). *Growing up with television: The cultivation perspective.* In J. Bryant & D. Zillmann (Eds.), *Media effects* (pp. 17–41). Hillsdale, NJ: Erlbaum.

Guerra, N. G., Huesmann, L. R., Tolan, P., Van Acker, R., & Eron, L. D. (1995). Stressful events and individual beliefs as correlates of economic disadvantage and aggression among urban children. *Journal of Consulting and Clinical Psychology, 63*(4), 518–528.

Hamilton, J. T. (1998). *Channeling violence: The economic market for violent television programming.* Princeton, NJ: Princeton University Press.

Hanna, E., & Meltzoff, A. N. (1993). Peer imitation by toddlers in laboratory, home, and day care contexts: Implications for social learning and memory. *Developmental Psychology, 29*(4), 701–710.

Howitt, D., & Cumberbatch, G. (1975). *Mass media violence and society.* New York: John Wiley & Sons.

Huesmann, L. R. (1988). An information processing model for the development of aggression. *Aggressive Behavior, 14,* 13–24.

Huesmann, L. R. (1995). *Screen violence and real violence: Understanding the link.* Brochure. Auckland, NZ: Media Aware.

Huesmann, L. R. (1997). Observational learning of violent behavior. In Raine et al. (Eds.), *Biosocial bases of violence*. New York: Plenum Press.

Huesmann, L. R. (1998). The role of social information processing and cognitive schemas in the acquisition and maintenance of habitual aggressive behavior. In R. G. Geen & E. Donnerstein (Eds.), *Human aggression: Theories, research, and implications for policy* (pp. 73–109). New York: Academic Press.

Huesmann, L. R. (1999). The effects of childhood aggression and exposure to media violence on adult behaviors, attitudes, and mood: Evidence from a 15-year cross-national longitudinal study. *Aggressive Behavior, 25*, 18–29.

Huesmann, L. R. (2003). Gender differences in the continuity of aggression from childhood to adulthood: Evidence from some recent longitudinal studies. In S. Fein, A. Goethals, & M. Sandstron (Eds.), *Gender and aggression: The 2001 G. Stanley Hall symposium*. Mahwah, NJ: Erlbaum.

Huesmann, L. R., & Eron, L. D. (1986). The development of aggression in children of different cultures: Psychological processes and exposure to violence. In L. R. Huesmann & L. D. Eron (Eds.), *Television and the aggressive child: A cross national comparison* (pp. 239–257). Hillsdale, NJ: Lawrence Erlbaum Associates.

Huesmann, L. R., & Guerra, N. G. (1997). Normative beliefs about aggression and aggressive behavior. *Journal of Personality and Social Psychology, 72*(2), 408–419.

Huesmann, L. R., & Miller, L. S. (1994). Long-term effects of repeated exposure to media violence in childhood. In L. R. Huesmann (Ed.), *Aggressive behavior: Current perspectives*. New York: Plenum Press.

Huesmann, L. R., & Moise, J. (1996). Media violence: A demonstrated public threat to children. *Harvard Mental Health Letter, 12*(12), 5–7.

Huesmann, L. R., Eron, L. D., Lefkowitz, M. M., & Walder, L. O. (1984). The stability of aggression over time and generations. *Developmental Psychology, 20*, 1120–1134.

Huesmann, L. R., Eron, L. D., Berkowitz, L., & Chaffee, S. (1992). The effects of television violence on aggression: A reply to a skeptic. In P. Suedfeld & P. E. Tetlock (Eds.), *Psychology and social policy* (pp. 191–200). New York: Hemisphere.

Huesmann, L. R., Guerra, N. G., Zelli, A., & Miller, L. (1992). Differing normative beliefs about aggression for boys and girls. In K. Bjorkqvist & P. Niemela (Eds.), *Of mice and women: Aspects of female aggression*. Orlando, FL: Academic Press.

Huesmann, L. R., Lagerspetz, K., & Eron, L. D. (1984). Intervening variables in the television violence—aggression relation: Evidence from two countries. *Developmental Psychology, 20*(5), 746–775.

Huesmann, L. R., Moise, J. F., & Podolski, C.-L. (1997). The effects of media violence on the development of antisocial behavior. In D. Stoff, J. Breiling, & J. D. Maser (Eds.), *Handbook of antisocial behavior* (pp. 181–193). New York: John Wiley & Sons.

Huesmann, L. R., Moise, J., Podolski, C. P., & Eron, L. D. (2003). Longitudinal relations between children's exposure to television violence and their aggressive and violent behavior in young adulthood: 1977–1992. *Developmental Psychology*.

Jo, E., & Berkowitz, L. (1994). A priming effect analysis of media influences: An update. In J. Bryant and D. Zillman (Eds.), *Media effects* (pp. 43–60). Hillsdale, NJ: Lawrence Erlbaum.

Jones, G. (2002). *Killing monsters: Why children need fantasy, super heroes, and make-believe violence*. New York: Basic Books.

Josephson, W. L. (1987). Television violence and children's aggression: Testing the priming, social script, and disinhibition predictions. *Journal of Personality and Social Psychology, 53*(5), 882–890.

Leyens, J. P., Camino, L., Parke, R. D., & Berkowitz, L. (1975). The effects of movie violence on aggression in a field setting as a function of group dominance and cohesion. *Journal of Personality and Social Psychology, 32,* 346–360.

Meltzoff, A. N., & Moore, K. M. (1977). Imitation of facial and manual gestures by human neonates. *Science, 109,* 77–78.

Meltzoff, A. N., & Moore, K. M. (2000). Resolving the debate about early imitation (pp. 167–181). In D. Muir (Ed.), *Infant development: The essential readings.* Malden, MA: Blackwell Publishers.

Milavsky, J. R., Kessler, R., Stipp, H., & Rubens, W. S. (1982). Television and aggression: Results of a panel study. In D. Pearl, L. Bouthilet, & J. Lazar (Eds.), *Television and behavior: Ten years of scientific progress and implications for the 80's: Vol. 2. Technical reviews.* Washington, DC: Government Printing Office.

Moise-Titus, J. (1999). *The role of negative emotions in the media violence-aggression relation.* Unpublished doctoral dissertation, University of Michigan, Ann Arbor, MI.

Murray, J. P. (1984). Results of an informal poll of knowledgeable persons concerning the impact of television violence. *Newsletter of the American Psychological Association Division of Child, Youth and Family Services, 7*(1), 2.

Paik, H., & Comstock, G. (1994). The effects of television violence on antisocial behavior: A meta-analysis. *Communication Research, 21*(4), 516–546.

Petty, R. E., & Cacioppo, J. T. (1986). The elaboration likelihood model of persuasion. In L. Berkowitz (Ed.), *Advances in experimental social psychology: Vol. 19.* Orlando, FL: Academic Press.

Rizzolati, G., Fadiga, L., Gallese, V., & Fogassi, L. (1996). Premotor cortex and the recognition of motor actions. *Cognitive Brain Research, 3,* 131–141.

Rosenthal, R. (1986). Media violence, antisocial behavior, and the social consequences of small effects. *Journal of Social Issues, 42,* 141–154.

Schweitzer, K., Zillmann, D., Weaver, J. B., & Luttrell, E. S. (1992). Perception of threatening events in the emotional aftermath of a televised college football game. *Journal of Broadcasting & Electronic Media, 36*(1), 75–82.

Steinfeld, J. (1972). Statement in hearings before Subcommittee on Communications of Committee on Commerce (United States Senate, Serial nos. 92–52, pp. 25–27). Washington, DC: United States Government.

Strasburger, V. C., & Wilson, B. J. (2003). Television violence. In D. Gentile (Ed.), *Media Violence and Children.* Greenwood, CT: Praeger.

Tremblay, R. E. (2000). The development of aggressive behavior during childhood: What have we learned in the past century? *International Journal of Behavioral Development, 24,* 129–141.

Turner, C. W., & Simons, L. S. (1974). Effects of subject sophistication and evaluation apprehension on aggressive responses to weapons. *Journal of Personality and Social Psychology, 30,* 341–348.

Valkenburg, P. M., Cantor, J., Peeters, A. L. (2000). Fright reactions to television: A child survey. *Communication Research, 27*(1), 82–97.

Wyrwicka, W. (1996). *Imitation in human and animal behavior.* New Brunswick, NJ: Transaction Publishers.

Zillmann, D. (1979). *Hostility and aggression*. Hillsdale, NJ: Lawrence Erlbaum.

Zillmann, D. (1983a). Arousal and aggression. In R. Geen & E. Donnerstein (Eds.), *Aggression: Theoretical and empirical review: Vol. 1* (pp. 75–102). New York: Academic Press.

Zillmann, D. (1983b). Transfer of excitation in emotional behavior. In J. T. Cacioppo & R. E. Petty (Eds.), *Social psychophysiology: A sourcebook* (pp. 215–240). New York: Guilford Press.

Zillmann, D. (1988). Mood management through communication choices. *American Behavioral Scientist, 31*(3), 327–340.

CHAPTER 7

American Academy of Pediatrics, American Psychological Association, American Academy of Child & Adolescent Psychiatry, & American Medical Association. (2000). *Joint statement on the impact of entertainment violence on children* [Web Page]. URL http://www.aap.org/advocacy/releases/jstmtevc.htm.

Anderson, C. A. (2002). Violent video games and aggressive thoughts, feelings, and behaviors. In S. L. Calvert, A. B. Jordan, & R. R. Cocring (Eds.), *Children in the digital age* (pp. 101–119). Westport, CT: Praeger.

Anderson, C. A. (2003). Video games and aggressive behavior. In D. Ravitch and J. P. Viteritti (Eds.), *Kids' stuff: Marketing violence and vulgarity in the popular culture* (pp. 143–167). Baltimore, MD: Johns Hopkins University Press.

Anderson, C. A., & Bushman, B. J. (1997). External validity of "trivial" experiments: The case of laboratory aggression. *Review of General Psychology, 1*, 19–41.

Anderson, C. A. & Bushman, B. J. (2001). Effects of violent games on aggressive behavior, aggressive cognition, aggressive affect, physiological arousal, and prosocial behavior: A meta-analytic review of the scientific literature. *Psychological Science, 12*, 353–359.

Anderson, C. A., & Bushman, B. J. (2002a). Human Aggression. *Annual Review of Psychology, 53*, 27–51.

Anderson, C. A., & Bushman, B. J. (2002b). The effects of media violence on society. *Science, 295*, 2377–2378.

Anderson, C. A., & Dill, K. E. (2000). Video games and aggressive thoughts, feelings, and behavior in the laboratory and in life. *Journal of Personality and Social Psychology, 78*, 772–790.

Anderson, C. A., & Ford, C. M. (1986). Affect of the game player: Short-term consequences of playing aggressive video games. *Personality and Social Psychology Bulletin, 12*, 390–402.

Anderson, C. A., & Huesmann, L. R. (in press). Human aggression: A social-cognitive view. In M. A. Hogg & J. Cooper (Eds.), *Handbook of social psychology*. London: Sage Publications.

Anderson, C. A., Lindsay, J. J., & Bushman, B. J. (1999). Research in the psychological laboratory: Truth or triviality? *Current Directions in Psychological Science, 8*, 3–9.

Associated Press. (2002, July 2). *Be all you can be in computer game*. http://www.msnbc.com, accessed July 2, 2002.

Austin, E. W. (1993). Exploring the effects of active parental mediation of television content. *Journal of Broadcasting & Electronic Media, 37*, 147–158.

Ballard, M. E., & Lineberger, R. (1999). Video game violence and confederate gender: Effects on reward and punishment given by college males. *Sex Roles, 41,* 541–558.

Ballard, M. E., & West, J. R. (1996). *Mortal Kombat*: The effects of violent video game play on males' hostility and cardiovascular responding. *Journal of Applied Social Psychology, 26,* 717–730.

Banaji, M. R., & Crowder, R. G. (1989). The bankruptcy of everyday memory. *American Psychologist, 44,* 1185–1193.

Berkey, C. S., Rockett, H. R., Field, A. E., Gillman, M. W., Frazier, A. L., Camargo, C. A., Jr., & Colditz, G. A. (2000). Activity, dietary intake, and weight changes in a longitudinal study of preadolescent and adolescent boys and girls. *Pediatrics, 105*(4), E56.

Berkowitz, L., & Donnerstein, E. (1982). External validity is more than skin deep: Some answers to criticism of laboratory experiments. *American Psychologist, 37,* 245–257.

Buchman, D. D., & Funk, J. B. (1996). Video and computer games in the '90s: Children's time commitment and game preference. *Children Today, 24,* 12–16.

Bushman, B. J., & Anderson, C. A. (2001). Media violence and the American public: Scientific facts versus media misinformation. *American Psychologist, 56,* 477–489.

Bushman, B. J., & Anderson, C. A. (2002). Violent video games and hostile expectations: A test of the general aggression model. *Personality and Social Psychology Bulletin, 28,* 1679–1686.

Bushman, B. J., & Huesmann, L. R. (2000). Effects of televised violence on aggression. In D. Singer & J. Singer (Eds.), *Handbook of children and the media* (pp. 223–254). Thousand Oaks, CA: Sage Publications.

Calvert, S. L., & Tan, S. L. (1994). Impact of virtual reality on young adults' physiological arousal and aggressive thoughts: Interaction versus observation. *Journal of Applied Developmental Psychology, 15,* 125–139.

Cantor, J. R., Zillmann, D., & Bryant, J. (1975). Enhancement of experienced sexual arousal in response to erotic stimuli through misattributions of unrelated residual excitation. *Journal of Personality and Social Psychology, 32,* 69–75.

Carlson, M., Marcus-Newhall, A., & Miller, N. (1989). Evidence for a general construct of aggression. *Personality and Social Psychology Bulletin, 15,* 377–389.

Chambers, J. H., & Ascione, F. R. (1987). The effects of prosocial and aggressive video games on children's donating and helping. *Journal of Genetic Psychology, 148,* 499–505.

Children Now. (2001). *Fair play? Violence, gender and race in video games.* Los Angeles, CA: Children Now.

Cohen, A. (2000, October 30). New game [PlayStation 2]. *Time, 156,* 58–60.

Cook, W. W., & Medley, D. M. (1954). Proposed hostility and parisaic-virtue scales for the MMPI. *Journal of Applied Psychology, 38,* 414–418.

Cooper, J., & Mackie, D. (1986). Video games and aggression in children. *Journal of Applied Social Psychology, 16,* 726–744.

Creasey, G. L., & Myers, B. J. (1986). Video games and children: Effects on leisure activities, schoolwork, and peer involvement. *Merrill-Palmer Quarterly, 32,* 251–262.

Crick, N. R., & Dodge, K. A. (1994). A review and reformulation of social information-processing mechanisms in children's social adjustment. *Psychological Bulletin, 115*, 74–101.

Dietz, T. L. (1998). An examination of violence and gender role portrayals in video games: Implications for gender socialization and aggressive behavior. *Sex Roles, 38*, 425–442.

Dill, K. E., & Dill, J. C. (1998). Video game violence: A review of the empirical literature. *Aggression and Violent Behavior: A Review Journal, 3*, 407–428.

Dill, K. E., Gentile, D. A., Richter, W. A., & Dill, J. C. (2001, August). *Portrayal of women and minorities in video games.* Paper presented at the 109th Annual Conference of the American Psychological Association, San Francisco, CA.

Dominick, J. R. (1984). Videogames, television violence, and aggression in teenagers. *Journal of Communication, 34*, 136–147.

Donnerstein, E., Slaby, R. G., & Eron, L. D. (1994). The mass media and youth aggression. In L. D. Eron, J. H. Gentry, & P. Schlegel (Eds.), *Reason to hope: A psychosocial perspective on violence and youth* (pp. 219–250). Washington, DC: American Psychological Association.

Dorr, A., & Rabin, B. E. (1995). Parents, children, and television. In M. Bornstein (Ed.), *Handbook of parenting: Vol. 4* (pp. 323–351). Mahwah, NJ: Erlbaum.

Funk, J. B. (1993). Reevaluating the impact of video games. *Clinical Pediatrics, 32*, 86–90.

Funk, J. B. (2001). *Children and violent video games: Are there "high risk" players?* Paper presented at "Playing by the Rules: Video Games and Cultural Policy Conference," Chicago, IL.

Funk, J. B. (2003). Violent video games: Who's at risk? In D. Ravitch and J. P. Viteritti (Eds.), *Children and the popular culture* (pp. 168–192). Baltimore, MD: Johns Hopkins University Press.

Funk, J. B., & Buchman, D. D. (1996). Playing violent video and computer games and adolescent self-concept. *Journal of Communication, 46*, 19–32.

Funk, J. B., Buchman, D. D., & Germann, J. N. (2000). Preference for violent electronic games, self-concept, and gender differences in young children. *American Journal of Orthopsychiatry, 70*, 233–241.

Funk, J., Hagan, J., & Schimming, J. (1999). Children and electronic games: A comparison of parents' and children's perceptions of children's habits and preferences in a United States sample. *Psychological Reports, 85*, 883–888.

Gadberry, S. (1980). Effects of restricting first graders' TV-viewing on leisure time use, IQ change, and cognitive style. *Journal of Applied Developmental Psychology, 1*, 45–57.

Geen, R. G. (2001). *Human aggression.* Philadelphia, PA: Open University Press.

Gentile, D. A., Lynch, P. J., Linder, J. R., & Walsh, D. A. (in press). The effects of violent video game habits on adolescent hostility, aggressive behaviors, and school performance. *Journal of Adolescence.*

Gentile, D. A., & Walsh, D. A. (2002). A normative study of family media habits. *Journal of Applied Developmental Psychology, 23*, 157–178.

Giancola, P. R., & Chermack, S. T. (1998). Construct validity of laboratory aggression paradigms: A response to Tedeschi and Quigley (1996). *Aggression and Violent Behavior, 3*, 237–253.

Graybill, D., Kirsch, J. R., & Esselman, E. D. (1985). Effects of playing violent versus nonviolent video games on the aggressive ideation of aggressive and nonaggressive children. *Child Study Journal, 15,* 199–205.

Grossman, D. (1996). *On killing.* Boston, MA: Little, Brown & Co.

Grossman, D. (1998, August 10). Trained to kill. *Christianity Today,* 31–39.

Gwinup, G., Haw, T., & Elias, A. (1983). Cardiovascular changes in video-game players: Cause for concern? *Post Graduate Medicine, 245–248.*

Harris, M. B., & Williams, R. (1985). Video games and school performance. *Education, 105*(3), 306–309.

Huston, A. C., Donnerstein, E., Fairchild, H., Feshbach, N. D., Katz, P. A., Murray, J. P., Rubinstein, E. A., Wilcox, B. L., & Zuckerman, D. M. (1992). *Big world, small screen: The role of television in American society.* Lincoln, NE: University of Nebraska Press.

"Industrial strengths: New vs. old economy earnings." (2000, November). *Wired.* p. 122.

Irwin, A. R., & Gross, A. M. (1995). Cognitive tempo, violent video games, and aggressive behavior in young boys. *Journal of Family Violence, 10,* 337–350.

Kasper, D., Welsh, S., & Chambliss, C. (1999). Educating students about the risks of excessive videogame usage. ERIC Document Reproduction Service, ED 426 315.

Keller, S. (1992). Children and the Nintendo. ERIC Document Retrieval Service, ED 405 069.

Kent, S. L. (2001). *The ultimate history of video games.* Roseville, CA: Prima Publishing.

Kestenbaum, G. I., & Weinstein, L. (1985). Personality, psychopathology and developmental issues in male adolescent video game use. *Journal of the American Academy of Child Psychiatry, 24,* 329–333.

Kirsh, S. J. (1998). Seeing the world through Mortal Kombat–colored glasses: Violent video games and the development of a short-term hostile attribution bias. *Childhood, 5,* 177–184.

Koepp, M. J., Gunn, R. N., Lawrence, A. D., Cunningham, V. J., Dagher, A., Jones, T., Brooks, D. J., Bench, C. J., & Grasby, P. M. (1998). Evidence for striatal dopamine release during a video game. *Nature, 393,* 266–268.

Kruglanski, A. W. (1975). The human subject in the psychology experiment: Fact and artifact. In L. Berkowitz (Ed.), *Advances in experimental social psychology: Vol. 8* (pp. 101–147). New York: Academic Press.

Lieberman, D. A. (1997). Interactive video games for health promotion: Effects on knowledge, self-efficacy, social support, and health. In R. L. Street, W. R. Gold, & T. Manning (Eds.), *Health promotion and interactive technology: Theoretical applications and future directions* (pp. 103–120). Mahwah, NJ: Lawrence Erlbaum.

Lieberman, D. A., Chaffee, S. H., & Roberts, D. F. (1988). Computers, mass media, and schooling: Functional equivalence in uses of new media. *Social Science Computer Review, 6,* 224–241.

Lin, C. A., & Atkin, D. J. (1989). Parental mediation and rulemaking for adolescent use of television and VCRs. *Journal of Broadcasting & Electronic Media, 33,* 53–67.

Lynch, P. J. (1994). Type A behavior, hostility, and cardiovascular function at rest and after playing video games in teenagers. *Psychosomatic Medicine, 56,* 152.

Lynch, P. J. (1999). Hostility, Type A behavior, and stress hormones at rest and after playing violent video games in teenagers. *Psychosomatic Medicine, 61,* 113.

Lynch, P. J., Gentile, D. A., Olson, A. A., & van Brederode, T. M. (2001, April). The effects of violent video game habits on adolescent aggressive attitudes and behaviors. Paper presented at the Biennial Conference of the Society for Research in Child Development, Minneapolis, MN.

Mook, D. G. (1983). In defense of external invalidity. *American Psychologist, 38*, 379–387.

Murphy, J. K., Alpert, B. S., & Walker, S. S. (1992). Ethnicity, pressor reactivity, and children's blood pressure: Five years of observations. *Hypertension, 20*, 327–332.

Nintendo sells one billionth video game. (1995, October 3). Nintendo of America Inc. Home Page, http://www.nintendo.com.

Paik, H., & Comstock, G. (1994). The effects of television violence on antisocial behavior: A meta-analysis. *Communication Research, 21*(4), 516–546.

Potter, W. J. (1999). *On media violence.* Thousand Oaks, CA: Sage Publications.

Roberts, D. F., Foehr, U. G., Rideout, V. J., & Brodie, M. (1999). *Kids & media @ the new millennium.* Menlo Park, CA: Kaiser Family Foundation.

Robinson, T. N., Wilde, M. L., Navracruz, L. C., Haydel, K. F., & Varady, A. (2001). Effects of reducing children's television and video game use on aggressive behavior: A randomized controlled trial. *Archives of Pediatric Adolescent Medicine, 155*, 17–23.

Schutte, N. S., Malouff, J. M., Post-Gorden, J. C., & Rodasta, A. L. (1988). Effects of playing video games on children's aggressive and other behaviors. *Journal of Applied Social Psychology, 18*, 454–460.

Segal, K. R., & Dietz, W. H. (1991). Physiologic responses to playing a video game. *American Journal of Diseases of Children, 145*, 1034–1036.

Silvern, S. B., & Williamson, P. A. (1987). The effects of video game play on young children's aggression, fantasy and prosocial behavior. *Journal of Applied Developmental Psychology, 8*, 453–462.

Strasburger, V. C., & Donnerstein, E. (1999). Children, adolescents, and the media: Issues and solutions. *Pediatrics, 103*, 129–139.

Subrahmanyam, K., Kraut, R. E., Greenfield, P. M., & Gross, E. F. (2000). The impact of home computer use on children's activities and development. *Children and Computer Technology, 10*(2), 123–144.

Surgeon General (2001). *Youth violence: A report of the Surgeon General.* Rockville, MD: U.S. Department of Health and Human Services.

Thompson, K. M., & Haninger, K. (2001). Violence in E-Rated Video Games. *JAMA, 286*, 591–598.

Ubi Soft. (2001). *Ubi Soft licenses Tom Clancy's Rainbow Six Rogue Spear game engine to train U.S. soldiers* [Web Page]. URL http://corp.ubisoft.com/pr_release_010829a.htm [2002, February 12].

van Schie, E.G.M., & Wiegman, O. (1997). Children and videogames: Leisure activities, aggression, social integration, and school performance. *Journal of Applied Social Psychology, 27*, 1175–1194.

Walsh, D. (2000). *5th Annual video and computer game report card.* Minneapolis, MN: National Institute on Media and the Family.

Walsh, D. A., & Gentile, D. A. (2001). A validity test of movie, television, and video-game ratings. *Pediatrics, 107*, 1302–1308.

Wiegman, O., & van Schie, E.G.M. (1998). Video game playing and its relations with aggressive and prosocial behavior. *British Journal of Social Psychology, 37,* 367–378.

Williams, P. A., Haertel, E. H., Haertel, G. D., & Walberg, H. J. (1982). The impact of leisure-time television on school learning: A research synthesis. *American Educational Research Journal, 19,* 19–50.

Woodard, E. H., & Gridina, N. (2000). *Media in the home.* Philadelphia, PA: Annenburg Public Policy Center of the University of Pennsylvania.

CHAPTER 8

Adoni, H. (1978). The functions of mass media in the political socialization of adolescents. *Communication Research, 6,* 84–106.

Anderson, C. A., Carnagey, N. L., & Eubanks, J. (2003). Exposure to violent media: The effects of violent song lyrics on aggressive thoughts and feelings. *Journal of Personality & Social Psychology, 84,* 960–971.

Arnett, J. (1991a). Adolescence and heavy metal music: From the mouths of metalheads. *Youth and Society, 23*(1), 76–98.

Arnett, J. (1991b). Heavy metal music and reckless behavior among adolescents. *Journal of Youth and Adolescence, 20,* 573–592.

Ballard, M. E., & Coates, S. (1995). The immediate effects of homicidal, suicidal, and nonviolent heavy metal and rap songs on the moods of college students. *Youth & Society, 27,* 148–168.

Barongan, C., & Hall, G.C.N. (1995). The influence of misogynous rap music on sexual aggression against women. *Psychology of Women Quarterly, 19,* 195–207.

Berman, A. L., & Jobes, D. A. (1991). *Adolescent suicide: Assessment and intervention.* Washington, DC: American Psychological Association.

Brown, J. D., Campbell, K., & Fischer, L. (1986). American adolescents and music videos: Why do they watch? *Gazette, 37,* 19–32.

Brown, J. D., Childers, K., Bauman, K., & Koch, G. (1990). The influence of new media and family structure on young adolescents' television and radio use. *Communication Research, 17,* 65–82.

Brown, R., & O'Leary, M. (1971). Pop music in an English secondary school system. *American Behavioral Scientist, 14,* 401–413.

Carey, J. (1969). Changing courtship patterns in the popular song. *American Journal of Sociology, 4,* 720–731.

Chaffee, S. H. (1977). Mass media effects: New research perspectives. In D. Lerner and L. Nelson (Eds.), *Communication research—a half century appraisal* (pp. 210–241). Honolulu: East-West Center Press.

Christenson, P. (1992a). The effects of parental advisory labels on adolescent music preferences. *Journal of Communication, 42*(1), 106–13.

Christenson, P., & DeBenedittis, P. (1986). "Eavesdropping" on the FM band: Children's use of radio. *Journal of Communication, 36*(2), 27–38.

Christenson, P., DeBenedittis, P., & Lindlof, T. (1985). Children's use of audio media. *Communication Research, 12,* 327–343.

Christenson, P. G., & Roberts, D. F. (1998). *It's not only rock & roll: Popular music in the lives of adolescents.* Cresskill, NJ: Hampton Press.

Christenson, P., & van Nouhuys, B. (1995, May). *From the fringe to the center: A com-*

parison of heavy metal and rap fandom. Paper presented at the annual meeting of the International Communication Association, Albuquerque.

Dominick, J. (1974). The portable friend: Peer group membership and radio usage. *Journal of Broadcasting, 18*(2), 164–69.

Eaton, L. (1997, August 3). Teen proves hard rock's bad for you. *The News Herald.* Retrieved July 8, 2002, from http://www.newsherald.com/EDUCATION/ ROCK86.HTM.

Egan, T. (1998, June 14). From adolescent angst to shooting up schools. *New York Times,* p. 1.

Fedler, F., Hall, J., & Tanzi, L. (1982). Popular songs emphasize sex, de-emphasize romance. *Mass Communication Review, 9,* 10–15.

Frith, S. (1981). *Sound effects: Youth, leisure and the politics of rock'n'roll.* New York: Pantheon, 1981.

Gantz, W., Gartenberg, H., Pearson, M., & Schiller, S. (1978). Gratifications and expectations associated with popular music among adolescents. *Popular Music and Society, 6*(1), 81–89.

Gentile, D. A., Linder, J. R., & Walsh, D. A. (2003, April). *Looking through time: A longitudinal study of children's media violence consumption at home and aggressive behaviors at school.* Poster presented at the Biennial Conference of the Society for Research in Child Development, Tampa, FL.

Gentile, D. A., Lynch, P. J., Linder, J. R., & Walsh, D. A. (2003, in press). The effects of violent video game habits on adolescent hostility, aggressive behaviors, and school performance. *Journal of Adolescence.*

Gentile, D. A., Pick, A. D., Flom, R. A., & Campos, J. J. (1994). *Adults' and preschoolers' perception of emotional meaning in music.* Poster presented at the 13th Biennial Conference on Human Development, Pittsburgh, PA.

Gentile, D. A., & Pick, A. D. (2003, under review). Infants' discrimination of musical affective expressiveness.

Gentile, D. A., Stoerzinger, R.L.C., Finney, P. A., & Pick, A. D. (1996). *Preschoolers can perceive emotional meaning in music: Converging evidence.* Presented at the 14th Biennial Conference on Human Development, Birmingham, AL.

Gentile, D. A., & Walsh, D. A. (1999). *MediaQuotient™: National survey of family media habits, knowledge, and attitudes.* Minneapolis, MN: National Institute on Media and the Family.

Goleman, D. (1995). *Emotional intelligence.* New York: Bantam Books.

Gordon, T., Hakanen, E., & Wells, A. (1992, May). *Music preferences and the use of music to manage emotional states: Correlates with self-concept among adolescents.* Paper presented at the annual meetings of the International Communication Association, Miami.

Greenberg, B., Ku, L., & Li, H. (1989, June). *Young people and their orientation to the mass media: An international study, Study #2: United States.* East Lansing, MI: College of Communication Arts, Michigan State University.

Greeson, L., & Williams, R. A. (1986). Social implications of music videos for youth: An analysis of the content and effects of MTV. *Youth and Society, 18,* 177–189.

Hakanen, E., & Wells, A. (1993). Music preference and taste cultures among adolescents. *Popular Music and Society, 17*(1), 55–69.

Hansen, C., & Hansen, R. (1990a). Rock music videos and antisocial behavior. *Basic and Applied Psychology, 11,* 357–369.

Hansen, C., & Hansen, R. (1990b). The influence of sex and violence on the appeal of rock music videos. *Communication Research, 17,* 212–234.

Hansen, C., & Hansen, R. (1991). Constructing personality and social reality through music: Individual differences among fans of punk and heavy metal music. *Journal of Broadcasting and Electronic Media, 35,* 335–350.

Health, Wealth, & Happiness (n.d.). Hard rock music creates killer mice! Retrieved July 8, 2002, from http://www.relfe.com/hard_rock.html.

Johnson, J. D., Jackson, L. A., & Gatto, L. (1995). Violent attitudes and deferred academic aspirations: Deleterious effects of exposure to rap music. *Basic and Applied Social Psychology, 16*(1&2), 27–41.

Kenealy, P. M. (1988). Validation of a music mood induction procedure: Some preliminary findings. *Cognition and Emotion, 2,* 41–48.

Kubey, R., & Larson, R. (1989). The use and experience of the new video media among children and young adolescents: Television viewing compared to the use of videocassettes, video games, and music videos. *Communication Research, 17,* 107–130.

Kuwahara, Y. (1992). Power to the people, y'all: Rap music, resistance, and black college students. *Humanity and Society, 16*(1), 54–73.

Larson, R., Kubey, R., & Colletti, J. (1989). Changing channels: Early adolescent media choices and shifting investments in family and friends. *Journal of Youth and Adolescence, 18*(6), 583–599.

Leming, J. (1987). Rock music and the socialization of moral values in early adolescence. *Youth and Society, 18,* 363–383.

Levy, C. J., & Deykin, E. Y. (1989). Suicidality, depression, and substance abuse in adolescence. *American Journal of Psychiatry, 146,* 1462–1467.

Litman, R. E., & Farberow, N. L. (1994). Pop-rock music as precipitating cause in youth suicide. *Journal of Forensic Sciences, 39,* 494–499.

Lull, J. (1987). Listeners' communicative uses of popular music. In J. Lull (Ed.), *Popular music and communication* (pp. 140–174). Newbury Park, CA: Sage.

Lull, J. (1992). Popular music and communication: An introduction. In J. Lull (Ed.), *Popular music and communication,* 2nd ed. (pp. 1–32). Newbury Park, CA: Sage.

Lyle, J., & Hoffman, H. (1972). Children's use of television and other media. In E. Rubinstein, G. Comstock, & J. Murray (Eds.), *Television in Day-to-day Life: Patterns of Use* (pp. 129–256). Washington, DC: Government Printing Office.

Martin, G., Clarke, M., & Pearce, C. (1993). Adolescent suicide: Music preference as an indicator of vulnerability. *Journal of the Academy of Child and Adolescent Psychiatry, 32*(3), 530–535.

National Television Violence Study 3. (1998). Thousand Oaks, CA: Sage Publications.

Peterson, D. L., & Pfost, K. S. (1989). Influence of rock videos on attitudes of violence against women. *Psychological Reports, 64,* 319–322.

Pignatiello, M. F., Camp, C. J., & Rasar, L. A. (1986). Musical mood induction: An alternative to the Velten technique. *Journal of Abnormal Psychology, 95,* 295–297.

Pignatiello, M., Camp, C. J., Elder, S. T., & Rasar, L. A. (1989). A psychophysiological comparison of the Velten and musical mood induction techniques. *Journal of Music Therapy, 26,* 140–154.

Roberts, D. F., & Foehr, V. (2003, in press). *Kids and media in America: Patterns of use at the millennium.* New York: Cambridge University Press.

Roberts, D. F., Foehr, U. G., Rideout, V. J., & Brodie, M. (1999). *Kids & media @ the new millennium*. Menlo Park, CA: Kaiser Family Foundation.

Roberts, D. F., & Henriksen, L. (1990, June). *Music listening vs. television viewing among older adolescents*. Paper presented at the annual meeting of the International Communication Association, Dublin, Ireland.

Roberts, D. F., Henriksen, L., & Christenson, P. (1999, April). *Substance use in popular movies and music*. Washington, DC: Office of National Drug Control Policy.

Rock on trial. (1988, Oct. 15). *The Economist*, p. 38.

Roe, K. (1984, August). *Youth and music in Sweden: Results from a longitudinal study of teenagers' media use*. Paper presented at the meeting of the International Association of Mass Communication Research, Prague.

Roe, K. (1985). Swedish youth and music: Listening patterns and motivations. *Communication Research, 12*(3), 353–62.

Roe, K., (1995). Adolescents' use of socially disvalued media: Towards a theory of media delinquency. *Journal of Youth and Adolescence, 24*, 617–631.

Rouner, D. (1990). "Rock Music Use as a Socializing Function." *Popular Music and Society, 14*(1), 97–107.

Rubin, A. M., West, D. V., & Mitchell, W. S. (2001). Differences in aggression, attitudes toward women, and distrust as reflected in popular music preferences. *Media Psychology, 3*, 25–42.

St. Lawrence, J. S., & Joyner, D. J. (1991). The effects of sexually violent rock music on males' acceptance of violence against women. *Psychology of Women Quarterly, 15*, 49–63.

Sullivan, S. E., Gentile, D. A., & Pick, A. D. (1998). The perception of emotion in music by eight-month-old infants. Presented at 11th Biennial International Conference on Infant Studies, Atlanta, GA.

Sun, S., & Lull, J. (1986). The adolescent audience for music videos and why they watch. *Journal of Communication, 36*(1), 115–25.

Took, K. J., & Weiss, D. S. (1994). The relationship between heavy metal and rap music and adolescent turmoil: Real or artifact? *Adolescence, 29*, 613–621.

2 Live Crew. (1986). We Want Some Pussy! On *Is What We Are* [record]. Miami, FL: Lil' Joe Records.

Vance v. Judas Priest, 1990 WL 130920 (Nev. Ct. August 24, 1990).

Wanamaker, C. E., & Reznikoff, M. (1989). Effects of aggressive and nonaggressive rock songs on projective and structured tests. *The Journal of Psychology, 123*, 561–570.

Wartella, E., Heintz, K., Aidman, A., & Mazzarella, S. (1990). Television and beyond: Children's video media in one community. *Communication Research, 17*, 45–64.

Wass, H., Miller, D., and Reditt, C. (1991). Adolescents and destructive themes in rock music: A follow-up. *Omega, 23*(3), 193–206.

Wass, H., Miller, D., and Stevenson, R. (1989). Factors affecting adolescents' behavior and attitudes toward destructive rock lyrics. *Death Studies, 13*, 287–303.

Wells, A. (1990). Popular music: Emotional use and management. *Journal of Popular Culture, 24*(1), 105–117.

Wester, S. R., Crown, C. L., Quatman, G. L., & Heesacker, M. (1997). The influence of sexually violent rap music on attitudes of men with little prior exposure. *Psychology of Women Quarterly, 21*, 497–508.

CHAPTER 9

Abelman, R., & Atkin, D. (2000). What children watch when they watch TV: Putting theory into practice. *Journal of Broadcasting & Electronic Media, 44*(1), 143–154.

Acuff, D. S. (1997). What kids buy and why: The psychology of marketing to kids. New York: Free Press.

Anderson, C. A., & Bushman, B. J. (2001). Effects of violent video games on aggressive behavior, aggressive cognition, aggressive affect, physiological arousal, and prosocial behavior: A meta-analytic review of the scientific literature. *Psychological Science, 12,* 353–359.

Anderson, C. (2002). Violent video games and aggressive thoughts, feelings, and behaviors. In S. Calvert, A. Jordan, & R. Cocking (Eds.), *Children in the digital age: Influences of electronic media on development.* Westport, CT: Praeger.

Ashdown, S. (2002, May). Nick and THQ try on next-gen studio-gameco relationship for size. *Kidscreen,* 37–38, 42.

Bandura, A. (1997). *Self-efficacy: The exercise of control.* New York: W. H. Freeman & Co.

Bates, B. R. & Garner, T. (2001). Can you dig it? Audiences, archetypes, and John Shaft. *The Howard Journal of Communications, 12*(3), July–Sept., 137–157.

Berkowitz, L. (1970). Aggressive humor as a stimulus to aggressive responses. *Journal of Personality & Social Psychology, 16*(4), 710–717.

Boyatzis, C. J., Matillo, G. M., Nesbitt, K. M. (1995). Effects of the "Mighty Morphin Power Rangers" on children's aggression with peers. *Child Study Journal 25*(1) 45–55.

Breton, J., Valla, J., & Lambert, J. (1993). Industrial disaster and mental health of children and their parents. *Journal of the American Academy of Child and Adolescent Psychiatry, 32,* 438–445.

Bryant, J., & Zillmann, D. (1991). *Responding to the screen.* Hillsdale, NJ: Erlbaum.

Buchman, D. D., & Funk, J. B. (1996). Video and computer games in the '90s: Children's time commitment and game preference. *Children Today, 24,* 12–15.

Bushman, B. J. & Anderson, C. A. (2001). Is it time to pull the plug on hostile versus instrumental aggression dichotomy? *Psychological Review, 108*(1), 273–279.

Calvert, S. L. (1999). *Children's journeys through the information age.* Boston: McGraw Hill.

Calvert, S. L., Kondla, T., Ertel, K. & Meisel, D. (2001). Young adults' perceptions and memories of a televised woman hero. *Sex Roles, 45,* 31–52.

Calvert, S. L. & Tan, S. L. (1994). Impact of virtual reality on young adults' physiological arousal and aggressive thoughts: Interaction versus observation. *Journal of Applied Developmental Psychology, 15,* 125–139.

Campbell, J. (1949). *The hero with a thousand faces.* Princeton, NJ: Princeton University Press.

Cassell, J. (2002). We have these rules within: The effects of exercising voice in a children's online forum. In S. Calvert, A. Jordan, & R. Cocking (Eds.), *Children in the digital age: Influences of electronic media on development.* Westport, CT: Praeger.

Children Now. (1994). Tuned in or tuned out? America's children speak out on the news media. Available at www.childrennow.org/publications.html.

Children Now. (2001, December). Fair play? Violence, gender, and race in video games. Available at http://www.childrennow.org/media/video-games/2001/ .

Coie, J., & Dodge, K. (1998). Aggression and antisocial behavior. In W. Damon (Gen. Ed.) and N. Eisenberg (Vol. Ed.). *Handbook of Child Psychology. 5th ed.* NY: John Wiley & Sons (pp. 779–862).

Collins, W.A. (1973). Effects of temporal separation between motivation, aggression, and consequences: A developmental study. *Developmental Psychology, 8,* 215–221.

Connell, M. (2002, May). Cool new games. *Kidscreen,* 40–41.

Drabman, R. S., & Thomas, M. H. (1974). Does media violence increase children's toleration of real-life aggression? *Developmental Psychology, 10*(3), 418–421.

Finkelhor, D., Mitchell, K. J., & Wolak, J. (2000, June). Online victimization: A report on the nation's youth. Alexandria, VA: National Center for Missing and Exploited Children.

Fraczek, A. (1985). Moral approval of aggressive acts: A Polish-Finnish comparative study. *Journal of Cross-Cultural Psychology, 16*(1), 41–54.

Funk, J. B. (2002). Children and violent video games: Strategies for identifying high risk players. In D. Ravitch & J. Viteritti (Eds.), *Children and the Popular Culture.* Baltimore, MD: Johns Hopkins University Press.

Funk, J. B., Germann, J. N., & Buchman, D. D. (1997). Children and electronic games in the United States. *Trends in Communication, 2,* 111–126.

Gailey, C. W. (1996). Mediated messages: Gender, class, and cosmos in home video games. In I. E. Sigel (Series Ed.), & P. M. Greenfield & R. R. Cocking (Vol. Eds.), *Interacting with video: Vol. 11. Advances in applied developmental psychology* (pp. 9–23). Norwood, NJ: Ablex.

Gerbner, G., & Gross, L. (1976). Living with television: The violence profile. *Journal of Communication,* 184–196.

Gershoff, E. T., Aber, J. L., & Kotler, J. A. (2003, April). *The impact of September 11 on anxiety and prejudice in New York City youth.* Presentation at the Biennial Conference of the Society for Research in Child Development, Tampa, FL.

Ginzler, J. A. (1998). Children's moral reasoning about reactions to varying levels of physical aggression: The effect of informational assumptions on judgments of self-defense. *Dissertation Abstracts International: Section B: the Sciences & Engineering, 9,* 1-B.

Gollob, H. F., & Levine, J. (1967). Distraction as a factor in the enjoyment of aggressive humor. *Journal of Personality & Social Psychology, 5*(3), 368–372.

Greenfield, P. M. (2000, December). *Effect of exposure to pornographic and other inappropriate material on the Internet.* Presentation to the Committee on Tools and Strategies for Protecting Children from Pornography and Other Inappropriate Material on the Internet, National Academy of Sciences, Washington, DC.

Hall, C., & Nordby, V. (1973). *A primer of Jungian psychology.* New York: Mentor Books.

Handford, H. A., Mayes, S. D., Matson, R. E., Humphrey, F. J., II, Bagnato, S., Bixler E. O., & Kales, J. D. (1986). Child and parent reaction to the Three Mile Island nuclear accident. *Journal of the American Academy of Child Psychiatry, 25,* 346–356.

Huston-Stein, A., Fox, S., Greer, D., Watkins, B.A., & Whitaker, J. (1981). The effects of TV action and violence on children's social behavior. *The Journal of Genetic Psychology, 138,* 183–191.

Jung, C. (1954). *Collected works: Vol. 9: The archetypes and the collective unconscious.* Princeton, NJ: Princeton University Press.

Jung, C. (1959). *The basic writings of C. G. Jung.* New York: Modern Library.

Jung, C. (1968). *Aion: Researches into the phenomenology of the self.* In Sir H. Read, M. Fordam, G. Adler, & W. McGuire (Eds.), *The collected works of C. G. Jung.* Princeton, NJ: Princeton University Press.

Krcmar, M., & Cooke, M. C. (2001). Children's moral reasoning and their perceptions of television violence. *Journal of Communication, 51*(2), 300–316.

Lahey, B. S., Schwab-Stone, M., Goodman, S. H., Waldman, I. D., Canino, G., Rathouz, P. J., Miller, T. L., Dennis, K. D., Bird, H., Jensen, P. S. (2000). Age and gender differences in oppositional behavior and conduct problems: A cross-sectional household study of middle childhood and adolescence. *Journal of Abnormal Psychology, 109*(3), 488–503.

Lemish, D. (1988). Girls can wrestle too: Gender differences in the consumption of a television wrestling series. *Sex Roles,* 833–849.

Liss, M. B., Reinhardt, L. C., & Fredriksen, S. (1983). TV heroes: The impact of rhetoric and deeds. *Journal of Applied Developmental Psychology, 4*(2), 175–187.

McGhee, P. E. (1979). *Humor: Its origins and development.* San Francisco: Freeman.

McGhee, P. E., & Lloyd, S. A. (1981). A developmental test of the disposition theory of humor. *Child Development, 52,* 925–931.

McKenna, M. W., & Ossoff, E. P. (1998). Age differences in children's comprehension of a popular television program. *Child Study Journal, 28*(1), 53–68.

Molitor, F., & Hirsch, K. W. (1994). Children's toleration of real-life aggression after exposure to media violence: A replication of the Drabman & Thomas studies. *Child Study Journal, 24*(3), 191–207.

Murray, J. (1995) Children and television violence. *Kansas Journal of Law & Public Policy, 4*(3), 7–14.

Nader, K. O., Pynoos, R. S., Fairbanks, L. A., Al-Ajeel, M., & Al-Asfour, A. (1993). A preliminary study of PTSD and grief among the children of Kuwait following the Gulf crisis. *British Journal of Clinical Psychology, 32,* 407–416.

Nathanson, A. I., & Cantor, J. (2000). Reducing the aggression-promoting effect of violent cartoons by increasing children's fictional involvement with the victim. *Journal of Broadcasting & Electronic Media, 44,* 125–142.

National Television Violence Study (1997). *National Television Violence Study: Vol. 2.* Thousand Oaks, CA: Sage Publications.

Osterweil, Z., & Nagano-Nakamura, K. (1992). Maternal views on aggression: Japan and Israel. *Aggressive Behavior, 18*(4), 263–270.

Pfefferbaum, B., Nixon, S. J., Tivis, R. D., Doughty, D. E. (2001). Television exposure in children after a terrorist incident. *Psychiatry, 64*(3), 202–211.

Poling, K. (2001, December 17). A national narrative: Children and adults need stories that put words to their desires. *St. Louis Post–Dispatch,* p. C7.

Potter, W. James. (1999). *On media violence.* Thousand Oaks, CA: Sage Publications.

Pynoos, R. S., & Nader, K. (1989). Case study: Children's memory and proximity to violence. *Journal of the American Academy of Child and Adolescent Psychiatry, 28*(2), 236–241.

Rose, A. J., & Asher, S. R. (1999). Children's goals and strategies in response to conflicts within a friendship. *Developmental Psychology, 35*(1), 69–79.

Rubin, A. (1994). Media uses and effects: A uses-and-gratifications perspective. In J. Bryant & D. Zillmann (Eds.), *Media effects: Advances in theory and research.* Hillsdale, NJ: Erlbaum.

Schneider, W. (2002, February 24). A Reagan echo: Bush's version of cowboy diplo-macy has our allies reeling, but the "axis of evil" is running scared. *The Los Angeles Times*, M1.

Schultz, T. R., & Horibe, F. (1974). Development of appreciation of verbal jokes. *Developmental Psychology, 40*, 13–20.

Schultz, T. R., & Pilon, R. (1973). Development of the ability to detect linguistic ambiguity. *Child Development, 44*, 728–733.

Schutte, N., Malouff, J., Post-Garden, J., & Rodasta, A. (1988). Effects of playing video games on children's aggressive and other behaviors. *Journal of Applied Social Psychology, 18*, 454–460.

Shannon, P., Kameenui, E. J., & Baumann, J. F. (1988). An investigation of children's ability to comprehend character motives. *American Educational Research Journal, 25*(3), 441–462.

Silvern, S. B., & Williamson, P. A. (1987). The effects of video game play on young children's aggression, fantasy, and prosocial behavior. *Journal of Applied Devel-opmental Psychology, 8*, 453–462.

Smith, C. R. (2002). *Television violence.* Constitutional and Research Issues, Center for First Amendment Studies, at www.csulb/~crsmith/1amendment.html.

Smith, S., & Wilson, B. J. (2002). Children's comprehension of and fear reactions to television news. *Media Psychology, 4*(1), 1–26.

Spector, C. C. (1996). Children's comprehension of idioms in the context of humor. *Language, Speech, and Hearing Services in Schools, 27*, 307–313.

Stein, A. H., & Friedrich, L. K. (1972). Television content and young children's be-havior. In J. P. Murray, E. A. Rubinstein, & G. A. Comstock (Eds.), *Television and social behavior: Vol. 2, Television and social learning* (pp. 202–317). Washing-ton, DC: United States Government Printing Office.

Subramanyam, K., Greenfield, P., Kraut, R., & Gross, E. (2001). The impact of com-puter use on children's and adolescents' development. *Journal of Applied Devel-opmental Psychology, 22*, 7–30.

Turkle, S. (1995). *Life on the screen: Identity in the age of the Internet.* New York: Simon & Schuster.

Valenti, J. (2000, May). *The reel story?* Presentation on youth violence in America at the Creative Coalition, National Press Club, Washington, DC.

Valkenburg, P. M., Cantor, J., & Peeters, A. L. (2000). Fright reactions to television: A child survey. *Communication Research, 27*(1), 82–97.

Valkenburg, P. M., & Janssen, S. (1999). What do children value in entertainment programs? A cross-cultural investigation. *Journal of Communication, 49*, 3–21.

Vooijs, M.W., & van der Voort, T.H.A. (1993). Learning about television violence: The impact of a critical viewing curriculum on children's attitudinal judgments of crime series. *Journal of Research & Development in Education, 26*(3), 133–142.

Voytilla, S. (1999). *Myth and the movies: Discovering the mythic structures of 50 unforget-table films.* Studio City, CA: Michael Wiese Productions.

Walker, K. B., & Morley, D. D. (1991). Attitudes and parental factors as intervening variables in the television violence-aggression relation. *Communication Research Reports, 8*, 44–51.

Wallace, W. (1999). *Psychology of the Internet.* Cambridge: Cambridge University Press.

Warnars-Kleverlann, N., Oppenheimer, L., & Sherman, L. (1996). To be or not to be humorous: Does it make a difference? *Humor 9*(2), 117–141.

Weiss, A. J., & Wilson, B. J. (1996). Emotional portrayals in family television series that are popular among children. *Journal of Broadcasting & Electronic Media, 40,* 1–29.

Weiss, A. J., & Wilson, B. J. (1998). Children's cognitive and emotional responses to the portrayal of negative emotions in family-formatted situation comedies. *Human Communication Research, 24,* 584–609.

Wilson, B. J., Smith, S. L., Potter, W. J., Kunkel, D., Linz, D., Colvin, C., & Donnerstein, E. (2002). Violence in children's television programming: Assessing the risks. *Journal of Communication, 52,* 5–35.

Wright, J. C., Kunkel, D., Pinon, M. F., & Huston, A. C. (1989). How children reacted to televised coverage of the space shuttle disaster. *Journal of Communication, 39*(2), 27–45.

Zehnder, S. (2002). The hero and the shadow. Unpublished master's thesis, Georgetown University, Washington, DC.

Zillmann, D. (2000). Humor and comedy. In D. Zillmann & P. Vorderer (Eds.), *Media entertainment: The psychology of its appeal* (pp. 37–57). Mahwah, NJ: Lawrence Erlbaum.

CHAPTER 10

Applied Research and Consulting, LLC, Columbia University Mailman School of Public Health, & New York State Psychiatric Institute (2002). *Effects of the World Trade Center attack on NYC public school students.* New York: New York City Board of Education.

Badzinski, D. M., Cantor, J., & Hoffner, C. (1989). Children's understanding of quantifiers. *Child Study Journal, 19,* 241–258.

Birnbaum, D. W., & Croll, W. L. (1984). The etiology of children's stereotypes about sex differences in emotionality. *Sex Roles, 10,* 677–691.

Blumer, H. (1933). *Movies and conduct.* New York: Macmillan.

Bowlby, J. (1973). *Separation: Anxiety and anger.* New York: Basic Books.

Buzzuto, J. C. (1975). Cinematic neurosis following *The Exorcist. Journal of Nervous and Mental Disease, 161,* 43–48.

Cantor, J. (1998). *"Mommy, I'm scared": How TV and movies frighten children and what we can do to protect them.* San Diego, CA: Harvest/Harcourt.

Cantor, J. (2002). Fright reactions to mass media. In J. Bryant & D. Zillmann (Eds.), *Media effects: Advances in theory and research* (2nd ed., pp. 287–306). Mahwah, NJ: Erlbaum.

Cantor, J., & Hoffner, C. (1990). Children's fear reactions to a televised film as a function of perceived immediacy of depicted threat. *Journal of Broadcasting & Electronic Media, 34,* 421–442.

Cantor, J., Mares, M. L., & Oliver, M. B. (1993). Parents' and children's emotional reactions to televised coverage of the Gulf War. In B. Greenberg & W. Gantz (Eds.), *Desert storm and the mass media* (pp. 325–340). Cresskill, NJ: Hampton Press.

Cantor, J., & Nathanson, A. (1996). Children's fright reactions to television news. *Journal of Communication, 46*(4), 139–152.

Cantor, J., & Omdahl, B. (1991). Effects of fictional media depictions of realistic threats on children's emotional responses, expectations, worries, and liking for related activities. *Communication Monographs, 58,* 384–401.

Cantor, J., & Sparks, G. G. (1984). Children's fear responses to mass media: Testing some Piagetian predictions. *Journal of Communication, 34*(2), 90–103.

Cantor, J., Sparks, G. G., & Hoffner, C. (1988). Calming children's television fears: Mr. Rogers vs. the Incredible Hulk. *Journal of Broadcasting & Electronic Media, 32,* 271–288.

Cantor, J., Stutman, S., & Duran, V. (1996). *What parents want in a television rating system: Results of a national survey.* Chicago, IL: National PTA. http://www. pta.org/ptacommunity/tvreport.asp.

Cantor, J., & Wilson, B. J. (1984). Modifying fear responses to mass media in preschool and elementary school children. *Journal of Broadcasting, 28,* 431–443.

Cantor, J., & Wilson, B. J. (1988). Helping children cope with frightening media presentations. *Current Psychology: Research & Reviews, 7,* 58–75.

Cantor, J., Wilson, B. J., & Hoffner, C. (1986). Emotional responses to a televised nuclear holocaust film. *Communication Research, 13,* 257–277.

Crouter, A. C., Manke, B. A., & McHale, S. M. (1995). The family context of gender intensification in early adolescence. *Child Development, 66,* 317–329.

Eisenberg, A. L. (1936). *Children and radio programs: A study of more than three thousand children in the New York metropolitan area.* New York: Columbia University Press.

Fabes, R. A., & Martin, C. L. (1991). Gender and age stereotypes of emotionality. *Personality and Social Psychology Bulletin, 17,* 532–540.

Flavell, J. (1963). *The developmental psychology of Jean Piaget.* New York: Van Nostrand.

Gentile, D. A., & Walsh, D. A. (2002). A normative study of media habits. *Applied Developmental Psychology, 23,* 157–178.

Grossman, M., & Wood, W. (1993). Sex differences in the intensity of emotional experience: A social role interpretation. *Journal of Personality and Social Psychology, 65,* 1010–1022.

Harrison, K., & Cantor, J. (1999). Tales from the screen: Enduring fright reactions to scary media. *Media Psychology, 1*(2), 97–116.

Harris, R. J., Hoekstra, S. J., Scott, C. L., Sanborn, F. W., Karafa, J. A., & Brandenburg, J. D. (2000). Young men's and women's different autobiographical memories of the experience of seeing frightening movies on a date. *Media Psychology, 2,* 245–268.

Hoekstra, S. J., Harris, R. J., & Helmick, A. L. (1999). Autobiographical memories about the experience of seeing frightening movies in childhood. *Media Psychology, 1*(2), 117–140.

Hoffner, C. (1995). Adolescents' coping with frightening mass media. *Communication Research, 22,* 325–346.

Hoffner, C., & Cantor, J. (1985). Developmental differences in responses to a television character's appearance and behavior. *Developmental Psychology, 21,* 1065–1074.

Hoffner, C., & Cantor, J. (1990). Forewarning of a threat and prior knowledge of outcome: Effects on children's emotional responses to a film sequence. *Human Communication Research, 16,* 323–354.

Hoffner, C., Cantor, J., & Badzinski, D. M. (1990). Children's understanding of adverbs denoting degree of likelihood. *Journal of Child Language, 17,* 217–231.

Johnson, B. R. (1980). General occurrence of stressful reactions to commercial motion pictures and elements in films subjectively identified as stressors. *Psychological Reports, 47*, 775–786.

Kelly, H. (1981). Reasoning about realities: Children's evaluations of television and books. In H. Kelly & H. Gardner (Eds.), *Viewing children through television* (pp. 59–71). San Francisco: Jossey-Bass.

Leeson, C. (1917). Statement for the report of and chief evidence taken by the Cinema Commission of Inquiry instituted by the National Council of Public Morals. In *The cinema: Its present position and future possibilities*. London: Williams and Norgate.

Manis, F. R., Keating, D. P., & Morison, F. J. (1980). Developmental differences in the allocation of processing capacity. *Journal of Experimental Child Psychology, 29*, 156–169.

Mathai, J. (1983). An acute anxiety state in an adolescent precipitated by viewing a horror movie. *Journal of Adolescence, 6*, 197–200.

Melkman, R., Tversky, B., & Baratz, D. (1981). Developmental trends in the use of perceptual and conceptual attributes in grouping, clustering and retrieval. *Journal of Experimental Child Psychology, 31*, 470–486.

Morison, P., & Gardner, H. (1978). Dragons and dinosaurs: The child's capacity to differentiate fantasy from reality. *Child Development, 49*, 642–648.

Owens, J., Maxim, R., McGuinn, M., Nobile, C., Msall, M., & Alario, A. (1999). Television-viewing habits and sleep disturbance in school children. *Pediatrics, 104*(3), 552, e 27. http://pediatrics.aappublications.org/cgi/content/full/104/3/e27.

Pavlov, I. P. (1960). *Conditioned reflexes* (G. V. Anrep, Trans.). London: Oxford University Press. (Original work published 1927).

Peck, E. Y. (1999). *Gender differences in film-induced fear as a function of type of emotion measure and stimulus content: A meta-analysis and a laboratory study.* Unpublished doctoral dissertation, University of Wisconsin–Madison.

Preston, M. I. (1941). Children's reactions to movie horrors and radio crime. *Journal of Pediatrics, 19*, 147–168.

Schofield, J., & Pavelchak, M. (1985). "The Day After": The impact of a media event. *American Psychologist, 40*, 542–548.

Schuster, M. A., Stein, B. D., Jaycox, L. H., Collins, R. L., Marshall, G. N., Elliott, M. N., Zhou, A. J., Kanouse, D. E., Morrison, J. L., & Berry, S. H. (2001). A national survey of stress reactions after the September 11, 2001, terrorist attacks. *New England Journal of Medicine, 345*, 1507–1512.

Silver, R. C. (2002). *New national study shows degree of exposure to 9/11—rather than the degree of loss—predicts level of distress.* (Press release). Washington, DC: American Psychological Association. www.apa.org/releases/911coping.html.

Simons, D., & Silveira, W. R. (1994). Post-traumatic stress disorder in children after television programs. *British Medical Journal, 308*, 389–390.

Singer, M. I., Slovak, K., Frierson, T., & York, P. (1998). Viewing preferences, symptoms of psychological trauma, and violent behaviors among children who watch television. *Journal of the American Academy of Child and Adolescent Psychiatry, 37*(10), 1041–1048.

Smith, S. L., Moyer, E., Boyson, A. R., & Pieper, K. M. (2002). Parents' perceptions of their children's fear reactions to TV news coverage of the terrorists' attacks.

In B. S. Greenberg, (Ed.), *Communication and terrorism* (pp. 193-209). Cresskill, NJ: Hampton Press.

Smith, S. L., & Wilson, B. J. (2002). Children's comprehension of and fear reactions to television news. *Media Psychology, 4,* 1–26.

Sparks, G. G. (1986). Developmental differences in children's reports of fear induced by the mass media. *Child Study Journal, 16,* 55–66.

Sparks, G. G., & Cantor, J. (1986). Developmental differences in fright responses to a television program depicting a character transformation. *Journal of Broadcasting and Electronic Media, 30,* 309–323.

Twenge, J. M. (2000). The age of anxiety? Birth cohort change in anxiety and neuroticism, 1952–1993. *Journal of Personality and Social Psychology, 79,* 1007–1021.

Valkenburg, P. M., Cantor, J., & Peeters, A. L. (2000). Fright reactions to television: A child survey. *Communication Research, 27,* 82–99.

Weiss, A. J., Imrich, D. J., & Wilson, B. J. (1993). Prior exposure to creatures from a horror film: Live versus photographic representations. *Human Communication Research, 20,* 41–66.

Wilson, B. J. (1987). Reducing children's emotional reactions to mass media through rehearsed explanation and exposure to a replica of a fear object. *Human Communication Research, 14,* 3–26.

Wilson, B. J. (1989a). Desensitizing children's emotional reactions to the mass media. *Communication Research, 16,* 723–745.

Wilson, B. J. (1989b). The effects of two control strategies on children's emotional reactions to a frightening movie scene. *Journal of Broadcasting & Electronic Media, 33,* 397–418.

Wilson, B. J., & Cantor, J. (1987). Reducing children's fear reactions to mass media: Effects of visual exposure and verbal explanation. In M. McLaughlin (Ed.), *Communication yearbook 10* (pp. 553–573). Beverly Hills, CA: Sage.

Wilson, B. J., Hoffner, C., & Cantor, J. (1987). Children's perceptions of the effectiveness of techniques to reduce fear from mass media. *Journal of Applied Developmental Psychology, 8,* 39–52.

Wilson, B. J., & Weiss, A. J. (1991). The effects of two reality explanations on children's reactions to a frightening movie scene. *Communication Monographs, 58,* 307–326.

Wilson, B. J., & Weiss, A. J. (1993). The effects of sibling coviewing on preschoolers' reactions to a suspenseful movie scene. *Communication Research, 20,* 214–248.

Zoglin, R. (1984, June 25). Gremlins in the rating system. *Time,* p. 78.

Zuckerman, M. (1979). *Sensation seeking: Beyond the optimal level of arousal.* New York: Wiley.

CHAPTER 11

Allen, M., D'Alessio, D., & Brezgel, K. (1995). A meta-analysis summarizing the effects of pornography II: Aggression after exposure. *Human Communication Research, 22*(2), 258–283.

Andison, F. S. (1977). TV violence and viewer aggression: A cumulation of study results. *Public Opinion Quarterly, 41*(3), 314–331.

Attorney General's Commission on Pornography. (1986). *Final Report.* Washington, DC: U.S. Government Printing Office.

Bandura, A. (1986). *Social foundations of thought and action: A social cognitive theory.* Englewood Cliffs, NJ: Prentice Hall.

Bandura, A., Ross, D., & Ross, S. A. (1963a). Imitation of film-mediated aggressive models. *Journal of Abnormal and Social Psychology, 66*(1), 3–11.

Bandura, A., Ross, D., & Ross, S. A. (1963b). Vicarious reinforcement and imitative learning. *Journal of Abnormal and Social Psychology, 67*(6), 601–607.

Belson, W. A. (1978). *Television violence and the adolescent boy.* Westmead, England: Saxon House, Teakfield.

Bushman, B. J., & Anderson, C. A. (2001). Media violence and the American public: Scientific facts versus media misinformation. *American Psychologist 56*(6–7), 477–489.

Bushman, B. J., & Huesmann, L. R. (2001). Effects of television violence on aggression. In D. G. Singer & J. L. Singer (Eds.), *Handbook of children and the media* (pp. 223–254). Thousand Oaks, CA: Sage.

Cairnes, E., Hunter, D., & Herring, L. (1980). Young children's awareness of violence in Northern Ireland: The influence of Northern Irish television in Scotland and Northern Ireland. *British Journal of Social and Clinical Psychology, 19,* 3–6.

Celozzi, M. J., II, Kazelskis, R., & Gutsch, K. U. (1981). The relationship between viewing televised violence in ice hockey and subsequent levels of personal aggression. *Journal of Sport Behavior, 4*(4), 157–162.

Chaffee, S. H. (1972). Television and adolescent aggressiveness (overview). In G. A. Comstock & E. A. Rubinstein (Eds.), *Television and social behavior: Television and adolescent aggressiveness* (Vol. 3, pp. 1–34). Washington, DC: U.S. Government Printing Office.

Chaffee, S. H., McLeod, J. M., & Atkin, D. K. (1971). Parental influences on adolescent media use. *American Behavioral Scientist, 14,* 323–340.

Cohen, J. (1988). *Statistical power analysis for the behavioral sciences* (2nd ed.) Hillsdale, NJ: Lawrence Erlbaum Associates.

Comstock, G. (1991). *Television and the American child.* San Diego: Academic Press.

Comstock, G. & Scharrer, E., (1999). *Television: What's on, who's watching, and what it means.* San Diego, CA: Academic Press.

Comstock, G. (2003). Paths from television to aggression: Reinterpreting the evidence. In L. J. Shrum, (Ed.), *The psychology of entertainment media: Blurring the lines between entertainment and persuasion* (pp. 193–211). Mahwah, NJ: Lawrence Erlbaum.

Cook, T. D., & Campbell, D. T. (1979). *Quasi-experimentation: Design and analysis issues for field settings.* Chicago: Houghton Mifflin.

Cook, T. D., Kendzierski, D. A., & Thomas, S. A. (1983). The implicit assumptions of television research: An analysis of the 1982 NIMH report on television and behavior. *Public Opinion Quarterly, 47*(2), 161–201.

Cooper, H. (1989). *Homework.* New York: Longman.

Donnerstein, E., Linz, D., & Penrod, S. (1987). *The question of pornography: Research findings and policy implications.* New York: Free Press.

Fiore, M. C., Smith, S. S., Jorenby, D. E., & Baker, T. B. (1994). The effectiveness of the nicotine patch for smoking cessation. *Journal of the American Medical Association, 271,* 1940–1947.

Glass, G.V., (1976). Primary, secondary, and meta-analysis of research. *Educational Researcher, 5,* 3–8.

Hawkins, J. D., Herrenkohl, T. L., Farrington, D. P., Brewer, D., Catalano, R. F., and Harachi, T. W. (1998). A review of predictors of youth violence. In R. Loeber and D. P. Farrington (Eds.), *Serious and violent juvenile offenders: Risk factors and successful interventions* (pp. 106–146). Thousand Oaks, CA: Sage.

Hearold, S. (1986). A synthesis of 1,043 effects of television on social behavior. In G. Comstock (Ed.), *Public communication and behavior* (Vol. 1, pp. 65–133). New York: Academic Press.

Hemphill, J. F. (2003). Interpreting the magnitudes of correlation coefficients. *American Psychologist, 58,* 78–79.

Hennigan, K. M., Heath, L., Wharton, J. D., Del Rosario, M. L., Cook, T. D., & Calder, B. J. (1982). Impact of the introduction of television on crime in the United States: Empirical findings and theoretical implications. *Journal of Personality and Social Psychology, 42*(3), 461–477.

Hill, D., White, V., Jolley, D., & Mapperson, K. (1988). Self-examination of the breast: Is it beneficial? Meta-analysis of studies investigating breast self-examination and extent of disease in patients with breast cancer. *British Medical Journal, 297,* 271–275.

Hogben, M. (1998). Factors moderating the effect of television aggression on viewer behavior. *Communication Research, 25,* 220–247.

Hunt, M. (1997). *How science takes stock.* New York: Russell Sage.

Johnson, J. G., Cohen, P., Smailes, E. M., Kasen, S., and Brook, J. S. (2002). Television viewing and aggressive behavior during adolescence and adulthood. *Science, 295,* 2468–2471.

Josephson, W. L. (1987). Television violence and children's aggression: Testing the priming, social script, and disinhibition predictions. *Journal of Personality and Social Psychology, 53*(95), 882–890.

Kang, N. (1990). *A critique and secondary analysis of the NBC study on television and aggression.* Unpublished doctoral dissertation, Syracuse University, Syracuse, NY.

Lefkowitz, M. M., Eron, L. D., Walder, L. O., & Huesmann, L. R. (1977). *Growing up to be violent: A longitudinal study of the development of aggression.* Elmsford, NY: Pergamon.

Lipsey, M. W., & Derzon, J. H. (1998). Predictors of violent and serious delinquency in adolescence and early adulthood: A synthesis of longitudinal research. In R. Loeber & D. P. Farrington (Eds.), *Serious and violent juvenile offenders: Risk factors and successful interventions* (pp. 86–105). Thousand Oaks, CA: Sage.

McLeod, J. M., Atkin, C. K., & Chaffee, S. H. (1972). Adolescents, parents, and television use: Self-report and other-report measures from the Wisconsin sample. In G. A. Comstock & E. A. Rubinstein (Eds.), *Television and social behavior: Television and adolescent aggressiveness* (Vol. 3, pp. 239–313). Washington, DC: U.S. Government Printing Office.

Milavsky, J. R., Kessler, R., Stipp, H. H., & Rubens, W. S. (1982). *Television and aggression: A panel study.* New York: Academic Press.

Needleman, H. L., & Gatsonis, C. A. (1990). Low-level lead exposure and the IQ of children. *Journal of the American Medical Association, 263,* 673–678.

Paik, H. (1991). *The effects of television violence on aggressive behavior: A meta-analysis.* Unpublished doctoral dissertation, Syracuse University, Syracuse, NY.

Paik, H., & Comstock, G. (1994). The effects of television violence on antisocial behavior: A meta-analysis. *Communication Research, 21*(4), 516–546.

Robinson, J. P., & Bachman, J. G. (1972). Television viewing habits and aggression. In G. A. Comstock & E. A. Rubinstein (Eds.), *Television and social behavior: Television and adolescent aggressiveness.* (Vol. 3, pp. 372–382). Washington, DC: U.S. Government Printing Office.

Rosenthal, R. (1986). Media violence, antisocial behavior, and the social consequences of small effects. *Journal of Social Issues, 42*(3), 141–154.

Rosenthal, R., Rosnow, R. L., & Rubin, D. B. (2000). *Contrasts and effect sizes in behavioral research: A correlational approach.* New York: Cambridge University Press.

Rosenthal, R., & Rubin, D. B. (1982). A simple general purpose display of magnitude of experimental effect. *Journal of Educational Psychology, 74,* 166–169.

Rosenthal, R., & Rubin, D. B. (1978). Interpersonal expectancy effects: The first 345 studies. *Behavioral and Brain Sciences, 3,* 377–415.

Smith, A. H., Handley, M. A., & Wood, R. (1990). Epidemiological evidence indicates asbestos causes laryngeal cancer. *Journal of Occupational Medicine, 32,* 499–507.

Thornton, W., & Voigt, L. (1984). Television and delinquency. *Youth and Society, 15*(4), 445–468.

U.S. Department of Health & Human Services. (2001). *Youth violence: A report of the Surgeon General.* Rockville, MD: U.S. Department of Health and Human Services. Centers for Disease Control and Prevention, National Center for Injury Prevention and Control; Substance Abuse and Mental Health Services Administration, Center for Mental Health Services; and National Institutes of Health, National Institute of Mental Health.

Weaver, J. (1991). Responding to erotica: Perceptual processes and dispositional implications. In J. Bryant & D. Zillmann (Eds.), *Responding to the screen: Reception and reaction processes,* 329–354.

Weller, S. C. (1993). A meta-analysis of condom effectiveness in reducing sexually transmitted HIV. *Social Science and Medicine, 36,* 1635–1644.

Wells, A. J. (1998). Lung cancer from passive smoking at work. *American Journal of Public Health, 88,* 1025–1029.

Welten, D. C., Kemper, H.C.G., Post, G. B., & van Staveren, W. A. (1995). A meta-analysis of the effect of calcium intake on bone mass in young and middle aged females and males. *Journal of Nutrition, 125,* 2802–2813.

Wood, W., Wong, F., & Cachere, J. (1991). Effects of media violence on viewers' aggression in unconstrained social interaction. *Psychological Bulletin, 109*(3), 371–383.

Wynder, E. L, & Graham, E. A. (1950). Tobacco smoking as a possible etiological factor in bronchiogenic carcinoma. *Journal of the American Medical Association, 143,* 329–336.

CHAPTER 12

Abelman, R. (1999). Preaching to the choir: Profiling TV advisory ratings users. *Journal of Broadcasting & Electronic Media, 43,* 529–550.

Abelman, R. (2001). Profiling parents who do and don't use the TV advisory ratings. In B. Greenberg (Ed.), *The alphabet soup of television program ratings* (pp. 217–239). Cresskill, NJ: Hampton Press.

Action for Children's Television v. FCC, 58 F.3d 654 (D.C. Circuit, 1995).

Amercian Psychological Association. (1993). *Violence and youth: Psychology's response.* Washington, DC: Author.

American Medical Association. (1996). *Physician's guide to media violence.* Chicago: Author.

Baker, R., & Ball, S. (1969). *Mass media and violence: Staff report to the National Commission on the Causes and Prevention of Violence, Volume 9.* Washington, DC: U.S. Government Printing Office.

Ball-Rokeach, S. (2000, June). *The politics of studying media violence: Reflections thirty years after the Violence Commission.* Paper presented at the annual conference of the International Communication Association, Acapulco.

Bandura, A. (1963, October 22). What TV violence can do to your child. *Look*, pp. 46–52.

Bandura, A., Ross, D., & Ross, S. (1963). Transmission of aggression through imitation of aggressive models. *Journal of Abnormal and Social Psychology, 63,* 3–11.

Blumer, H., & Hauser, P. (1933). Movies, delinquency, and crime. New York: Macmillan.

Boffey, P., & Walsh, J. (1970). Study of TV violence: Seven top researchers blackballed from panel. *Science, 168*(3934), 949–952.

Bushman, B., & Anderson, C. (2001). Media violence and the American public: Scientific facts versus media misinformation. *American Psychologist, 56,* 477–489.

Bushman, B., & Stack, A. (1996). Forbidden fruit versus tainted fruit: Effects of warning labels on attraction to television violence. *Journal of Experimental Psychology: Applied, 2,* 207–226.

Cantor, J., Stutman, S., & Duran, V. (1997). *What parents want in a television rating system: Results of a national survey.* Chicago, IL: National PTA. Available at www.pta.org.

Cantor, J. (1998a). Ratings for program content: The role of research findings. *Annals of the American Academy of Political and Social Science, 557,* 54–69.

Cantor, J. (1998b). Mommy I'm scared: How TV and movies frighten children and what we can do to protect them. San Diego: Harcourt, Brace, & Company

Cantor, J., & Harrison, K. (1997). Ratings and advisories for television programming. In *National Television Violence Study* (Vol. 1). Thousand Oaks, CA: Sage.

Carter, T., Franklin, M., & Wright, J. (1999). *The First Amendment and the fifth estate: Regulation of electronic mass media* (5th ed.). New York: Foundation Press.

Cater, D., & Strickland, S. (1975). *TV violence and the child: The evolution and fate of the Surgeon General's report.* New York: Russell Sage Foundation.

Centers for Disease Control. (1991). *Position papers from the Third National Injury control in the 1990's.* Washington, DC: Department of Health and Human Services.

Charters, W. (1933). Motion pictures and youth. New York: Macmillan.

Cole & Oettinger. (1978). *Reluctant regulators: The FCC and the broadcast audience.* Readings, MA: Addison-Wesley.

Cooper, C. (1996). *Violence on television: Congressional inquiry, public criticism, and industry responses.* Lanham, MD: University Press of America.

Cooper, C. (2000, April). *The impact of citizen advocacy groups on the question of television ratings.* Paper presented at the annual conference of the Broadcast Education Association, Las Vegas, NV.

Cowan, G. (1979). *See no evil: The backstage battle over sex and violence on television.* New York: Simon & Schuster.

Derthick, M., & Quirk, P. (1985). *The politics of deregulation.* Washington, DC: The Brookings Institution.

Dysinger, W., & Ruckmick, C. (1933). *The emotional responses of children to the motion picture situation.* New York: Macmillan.

Edwards, H., & Berman, M. (1995). Regulating violence on television. *Northwestern University Law Review, 89,* 1487–1566.

Farhi, P. (1997, July 10). TV ratings agreement reached. *Washington Post,* pp. A1, A16.

Federal Communications Commission v. Pacifica Foundation. 438 U.S. 726 (Supreme Court, 1978).

Foehr, U., Rideout, V., & Miller, C. (2001a). Children and the TV ratings system: A national study. In B. Greenberg (Ed.), *The alphabet soup of television program ratings* (pp. 139–150). Cresskill, NJ: Hampton Press.

Foehr, U., Rideout, V., & Miller, C. (2001b). Parents and the TV ratings system: A national study. In B. Greenberg (Ed.), *The alphabet soup of television program ratings* (pp. 195–215). Cresskill, NJ: Hampton Press.

Freedman, J. (1984). Effect of television violence on aggressiveness. *Psychological Bulletin, 96,* 227–246.

Freedman, J. (2002). *Media violence and its effect on aggression: Assessing the scientific evidence.* Toronto: University of Toronto Press.

Gerbner, G., & Gross, L. (1976). Living with television: The violence profile. *Journal of Communication, 26*(2), 172–199.

Gerbner, G., Gross, L., Morgan, M., & Signorielli, N. (1986). Living with television: The dynamics of the cultivation process. In J. Bryant & D. Zillman (Eds.), *Perspectives on media effects* (pp. 17–40). Hillsdale, NJ: Lawrence Erlbaum.

Gould, J. (1972, January 11). TV violence held unharmful to youth. *The New York Times,* p. 1.

Greenberg, B., Eastin, M., & Mastro, D. (2001). The ratings distribution in 1998, according to TV Guide. In B. Greenberg (Ed.), *The alphabet soup of television program ratings* (pp. 19–37). Cresskill, NJ: Hampton Press.

Greenberg, B., & Rampoldi-Hnilo, L. (2001). Child and parent responses to the age-based and content-based television ratings (pp. 621–634). In D. Singer & J. Singer (Eds.), *Handbook of children and the media.* Thousand Oaks, CA: Sage Publications.

Greenberg, B., Rampoldi-Hnilo, L., & Hofschire, L. (2001). Young people's responses to the age-based ratings. In B. Greenberg (Ed.), *The alphabet soup of television program ratings* (pp. 83–115). Cresskill, NJ: Hampton Press.

Gruenwald, J. (1997, February 15). Critics say TV ratings system doesn't tell the whole story. *Congressional Quarterly, 55*(7), 424–425.

Guttman, M. (1994, May 9). Violence in entertainment: A kinder, gentler Hollywood. *U.S. News & World Report,* pp. 39–46.

Hamilton, J. (1998). *Channeling violence: The economic market for violent television programming.* Princeton, NJ: Princeton University Press.

Hicks, D. (1965). Imitation and retention of film-mediated aggressive peer and adult models. *Journal of Personality and Social Psychology, 2,* 97–100.

Hicks, D. (1968). Short- and long-term retention of affectively varied modeled behavior. *Psychonomic Science, 11*, 369–370.

Hoffner, C. (1998). Framing of the television violence issue in newspaper coverage. In J. T. Hamilton (Ed.), *Television violence and public policy* (pp. 313–333). Ann Arbor, MI: University of Michigan Press.

Hoffner, C., Buchanan, M., Anderson, J., Hubbs, L., Kamigaki, S., Kowalczyk, L., Pastorek, A., Plotkin, R., & Silberg, K. (1999). Support for censorship of television violence: The role of the third-person effect and news exposure. *Communication Research, 26*, 726–742.

Hoffner, C., Plotkin, R., Buchanan, M., Anderson, J., Kamigaki, S., Hubbs, L., Kowalczyk, L., Silberg, K., & Pastorek, A. (2001). The third-person effect in perceptions of the influence of television violence. *Journal of Communication, 51*(2), 283–299.

Hoffner, C., & Buchanan, M. (2002). Parents' responses to television violence: The third-person perception, parental mediation and support for censorship. *Media Psychology, 4*, 231–252.

Hofschire, L. (2001). Media advisories and ratings: What the experimental research tells us. In B. Greenberg (Ed.), *The alphabet soup of television program ratings* (pp. 241–250). Cresskill, N.J.: Hampton Press.

Holaday, P., & Stoddard, G. (1933). *Getting ideas from the movies.* New York: Macmillan.

Horwitz, R. (1989). *The irony of regulatory reform: The deregulation of American telecommunications.* New York: Oxford University Press.

Joint Statement on the Impact of Entertainment Violence on Children. (2000, July 26). Congressional Public Health Summit, Washington, DC. Available at www.aap.org/advocacy/releases/jstmtevc.htm.

Jones, G. (2002). *Killing monsters: Why children need fantasy, super-heroes, and make believe violence.* New York: Basic Books.

Kaiser Family Foundation. (2001). *Parents and the V-chip, 2001.* Menlo Park, CA: author.

Krcmar, M., Pulaski, M., & Curtis, S. (2001, November). Parent's use and understanding of the television rating system: A national survey. Paper presented at the annual conference of the National Communication Association, Atlanta, GA.

Kunkel, D., Farinola, W., Cope-Farrer, K., Donnerstein, E., Biely, E., & Zwarun, L. (2002). Deciphering the V-chip: An examination of the television industry's program rating judgments. *Journal of Communication, 52*(1), 112–138).

Liebert, R., & Sprakfin, J. (1988). *The early window: Effects of television on children and youth* (3rd ed.). New York: Pergammon Press.

MacCarthy, M. (1995). Broadcast self-regulation: The NAB Codes, Family Viewing Hour, and television violence. *Cardozo Arts & Entertainment Law Journal, 13*, 667–696.

Maccoby, E. (1954). Why do children watch television? *Public Opinion Quarterly, 18*, 239–244.

Maddox, L., & Zanot, E. (1984). Suspension of the NAB Code and its effect on regulation of advertising. *Journalism Quarterly, 61*, 125–130, 156.

Mifflin, L. (1997, 22 February). New ratings codes for television get mixed reviews from parents. *New York Times*, p. A6.

Milagros-Rivera, M. (1995). The origins of the ban on obscene, indecent, or profane language of the Radio Act of 1927. *Journalism & Mass Communication Monographs, 149,* 1–33.

Milagros-Rivera, M., & Ballard, M. (1998). A decade of indecency enforcement. *Journalism & Mass Communication Quarterly, 75,* 143–153.

Minsky, K. (1997). The constitutionality and policy ramifications of the violent programming provision of the Telecommunications Act of 1996. *Syracuse Law Review, 47,* 1301–1318.

Murray, J. (1995). Children and television violence. *Kansas Journal of Law and Public Policy, 4*(3), 7–14.

National Commission on the Causes and Prevention of Violence. (1969). *To Establish Justice, To Ensure Domestic Tranquility.* Washington, DC: Government Printing Office.

National Institute of Mental Health. (1982). *Television and behavior: Ten years of scientific progress and implications for the eighties.* (Vol. 1): *Summary report.* Rockville, MD: author.

National Television Violence Study (Vol. 1). (1997). Thousand Oaks, CA: Sage.

National Television Violence Study (Vol. 2). (1998a). Thousand Oaks, CA: Sage.

National Television Violence Study (Vol. 3). (1998b). Thousand Oaks, CA: Sage.

Nixon, R. (1969, March 24). Letter from President Richard M. Nixon to Senator John O. Pastore. As quoted in Cater & Strickland, 1975, pp. 19–20.

Pastore, J. (1962, February 28). *Remarks of United States Senator John O. Pastore at the luncheon meeting of the National Association of Broadcasters.* Washington, DC, Shoreham Hotel. As quoted in Cater & Strickland, 1975, pp. 15–16.

Pearl, D., Bouthilet, E., & Lazar, J. (Eds.) (1982). *Television and behavior: Ten years of scientific progress and implications for the eighties* (Vol. 2). Rockville, MD: National Institute of Mental Health.

Peterson, R., & Thurstone, L. (1933). *Motion pictures and the social attitudes of children.* New York: Macmillan.

Picture of violence. (1964, February 24). *Newsweek,* p. 91.

Potter, W. J. (1999). *On media violence.* Thousand Oaks, CA: Sage Publications.

Price, M. (Ed.). (1998). *The V-chip debate: Content filtering from television to the internet.* Mahwah, NJ: Lawrence Erlbaum.

Reiss, A., & Roth, J. (Eds.). (1993). *Understanding and preventing violence.* Washington, DC: National Academy Press.

Reno, J. (1993, October 20). *Statement concerning violent television programming.* Hearings before the U.S. Senate Committee on Commerce, Science & Transportation.

Rhodes, R. (2000, September 17). Hollow claims about fantasy violence. *New York Times,* p. 19.

Rowland, W. (1983). *The politics of TV violence: Policy uses of communication research.* Beverly Hills: Sage Publications.

Saunders, K. (1996). *Violence as obscenity: Limiting the media's First Amendment protection.* Durham, NC: Duke University Press.

Schlegel, J. (1993). The Television Violence Act of 1990: A new program for government censorship? *Federal Communication Law Journal, 46,* 187–217.

Spitzer, M. (1998). A first glance at the constitutionality of the V-chip ratings system. In J. T. Hamilton (Ed.), *Television violence and public policy* (pp. 335–383). Ann Arbor, MI: University of Michigan Press.

Stanger, J., & Gridina, N. (1999). *Media in the home 1999: The fourth annual survey of parents and children.* Philadelphia: University of Pennsylvania, Annenberg Public Policy Center.

Surgeon General's Scientific Advisory Committee on Television and Social Behavior. (1972). *Television and growing up: The impact of televised violence.* Report to the Surgeon General, U.S. Public Health Service. Washington, DC: U.S. Government Printing Office.

Times Mirror Center for People and the Press. (1993). *TV Violence: More objectionable in entertainment than in newscasts.* Washington, DC: Author.

U.S. Senate, Committee on Commerce, Science, & Transportation. (1997, February 27). *Hearing on television rating system* (105th Congress, 1st Session, Doc. No. 105-157). Washington, DC: U.S. Government Printing Office.

U.S. Senate, Committee on Governmental Affairs. (2001, July 25). *Rating entertainment ratings: How well are they working for parents and what can be done to improve them?* (107th Congress, Rep. No. 75480). Washington, DC: U.S. Government Printing Office.

U.S. Senate, Committee on the Judiciary. (1956, January 16). *Television and juvenile delinquency: Investigation of Juvenile delinquency in the United States* (84th Congress, 2nd Sess., Rep. No. 1466). Washington, DC: U.S. Government Printing Office.

U.S. Senate, Subcommittee on Communications. (1972, March 21–24). *Hearings on the Surgeon General's Report by the Scientific Advisory Committee on Television and Social Behavior.* (92nd congress, 2nd session). Washington, DC: U.S. Government Printing Office.

UCLA Center for Communication Policy. (1995). *The UCLA television violence monitoring report.* Los Angeles: Author.

UCLA Center for Communication Policy. (1996). *The UCLA television violence report, 1996.* Los Angeles: Author.

UCLA Center for Communication Policy. (1998). *The UCLA television violence report, 1997.* Los Angeles: Author.

Walsh, D. A. & Gentile, D. A. (2001). A validity test of movie, television, and video game ratings. *Pediatrics, 107,* 1302–1308.

Walsh, D. A., Gentile, D. A., & van Brederode, T. M. (2002). Parents rate the ratings: A test of the validity of the American movie, television, and video game ratings. *Minerva Pediatrica, 54,* 1–11.

Wartella, E., Reeves, B. (1985). Historical trends in research on children and the media: 1900–1960. *Journal of Communication, 35*(2), 118–133.

Welkos, R. (1995, June 14). The Times Poll: Public echoes Dole view on sex, violence. *Los Angeles Times,* pp. A1, A24–25.

Wilson, B., Linz, D., & Randall, B. (1990). Applying social science research to film ratings: A shift from offensiveness to harmful effects. *Journal of Broadcasting and Electronic Media, 34,* 443–468.

Windhausen, J. (1994). Congressional interest in the problem of television and violence. *Hofstra Law Review, 22,* 783–791.

Woodard, E. H., Jordan, A., Scantlin, R., & Fishman. (2002, November). Do families use the V-Chip? A field investigation of the V-Chip mandate. Presented at the annual conference of the National Communication Association Convention, New Orleans, LA.

Wurtzel, A., & Lometti, G. (1984). Determining the acceptability of violent program content at ABC. *Journal of Broadcasting, 28*, 89–97.

CHAPTER 13

Baron, R. A. (1977). *Human aggression.* New York: Plenum.

Berkowitz, L. (1970). Aggressive humors as a stimulus to aggressive responses. *Journal of Personality and Social Psychology, 16*, 710–717.

Berkowitz, L. (1974). Some determinants of impulsive aggression: The role of mediated associations with reinforcements for aggression. *Psychological Review, 81*, 165–176.

Berkowitz, L., & Alioto, J. T. (1973). The meaning of an observed event as a determinant of its aggressive consequences. *Journal of Personality and Social Psychology, 28*(2), 206–217.

Berkowitz, L., & Rawlings, E. (1963). Effects of film violence on inhibitions against subsequent aggression. *Journal of Abnormal and Social Psychology, 66*(5), 405–412.

Cantril, H. (1940). *The invasion from mars: A study in the psychology of panic.* Princeton, NJ: Princeton University Press.

Carver, C., Ganellen, R., Froming, W., & Chambers, W. (1983). Modeling: An analysis in terms of category assessibility. *Journal of Experimental Social Psychology, 19*, 403–421.

Charters, W. W. (1933). *Motion pictures and youth: A summary.* New York: Macmillan.

Comstock, G., Chaffee, S., Katzman, N., McCombs, M., & Roberts, D. (1978). *Television and human behavior.* New York: Columbia University Press.

Comstock, G., & Scharrer, E. (2003). The contribution of meta-analysis to the controversy over television violence and aggression. In D. A. Gentile (Ed.), *Media violence and children.* Westport, CT: Praeger.

Condry, J. (1989). *The psychology of television.* Hillsdale, NJ: Erlbaum.

Donnerstein, E., & Berkowitz, L. (1981). Victim reactions in aggressive erotic films as a factor in violence against women. *Journal of Personality and Social Psychology, 41*(4), 710–724.

Donnerstein, E., Slaby, R. G., & Eron, L. D. (1994). The mass media and youth aggression. In L. D. Eron, J. H. Gentry, & P. Schlegel (Eds.), *Reason to hope: A psychological perspective on violence and youth* (pp. 219–250). Washington, DC: American Psychological Association.

Geen, R. G. (1975). The meaning of observed violence: Real vs. fictional violence and consequent effects on aggression and emotional arousal. *Journal of Research in Personality, 9*, 270–281.

Gentile, D. A., & Anderson, C. A. (2003). The effects of violent video games. In D. A. Gentile (Ed.), *Media violence and children.* Westport, CT: Praeger.

Gerbner, G., Gross, L., Morgan, M. & Signorielli, N. (1980). The "mainstreaming" of America: Violence profile no. 11. *Journal of Communication, 30*(3), 10–29.

Ginsburg, H. P., & Opper, S. (1988). *Piaget's theory of intellectual development* (3rd ed.). Englewood Cliffs, NJ: Prentice Hall.

Goranson, R. (1969). *Observed violence and aggressive behavior: The effects of negative outcomes to the observed violence.* Unpublished doctoral dissertation, University of Wisconsin, Madison.

Greenberg, B. S., Edison, N., Korzenny, F., Fernandez-Collado, C., & Atkin, C. K. (1980). In B. S. Greenberg (Ed.), *Life on television: Content analysis of U.S. TV drama* (pp. 99–128). Norwood, NJ: Ablex.

Gunter, B. (1994). The question of media violence. In J. Bryant & D. Zillmann (Eds.), *Media effects: Advances in theory and research* (pp. 163–211). Hillsdale, NJ: Erlbaum.

Hapkiewicz, W. G., & Stone, R. D. (1974). The effect of realistic versus imaginary aggressive models on children's interpersonal play. *Child Study Journal, 4*(2), 47–58.

Hearold, S. (1986). A synthesis of 1043 effects of television on social behavior. In G. Comstock (Ed.), *Public communication and behavior* (Vol. 1, pp. 65–133). San Diego, CA: Academic Press.

Howitt, D., & Cumberbatch, G. (1975). *Mass media violence and society.* New York: Wiley.

Huesmann, L. R., & Eron, L. D. (1986). *Television and the aggressive child: A cross national comparison.* Hillsdale, NJ: Erlbaum.

Kotler, J. A., & Calvert, S. L. (2003). Children's and adolescents' exposure to different kinds of media violence: Recurring choices and recurring themes. In D. A. Gentile (Ed.), *Media violence and children.* Westport, CT: Praeger.

Leyens, J.-P., & Picus, S. (1973). Identification with the winner of a fight and name mediation: Their differential effects upon subsequent aggressive behavior. *British Journal of Social Clinical Psychology, 12,* 374–377.

Liebert, R. M., & Schwartzberg, N. S. (1977). Effects of mass media. *Annual Review of Psychology, 28,* 141–173.

Mares, M.-L., & Woodward, E. H. (2001). Prosocial effects on children's social interactions. In D. G. Singer & J. L. Singer (Eds.), *Handbook of children and the media* (pp. 183–205). Thousand Oaks, CA: Sage.

Morrison, D. E. (1993). The idea of violence. In A. M. Hargrave (Ed.), *Violence in factual television, Annual review 1993* (pp. 124–129). London: John Libbey.

National Television Violence Study. (1996). *Technical Report, Vol. 1.* Thousand Oaks, CA: Sage.

National Television Violence Study. (1997). *Technical Report, Vol 2.* Thousand Oaks, CA: Sage.

Paik, H., & Comstock, G. (1994). The effects of television violence on antisocial behavior: A meta-analysis. *Communication Research, 21,* 516–546.

Potter, W. J. (1987). Does television viewing hinder academic achievement among adolescents? *Human Communication Research, 14*(1), 27–46.

Potter, W. J. (1991a). The relationships between first and second order measures of cultivation. *Human Communication Research, 18,* 92–113.

Potter, W. J. (1991b). Examining cultivation from a psychological perspective: Component subprocesses, *Communication Research, 18,* 77–102.

Potter, W. J. (1994). A methodological critique of cultivation research. *Journalism Monographs,* vol. 147.

Potter, W. J. (1997). The problem of indexing risk of viewing television aggression. *Critical Studies in Mass Communication, 14,* 228–248.

Potter, W. J. (1999). *Media violence.* Thousand Oaks, CA: Sage.

Potter, W. J., Pashupati, K., Pekurny, R. G., Hoffman, E., & Davis, K. (2002). Perceptions of television violence: A schema explanation. *Media Psychology, 4*, 27–50.

Potter, W. J., & Vaughan, M. (1997). Aggression in television entertainment: Profiles and trends. *Communication Research Reports, 14*, 116–124.

Potter, W. J., Vaughan, M., Warren, R., Howley, K., Land, A., & Hagemeyer, J. (1995). How real is the portrayal of aggression in television entertainment programming? *Journal of Broadcasting & Electronic Media, 39*, 496–516.

Potter, W. J., & Ware, W. (1987). An analysis of the contexts of antisocial acts on prime-time television. *Communication Research, 14*, 664–686.

Potter, W. J., & Warren, R. (1998). Humor as camouflage of television violence. *Journal of Communication, 48*(2), 40–57.

Potter, W. J., Warren, R., Vaughan, M., Howley, K., Land, A., & Hagemeyer, J. (1997). Antisocial acts in reality programming on television. *Journal of Broadcasting & Electronic Media, 41*, 69–75.

Roberts, D. F., Christenson, P. G., & Gentile, D. A. (2003). The effects of violent music on children and adolescents. In Gentile, D. A. (Ed.), *Media violence and children*. Westport, CT: Praeger.

Schramm, W., Lyle, J., & Parker, E. (1961). *Television in the lives of our children*. Palo Alto, CA: Stanford University Press.

Signorielli, N. (1990). Television's mean and dangerous world: A continuation of the cultural indicators perspective. In N. Signorielli & M. Morgan (Eds.), *Cultivation analysis: New directions in media effects research* (pp. 85–106). Newbury Park, CA: Sage.

Strasburger, V. C., & Wilson, B. J. (2003). Television violence. In Gentile, D. A. (Ed.), *Media violence and children*. Westport, CT: Praeger.

Surgeon General's Scientific Advisory Committee on Television and Social Behavior. (1971). *Television and growing up: The impact of televised violence*. Report to the Surgeon General, United States Public Health Service. Washington, DC: U.S. Government Printing Office.

Thomas, M. H., & Drabman, R. S. (1978). Effects of television violence on expectations of other's aggression. *Personality and Social Psychology Bulletin, 4*, 73–76.

Thomas, M. H., & Tell, P. M. (1974). Effects of viewing real versus fantasy violence upon interpersonal aggression. *Journal of Research in Personality, 8*, 153–160.

Turner, C. W., & Berkowitz, L. (1972). Identification with film aggressor (covert role taking) and reactions to film violence. *Journal of Personality and Social Psychology, 21*, 256–264.

Van der Voort, T.H.A. (1986). *Television violence: A child's-eye view*. Amsterdam: North-Holland.

Index

About the Editor and Contributors

DOUGLAS A. GENTILE, Editor, is a developmental psychologist and the director of research for the National Institute on Media and the Family, an organization devoted to maximizing the benefits and minimizing the harm of media on children and families through research, education, and advocacy. Dr. Gentile received his doctorate in child psychology from the Institute of Child Development at the University of Minnesota. Prior to joining the National Institute, he worked as a market researcher, a math instructor, and served as test developer and data analyst for Educational Testing Service in Princeton, New Jersey. He is currently on the faculty of the psychology department at Iowa State University, where he teaches media and child development. His current research focuses on media violence and advertisements as risk factors for healthy development.

CRAIG A. ANDERSON received his Ph.D. in psychology from Stanford University. He is currently professor and chair of the Department of Psychology at Iowa State University. Dr. Anderson has been awarded fellow status from the American Psychological Society, the American Psychological Association, the International Society for Research on Aggression, and the American Association of Applied and Preventive Psychology. Dr. Anderson's current research focuses on the potentially harmful effects of exposure to violent video games. He recently testified on this topic to the U.S. Senate Commerce, Science, and Transportation Committee. His article with Karen E. Dill in the *Journal of Personality and Social Psychology* (April, 2000) was a key factor in leading both the City of Indianapolis and the County of St. Louis to enact legislation aimed at reducing exposure of children to the most extremely violent video games. He also served as an expert consultant to the National Institute of Mental Health in its preparation of the new Report of the Surgeon General on Youth Violence.

KATHRYN B. ANDERSON, Ph.D., is a social psychologist at Our Lady of the Lake University in San Antonio, Texas. Her research interests include personality and situational precipitators of aggression, and evolutionary and social structural theories of mate attraction.

BRUCE D. BARTHOLOW earned a B.A. in Psychology from Minnesota State University at Mankato in 1992, an M.S. in Experimental Psychology from Drake University in 1995, and a Ph.D. in Psychology from the University of Missouri in 2000. He also spent time as a postdoctoral research fellow at the University of Missouri before accepting in 2001 his present position as assistant professor in the Department of Psychology at the University of North Carolina at Chapel Hill. His research interests include studying the effects of media violence on aggressive behavior and aggression-related phenomena (e.g., desensitization to violence), interpersonal and intergroup perception, and effects of alcohol on these processes. In much of his work, these issues are studied by examining how brain activity at the time of perception corresponds to subsequent behavior.

SANDRA L. CALVERT, the director of the Children's Digital Media Center, is a professor of psychology at Georgetown University. She is author of *Children's Journeys through the Information Age* (1999), and coeditor of *Children in the Digital Age: Influences of Electronic Media on Development* (Praeger, 2002). Professor Calvert's research examines the role that interactivity and identity play in children's learning from entertainment media through studies conducted by the Children's Digital Media Center, which is funded by the National Science Foundation. She is also involved in media policy, recently completing research about children's learning from educational and informational television programs required by the Children's Television Act. Professor Calvert is a fellow of the American Psychological Association. She has consulted for Nickelodeon Online, Sesame Workshop, Blue's Clues, and Sega of America to influence the development of children's television programs, Internet software, and video games.

JOANNE CANTOR is professor emerita at the University of Wisconsin–Madison, where she taught in the Department of Communication Arts for 26 years. She has published more than 80 scholarly articles and chapters on the impact of the mass media, with an emphasis on children's emotional reactions to television and films. Her book, *Mommy, I'm Scared: How TV and Movies Frighten Children and What We Can Do To Protect Them* (1998), summarizes her research and its applications for an audience of parents, teachers, and childcare professionals. She is frequently quoted in the national press and maintains a web site titled "joannecantor.com" to keep these audiences abreast of the latest developments.

NICHOLAS L. CARNAGEY graduated from Iowa State University with a bachelor's degree in psychology. He is currently in the Ph.D. program at Iowa State University in social psychology. His research interests include aggressive priming, attitudes toward violence, and effects of violent media on aggression-related variables.

PETER G. CHRISTENSON is professor of communication at Lewis and Clark College. He received his B.A. from Dartmouth College and his Ph.D. from Stanford University. His primary current research interests are in health communication and the impact of media on children and adolescents. He has authored or coauthored a number of articles and monographs in these areas, including *It's Not Only Rock & Roll—Popular Music in the Lives of Adolescents* (1998, with Donald Roberts) and a recent series of monographs on substance portrayals in the mass media: *Substance Use in Popular Movies and Music* (1999), *Substance Use in Popular Prime Time Television* (2000), and *Substance Use in Popular Music Videos* (2002).

GEORGE COMSTOCK (Ph.D., Stanford University) is S.I. Newhouse Professor at the School of Public Communications, Syracuse University. He was science adviser to the Surgeon General's Scientific Advisory Committee on Television and Social Behavior that issued the 1972 federal report, *Television and Growing Up: The Impact of Televised Violence*. Interests include the art and science of research synthesis, the influence of media in the socialization of children, and the dynamics of public opinion. Publications include (with Steven Chaffee, Natan Katzman, Maxwell McCombs, and Donald Roberts) *Television and Human Behavior* (1978), *The Evolution of American Television* (1989), *Television in America*, second edition (1991), *Television and the American Child* (1991), and more recently with Erica Scharrer, *Television: What's On, Who's Watching, and What It Means* (1999), "Children's Use of Television and Related Visual Media" (in *The Handbook of Children and Media*, 2001), "Entertainment Televisual Media" (in *Faces Of Televisual Media: Teaching, Violence, Selling*, 2003), and "Television, Role of: 1975—present" (in the *Encyclopedia of International Media and Communications*, 2003).

KAREN E. DILL received her Ph.D. in Social Psychology from the University of Missouri–Columbia. Her work on the effects of violent video games on aggression has received wide interest from the media, including *Time*, CNN, *USA Today*, and the BBC. Dr. Dill has testified before the U.S. Congress about media violence effects and has led media literacy workshops in her community. She is currently an associate professor of psychology at Lenoir-Rhyne College in Hickory, North Carolina.

L. ROWELL HUESMANN is professor of psychology and communication studies at the University of Michigan and a senior research scientist at the Institute for Social Research, where he directs the Aggression Research Program. Professor Huesmann's research has focused on the psychological foundations of aggressive and antisocial behavior and social-cognitive models to explain aggression. He was the lead author on the 1997 Human Capital Initiative report on the causes of violence and is past president of the International Society for Research on Aggression. He received his B.S. at the University of Michigan in 1964 and his Ph.D. at Carnegie-Mellon University in 1969. Prior to being on the faculty at Michigan, he was on the faculty of Yale University and the University of Illinois at Chicago.

JENNIFER A. KOTLER is the assistant director of knowledge management at Sesame Workshop. When she coauthored her chapter in this volume, she worked at the National Center for Children in Poverty at Columbia University on an evaluation of a school-based violence prevention program. She received her Ph.D. in Child Development at University of Texas in 1999 and subsequently received postdoctoral training at Georgetown University.

DALE KUNKEL is professor of communication at the University of California, Santa Barbara, and Director of the UCSB Washington Program. His research examines children and media issues from several diverse perspectives, including television effects research as well as assessments of media industry content and practices. He specializes in children's media policy topics, and has served as a Congressional Science Fellow. He was a principal investigator on the National Television Violence Study, which examined the risks associated with different types of violent portrayals on television. More recently, he has conducted an ongoing series of studies for the Henry J. Kaiser Family Foundation tracking the treatment of sexual content on entertainment television.

JAMES J. LINDSAY received his Ph.D. in social psychology from the University of Missouri in 1999. His research has addressed both the best and worst sides of human nature. Specifically, he has published empirical studies on the antecedents of human aggression and the behavioral correlates of deception. He served as an evaluator and consultant for programs aimed at strengthening families in impoverished areas and preventing child abuse and neglect. He is presently a research associate at the University of Minnesota, where his work focuses on more positive aspects of human behavior, such as providing assistance to others in distress and volunteerism.

TANNIS M. MACBETH, Ph.D. (formerly Tannis MacBeth Williams), is a developmental psychologist in the Department of Psychology at the University of British Columbia in Vancouver, B.C., Canada. The common thread underlying her research has been her focus on social issues, including the role of stereotypes in beliefs and attitudes about the menstrual and other cycles (e.g., lunar, days of the week). Her media research began with her discovery in 1973 of a town without television. Since then she has published numerous articles, chapters, and books on various aspects of the content and effects of television.

W. JAMES POTTER is a professor in the department of communication at the University of California at Santa Barbara. He is the author of nine books, including *On Media Violence*, *The 11 Myths of Media Violence*, and *Media Literacy*. He is the former editor of the *Journal of Broadcasting & Electronic Media* and the current general editor of *The Encyclopedia of Media Violence*.

DONALD F. ROBERTS is the Thomas More Storke Professor in Communication at Stanford University, where he has taught and conducted research on children and media since 1968. He began his career examining the impact of television violence on children's behavior for the first *U.S. Surgeon General's Report on Television and Social Behavior*. Over the ensuing years, he has examined the influence of media exposure on children's and adolescents' beliefs and behavior in such areas as violence, prosocial behavior, school performance, political attitudes, and consumer knowledge and attitudes. His most recent books include an examination of the role of popular music in the lives of adolescents (*It's Not Only Rock & Roll*) and a large-scale, national survey of U.S. youths' media behavior (*Kids and Media in America; Patterns of Use at the Millennium*).

ERICA SCHARRER (Ph.D., Syracuse University, 1998) is an assistant professor in the department of communication at the University of Massachusetts Amherst. She studies media content, media effects, and media literacy, especially as they pertain to the topics of gender and violence. She has published articles in *Communication Research*, *Journal of Broadcasting & Electronic Media*, *Media Psychology*, and *Journalism Studies*. She is the coauthor (first author, Dr. George Comstock) of the book, *Television: What's On, Who's Watching, and What it Means* (1999).

ARTURO SESMA JR. is an applied developmental researcher at Search Institute, a nonprofit organization that provides leadership, knowledge, and resources to support healthy children, youth, and communities. His current research involves articulating models of positive development, as well as constructing survey tools and strategies for assessing positive development. He also works with communities in applying data and research methodologies in order to build a developmental infrastructure that promotes thriving youth. He completed his Ph.D. in developmental psychology at the University of Minnesota.

VICTOR C. STRASBURGER, M.D., is professor of pediatrics, professor of family and community medicine, and chief of the division of adolescent medicine at the University of New Mexico School of Medicine. He graduated from Yale College (where he studied fiction writing with Robert Penn Warren) and from Harvard Medical School. Dr. Strasburger has authored more than 10 books and 130 articles on the subjects of children, adolescents, and the media and adolescent medicine; he has appeared frequently on *Oprah* and *The Today Show* and has been heard on National Public Radio.

LARAMIE D. TAYLOR is a doctoral student in communication studies at the University of Michigan. His research focuses primarily on the effects of exposure to violent and sexual media messages on young people. He lives in Ann Arbor with his wife and two sons.

BARBARA J. WILSON (Ph.D., University of Wisconsin–Madison) is professor and head of the department of speech communication at the University of Illinois at Urbana–Champaign. Before joining the University of Illinois, she was on the faculty at the University of California, Santa Barbara for 12 years. Professor Wilson's research focuses on the social and psychological effects of the mass media, particularly on children. She is coauthor of *Children, Adolescents, and the Media* (2002) and three volumes of the *National Television Violence Study* (1997–1998). In addition, she has published more than 50 scholarly articles and chapters on media effects and their implications for media policy.

4/15

CPSIA information can be obtained at www.ICGtesting.com
Printed in the USA
LVOW01s1537130215

426956LV00004B/15/P

9 780313 361524